The Illuminating Lantern

An exposition of subtleties from the Qurʾān

Part Thirty

Shaykh Ḥabīb al-Kāḍhimī

Translated by Alexander Khaleeli

ISBN: 9780986295140

Published by:
Imam Mahdi Association of Marjaeya (I.M.A.M.)
22000 Garrison St.
Dearborn, MI 48124
Tel: 313 - 562 - IMAM (4626)
www.imam-us.org

Layout by Taqwa Media, LLC

www.taqwamedia.com

Contents

I.M.A.M's Foreword

In the Name of Allāh, the All-Beneficent, the All-Merciful

All praise belongs to God, Lord of all the worlds, and may the best of blessings and peace be upon the mercy sent to all nations, the seal of the prophets and messengers, Muḥammad, son of ʿAbd Allāh, and on his pure and infallible progeny from whom God repelled all impurity and purified with a thorough purification.

God, the Exalted, says, "Indeed this Qurʾān guides to what is most upright and gives the good news to the faithful who do righteous deeds that there is a great reward for them" (17:9).

Imam Mahdi Association of Marjaeya (I.M.A.M.) is glad to present its readers with another kind of knowledge and learning. It is indeed the source of all knowledge and learning for anybody who is searching for happiness, provided he really grasps it and acts upon it. This is testified to by all those specialized in knowledge and science who possess a free spirit and sound judgment. It is the gracious Qurʾān, the heavenly book that was revealed to the seal of the prophets and messengers, Muḥammad, son of ʿAbd Allāh, may Allāh shower him and his progeny with mercy (who was born in the year 53 before Hijrah and departed this world in 11 AH, 570–632 AD).

In the 1,400 years separating us from the revelation of the Qurʾān, numerous books have been written about it. Some spoke of its value, meaning, and fruitage. Others spoke of knowledge about it, such as knowing the Meccan and Medinan, miracle and revelation, infallibility, distortion and abrogation, definitive and metaphorical, and other issues known as the Qurʾānic sciences.

Still others, and they are the majority, undertook the task of explicating and constructing it. This reflects another aspect of its eternal transcendence. Throughout history, there have been a great number of singular compositions by exceptional authors that compelled scholars to dissect them and comment on them over and over. Although they commanded a great amount of analysis and interpretation, they faded as time passed. This is because the state of any composition mirrors the state of its author, and as long as the author is still learning and growing, human knowledge and its products throughout the ages remain open to criticism and to further integration. Allāh, the Exalted, says, "O man! You are laboring toward your Lord laboriously, and you will encounter Him" (84:6). However, since its revelation, this book has remained a rich banquet for admirers of knowledge and a field where scholars of diverse specialties have been tussling eagerly and relentlessly throughout the ages, whether they were believers in it, neutral prospectors, or opponents searching for stumbles and errors.

It is the gracious Qurʾān, the eternal miracle of the seal of the prophets, Muḥammad, son of ʿAbd Allāh, may Allāh shower him and his progeny with mercy.

Today, we live in an age in which various fields and branches of knowledge have advanced greatly. Some thinkers even went to the extreme and proposed the theory of the end of history, claiming that humans have reached the peak in knowledge and progress. This theory was annulled in less than a decade, and the Qurʾān had already invalidated it as it states, "And say, 'My Lord! Increase me in knowledge'" (20:114) and declares, "And you have not been given of knowledge except a little" (17:85). Despite all the progress we see in various sciences and fields, reality imposes itself again and again. Any prospector can tour the vast online libraries from around the world to face the glory of the Qurʾān with its elegant look and in-depth content. The mind is baffled again and again and one is filled with pride when reading the words and descriptions some great scholars from different religions, schools, faiths, and beliefs have written about this singular book.

Some characteristics that distinguish this divine book and make it peerless and matchless are briefly as follows:

- Generality and inclusiveness: The Qurʾān is an extensive book that speaks about many aspects of human life. It echoes and emulates humans' instinct, inner conscience, and internal call. It tells about the unseen and eliminates human fear and anxiety about the metaphysical and supernatural world. It also satisfies the human mind with comforting and calming faith and provides him with frameworks and regulations that enhance and protect his individual and social relations.
- Transcendence and defiance: The Qurʾān is the only book that defies finding any flaw or imperfection in itself. It challenges everybody to come up with one verse that resembles its 6,666 verses. It also challenges humanity to prove one thought or idea presented by it to be void or ineffective. Instead, we notice a unique transcendence that manifests itself in the confirmation of its prophecies throughout the ages.
- Perpetuity and endurance: Every idea, vision, or law has a limited duration. In contrast, the principles, resolutions, and laws presented by the Qurʾān are eternal, as it is in accordance with human nature.
- Universality and internationality: The gracious Qurʾān is God's book. It is God's word to all of His creatures with no exception. No wonder we find that only a small part of the Qurʾān contains teachings and instructions to believers while the majority of its verses speak to humanity as a whole and address the two main pillars of human thought which are beliefs and ethics. It presents them with a uniquely woven set of principles, standards, and laws that ensure a prosperous life for them.
- Progress and futurism: No matter how much the human mind advances and progresses with new inventions and discoveries, we see the Qurʾān keeping pace with it and find no conflicts whatsoever. Instead, we see the Qurʾān spur, support, and affirm any notion, research, or logical thought that could benefit humanity.

I would like to invite all my brothers and sisters in humanity, regardless of their religious, sectarian, racial, or ethnic affiliations, and regardless of any belief they have, as a brother or sister to observe the Qurʾān and have a neutral reading of it at least once. Let's read the Qurʾān with our mind, with our conscience, with our instinct as it is, without regard to any presuppositions, prejudgments, or indoctrinations, and let's see the latitude we can reach. I, personally, have tried this, and I would like to share this feeling with my brothers and sisters in humanity. I would also like for my brothers and sisters in religion to not settle for just reciting the Qurʾān or simply being proud of it, but to examine it daily to replenish their spirituality and to act upon its teachings in their daily conduct.

God, the Exalted, has chosen the Arabic language for His holy book because, on one hand, it is accurate and precise and can express the meaning perfectly and, on the other hand, it can express one meaning in several ways without changing the original content, thus suiting the Qurʾān as a permanent message that can meet different needs in different times, places, and domains. For this and other reasons, there has been an extensive field of explication. For over a millennium, numerous explications have been written and published around the world. Regardless of how much human knowledge advances, the gracious Qurʾān meets all the needs. New interpretations of it emerge, and new knowledge and information is discovered inside it. In Qurʾānic studies, this is called the rule of flow and application, meaning the Qurʾān flows like the flow of night and day and applies to the emerging issues and what humanity needs throughout life. This is strong evidence of the depth and greatness of this transcending book.

The book you are holding in your hands is one of the new explications. Although it explicates the thirtieth section only and the respected author hopes to have the chance to explicate all the thirty sections, it is a new and functional style to practically benefit from the gracious Qurʾān. The author has relied on the bulleting method instead of explaining every word and every expression as is customary in most explications. He collects the components of every short chapter and chooses the main points that pertain to our daily life. He then adds a moral and spiritual aspect with a language that speaks to the spirit and the mind to present practical Qurʾānic solutions that can shape human personality in the three dimensions of mind, spirit, and morals. Although readers of Arabic may be able to find such a style here and there, English readers are still deprived of such accurate works with consistent and precise translation.

The author, Shaykh Ḥabīb al-Kāḍhimī (may Allāh protect him), has received God's blessing to be able to produce such a work. I congratulate him and wish him success in completing the rest of this work. The Research and Education Department in I.M.A.M. is also thankful to him for trusting us with publishing this outstanding work in North America. We are also proud of and thankful to the translator, Alexander Khaleeli, who has presented a remarkable translation. Translating such a work is not an easy task. It requires strong religious qualifications in addition to an in-depth knowledge of both languages and how their speakers use their words in order to express the meaning with honesty and integrity.

I wish that everybody who is interested in religious preaching and providing guidance during activities in religious and social settings takes advantage of this book. Its content can save them much effort in finding and presenting what people need intellectually, spiritually, and morally. I ask God to accept this blessed effort and make our intentions sincere to His Highness.

Sayyid M. B. Kashmiri
Vice Chairman, I.M.A.M.
18 Dhū al-Ḥijjah 1436 AH
September 2, 2015 AD

Preface

In the name of Allāh, the All-Beneficent, the All-Merciful

Peace and blessings be upon the one to whom He sent down the Clear Book, Muḥammad, the Chosen Prophet, and upon his noble progeny, whom Allāh has made the balance of His noble book.

Dear reader,

When we look at the library of books written about the Qur᾿ān, we see that the methods of Qur᾿ānic commentary (*tafsīr*) vary considerably—there are those that focus on the linguistic and literary import of the scripture; others that rely on narrations to explain it; some that affirm its spiritual and ethical dimensions; others that set out to produce an erudite scholarly analysis of it; and others still that attempt to do all of the above. What unites all of these various commentaries is the great length and detail with which they speak, placing considerable strain on a reader who wishes to gather all relevant knowledge diffused throughout the pages of these texts, which are truly at the pinnacle of humanity's written heritage.

But in addition to these methods of Qur᾿anic commentaries, with their various sources, I saw fit, by Allāh's grace, to produce another kind of work, one which, first of all, divides *sūrahs* into collections of similar verses that share the same context and meaning and then extracts the subtleties of their meaning in the form of self-contained points. In doing so, I wanted to help the reader to focus on each individual idea and ponder it, even if one only has a little time to do so, whether at home or while traveling, so that we can be people who ponder (*mutadabbir*) on the Qur᾿ān and benefit from its verses in our movements towards Allāh, just as Allāh himself expects from all free-willed individuals:

> *Do they not contemplate the Qurʾan?*[1]
>
> *This is an explanation for mankind, and a guidance and advice for the Godwary.*[2]
>
> *Certainly We have made the Qurʾan simple for the sake of admonishment.*[3]
>
> *We have sent down the Book to you as a clarification of all things and as a guidance and mercy and good news for those who submit.*[4]
>
> *We have sent the Qurʾan in [discrete] parts so that you may read it to the people a little at a time*[5]
>
> *A blessed Book that We have sent down to you, so that they may contemplate its signs*[6]
>
> *This is a proclamation for mankind, so that they may be warned thereby*[7]
>
> *...there has come to you in this [surah] the truth and an advice and admonition for the faithful.*[8]
>
> *We have made it an Arabic Qurʾan so that you may apply reason*[9]
>
> *These are the signs of the Manifest Book.*[10]

I wanted this commentary to be like a helper for the reader in this regard so that Allāh's book could become a remembrance, a proclamation, a guidance, an admonition, a clarification, an

1. Sūrat al-Nisāʾ (4):82
2. Sūrat Āle ʿImrān (3):138
3. Sūrat al-Qamar (54):17
4. Sūrat al-Naḥl (16):89
5. Sūrat al-Isrāʾ (17):106
6. Sūrat Ṣād (38):29
7. Sūrat Ibrāhīm (14):52
8. Sūrat Hūd (11):120
9. Sūrat al-Zukhruf (43):3
10. Sūrat al-Shuʿarāʾ (26):2

explanation, a criterion, and a clear book for a reader—which is the essence we extract from the above verses.

Something that I should mention here is that this commentary has a hue of moral education to it in that I have tried to lead the one who ponders it towards the realm of spiritual refinement and self-development which was the Qur᾽ānic revelation's very *raison d'etre.* So it owes itself to this fact that I have, in some areas, chosen to focus on those points that are most useful for practically implementing the verse in our lives, rather than interrogating its corresponding concepts, to avoid making the verses appear inanimate and abstract. In this way, we have tried to stay true to the original goal of this work, which was to transform the *knowledge* gained from these verses into *action* in the sphere of our daily lives. I hope that this is possible by pondering the merest paragraph concerning any verse in this book.

I began this work, by Allāh's grace, dealing with the final part (*juz᾽*) of the Qur᾽ān, assuming that readers will have had a general familiarity with the short *sūrahs* therein from a young age because they have often recited them in prayer or at other times which would require them to have at least a basic grasp of their meanings. Hence, I present this work hastening to good deeds, and I hope to complete the commentary [of the entire Qur᾽ān] with Allāh's kindness and generosity in what days and nights remain of my life.

Finally, I would like to give thanks to the Lord Almighty who blessed me with success in this endeavor, for I know well that the hours spent reciting the Qur᾽ān and pondering its meanings were some of the sweetest hours of my life because it was pondering the words of someone I love, and when you love someone, you love to speak to them, you love to understand their speech, and you love to comprehend their meaning.

And there is no doubt that the best books to be composed, read, studied, or pondered are those whose subject is the best book in existence—namely, the book that falsehood cannot approach from any direction.

Sūrat al-Nabaʾ (no. 78: The Tiding)

Verses 1–5

In the name of Allāh, the All-Beneficent, the All-Merciful

78:1 *What is it about which they question each other?!*

78:2 *[Is it] about the tremendous tiding,*

78:3 *the one about which they differ?*

78:4 *No indeed! They will soon know!*

78:5 *Again, no indeed! They will soon know!*

1. The tiding

Describing the tiding (*nabaʾ*) which, according to one opinion, refers to the Day of Resurrection, as tremendous (*aḍhīm*) demonstrates the important place that belief in the resurrection has in a person's spiritual development. Belief in the resurrection causes a person to vigilantly observe their own behavior (*murāqaba*), as not everyone can [otherwise] experience the fear of standing before their Lord.[1]

The Day of Resurrection has been described as tremendous in another verse, "Do they not know that they will be resurrected on a tremendous day…?"[2] The tiding has been described as tremendous elsewhere, too, "Say, 'It is a great tiding.'"[3]

---

1. Reference to Sūrat al-Raḥman (55):46: "For him who stands in fear of his Lord will be two gardens." And Sūrat al-Nāziʿāt (79):40: "But as for him who is afraid to stand before his Lord and forbids the soul from desire"
2. Sūrat al-Muṭaffifīn (83):4–5
3. Sūrat Ṣād (38):67

2. Denying the resurrection

Despite being unanimous in their disbelief, the faithless still differ amongst themselves, even in their false doctrines. We understand this from the expression "they differ" (*mukhtalifūn*). Those who deny the resurrection in its true Qurʾānic sense fall into a number of groups:

- Those who deny bodily resurrection: "Who shall revive the bones when they have decayed? Say, 'He will revive them who produced them the first time....'"[4]
- Those who consider it to be far-fetched: "Far-fetched, far-fetched is what you are promised!"[5]
- Those who are in doubt concerning it: "No, they are in doubt about it."[6]

The expression "question each other" (*yatasāʾalūn*) shows that this was an issue they were discussing amongst themselves, even if only to deride the idea of the resurrection.

3. Asking questions

When a question is asked with a genuine innocence and desire to understand, it is appropriate to give a proper answer, such as when the Prophet (s) was questioned about the nature of the Spirit,[7] the division of spoils,[8] or wine and gambling.[9] But this is not the case when the question is asked out of obstinacy and derision, whereat the answer is connected to a kind of threat, as we can see in Allāh's words, "No indeed! They will soon know!" Moreover, Allāh disparages the questioning of the faithless with the words "What is it about which they question each other?!" because they are asking a question to which they already know the answer!

4. Sūrat Yā Sīn (36):78–79
5. Sūrat al-Muʾminūn (23):36
6. Sūrat al-Naml (27):66
7. Sūrat al-Isrāʾ (17):85: "They question you concerning the Spirit..."
8. Sūrat al-Anfāl (8):1: "They ask you concerning the spoils..."
9. Sūrat al-Baqarah (2):219: "They ask you concerning wine and gambling..."

4. Doctrinal challenges

Doctrinal challenges must be met firmly and frankly without any deference. The verses of the Qurʾān repeat the expression "no indeed!" (*kallā*) as an explicit rejection of the claims of the faithless group. The verse repudiates their very act of questioning without undertaking to offer an answer. Whoever sees the signs of Allāh's power in this creation cannot rightly deny His ability to produce another, and nor can anyone who sees the wisdom of the Creator in this fleeting abode deny His wisdom that necessitates an accounting and recompense in the everlasting one!

5. Genuine knowledge of the resurrection

In terms of outcome, the main difference between those who believe in the resurrection and those who doubt it is that the former will live with genuine knowledge of what will come after the resurrection. The Commander of the Faithful (as) describes them, "They are, with regards to paradise, like one who has seen it already!"[10] This is in contrast to the faithless who "will soon know" but only after they have lost the opportunity to attain it. When the veils are lifted from them, they will see the truth of the matter, but this revelation will not help them in the slightest.

6. Resurrection is close

The words 'they will soon know,' which suggest something soon to occur, show that while we imagine the resurrection as though it is an event far off in the future, it is actually near at hand, but we do not sense it. Death is all that stands between us and our resurrection—as soon as we die, it sets in. From the Prophet (s), it is narrated that he said, "Whoever dies, his Resurrection has set in."[11] The Qurʾān affirms this fact in another verse, "Indeed they see it to be far off, and We see it to be near."[12] Assuming that 'near' (*qarīb*) in this verse means an impending reality and not merely a possible one.

---

10. *Nahj al-balāgha,* sermon no. 193
11. *Biḥār al-anwār* 58/7
12. Surat al-Maʿārij (70):6–7

Verses 6–16

78:6 *Did We not make the earth a cradle?*

78:7 *and the mountains stakes?*

78:8 *and create you in pairs?*

78:9 *and make your sleep for rest?*

78:10 *and make the night a covering?*

78:11 *and make the day for livelihood?*

78:12 *and build above you the seven mighty heavens?*

78:13 *and make [the sun for] a radiant lamp?*

78:14 *and We send down water pouring from the wringing rain-clouds,*

78:15 *that with it We may bring forth grains and plants,*

78:16 *and luxuriant gardens?*

7. Looking for the source

A believing person looks at everything as being ultimately connected to the Cause of Causes. Hence, one turns their attention to the Maker whenever they look at what He has made, recalling the words of their Lord, "Did We not make...?" When they look to the earth, they see "a resting place." When they look to the mountains, they see "stakes." An insightful person's gaze does not look merely at the act, nor at the proximate causes for that act, but towards the original cause, which is considered the source of its emanation and not merely its visible traces. Imām Ḥusayn (as) says in his supplication for the Day of ʿArafa, "Hesitancy in following the trail makes one's arrival unlikely."[13]

8. Allāh's signs in creation

Mentioning Allāh's signs in creation after mentioning the resurrection could allude to the fact that one of the proofs of the resurrection is the power of the Creator we see manifested in this

13. *Biḥār al-anwār* 95/225

first creation—whoever has the power to initiate something must also have the power to conclude it!

This is why these verses use the first person plural pronoun ("We built," "We made," "We sent down," "That We may bring forth") to continuously remind the audience of the active force behind the changing phenomena of this existence. The speaker attributes this to Himself in these verses that incorporate both affirmative ("We did") and negative ("Did We not?") statements.

9. Correct beliefs through reasoned arguments

After denying those false ideas in the first set of verses, we must establish the correct beliefs through reasoned arguments and evidence, to have the power of denial and affirmation at the same time. Just as the rule of "purification followed by illumination" (*takhliya thumma tajliya*) applies in the realm of spiritual purification, this also applies in the realm of intellectual purification. Without first freeing the mind of the audience from falsehoods, it is not easy to convince them of truths, and this meaning is realized in the first testimony of faith ("there is no god except Allah"—*lā ilāha ill allāh*) as well.

10. A wise, controlling power

When obstinacy and stubbornness are removed from a person and one considers the material phenomena that surround us—whether these appear to be fixed like the earth and mountains or ephemeral and changing like the restfulness of sleep or the livelihood we seek by day—we will connect to the Origin and the Destination. This is because the wisdom manifest in the particular phenomena of this existence did not spontaneously kindle from their inert matter. There must be a wise, controlling power that is beyond them that acts throughout this amazing universe.

11. Cradle

Calling the earth a cradle ("Did we not make the earth a cradle?") reminds us of the cradle of a newborn infant. This cradle is a temporary resting place for us because we will soon depart from it in this life to something that is more spacious and comfortable, like an enormous palace!

Hence we say that the earth and everything upon it, when compared to the hereafter, is like a small cradle in comparison to that enormous palace. In fact, the difference between the two is even greater because anyone who is familiar with this earth is like a newborn child who is barely familiar with a tiny cradle, let alone a great palace!

12. Annihilation

Allāh, who created the mountains and made them stakes, is He who will one day reduce these mountains to dunes of shifting sand,[14] carded wool,[15] scattered dust,[16] and a level plain,[17] as has been described in the Qurʾān. This, in turn, shows that all the beautiful and majestic phenomena of this world will one day be returned to nothingness and annihilation. All that will remain is the countenance of our Lord, the Master of Majesty and Nobility.

13. Day

The health of the body is, in some way, connected to its continuous alternation between movement and rest. So it is Allāh who made the day a time for livelihood after the slumber of sleep.

Therefore, someone who does not set aside time for rest—represented by the cover of night—after his daily striving for livelihood is opposing the law of nature and shall suffer afflictions as a result.

14. Waking and resurrection

The act of sleeping then waking is very similar to the process of death and resurrection, so servants who vigilantly observe

---

14. Sūrat al-Muzzammil (73):14: "...and the mountains will be like dunes of shifting sand."
15. Sūrat al-Qāriʿah (101):5: "...and the mountains will be like carded wool."
16. Sūrat al-Furqān (25):23: "...and then turn them into scattered dust."
17. Sūrat Ṭa Ha (20):106: "...then He will leave it a level plain."

themselves will be reminded of the coming resurrection every time they awaken, which in turn reminds them to prepare themselves for that critical day.

It is on this basis that the supplication prescribed to be recited when waking from sleep draws a connection between waking and resurrection, "Praise be to Allah who made me live after causing me to die, to Him is the Resurrection, and praise be to Allah who returned to me my spirit that I might praise and serve Him."[18]

15. Specific purposes

Allāh, the All-Powerful and All-Wise, has made every single thing in this existence disposed to a specific purpose, as the verses of this *sūrah* mention:

- Sleep is necessary for rest and relaxation: "and make your sleep for rest."
- Wakefulness during the day is necessary to seek one's livelihood: "and make the day for livelihood."
- Being pairs is necessary for mankind to produce offspring and multiply: "and create you in pairs."
- The gravitational attraction of planets and stars in the firmament is necessary for the earth to be a proper home for the human race: "and build above you the seven mighty heavens."
- And sending down rain is necessary for the earth to produce crops and beautiful vegetation: "that with it We may bring forth grains and plants."

Of course, we know that Allāh intends another goal beyond this universe, or else this worldly existence would end with death. Namely, He desires to bring His servants to the perfection for which they were created. This is also one of the evidences for the resurrection because the events that take place therein represent the ultimate purpose of bringing the universe into being.

18. *Biḥār al-anwār* 73/204

16. Revival

After mentioning the resurrection, this *sūrah* mentions many of Allāh's signs in creation such as reviving the earth and bringing forth vegetation. But all of these point to a single power in both creations (the first and the next)—one that is able to revive the dead in all forms. This is why it calls revival (*iḥyāʾ*) 'bringing forth' (*ikhrāj*), an expression that refers to both bringing forth vegetation and the dead from the earth.

17. Death

By calling rainclouds *muʿṣirāt,* the Qurʾān ascribes the act of wringing out to the clouds themselves ("from the wringing rain clouds") which wring themselves out to bring forth pouring water. But from another aspect, Allāh ascribes this to Himself ("and We send down...") so He is the one who sends down this water as a cause behind all causes. This is true in all cases where Allāh acts through intermediaries in this existence, including causing death:

- Allāh ascribes death to Himself sometimes: "Allah takes the souls at the time of their death..."[19]
- But at others He ascribes it to the angel of death: "Say, 'You will be taken away by the angel of death, who has been charged with you...'"[20]

18. Directing efforts

We must adorn ourselves with Allāh's manners in that every one of His actions is motivated by a penetrating wisdom. The sending down of water is followed by the bringing forth of plants and vegetation, but He uses the *lām* of causation (translated as "that... way may...") to convey this meaning, as in His words "that with it We may bring forth grains and plants."

In the same way, wise servants must never act haphazardly as they direct all of their efforts in this world toward their everlasting

19. Sūrat al-Zumar (39):42; see also Sūrat al-Naḥl (16):70: "Allah has created you, then He takes you away..."
20. Sūrat al-Sajdah (32):11

happiness, as alluded to by the verse "Say, 'Indeed my prayer and my worship, my life and my death are for the sake of Allah, the Lord of all the worlds.'"[21]

Verses 17–30

78:17 *Indeed the Day of Separation was the tryst,*

78:18 *the day the Trumpet will be blown, and you will come in groups,*

78:19 *and the sky will be opened and become gates,*

78:20 *and the mountains will be set moving and become a mirage.*

78:21 *Indeed hell is an ambush,*

78:22 *a resort for the rebels,*

78:23 *to reside therein for ages,*

78:24 *tasting in it neither any coolness nor drink,*

78:25 *except boiling water and pus*

78:26 *—a fitting requital.*

78:27 *Indeed they did not expect any reckoning,*

78:28 *and they denied Our signs mendaciously,*

78:29 *and We have figured everything in a Book.*

78:30 *So taste! We shall increase you in nothing but punishment!*

19. Maintaining ties with relatives

Calling the Day of Judgement the "Day of Separation" (*yawm al-faṣl*) alludes to the severing of social bonds, even that between a father and his son, and this strengthens the bonds that join a servant to his Lord between whom and His servant there is no separation in either of the creations, unlike the bond between one servant and another, "Your relatives and your children will not avail you on the Day of Resurrection: He will separate you from one another...."[22]

21. Sūrat al-Anʿām (6):162
22. Sūrat al-Mumtaḥanah (60):3

This motivates us to turn ourselves voluntarily towards our Master before we are forced to turn towards Him with the rest of mankind.

Of course, what we have said here does not contradict having relations with other people that attain the pleasure of our creator. For example, maintaining our ties with relatives and the faithful is important because these ties are one of the affairs of our Lord who has placed observing the rights of relatives (*arḥām*) next to wariness of Himself, "Be wary of Allah, in whose Name you adjure one another, and the relatives...."[23]

20. Oppression

People who have suffered injustice but are certain the resurrection will come to pass will not be thirsty for revenge because they know that there will be a reckoning. By the same token, the sense that the victims of injustice are powerless will not embolden their oppressors, because they too know that there will be a day when their deeds are weighed upon the scales of justice[24] and all disputes will be settled. These are all blessings that result from paying attention to the fact that the Day of Resurrection is a tryst and that people will be completely cut off from one another on that day, "Indeed the Day of Separation was the tryst."

21. A meeting

When we talk about a time being a tryst (*mīqāt*), this expression suggests that the fruit of all our struggles will appear at the time in which we will be called to account. Any rational person who is sure that this tryst will come to pass will prepare for this meeting that shall be without punishment or rebuke.

22. Worldly pleasures

Even those transient, worldly pleasures that are without benefit will seem worthless to someone who believes in the truth of this

---

23. Sūrat al-Nisā᾿ (4):1

24. A reference to Sūrat al-Anbiyā᾿ (21):47: "We shall set up the scales of justice on the Day of Resurrection..."

tryst, let alone those things which are forbidden to him. This is because he knows he will meet the Master of the Heavens and the Earth...obviously, the rebuke that one would receive for unnecessary worldly concerns and speech contains an element of punishment for those who understand the gravity of standing before their Lord in those tremendous stations.

23. Resurrection

The tryst of the resurrection was promised from pre-eternity, on the day that Allāh created the heavens and the earth, and this is why Allāh uses the past tense ("...was the tryst"). Because those who are wise pay attention to the outcomes of their actions even when they are only beginning them, as without this outcome the very wisdom behind creation and origination is lost, and the righteous and the sinner will be equal in their requital!

24. Groups and individuals

There is no contradiction between the statements "you will come in groups" and "and each of them will come to Him alone on the Day of Resurrection"[25] as we can say:

- These two statements refer to two different stages of the final judgement—everyone will be brought forth together, but each person will be held to account individually.
- Even if the outward manifestation of mankind being brought forth will be as a group, as we understand from the first verse, the inner reality will be as individuals because each person will be completely focused on his own fate and indifferent to that of others—a mother will even neglect her suckling child!

It should be remembered that the people mentioned in both of the above states, coming forth in groups and as individuals, will be resurrected under a single banner according to their state in

25. Sūrat Maryam (19):95

this world, as we understand from Allāh's words "The day We shall summon every group of people with their imam...."[26]

25. "Lowering, exalting"

The nature of the heavens is such that they are firmly sealed on all sides without opening while the nature of the mountains is that they are fixed as pegs in the earth...but on the Day of Resurrection, the very essence of things will change. Sealed doors will be thrown open ("the sky will be opened") and things that appear fixed will be set in motion ("the mountains will be set moving"). The same applies to the measuring of deeds—they will transform. That which appeared true will be shown false and vice versa, hence, why it is called "lowering, exalting."[27]

26. "A mirage"

All forms of enjoyment in this worldly life are like a fleeting mirage. Their outward appearance entices, but they are hollow and devoid of reality. Yet, this statement, which is a figure of speech in this world, will become manifestly real on the Day of Judgement. Mountains, which are the firmest manifestation and the most towering creation on the face of the earth, will become, as the Qurʾān says, "a mirage" which refers to the fading of their very reality, not merely their visible appearance.

27. Ambush

Calling hell an ambush, as Allāh does in His saying "Indeed hell is an ambush" suggests that there is someone waiting to ambush wayfarers, even if they do not perceive them, as is the common practice of bandits. Therefore, someone who lives in this world and knows that hell exists and that it is lying in wait or that it is the place where an ambush will be sprung—according to the two meanings of the Arabic word for 'ambush' (*mirṣād*)—should live with a fear that restrains one from forbidden things.

---

26. Sūrat al-Isrāʾ (17):71
27. Sūrat al-Wāqiʿah (56):3

28. Hell is like a path

Hell is like a path that one must traverse, a road upon which there are people who ambush travelers ("There is none of you but will come to it..."[28]), but the question is who will traverse it safely (the believers) and those who will fall into the ambush (the wrongdoers).

29. Rebellion

One of the attributes of hellfire's inhabitants is rebellion (*ṭughyān*), which means to overstep the bounds of moderation (iʿtidāl). Therefore, every act of rebellion that takes the servant beyond the bounds of moderation in everything, no matter how little it may be, is a step towards amassing sins to the extent that one of them becomes a rebel (*ṭāghūt*), in which case they become a manifestation of their own corruption and the corruption of others.

30. Excessive punishment

Hell is described as "a resort for the rebels" as though it is their natural place of return. They were familiar with it, even if they did not realize this, in the abode of this world, so they returned to it in the hereafter. Their rebellious nature is only compatible with remaining in this place of return.

From this perspective, we can also understand why they must remain forever in hellfire. Their immutable nature (*ṭabīʿa thābita*) requires this constant punishment, as the recompense on the Day of Resurrection, is appropriate to the deeds of the servant ("a fitting requital") So there is no reason to imagine that this punishment is excessive once we understand the essential kinship between hellfire and its inhabitants. The one who metes out this requital is absolutely just and the wisest of the wise!

---

28. Sūrat Maryam (19):71

31. Eternity in hell

Some inhabitants of hellfire are not condemned to remain therein forever. Sinners who are not faithless will actually "reside therein for ages." But residing in hellfire, even for merely ages of time, should still give us cause to tremble! We must imagine remaining in hellfire for a prolonged and uncertain amount of time as we can grasp from the word 'ages' (*aḥqāb*). This is a recompense that the servant would not have expected in the abode of this world.

32. Boiling water

Hell is a view of utter punishment, for there is nothing to drink nor even anything drinkable, or any shade in which to seek the slightest respite. Whoever has any hope of coolness, their recompense can be gleaned from Allāh's words "tasting in it neither any coolness nor drink." In fact, there is nothing to give relief to the inhabitants of hell, not even a transient moment of pleasure or a fleeting hope. We know this because the words 'coolness' (*bard*) and 'drink' (*sharāb*) appear as indefinite nouns in the context of a negation.

Graver still is that instead of drink they shall be quenched with boiling water (*ḥamīm*) that shall be poured over them as well ("and drink boiling water on top of it"[29]).

33. Denying the resurrection

Denying the resurrection is one of the causes of rebellion because it entails a denial of any recompense for one's actions that, in turn, would act as a check on man's defiance. About this, the verse says they "did not expect any reckoning" so, in practice, someone who does not expect any recompense is like one who denies it outright, even if they accept it on a theoretical level.

29. Sūrat al-Wāqiʿah (56):54

34. Continuous vigilance

One of the ways in which a servant can become righteous in life is through continuous vigilance (*murāqaba muttaṣila*), and this vigilance has two corollaries:

- First: Reminding oneself of the Day of Recompense: "when a person will observe what his hands have sent ahead."
- Second: Certainty that Allāh will figure every deed, whether great or small, in a book in which all of that is recorded: "We have figured everything in a Book."

In short, the source from which vigilance springs is reminding oneself of one's origin and return in a way that penetrates the very depths of one's soul.

35. Rebuke

When the person who has been wronged (*ṣāḥib al-ḥaqq*) rebukes the wrongdoer directly, this causes greater psychological pain for the latter when they face judgement, even more so when the person who has been wronged has power (*qudra*) as well. So the verse "So taste...!" represents a transition from referring to them in the third person ('they') to addressing them directly. This is a more eloquent form of censure and reproach, as it emanates directly from the creator of hell and the one who sustains its fires.

36. Aversion of rebels

In the abode of this world, the rebels only increase in aversion the more they are preached to ("but it increases them only in aversion"[30]). So their recompense in hell reflects this condition of theirs. Their pleas for relief are only followed by an increase in punishment ("So taste! We shall increase you in nothing but punishment!"). Just as the preaching of the prophets had no effect on them save to increase them in aversion, so too do their entreaties in hellfire have no effect save to increase their punishment!

---

30. Sūrat al-Isrā' (17):41

It has been narrated that this verse is one of the harshest descriptions of the condition in which the inhabitants of hellfire will find themselves. The Prophet (s) is narrated to have said, "This verse is the harshest part of the Qurʾān for the inhabitants of hellfire."[31]

Verses 31–38

78:31 *Indeed a triumph awaits the Godwary:*

78:32 *gardens and vineyards,*

78:33 *and buxom maidens of a like age,*

78:34 *and brimming cups.*

78:35 *They shall hear neither vain talk therein, nor lies*

78:36 *—a reward from your Lord, a bounty sufficing,*

78:37 *the Lord of the heavens and the earth and whatever is between them, the All-beneficent, whom they will not be able to address*

78:38 *on the day when the Spirit and the angels stand in an array. None shall speak except whom the All-beneficent permits and who says what is right.*

37. Fear and hope

The method of the Qurʾān alternates between instilling fear (*tarhīb*) and hope (*targhīb*), After mentioning the different kinds of painful punishment in hell, the verses shift and mention the different kinds of eternal comforts in paradise. This is a practical lesson for preachers, both then and now, that both methods must be used to kindle people's innermost feelings. Too much fear might cause them to despair, just as too much hope might lead them to feel complacent and assume they are safe from Allāh's stratagems.

31. *Tafsīr al-Kashshāf* 4/690

38. Gardens

Just as gardens (*ḥadā'iq*) represent paradise's material comforts, so too does its elevation above vain speech and lies represent its spiritual comforts. This means that a worldly life that is free from vain talk and lies is already imbued with a kind of blessing enjoyed by the inhabitants of paradise, and this can only be found in the lives of righteous men and women and a faithful family.

39. Vanity in talk

It is the nature of worldly comforts to remove the inhibitions of those who enjoy them and turn their conversations towards vanity, whereas the inhabitants of paradise, who enjoy the ultimate degrees of comfort, remain vigilant of their Master in such a way that prevents them from allowing vanity into their talk. They "shall hear neither vain talk therein" in the form of them calling one another liars, "nor lies" for there is no quarrelling between them, as Allāh says, "We will remove whatever rancour there is in their breasts...."[32]

We know that every form of vanity and deceit is removed from paradise because both of these words appear as indefinite nouns in the context of a negation which indicates a general negation.

40. Compensation

The choice not to call others liars as one of the blessings of paradise might be a kind of compensation (*taʿwīḍ*) for the faithful who suffered in the abode of this world because the faithless called them liars. We know that they only suffered this for the sake of Allāh (*fī sabīl illāh*), so it is as though the verse alludes to the fact that they will be relieved of this terrible persecution in the everlasting abode of paradise having endured it in this world. This compensation is like a type of reward that matches their good deeds as required by the wisdom of the one bestowing rewards upon them.

---

32. Sūrat al-Aʿrāf (7):43

41. Accounting and giving

Recompense on the Day of Resurrection is a combination of being through accounting (*ḥisāb*) first and through giving (*ʿaṭāʾ*) second, which is why the verse puts these two together saying, "a reward sufficing" (*ʿatāʾan ḥisāban*). So the matter is never beyond the compass of precise accounting, which is the mark of existence (*simat al-wujūd*), nor beyond the compass of liberal giving, which is the mark of generosity (*simat al-jūd*), otherwise how could a few years of obedience possibly compare to the eternal recompense!?

42. Never feel complacent

The careful accounting of recompense that is attributed to the Lord Almighty requires the servant to be unswerving in obedience to Him because of the inseparability of abundant obedience from abundant reward that is without limit ("There they will have whatever they wish, and with Us there is yet more."[33]).

Therefore, we must never feel complacent or content with a certain level of obedience, taking the magnanimity of our Master for granted, because even His magnanimity is proportional to the servant's good deeds.

43. Recompense of the faithful and faithless

Were we to ponder the recompense of the faithful and the faithless, we would see a reciprocity like that found between opposites that reflects the fate of each group on that day:

- The believers drink "a pure drink"[34] while the faithless consume "boiling water and pus."
- The outcome of the faithful is "a triumph" while the fate of the faithless is "an ambush."
- The recompense of the faithful is a "reward" (*ʿatāʾ*) which signifies generosity and open-handedness while that of the

---

33. Sūrat Qāf (50):35
34. Sūrat al-Insān (76):21

faithless is a "requital" (*wifāq*) befitting their crimes in this world.

44. Allāh appends the Prophet (s) to Himself

Allāh appends the Prophet (s) to Himself in the station of recompense saying, "a reward from your (sing.) Lord" before appending to that the heavens and the earth saying, "the Lord of the heavens and the earth" as though the universe in its entirety is in one hand and His beloved Muṣtafā (s) is in the other. This is the natural corollary of the entire universe having been created for his (s) sake and those noble members of his Household who are attached to him.

45. Ranks

Standing in ranks is usually the mark of those disciplined in affairs. The angels who do not precede Him in speech are organized in their affairs, as on the Day of Resurrection they will stand in ranks and not speak save with His permission ("...in an array. None shall speak except whom the All-beneficent permits."). Silence is the natural state for all creations on the day of gathering, while speaking requires someone to permit it.

46. Saying what is right

The presence of the Lord is a presence in which manners are observed and attention is given, so anyone who will not say what is right will not be permitted to speak as he will fall in the estimation of his Master! This means, even if the context in which it will be realized is the hereafter (as the verse itself states), the believer is attentive to this rule in the worldly life too. Believers know that if they does not say what is right, they will fall in the estimation of their aster, and this is a most difficult thing to bear for servants who are vigilant of their Lord.

47. Intercession on the Day of Resurrection

This verse demonstrates that intercession on the Day of Resurrection will only happen by Allāh's leave, for it is a kind of right speech that is permitted to emanate from the intercessor. This matter goes back to divine wisdom that judges that only that which is true and right shall come to pass on the side of sanctity. It has been narrated that when Imām al-Ṣādiq (as) was asked about this verse, he said, "We – by Allah! – are those permitted [to speak] on the Day of Judgement, and those who will say what is right."[35]

48. Permission to speak

The utmost pride servants shall feel is when they are permitted to speak with their Master in this world or in the hereafter. This is granted to everyone who becomes worthy thereof. The way to attain this worthiness is as follows:

- First, the person must be upon what is right ("and says what is right") and we know that anyone who wishes to be right must first know what right is! This is why we seek guidance from Him by saying, "Guide us to the straight path."[36]
- Second, that they prepare themselves to enter the compass of divine attraction (*jadhb ilāhī*) so that they will be permitted to speak ("whom the All-Beneficent permits"). It should be noted that the choice of the word 'the All-Beneficent' (*al-raḥmān*) has a subtle meaning here. It alludes to the fact that one of the causes for this divine providence (*ʿināya*) is a servant's acquisition of this attribute as well.

35. *Al-Kāfī* 1/435
36. Sūrat al-Fātiḥah (1):6

Verses 39–40

78:39 *That is the day of truth. So let anyone who wishes take resort with his Lord.*

78:40 *Indeed We have warned you of a punishment near at hand—the day when a person will observe what his hands have sent ahead and the faithless one will say, 'I wish I were dust!'*

49. No compulsion

Wayfaring on the path to Allāh is not by compulsion and force or else there would be no point in the struggle required when seeking divine proximity. In fact, He has made the fact of being guided to the way conditional upon struggling for Him ("As for those who strive in Us, We shall surely guide them in Our ways..."[37]).

So whoever wants their destination and their fate to be with Allāh must first of all sincerely desire and wish for that ("So let anyone who wishes...") and secondly, they must be resolved to traverse the path laid down to Him ("...take resort with his Lord.").

50. The original warner

The original warner (*mundhir*) is the Lord of the Worlds ("We have warned you of a punishment near at hand") followed by the messenger ("Messengers, as bearers of good news and warners"[38]) followed by scholars ("and to warn their people"[39]). From this, we can grasp the importance of scholars and their position in that they have become an extension of the divine will from one side and emulators of the actions of the prophets from the other.

51. Warnings

Warnings (*indhār*) are more suited to awaken those who are unaware than good tidings (*bashāra*), which is why this verse only mentions warning, "We have warned you of a punishment near at

37. Sūrat al-ʿAnkabūt (29):69
38. Sūrat al-Nisāʾ (4):165
39. Sūrat al-al-Tawbah (9):122

hand," without mentioning good tidings when discussing "the day of truth" because the *sūrah* concludes by mentioning the faithless.

52. Very near

Some people see the hereafter as though it is far off in the future while the truth is that the only thing separating us from the hereafter is death, which could overtake us at any moment. This is why the verse announces that the punishment it warns of is very near indeed ("We have warned you of a punishment near at hand."). This verse explains nearness according to reality while the other verse above explains it from the viewpoint of the All-Wise ("We see it to be near") and this previous warning is only another proof against the faithless on the Day of Resurrection.

53. Physical reality of deeds

On the Day of Judgement, a person's deeds will take on a physical reality. Verses of the Qurʾān talk about physically seeing deeds (*ruʾya*) in numerous contexts such as the verse in this *sūrah*: "the day when a person will observe what his hands have sent ahead" when actually, it is more fitting that servants should observe their deeds in this world, both because they are nearer to them and because there is still an opportunity for them to change their ways. The problem is that many people lack the insight to see things that will only be revealed to them when it is too late for them to do anything about it.

54. Extreme regret

The fact that someone who was once a candidate for divine vicegerency (*al-khilāfa al- ilāhiyya*) should wish that he were dust reveals the extreme regret experienced by a disbeliever on the Day of Judgement ("and the faithless one will say, 'I wish I were dust!'"). In fact, one can even say that the dust is better than him because it allows the seed deposited within it to become an expansive tree. On the other hand, the disbelievers' Master has placed the seeds of goodness in their hearts, but they have done nothing to cultivate them in the depths of their souls. They have covered them with their deformed hearts, and with this act of concealment that Allāh alludes to saying, "and one who betrays it fails,"[40] they have failed. This is one of the ways in which the Arabic word *kufr* meaning "disbelief" corresponds to its original sense which is "to cover up."[41]

40. Sūrat al-Shams (91):10

41. *Muʿjam Maqāyīs al-Lugha* 5/191

Sūrat al-Nāziʿāt (no. 79: Those Who Wrest Violently)

Verses 1–14

79:1 *By those who wrest violently,*

79:2 *by those who draw out gently,*

79:3 *by those who swim smoothly,*

79:4 *by those who take the lead, racing,*

79:5 *by those who direct an affair:*

79:6 *the day when the Quaker quakes*

79:7 *and is followed by the Successor,*

79:8 *hearts will be trembling on that day,*

79:9 *bearing a humbled look.*

79:10 *They will say, 'Are we being returned to our earlier state?*

79:11 *What, when we have been decayed bones?!'*

79:12 *They will say, 'This, then, is a ruinous return!'*

79:13 *Yet it will be only a single shout,*

79:14 *and behold, they will be upon a barren plain.*

1. Different kinds of angels

This *sūrah* opens with a number of oaths sworn in the name of different kinds of angels including:

- *Nāziʿāt,* "Those who wrest," who pull the spirits of the faithless violently from their bodies
- *Nāshiṭāt,* "Those who draw out," who gently unsheathe the spirits of faithless from their bodies
- *Sābiḥāt,* "Those who swim," who hasten to execute the divine commands such as quickly taking the spirits of the faithful and conveying them to their abode in the seat of veracity with the Mighty King
- *Sābiqāt,* "Those who take the lead," who are at the forefront in their journeys, whether it is to take people's spirits or convey the revelatory address to prophets
- *Mudabbirāt,* "Those who direct." who manage the affairs of the universe; they are an intermediary between divine commands when they are issued and their implementation as worldly determinations (*muqaddirāt*)

These oaths, in turn, serve to show us the tasks of the angels that vary according to the differing degrees of their servitude. From this it is clear that the angels are occupied with managing important affairs as the word 'affair' (*amr*) appears as a singular indefinite noun ("By those who direct an affair") which conveys this sense of importance.

2. Actions of the angels

The time of death, in which the spirit is taken, is one of the most important times in a person's life, which is why it is worthy of Allāh classifying the different tasks of the angels according to the differing states, whether they are seizing the spirit of a disbeliever or anyone else, and conveying these spirits to the place that is appropriate to them. This, in its entirety, is when the verse is looking at the actions of the angels. But there are also indications that the verses are looking at the conditions of the stars according to their movement in the heavens,[1] and that they are looking at the conditions of the *mujāhidīn* in battle. This supports the

1. *Al-Tibyan* 10/251; *Majmaʿ al-bayān fi tafsīr al-Qurʾān* 10/651

opinion that the Qurʾān carries multiple dimensions of meaning simultaneously.

3. Difficulty in removal of a spirit from its body

The difficulty in removal of a spirit from its body is proportional to its attachment to the world of desires, just as it is difficult to pull an arrow from a person's body because its head causes it to lodge in it. The same is true of the spirits of the faithless—the angels must wrest their sprits from their bodies like someone mercilessly pulling out an arrow [because it is buried so deep]. It is a long, hard, and violent process to remove it, and this is the meaning given for the verse "By those who wrest violently...."

4. Angels directing the affair

The importance of the angels is manifested in the fact that they direct the affair ("By those who direct an affair") in addition to the oaths sworn by them in a number of *sūrahs* such as in *al-Ṣāffāt* and *al-Mursalāt.* Angels are the means of conveyance. In fact, Allāh attaches this grave affair to Himself when He says, "...then settled on the Throne, directing the affair...."[2] The difference is that while the angels have been entrusted with directing the command, it is Allāh who is the ultimate authority in all matters.

Is it any surprise, then, that Allāh should entrust this to His greatest *awliyāʾ* who are intermediaries in emanation (*fayḍ*) and who are served by these same angels!?

5. A station of nearness

The occupation of the angels with directing the affairs of the universe by Allāh's command does not contradict their utter absorption in the glorification and praise of Allāh as implied by His words "and those who are near Him do not disdain to worship Him, nor do they become weary. They glorify night and day, and they do not flag."[3] So what is desired of man—who is like a deputy (*khalīfa*)

2. Sūrat Yūnus (10):3
3. Sūrat al-Anbiyāʾ (21):19–20

of Allāh upon this earth and who resembles being amongst the rank of the angels—is to reach this level whereby he unites (*jamᶜ*) occupation in the creation with utter absorption in the creator!

This verse might indicate how this can be achieved. Human beings must sense that they have a station of nearness (*ᶜindiyya*), as derived from the words 'who are near Him' (*wa man ᶜindahu*). It is as though this is the key to attaining this all-consuming remembrance [of Allāh.]

6. The ultimate cause in all situations

Ascribing worldly phenomena such as death, sustenance, etc. to various causes (*asbāb*) after having already ascribed them to Allāh is like ascribing the act of writing to the pen or the hand. These are subsidiaries of the human being in relation to the act and are not co- equal with the human being. Therefore, it is not unusual to attribute worldly phenomena to various causes such as ascribing death to the angel of death,[4] once again after already being ascribed to Allāh. In this way, the magnificence of Lordship remains untouched by seeing it as the ultimate cause in all situations.

7. Two great cries

One of the unique features of the resurrection is that it contains two great cries (*ṣayḥa*) that induce panic. They are referred to as "the quaker" (*al-rājifa*) and "the successor" (*al- rādifa*) which follows it. It is noteworthy that the Qurʾān has used a word derived from the same root meaning as the first for the hypocrites (*munāfiqūn*) of Madīnah ("the rumourmongers (*murjifūn*) in the city"[5]) as though their speech in which they spread rumors is like an earthquake that shakes the peace of the community.

4. Sūrat al-Sajdah (32):11: "Say, 'You will be taken away by the angel of death, who has been charged with you. Then you will be brought back to your Lord.'"
5. Sūrat al-Aḥzāb (33):60

8. Self-refinement

On the Day of Resurrection, the condition of the faithless who denied the resurrection will resemble the condition of the hearts of the faithful in this world in that they will be:

- "trembling" (*wājifa*) which means they will be panicking in fear of Allāh, just as the hearts of the faithful trembled in this world.
- "bearing a humbled look" (*abṣāruhā khāshiʿa*) because their hearts are humbled, and this is one of the most sublime qualities of the faithful in this world!

But as well as these attributes that are shared in the hereafter, there is one quality that belongs only to the faithful in this world—namely, that "they will have no fear, nor will they grieve."[6] So the perfection of all perfection is for the attributes of the hearts in the hereafter to be realized in the life of this world, which is the abode of self-refinement and attaining nearness to Allāh.

9. "A barren plain"

After the second blowing in the trumpet, the ground of resurrection will transform into what the Qurʾān describes as "and behold, they will be on a barren plain." In other words, they will find themselves upon a vast, flat expanse without vegetation. This means people should, when they see the delightful sights of this world, remember the day when every sight on the earth will vanish. There will remain but a single sight, represented in everything that was ascribed to Allāh, because the only thing that shall endure is His countenance (*wajh*), and this includes everything that is properly ascribed to Him.

6. Sūrat al-Aḥqāf (46):13

Verses 15–26

79:15 *Did you receive the story of Moses,*

79:16 *when his Lord called out to him in the holy valley of Tuwa?*

79:17 *'Go to Pharaoh, for indeed he has rebelled,*

79:18 *and say, "Would you refine yourself?*

79:19 *I will guide you to your Lord, that you may fear [Him]?"'*

79:20 *Then he showed him the greatest sign.*

79:21 *But he denied, and disobeyed.*

79:22 *Then he turned back, striving,*

79:23 *and mustered [the people] and proclaimed,*

79:24 *saying, 'I am your lord, the most-high!'*

79:25 *So Allah seized him with the punishment of this life and the Hereafter.*

79:26 *There is indeed a moral in that for someone who fears!*

10. Divine providence

Someone who receives the divine providence (*ʿināya ilāhiyya*), by which they become one summoned to their Master, is best able to confront the Pharaonic tyrants. Sometimes, this requires the ability to master the hearts of those who advance towards you. At other times, it requires the ability to face those who turn away—namely, to confront their numbers and strength. Neither of these can be achieved without assistance from the realm of the unseen. Allāh certainly gave assistance to Moses (as) with both of these abilities according to the stories of him in the Qurʾān.

11. Physical and spiritual purity

Conversing with the Holy of Holies can only happen in venues which are sacred and pure which is why Allāh chose the holy valley to speak directly to Moses (as) and commanded

Abraham (as), His confidant, to purify His house for those who go around it ("Purify..."),[7] forbade the idolaters from maintaining Allāh's mosques ("The polytheists may not maintain..."),[8] and bid us to put on our adornment for every occasion of prayer ("Put on your adornment on every occasion of prayer."[9]).

On this basis, it can be said that anyone who wishes to be in a proper state to converse intimately (*munājā*) with his Master must purify themselves outwardly from physical impurities and inwardly from spiritual ones—such as disobedience and sinning.

12. Tyrannical rulers

Anyone who wishes to combat corruption in society can only remove it by combating its sources. At the head of these sources is the conduct of tyrannical rulers ("people follow the religion of their sovereigns"[10] and "Indeed when kings enter a town, they corrupt it..."[11]).

This is why Allāh commands Moses (as) to confront Pharaoh as the first step in his program of reform ("Go to Pharaoh, for indeed he has rebelled.").

13. Enjoining good and forbidding evil

Just because your audience is rebellious, this should never prevent you from undertaking your duty to enjoin the good and forbid the evil:

- You might still have an effect on them, even if it is delayed. There is always hope that even the greatest of sinners will see the error of his ways, as Pharaoh's magicians did.

---

7. Sūrat al-Baqarah (2):125: "Purify My House for those who go around it, [for] those who make it a retreat and [for] those who bow and prostrate."

8. Sūrat al-Tawbah (9):17: "The polytheists may not maintain Allah's mosques..."

9. Sūrat al-Aʿrāf (7):31: "O Children of Adam! Put on your adornment on every occasion of prayer..."

10. *ʿIlal al-sharāʾiʿ* 1/14

11. Sūrat al-Naml (27):34

- Or to leave them without any excuse (*itmām al-ḥujja*), which will make their fate more severe and their punishment more fitting.

14. Allāh's stratagems

The verses that mention Pharaoh's destruction demonstrate Allāh's power to seize even the mightiest of tyrants, which, in turn, gives consolation to the faithful when they suffer under the oppressors of their own times, who are weaker than Pharaoh. But these verses should also cast terror into the hearts of the wrongdoers when they see the subtlety of Allāh's stratagems (*makr*), and He directs these against the faithless people.

15. Kindness and beautiful preaching

The Qurʾān teaches us to use kindness and beautiful preaching when calling Allāh's servants to Him:

- Pharaoh was the most vicious of Allāh's creation, and yet he was called to purify himself gently ("Would you refine yourself?").
- And in a soft manner ("Speak to him in a soft manner..."[12]). This was with someone who claimed to be the Highest Lord and ordered the slaughter of suckling infants!
- Here, Moses (as) connects the Lord to Pharaoh, saying, "to your Lord." Even though he did not acknowledge the God of Moses.

16. Self-purification

What is desired from servants is to produce a change in our selves through our own efforts, otherwise Allāh is easily able to produce this change without any effort from His servant, as happens with all the other changes in the universe. This is why we see Moses (as) asking Pharaoh to purify himself ("Would you refine yourself?") He does not say, for instance, "I will refine you!"

---

12. Sūrat Ṭa Ha (20):44

17. Self-refinement

The expression "self-refinement" (*tazkiya*) is repeated in the calls of all the prophets (as), so if it is:

- with the meaning of growth (*namw*), it indicates continuous human self- development (*takāmul*) and growth that is achieved through following the message of the prophets.
- with the meaning of cleansing and purification, it indicates freeing oneself of contaminants in the human soul, also by following their message.

18. Addressing those who are far from the path

When addressing those who are far from the path of guidance, you must always mention things that will attract them to the path and be in harmony with their nature (*fiṭra*) rather than demanding them to blindly accept things that are difficult for them! This is why we see that Moses (as) does not call on Pharaoh to follow the laws of his *sharīʿa* but only asks him to refine himself in a manner that no one with a healthy nature would disagree with and which even someone with no religion would desire!

19. The message of the prophets

The message of the prophets is represented in guiding those who can be guided sometimes and by confronting those who are averse to accepting guidance of others. This is clearly manifested in the lives of Abraham (as) and Moses (as), and this is what we mean when we say that religion is not separated from the politics of Allāh's servants! The verses of the Qurʾān are replete with instances that demonstrate these two affairs, by which I mean sending messengers to guide all mankind ("We did not send you except as a bearer of good news and warner to all mankind..."[13]) and fighting against all those who obstruct divine guidance as well ("Fight all the polytheists, just as they fight you all..."[14]).

---

13. Sūrat Sabaʾ (34):28
14. Sūrat al-al-Tawbah (9):36

20. Levels

There is a connection, in the logic of the Qurʾān, between guidance ("I will guide you"), self-refinement ("refine yourself"), and fear ("that you may fear") because faith is not restricted to the worshipping of the limbs, which may not entail any of these affairs. Hence, we know that anyone who wants to guide others must have attained these levels and embodied them in themselves. Someone who lacks fear and refinement cannot bring these about in others.

21. Pharaoh and Moses (as)

Allāh commanded Moses (as) to raise the level of what was being demanded of Pharaoh, who claimed lordship for himself. So Moses asked of him things that some people might not have thought him obliged to do, such as self-refinement and fear. If this is the case, how can some people excuse themselves from such duties while they are at an acceptable level of faith?

22. Fear of Allāh

We can say that the stages of being affected by the preaching of the prophets and successors (as) are represented first by learning ("and teach them the Book and wisdom"[15]) followed by fear ("Only those of Allah's servants having knowledge fear Him..."[16]). Their fruit is fearing Allāh and avoiding His prohibitions ("You can only warn those who fear their Lord..."[17]) because this internal transformation requires a foundation of fear, which is why the Qurʾān makes fear a precondition of taking a moral ("There is indeed a moral in that for someone who fears!"[18]).

23. Self-refinement

Self-refinement is accomplished in two stages:

---

15. Sūrat al-Baqarah (2):129
16. Sūrat Fāṭir (35):28
17. Sūrat Fāṭir (35):18
18. Sūrat al-Nāziʿāt (79):26

- First, 'general self-refinement' (*al-tazkiya al-ijmāliyya*) as represented by avoiding sins and receiving general guidance (*al-hidāya al-ijmāliyya*)
- Second, 'detailed self-refinement' (*al-tazkiya al-tafṣīliyya*) that accompanies fear after which the servant becomes ready for select and detailed guidance (*al-hidāya al-khāṣṣa*)

The verse mentions self-refinement first, followed by guidance, followed by fear ("refine yourself...I will guide you...that you might fear").

24. Moses' miracles

Acting on the psychological dimension comes before acting visibly on the external one. As you can see:

- Moses (as) acted to bring about an emotional and intellectual opening in the psychological realm by using soft words and calling [Pharaoh] to refine himself and fear [Allāh] in the manner of a suggestion or a request, rather than that of a forceful command.
- Moses (as) showed Pharaoh the greatest signs in the visible realm, including the transformation of his staff, his white hand, and others in order to leave him without any excuse.

It is well-known that miracles are rarely employed to convince people, but the same cannot be said of psychological influence—this option is always open for anyone who wishes to utilize the methods of the prophets.

25. Guiding other people

The duty of anyone to whom Allāh turns towards and singles out for special graces is represented in utilizing that to guide other people and confront the wrongdoers. Rather than being absorbed by spiritual prosperity, as is the practice of monks, the first action the prophets (as) undertook after receiving their mission was to guide those who were astray and confront those who had earned

Allāh's wrath. This is something we can also see clearly in the life of the Final Prophet (s).

26. Prophets

Allāh endowed His prophets with powers that corresponded to those of their enemies. So He gave Moses numerous signs, including the one mentioned in this *sūrah* ("Then he showed him the greatest sign") because of the power of his opponent who claimed not only lordship for himself but the *highest* lordship ("I am your lord, the most-high!") in addition to the fact that his civilization had reached the pinnacle of development in architecture and other fields, as attested to by the construction of the pyramids. This power belongs to the hearts of everyone who calls to Allāh in all times and places, as there is some power that provides them with that which they need in order to match that of their enemies, such that there is no fear upon them in this regard, and nor shall they grieve!

27. Employing falsehood

Those who have strayed from the path of guidance do not hesitate in employing any falsehood, no matter how obvious. This is why Pharaoh insists on calling the most honest man alive, Moses (as), a liar ("But he denied") in spite of the manifest signs he brought, not least of which was showing Pharaoh's magic to be false—something the magicians themselves confessed to![19]

28. False beliefs

The people of falsehood are committed to their false beliefs. In fact, they struggle for them. Pharaoh "turned back, striving" as striving shows seriousness and determination, but the faithful are more entitled to strive for the sake of their rights. This is why the Commander of the Faithful (as) had every right to complain about his people when he said, "How strange it is! By Allah, my heart

---

19. Sūrat al-Aʿrāf (7):119–120

sinks and I grieve to see these people united upon their falsehood while you scatter from your right; So woe to you! And grief!"[20]

In another verse, the Qurʾān alludes to the fact that whatever harm befalls you, the faithful, in Allāh's way also befalls the faithless, with the caveat that there is an immeasurable divide between the fate of these two sides ("If you are suffering, they are also suffering like you, but you expect from Allah what they do not expect..."[21]).

29. The media

Tyrants in every age exploit the media for their own ends. Pharaoh had the ability to gather the people and tell them whatever he wanted, as we see from Allāh's words "and mustered [the people] and proclaimed" and His words "Then Pharaoh sent heralds to the cities."[22] This shows us that someone like this can only be confronted by using similar means—namely, the media power to assemble one's allies and helpers in the path of guidance.

30. Two kinds of punishment

Allāh holds two kinds of punishment for people; a punishment deferred until a day on which the eyes will be glazed[23] and an immediate punishment! Allāh will show some people abasement in this world before the hereafter, and that is what happened to Pharaoh and his clan—as for the punishment of this world, "So We...drowned them in the sea"[24] and in the hereafter, "And on the day when the Hour sets in Pharaoh's clan will enter the severest punishment."[25] Allāh combines these two meanings in His words "So Allah seized him with the punishment of this life and the Hereafter." It is possible to say that whoever disputes Allāh's authority will face punishment in this world, unlike the sinner who not only does not see in himself the power to contend with

20. *Nahj al-balāgha*, sermon no. 27
21. Sūrat al-Nisāʾ (4):104
22. Sūrat al-Shuʿarāʾ (26):53
23. Sūrat Ibrāhīm (14):42: "He is only granting them respite until the day when the eyes will be glazed."
24. Sūrat al-Aʿrāf (7):136
25. Sūrat Ghāfir (40):46

his Lord once he dies, but, in truth sees his own abasement in the sins he has committed.

31. Lessons

The Qurʾān does not set forth stories of the prophets (as) to offer us consolation from listening to their tales or to cast them in purely artistic forms. Rather these stories are there for us to consider and take lessons from. This is only possible for those who already possess a foundation of fearing their Lord ("There is indeed a moral in that for someone who fears!").

Verses 27–36

79:27 *Is it you whose creation is more prodigious or the sky which He has built?*

79:28 *He raised its vault, and fashioned it,*

79:29 *and darkened its night, and brought forth its day;*

79:30 *and after that He spread out the earth,*

79:31 *and brought forth from it its water and pastures,*

79:32 *and set firm the mountains,*

79:33 *as a provision for you and your livestock.*

79:34 *When the Greatest Catastrophe befalls,*

79:35 *the day when man will remember his endeavors,*

79:36 *and hell is brought into view for one who sees,*

32. The universe

One verse says, "Is it you whose creation is more prodigious or the sky which He has built?" Another, elsewhere, says, "Surely the creation of the heavens and the earth is more prodigious than the creation of mankind...."[26] In these verses, the Qurʾān affirms the fact that the act of creating of the heavens is greater than that

26. Sūrat Ghāfir (40):57

of creating the human being. In this way, it makes the power of creation more complex, as proof that Allāh can repeat the creation of something lesser. This reveals the state of believers when they ponder the creation of the heavens, especially when they wake for prayer in the depths of the night. They realize, in truth, that the object of contemplation, the universe, is greater than the one contemplating it–the person themselves. This realization, in turn, should give occasion to feel small and humbled indeed!

33. Posing a question

One of the ways to engage your audience is to pose them a question, even if the answer to it seems obvious, in order to arouse their interest in the subject under discussion, which is why the Almighty asks the question, "Is it you whose creation is more prodigious or the sky which He has built?" so that the audience will acknowledge their own weakness in their own hearts.

34. Mentioning signs

The common approach to remind mankind of their creator is by mentioning His signs in the external world. That is why the Qurʾān frequently mentions the heavens and the earth, including these signs, so that the audience's minds will move from the sensory to the intelligible. But there are also servants who do not need this common approach—these are those for whom Allāh manifests within their own selves in some form.

35. Enjoying the provisions of this world

There is no fault whatsoever in people enjoying the provisions of this world, so long as this does not hinder them from worshipping their Lord. Allāh mentions the blessings of the earth—and the things He brings forth from it such as water, pasture, and mountains—in the context of divine blessings. Far be it from Allāh to give His servants something that would bar them from His way! The Qurʾān affirms this fact when it says, "Say: 'Who has forbidden the adornment of

Allah which He has brought forth for His servants, and the good things of provision?'"[27]

36. Masters of provision

When some provision is attributed to another person, this implies that its owner occupies a higher level than it because the owner possesses it and uses it as he wishes, making him its master (*mālik*) and owner. Whereas someone who loves this provision becomes its servant (*mamlūk*). The Qur'ān wants us to be masters of provision ("as a provision for you") not for worldly provisions to become masters of us! This is why some say that the essence of asceticism (*zuhd*) is that nothing owns the human being, not that the human being owns nothing.[28]

37. Reflection

Allāh attributes the provisions of this world to mankind and cattle equally ("...for you and your cattle"), but the distinction between them lies in other areas—namely, reflection and thought. It is only through these activities that the human being becomes a rational animal (*ḥaywān nāṭiq*).

38. Catastrophe

The tribulation servants face on the Day of Judgement as a consequence of their actions is graver than any other they have experienced. That is why Allāh calls it "the greatest catastrophe." A catastrophe (*ṭāmma*) means something overwhelming. It is described as "greatest" (*kubrā*) to emphasize its gravity. Once we comprehend this, we will come to realize that we should endure the hardships of this world to avoid something worse than them!

39. Self-accounting

During the events of the resurrection, and especially when hell comes into view for its inhabitants, the human being will be

---

27. Sūrat al-Aʿrāf (7):32
28. *Taḥqīq fī kalimāt al-Qur'ān* 4/356

constantly reminded of their efforts in this world ("the day man will remember his endeavors") and this in and of itself is a kind of punishment for hell's inhabitants because it associates their past actions with their immediate consequences. They will see that their worldly pleasures have truly vanished and their suffering has now begun!

How appropriate it is that this remembrance, which is in the abode of this world, should be an opportunity for us to change our ways, as this lies at the very core of self- accounting (*muḥasaba*) and self-observation (*murāqaba*). Imām al-Kāḍhim (as) disassociates from anyone who neglects these duties when he says, "Not of us is whoever does not hold himself to account every day!"[29]

Verses 37–46

79:37 *as for him who was rebellious*

79:38 *and preferred the life of this world,*

79:39 *his refuge will indeed be hell.*

79:40 *But as for him who fears standing before his Lord and forbids the soul from desire,*

79:41 *his refuge will indeed be paradise.*

79:42 *They ask you concerning the Hour, 'When will it set in?'*

79:43 *What have you to say thereof?*

79:44 *Its outcome is with your Lord.*

79:45 *You are only a warner for those who fear it.*

79:46 *The day they see it, it shall be as if they had not stayed [in the world] except for an evening or forenoon.*

40. Internal foundation

If the foundation of rebelliousness is laid down in servants ("as for him who was rebellious"), this will cause them to prefer the

29. *Biḥār al-anwār* 1/152

life of this world over the hereafter ("and preferred the life of this world") as the above verses have joined together these two qualities. Likewise, a foundation of fearing the encounter with one's Lord ("But as for him who fears standing before his Lord") will cause them to forbid themselves from following their desires ("and forbids the soul from desire") as we also glean from this *sūrah*. The general rule we can derive from the Qurʾān as a whole is that a person's internal foundation is the source for many external effects.

41. Worldly life

The human being's problem does not lie in any distinct feature of worldly life, as represented by women, sons, accumulated piles of gold and silver, and livestock and farms.[30] Rather it lies in preferring these things to the satisfaction of the Lord Almighty ("and preferred the life of this world") in the fact that they are made decorous in our minds ("I will surely glamorize for them [life] upon the earth"[31]) and that they lead to servants becoming rebelliousness ("Indeed man becomes rebellious when he considers himself without need."[32]). In other words, the problem lies in not in ownership (*ʿalāqa*) but in the level of attachment (*ʿulqa*).

42. Actions of the heart

When interpreting "standing before his Lord," which makes one fear Him, several meanings are mentioned:

- Standing before Him for judgement, in which it means standing before our Lord means when the scales are set up.
- Allāh's knowledge of the actions of His servant and His watchfulness over him, in the sense that He stands over every soul and is aware of what it earns.[33]

30. Sūrat Āle ʿImrān (3):14: "To mankind has been made to seem decorous the love of desires, including women and children, accumulated piles of gold and silver, horses of mark, livestock, and farms. Those are the wares of the life of this world; but Allah - with Him is a good destination."

31. Sūrat al-Ḥijr (15):39

32. Sūrat al-ʿAlaq (96): 6–7

33. Sūrat al-Raʿd (13):33: "Is He who sustains every soul in spite of what it earns [comparable to the idols]?"

- In the sense of the station of Lordship and all that Lordship entails

All of these interpretations are in agreement that it is the deeds of servants that nurture the heart, which, in turn, comprehends these spiritual truths and causes them to abstain from their desires and which ultimately leads to their physical well-being. This shows that the actions of the heart precede the actions of the body, just as a cause precedes an effect, or just as unrolling a scroll of paper precedes writing something upon it.

43. Standing before one's Lord

Being aware of standing before one's Lord means that the human being views all the vicissitudes of life as being from Allāh, and this awareness is one of the causes for someone to follow the right path in public and in private and thereby eliminate or minimize oscillations between turning towards Allāh and turning away from Him, of which even the *awliyāʾ* complain.

One piece of evidence that the meaning of standing before one's Lord is what we mentioned above is a tradition narrated from Imām al-Ṣādiq (as), in which he says, "Whoever knows that Allah sees him, hears his what he says and knows any good or evil [he does], and this prevents him from immoral deeds, then this person is one who fears standing before his Lord and forbids his soul from desire."[34]

44. Fear

People's fear could be:

- due to an external factor, such as fear of a wild animal or a human enemy.
- because of some fault of their own, such as a criminal's fear of punishment.

---

34. *Al-Kāfi* 2/70

- because they sense the greatness of someone they believe to be great, such as a student's fear of a teacher that accompanies a sense of the teacher's importance.

So when the *awliyāʾ* fear Allāh, this fear belongs in the third category. They do not feel fear because something fearsome threatens them, nor because of any fault of their own doing. Rather it is because they are aware of the station of greatness that inspires them with a holy sense of fear.

45. Desires

People must deal with their desires ("and forbids the soul from desire") as a father deals with a child who, unaware of his own best interests, desires something that will bring him to ruin, so his father prevents him from pursuing it. This is different from forbidding evil, which is accomplished purely through admonition.

Therefore, the way we deal with our own desires is not like one equal giving advice to another.

46. Divine law

The divine law applies to all creations, whether they exist in the external realm or the internal one. One this basis, the verse invokes a general principle: He "who was rebellious" will fall into the path of ruin, for hell is his refuge, while he "who fears standing before his Lord" will attain the peak of guidance, for paradise is his, as it is clear that whoever follows the path of causes will reach their effects, just as it is in the material realm.

47. Details that have no practical benefit

Some people become fixated on details that have no practical benefit, and in this they resemble the polytheists who were asking about the time of the hour. The Qurʾān answers them, "What have you to say thereof?" to dissuade them from this childishness that is of no avail. The same is true of Allāh's saying, "They ask you concerning the Hour, 'When will it set in?'"

Perhaps we can apply the same rebuke to those who try to work out when Allāh's relief (*faraj*) will come, for example, while doing nothing to prepare themselves to assist the bringer of that relief. Or we can apply the same rebuke to those who try to work out the philosophy behind certain rulings rather than applying them to their lives!

48. Hidden knowledge

Even though Allāh has opened the door of exoteric knowledge to all of His servants and the door of esoteric knowledge to His elect, the prophets and the successors (as), there is some knowledge that He has reserved of which no human being has any inkling. One such piece of knowledge concerns the time of the Day of Judgement, whose knowledge is in the sole preserve of the One who knows everything visible and the unseen ("Its outcome is with your Lord.").

None of this, in any way, shape, or form, prevents servants from seeking abundant and copious knowledge from our Lord, according to our innate capacity for that. In fact, we should first ask Him to expand our capacity and then to shower His blessings upon us!

49. Glad tidings and warnings

The prophets (as) were sent as bearers of glad tidings and as warners, but that does not mean that the ratio of warnings to glad tidings is equal for all kinds of people. Warnings, rather than glad tidings, are emphasized for those who are negligent or oppositional, and that is why this verse only mentions a warning for those who deny the resurrection ("You are only a warner for those who fear it.").

This means that when believers are calling others towards Allāh, they must balance warnings and glad tidings according to the condition of those with whom they are interacting.

50. Personal development

The prophets (as) came to raise each individual person's level of development, but in order to have an effect, their preaching requires there be a general foundation for the acceptance of their message. This in turn necessitates a state, even if only a very general one, of fear towards the Origin sometimes ("You can only warn someone who follows the Reminder and fears the All-beneficent..."[35]) and towards the Return at others ("You are only a warner for those who fear it.").

This shows that someone who has not based their life on being open [to the prophetic message] and followed [it] within themselves, cannot bring themselves to follow the prophets externally. This is what Allāh means when He says, "...it is the same to them whether you warn them or do not warn them...."[36]

51. A short sojourn

Being aware of the transient nature of this world and its insignificance compared to the hereafter is something that will prevent servants from being consumed by lusts. This is because any rational person will naturally forgo a small gain for a greater one. So what about when the two are incomparable? As compared to the eternal life of the hereafter, this world is nothing more than a morning or evening's sojourn ("The day they see it, it shall be as if they had not stayed for an evening or a forenoon") or even less; an hour! Allāh says, "And on the day when the Hour sets in the guilty will swear that they had remained only for an hour...."[37]

35. Sūrat Yā Sīn (36):11
36. Sūrat al-Baqarah (2):6
37. Sūrat al-Rūm (30):55

Sūrat ʿAbasa (no. 80: He Frowned)

Verses 1–10

80:1 *He frowned and turned away*

80:2 *when the blind man approached him.*

80:3 *And how do you know, maybe he would refine himself,*

80:4 *or take admonition, and the admonition would benefit him!*

80:5 *But as for someone who is self-complacent,*

80:6 *you attend to him,*

80:7 *though you care not if he does not purify himself.*

80:8 *But he who comes hurrying to you,*

80:9 *while he fears,*

80:10 *you are neglectful of him.*

1. Rebuke

Because of the rebuke these verses contain, which should be obvious to anyone who ponders them, it does not make sense that they should be referring to the Prophet (s), whom the Qurʾān describes as being possessed of a great character (*khuluq ʿaḍhīm*).[1]

If the Prophet (s) was not known to scowl even in the face of a disbeliever, then how could he in the face of the faithful? What about one whom the Qurʾān describes as blind, which would make him even more entitled to kindness? What about someone who came "hurrying" with great effort, desiring to be one of those who "feared"?

1. Sūrat al-Qalam (68):4: "and indeed you possess a great character."

2. Scowling

The moral qualities that emanate from believers originate only from their own spiritual perfection (*kamāl dhātī*) and not out of a desire to be praised, thanked, or otherwise rewarded! Scowling to other people's faces is something reprehensible, even to the face of a blind man who cannot see the scowl! Believer hold themselves to a higher standard than that because this is a quality that is detestable in the eyes of our Lord and in the eyes of one's own self.

3. Free from enslavement

When the Qur'ān speaks of guidance (*hidāya*), it mentions self-refinement (*tazkiya*) as the axis for the movement of the prophets.[2] Their teachings in their entirety exist only to release humankind from enslavement to their desires and free them to accept guidance. We know that the way to self-refinement is through being given admonition that awakens us from indolence, which is why the verses mention refinement and admonition together.

4. Unawareness

The preaching of those who call to Allāh is not always to bring people out of ignorance (*jahl*), such that their mission is merely teaching. Rather, it is also to bring people out of unawareness (*ghafla*), so their mission is also admonition! This is why this verse mentions admonition as benefitting some people, even if they are unaware ("or take admonition, and the admonition would benefit him!"). It is obvious that this does not apply to those who are opposed to the message. In fact, it will only increase their animosity and disbelief.

5. Complacency

It is the habit of worldly people to incline to whatever they think is a benchmark of success, and behold—one such benchmark is complacency ("But as for someone who is self-complacent, you attend to him") because this is an apparent virtue that is in

2. Sūrat al-Baqarah (2):151: "As We sent to you an Messenger from among yourselves, who recites to you Our signs, and purifies you, and teaches you the Book and wisdom, and teaches you what you did not know."

harmony with their own disposition, unlike someone who comes earnestly in a state of fear of Allāh, for their disposition renders them incapable of perceiving his virtue, causing them to dismiss those who possess it. Complacency, which is common amongst worldly persons, also does not accord with the spiritual rank of the Prophet (s), and thus it also serves to demonstrate again that this rebuke cannot have been directed against him.

6. Piety

Those verses rebuking he who turned away from the blind man because of the latter's lack of social rank, want us to form our preferences about people according to religious standards—namely the principle that someone is only nobler in God's eyes because of his piety (*taqwā*),[3] which was never given any regard during the Age of Ignorance, nor even after the advent of Islām in many circles. The above verse explicitly cites one of the harmful effects of failing to use this principle as a guide—namely, turning away while scowling at someone who possesses two very great attributes: striving to refine himself ("comes hurrying to you") and attiring himself with a continuous state of fear as is indicated by the verse "while he fears." In fact, the verse mentions an effect worse still, by which I mean attending to someone else as indicated by the verse "you are neglectful of him."

7. Neglecting other people's refinement

One of the qualities of worldly people (*ahl al-dunyā*) and those who seek complacency is a lack of concern with guiding people to the right path because they are fundamentally uninterested in their own guidance and self-refinement—why should they bother with the refinement of others? This is why the verse in front of us makes the condition of neglecting other people's refinement an occasion for reprimand ("though you care not if he does not purify himself"). We could say that this state of indifference is an instance of "Whoever does not concern himself with the affairs of

3. Sūrat al-Ḥujurāt (49):13: "Indeed the noblest of you in the sight of Allah is the most Godwary among you. Indeed Allah is all-knowing, all-aware."

the Muslims is not of them,"[4] as one of the most important affairs of the Muslims is striving for the refinement of others.

Verses 11–23

80:11 *No indeed! These are a reminder*

80:12 *—so let anyone who wishes remember it—*

80:13 *in honored scriptures,*

80:14 *exalted and purified,*

80:15 *in the hands of envoys,*

80:16 *noble and pious.*

80:17 *Perish man! How ungrateful is he!*

80:18 *From what has He created him?*

80:19 *He has created him from a drop of fluid, and then proportioned him.*

80:20 *Then He made the way easy for him;*

80:21 *then He made him die and buried him;*

80:22 *and then, if He wished, resurrected him.*

80:23 *No indeed! He has not yet carried out what He had commanded him.*

8. Greatness of Qurʾān

The verses in this section that pertain to the Qurʾān demonstrate its greatness insofar as it is:

- a collection "in honored scriptures" in the unseen realm and not those physical scriptures that we possess.
- of a lofty degree, "exalted" because of the measure of its rank.

4. *Al-Kāfi* 2/164

- "purified" from every impurity and beyond the reach of any distortion.
- "in the hands of envoys noble" who are the assistants of the greatest angel, Gabriel (as), who is the deliverer of revelation, and it is in this sense that he was obeyed (*muṭāʿ*) ("obeyed and trustworthy"[5]). Valuable things are usually entrusted to a number of hands to ensure that they are honored or protected to the utmost.

9. The infallibles (as)

Just as the Qurʾān was borne by the hands of "envoys noble and pious" in the realm from whence it is dispatched, so too is it borne by the noblest of the final *umma* in the realm in which it was received—namely, the infallibles (as) who bear the realities of the Qurʾān in every age, followed by those who are most exemplary in purity and nobility after them. Honored and purified scriptures require receptacles approximate to them in purity and sanctity, hence no one grasps the realities of the Qurʾān, not even amongst the scholars, save he who is pure and purified ("no one touches it except the pure ones").[6]

10. Ingratitude

The Lord who calls the immoderate to His mercy and shows affection for His creatures who are sinners,[7] calls a group of His creatures, namely, those who are ungrateful His blessings, with the harshest expression, being slain ("Perish man!"). The difference between the arches of divine mercy and divine wrath is vast indeed, and that is because ingratitude (*kufr*) contains a kind of challenge to the station of lordship. After reflecting on this, perhaps we can say that His wrath is actually a branch of His mercy as erecting justice and cultivating His servants by effectuating His wrath in

---

5. Sūrat al-Takwīr (81):21
6. Sūrat al-Wāqiʿah (56):79
7. Sūrat al-Zumar (39):53: "Say: 'O My servants who have committed excesses against their own souls, do not despair of the mercy of Allah.'"

its proper place is to make known His mercy in its proper place as well.

11. Ingratitude

The greatest act of ingratitude (*kufr*) is represented by covering the source of blessings with the veil of denial ("How ungrateful he is!"), and a lesser act of ingratitude is represented by covering the blessings themselves. The perpetrators of both of these sins can be called "faithless" (*kāfir*), but the harsh rebuke contained in these verses is appropriate for denying lordship.

However, this rebuke may also encompass ingratitude towards His blessings (*kufr bil- niʿma*) on some level, and even if we were to lighten this rebuke, what remained would still weigh heavy on the servants. That is why those who squander His blessings are called "brothers of the devils"[8] because this is a kind of ingratitude for them.

12. Ingratitude

If the creator of the universe uses an expression of astonishment for anything, this is striking indeed! When One who sees nothing exceptional in the universe because of His great authority and boundless sovereignty displays astonishment in His book ("How ungrateful he is!"), this shows how severe the matter is. What calamity is graver than denying the One who describes Himself elsewhere in this manner ("Is there any doubt about Allah, the originator of the heavens and the earth?"[9])?!

13. Dead but living

When Allāh invokes perishing upon a disbeliever, an expression which is more eloquent than a curse (*laʿn*), in illustrating his exclusion from the compass of divine mercy, the object of His invocation does not always come to pass in this world. People who have had death invoked upon them by their Lord might live a full

8. Sūrat al-Isrāʾ (17):27
9. Sūrat Ibrāhīm (14):10

and comfortable life. However, worse than the death of the body is the death of the spirit, which is like killing it ("They are dead, not living, and are not aware when they will be resurrected."[10]). This is because their inner faculties, such as hearing, sight, and thought, are idle and unused. What kind of life is this?

14. Origins

The Qurʾān frequently reminds humankind of their origins with various phrases ("Was he not a drop of emitted semen?"[11] "from an extract of a base fluid"[12]) just as this verse reminds disbelievers of their origins, firstly so that they may remember their lowly beginnings ("He fashioned him from a drop of fluid" so they are made from an impure liquid with an unpleasant odor) and, secondly, to demonstrate the magnificence of His creation. In three months, Allāh brings forth from the shadows of the womb things that amaze human minds by virtue of their beautiful and precise fashioning. This is why humankind is worthy of perishing when they deny the source of their being!

In short, any being whose beginnings were such has no right to pronounce anything that would suggest ingratitude.

15. Moral excellence

The expression "then proportioned him" suggests that there are two proportioning hands that want to intervene in this short time to produce wonderful things, after which the Creator leaves the affairs of the servants to themselves to do as they please! But if servants were to entreat their Master to watch over them, after emerging from the world of the womb, with their speech in the same manner as the servants entreated Him to watch over them in the womb through their state therein, would they not attain that moral excellence in this world just as they attained their physical excellence in the womb, when the hands that shape them in each are actually one and the same!?

---

10. Sūrat al-Naḥl (16):21
11. Sūrat al-Qiyāmah (75):37
12. Sūrat al-Sajdah (32):8

16. Beneath the guardianship of Satan

Allāh created mankind, and everything is made easy for the purpose for which they were created ("Then He made the way easy for him."). Servants can see this ideal clearly at the beginning of their journeys, even if they are sinners. But, with repeated sinning, and especially of major sins, they will reach a state where they no longer see the way as made easy. Rather "We shall surely ease him into hardship"[13] and they see themselves inclining against their will towards falsehood. The devils who have taken over their lives drive them towards things that will cause them hardship. This is what it means to be beneath the guardianship (*wilāya*) of Satan for some of those who do not follow the path of guidance.

17. Death and burial

Being attentive to the first stage of the life of this world ("He has created him from a drop of fluid and then proportioned him") and to its last ("then He made him die and buried him") breaks a person's selfish conceits, especially when they see themselves destined for that such as those of the person being mentioned at the beginning of this *sūrah* who was attentive to a complacent person but neglected a fearful one.

The Qur'ān's mentioning death and burial in the context of reprimanding people whom it has invoked death upon might be a way of deriding people who live a life of conceited faithlessness. Sometimes they have been reminded that they sprang from a lowly fluid ("Have We not created you from a base fluid"[14]), and, in this *sūrah,* they are reminded that they will ultimately become a rotting corpse[15] that has to be buried to contain its stench, so how can they be conceited when confronted by the exalted Lord of the Worlds?!

---

13. Sūrat al-Layl (92):10

14. Sūrat al-Mursalāt (77):20

15. *Nahj al-balāgha,* aphorism no. 451

18. Regression of bodies

The kind of death that is followed by burial is the external death of the body that will return to the dust. Were it not for the fact that the earth absorbs these bodies, these corpses would cause disgust and revulsion to their (former) comrades! However, this regression of bodies generally stands in marked contrast to the ascension of some spirits. There are some spirits whose final destination lies "in the abode of truthfulness with an omnipotent King."[16]

19. Resurrection

Divine wisdom demands that the dead be returned to life to receive the punishment or reward they deserve as recompense for their deeds in this world. All of this falls within the remit of the divine will, which is why this verse says, "if He wished, resurrected him," for He is the Master of these bondsmen in their origin and their end—their duties and their recompense.

20. Covetousness and anxiety

Many verses say that it is in humankind's nature to incline towards covetousness and anxiety,[17] that humankind is unfair and senseless,[18] and that we are in a state of loss.[19] These verses call to mind a question: Has a human being (who is in the palm of the Master's hand throughout all the ups and downs of life and who pays no heed to anything the verse says about creation and burial) truly discharged what his Lord commanded him to do? The answer is "No indeed! He has not yet carried out what He had commanded him."

---

16. Sūrat al-Qamar (54):55

17. Sūrat al-Maʿārij (70):19–20: "Indeed man has been created covetous, anxious when an ill befalls him..."

18. Sūrat al-Aḥzāb (33):72: "Indeed he is most unfair and senseless."

19. Sūrat al-ʿAṣr (103):2: "Indeed man is in loss"

Verses 24–32

80:24 *So let man observe his food:*

80:25 *We poured down water plenteously,*

80:26 *then We split the earth into fissures*

80:27 *and made the grain grow in it,*

80:28 *and vines and vegetables,*

80:29 *olives and date palms,*

80:30 *and densely-planted gardens,*

80:31 *fruits and pastures,*

80:32 *as a sustenance for you and your livestock.*

21. Food

The command for people to observe their food includes all dimensions of observation, whether the source, the means of obtaining it, the variety of its yields, or the many hands involved in preparing it... and we can even move from discussing physical food that sustains the body to discuss spiritual food that sustains the spirit. It has been narrated that Imām al-Bāqir (as) explained the meaning of 'food' (*ṭaʿām*) in the verse "So let man observe his food" as follows: "His knowledge which he obtains, from whom he obtains it."[20]

22. Pondering food and drink

After directing a rebuke to those who are ungrateful to their Lord, the verses shift their address to all mankind to encourage them to ponder and reflect within themselves. They call on them to look at the effects of Allāh's mercy upon the earth for Allāh has placed at their disposal pouring water ("We poured down water plenteously") and the earth that brings forth all kinds of vegetation ("then We split the earth into fissures") in order to satisfy mankind's hunger ("and made the grain grow in it") and for them to enjoy sights

20. *Al-Kāfī* 1/50

such as its towering trees ("and densely-planted gardens!") These sensory enjoyments are the most common amongst all people, and perhaps the verse singles out these blessings in order to remind people of the boons that are clearest to them—namely, the food and drink they consume.

23. Food

These verses unequivocally state that it is Allāh who causes plants to grow and sends down water from the skies, while some negligent servants of His think that it is obviously the farmers who cultivate the land, unaware that He is the cause behind all causes ("Is it you who make it grow, or are We the grower?"[21]

So, when servants eat foods like those mentioned in the verse ("vines and vegetables, olives and date palms" and "fruits" and herbs), then they are living in a state of receiving blessings and giving thanks towards the creator more than towards the one who presents them with it. How can the creator of the very origin of food be compared to someone who gives it to another creature like himself?

24. Humans and animals

When the Qurʾān mentions eaten provisions, it joins cattle to human beings ("a sustenance for you and your livestock"), and it also mentions in this *sūrah* what is eaten by humans ("fruits") and what is eaten by animals ("pastures") in the same context. However, when the discussion turns to intelligible provisions, it places humans in the context of the angels who have knowledge of Allāh ("Allah bears witness that there is no god except Him—as do the angels and those who possess knowledge—maintainer of justice...").[22]

---

21. Sūrat al-Wāqiʿah (56):64
22. Sūrat Āle ʿImrān (3):18

Verses 33–42

80:33 *So when the deafening Cry comes*

80:34 *—the day when a man will flee his brother,*

80:35 *his mother and his father,*

80:36 *his spouse and his sons—*

80:37 *that day each of them will have a task to keep him preoccupied.*

80:38 *That day some faces will be bright,*

80:39 *laughing and bright.*

80:40 *And some faces on that day will be covered with dust,*

80:41 *overcast with gloom.*

80:42 *It is they who are the faithless, the vicious.*

25. Cries

The Qurʾān repeatedly mentions different kinds of cry (*ṣayḥa*) on the Day of Resurrection:

- A cry on its own ("A single cry"[23])
- The quaker (*rājifa*), which is a terrible cry which causes shaking and confusion[24]
- The deafening cry (*ṣākha*), which is a cry so loud that it deafens those who hear it
- The trumpet (*nāqūr*), which will emit a sound that rends the heavens asunder[25]

The meaning that unites all of these sounds together is that, on the Day of Resurrection, there will be a terrifying sound announcing the time for judgement has come. In contrast to this, Allāh frequently used an affectionate style of speech in this world, to encourage His servants to hold themselves to account before the

23. Sūrat Yā Sīn (36):53
24. Sūrat al-Nāziʿāt (79):6
25. Sūrat al-Muddaththir (74):8

accounting of the resurrection ("Account yourselves before you are accounted."[26]) and to die of their own choice before being made to die ("Die before you die."[27]) and to weigh their own deeds in this world before they are weighed in the hereafter ("Weigh them before you are weighed."[28]). This is all because there is no opportunity for them to change their ways after they die.

26. Fleeing

When the verse speaks of fleeing ("the day when a man will flee his brother…"), this shows us the grave situation that the resurrected people find themselves in. A person will flee because:

- he is preoccupied with his own situation so that he is distracted from the terrors of the Day of Resurrection.
- he is afraid that those mentioned will come to demand the rights he deprived them of in this world.
- he wants to avoid becoming ensnared by them, as they might be asking that he give them some of his good deeds, which he has the greatest need of!

27. Helpers for the hereafter

Anyone who remembers this verse while in this world will experience a sense of wariness towards those people around him, even his nearest and dearest! The ideal way for him to alleviate himself of this burden is to make them into helpers for the hereafter, rather than merely helpers for this worldly existence. The latter is the habit of worldly people, who only desire sons for strength, honor, and the amassing of wealth, whereas the faithful want their children to be a good deed of theirs that will continue after their death (*sadaqa jāriya*).

Whereat it is only natural that parents would be pleased to see their children in the stages of the resurrection. In fact, they will

26. *Biḥār al-anwār* 67/73
27. Ibid. 69/59
28. Ibid. 73/67

seek them out to be reunited and to dwell together on a single level of paradise, as the fulfilment of Allāh's word, "The faithful and their descendants who followed them in faith — We will make their descendants join them...."[29]

28. Preoccupation with the self

One of the most striking aspects of this *sūrah* is the appearance of the verse "that day each of them will have a task to keep him preoccupied" after those saying that man will flee from those nearest and dearest to him. This suggests that it is his preoccupation with his own self that causes him to neglect others, and he is only preoccupied with his own self because the veil has been lifted from him, and he now stands before Allāh for questioning.

Therefore, we say that if servants live their lives as though they are in the presence of their Lord in this world, they will attain two important results together. First, they will not be attached to anything that will distract them from Allāh, and, secondly, they will be occupied with their own selves. This is a state encouraged by numerous narrations—namely, that people should attend to their own self before looking at others. The verse "Save yourselves and your families"[30] also bears witness to this.

29. Emotional attachment

The order of relatives mentioned in the verse—brother, mother, father, spouse, and child—might be according to their increasing level of emotional attachment ("the day when a man will evade his brother, his mother, and his father, his spouse, and his sons"). The first is brothers and the last is sons because the child is a piece of the parents, but they are not a piece of him.

Perhaps it is from this very dimension that the Qur᾿ān mentions children together with wealth in the context of being tested

29. Sūrat al-Ṭūr (52):21
30. Sūrat al-Taḥrīm (66):6

thereby ("Know that your possessions and children are only a test..."[31]).

30. Facial expressions

People's facial expressions are a manifestation of the spiritual states they experience in this world and the hereafter:

- In the hereafter, this is clear as the verse mentions that it is to the degree that it is visibly perceptible. On the side of good, the face is illuminated ("bright") while on the side of evil there is gloom and darkness ("overcast with gloom") such that other resurrectees will see and know this because the cover will be removed from all of them.
- In this world, there is a touch of brightness that surrounds a believer's face, and the believer is aware of it. In fact, anyone who has been given the power of divine discernment (*firāsa īmāniyya*), to see by Allāh's light, also sees it.

Clearly, the light of someone's face on the Day of Resurrection is something won in this world, especially by offering night prayers and reciting the Qurʾān.

31. Dark face

The sort of deviation that causes darkness to appear in someone's face ("And some faces on that day will be covered with dust") is caused by two things:

- Deviation in beliefs—most visibly represented in disbelieving in Allāh ("It is they who are the faithless")
- Deviation in practice—as alluded to by the words "the vicious"

So it is not enough for someone whose beliefs are correct, or even sees the love of Allāh's *awliyāʾ* in his heart, to rely on this when he is not righteous in his practice. Profligacy is equal to faithlessness as the above verse mentions them together in a single context.

31. Sūrat al-Anfāl (8):28

Sūrat al-Takwīr (no. 81: The Winding)

Verses 1–14

81:1 *When the sun is wound up,*

81:2 *when the stars scatter,*

81:3 *when the mountains are set moving,*

81:4 *when the pregnant camels are neglected,*

81:5 *when the wild beasts are mustered,*

81:6 *when the seas are set afire,*

81:7 *when the souls are paired,*

81:8 *when the girl buried-alive will be asked*

81:9 *for what sin she was killed.*

81:10 *When the scrolls are unrolled,*

81:11 *when the heavens are stripped away,*

81:12 *when hell is set ablaze,*

81:13 *when paradise is brought near,*

81:14 *then a soul shall know what it has readied [for itself].*

1. Future events

The resurrection is often discussed by the Qurʾān in the past tense. For example, Allāh says, "When the Sun is wound up" and "When the Imminent Hour befalls..."[1] [both of these appear in the past tense in Arabic.] Future events that the Lord of the Worlds informs

1. Sūrat al-Wāqiʿah (56):1

us about as though they are in the past signify that they will as surely come to pass as the past itself. Of course, discussing events ordained in the future is more beneficial than discussing the past because there is still an opportunity to prepare for it, to make amends, and to change a dark past into a bright present.

2. Nothing is truly stable

When Allāh wishes to convey the terrors of the resurrection, He refers to stable worldly phenomena such as the sun, the stars, and the firm, unshakable mountains. All of this is in order to show us that there is never anything truly stable and unchanging in this universe. Everything will eventually fall apart ("When the Sun is wound up") and fade ("when the stars scatter"), and the only being that can be depended upon is one whose essence and effects are unchanging. Is He not the only one who answers the question, "To whom does the sovereignty belong today?" by saying, "To Allah, the One, the All- paramount!"

3. Distraction from worldly possessions

She-camels like those mentioned in the verse "when the pregnant camels are neglected" were extremely valuable to the Arabs when the Qurʾān was revealed. They were pregnant she-camels in their tenth month. By them being neglected, this means during the stages of the resurrection, the terrors of that day will distract Allāh's servants from even their most valuable possessions! Were a servant's heart, while he is in this world, to be occupied with thoughts of the terrors of that day (as ʿAlī (as) says in his sermon about the *muttaqīn*), then he too will be distracted from the things worldly people deem precious. They do not seem valuable to him because his measure of value differs dramatically!

4. The resurrection of animals

Qurʾānic commentaries have disagreed concerning the resurrection of animals—how can they be resurrected when they have not been placed under any moral obligation? One opinion is that they shall be raised according to the extent they comprehended their own mistreatment of other animals. This view finds support in Allāh's words "There is no animal on land, nor a bird that flies with its wings, but they are communities like yourselves."[2] A corollary of this resemblance between communities of animals and birds and those of mankind is shared ends as represented in their ultimate fate, by which I mean being resurrected on a single level.

Therefore, servants should pay attention to every fault that transpires with their knowledge as this knowledge alone is enough to necessitate the resurrection and judgement of animals. It is even said that "a wounded sheep will seek redress against the one with horns who gored it!"[3]

5. The sea

The sea contains two extremely flammable and explosive substances, but Allāh joined them together and, through their reaction, made them coolness and safety for His servants! Water puts out fire, but if you separate it into its constituent elements, they become a source of fire, and there you see "when the seas are set afire."

The Lord, who from two substances with volatile natures, created a third that is a symbol of coolness and safety, can also combine different tempestuous personalities in a family and spread love and kindness therein. In society, He can join different individuals together, just as He joined the first Muslims together, whose hearts would have never been united had Allāh not united them ("Had you spent all that is in the earth, you could not have united their hearts, but Allah united them together."[4]).

6. "When the souls are paired"

People's souls acquire their propensity to dwell in paradise or to be consigned to hellfire in the life of this world. So it is as though

2. Sūrat al-Anʿām (6):38
3. *Maʿālim al-tanzīl fī tafsīr al-Qurʾān* 5/203
4. Sūrat al-Anfāl (8):63

they are already engaged to the maidens of paradise or bound to the malevolent devils! But the actual marriage is delayed until that promised day, about which Allāh says, "when the souls are paired." That is the wedding day of the righteous believers, and that is why the bounties of the maidens are suited to them. As for the others, who are the vicious ones, the malevolence of the devils to whom they are bound best befits them!

7. Cutting off near relatives

Burying infant girls alive is one example of severing family ties. In fact it is the destruction of family itself. The murdered child was nothing more than a newborn infant, and we do not know what she would have become had she lived in this world. So even worse, then, is the crime of cutting off the near relatives of Allāh's messenger (s) and murdering their children!

Hence, one of the first acts of judgement on the Day of Resurrection, before even the infant buried alive is asked for what crime she was slain ("when the girl buried alive will be asked"), shall be when Allāh asks for what crime Ḥusayn (as) and his closest companions were butchered!

8. Burying innocent children

When souls stray from the compass of guidance, they are actually leaving the bounds of healthy human nature. How can a mother, who is the very manifestation of kindness and affection, bury her own daughter alive as women did in the Age of Ignorance. When their time for birth drew near, they would dig a grave and sit in front of it, and if they gave birth to a girl they put her into the grave, but if they gave birth to a son they kept him!

Even if this practice is no longer common in our modern Age of Ignorance, burying children alive has taken on new forms. One of these is aborting fetuses with special equipment. The other is exposing them to harm and corruption [while in the womb]. There are narrations that mention still other forms of burying innocent children alive. For example, when Imām al-Bāqir (as) was asked about the meaning of the verse, he said, "Whoever was killed for loving us and adhering to our cause."[5] There are many such victims throughout history!

9. Disgrace

There are some sinners who sin in private, afraid of disgrace amongst some of Allāh's servants, but sometimes the person who witnesses them is not who they expect. It could even be a young child! The truth is that the Day of Judgement is a day sinners will be disgraced in the presence of witnesses. Their records of deeds were rolled up in the abode of this world, but behold, on the Day of Judgement they "are unrolled."

And the greatest cause for embarrassment, after that of knowing Allāh is aware of our [wicked] deeds, is the thought of the Final Prophet (s) being informed of the sins of his *umma* in the presence of the other prophets.

10. Lifting of the veil

One of the most important features of the Day of Resurrection is the lifting of the veil from the eyes of Allāh's servants. The heavens that used to interpose between the inhabitants of the earth and those of the heavens will be "stripped away." In other words, the cloak will be removed from them, and a person will thereafter see clearly that which was hidden from him, including paradise and hellfire, and even the angels. The Qurʾān has clearly announced this awe-inspiring event in another verse which is the splitting of the heavens accompanied by the descent of the angels ("The day when the sky with its clouds will split open, and the angels will be sent down in a majestic descent."[6]).

Here, we must say how appropriate it is for those people with lofty goals in this world to strive to remove the veil of heedlessness (*ghafla*) from their hearts by continuous and vigilant self-observation (*murāqaba*) and constant remembrance (*dhikr*) so that

5. *Al-Kāfī* 1/295
6. Sūrat al-Furqān (25):25

they may glimpse in this world what they shall see clearly in the next, as this is something possible in both worlds!

11. Paradise near

If a man has some standing amongst people, then would-be brides pursue him and try to win him for themselves, and this magnifies his character. And the opposite is also true! On the Day of Resurrection, paradise will be like a bride rushing towards her ideal suitor, which is why the creator says of His paradise, "When Paradise is brought near." Paradise, with its maidens and palaces, is described as if it is coming to its inhabitants out of love for them, as they are the purpose for which it was created.

These verses show us that paradise and hellfire encompass the inhabitants of this world, but the veil of matter prevents them from being seen. Yet other narrations tell us that the maidens are longing to meet their spouses from this world. What a difference there is between paradise being brought near to its inhabitants and the hell created before the creation of the hereafter such that its flames are "set blaze" ready to swallow its inmates!

12. Self-observation

This *sūrah* is one of those distinguished by the many conditional statements (*sharṭ*) it contains. In total, it contains twelve antecedents, but all of them are followed by a single consequence—"then a soul shall know what it has readied." This shows how important it is to practice self-observation in this world, lest a servant has an unpleasant surprise in store in the next. If a servant could see the physical manifestation of deeds and the effects they have in this world, whether good or evil, he would be more disciplined in his behavior and would not need much admonition. Every deed, righteous or wicked, would appear as a provision in this world that he would have to carry with him until that day. This is why people's knowledge is described with "certainty" in the verse "No indeed! Were you to know with certain knowledge...."[7] Their

7. Sūrat al-Takāthur (102):5

deeds are described as being "found" in the verse "They will find present whatever they had done...."[8]

13. Seeing our deeds

This condition of finding present one's deeds is actually for all people ("The day when every soul will find present whatever good it has done..."[9]), and this includes good deeds and evil ones. It is not unlikely that servants will see their deeds on that day in a form that is different from the carnal form (*sūrah mulkiyya*) it possessed in this world. In fact, they will see them in their imaginal form (*sūrah malakūtiyya*). This is because the hereafter is the abode of unveiling and seeing clearly, which is why the sin of wrongfully consuming the property of orphans may appear in the form mentioned for it in the Qurʾān, "Indeed those who consume the property of orphans wrongfully, only ingest fire into their bellies...."[10]

In fact, we can say that if our senses were fully opened in this world, it is possible that our actions would take on their imaginal form even here. It has been narrated from Imām al-Ṣādiq (as) that he said, "When the believer relinquishes this world, he ascends."[11] A corollary of such an ascent (*samw*) is that some hidden realities will be unveiled to him while he is still in this world.

Verses 15–29

81:15 *So I swear not by the stars that withdraw,*

81:16 *the planets that hide,*

81:17 *by the night as it approaches,*

81:18 *by the dawn as it breathes,*

81:19 *it is indeed the speech of a noble Messenger,*

81:20 *powerful and eminent with the Lord of the Throne,*

---

8. Sūrat al-Kahf (18):49
9. Sūrat Āle ʿImrān (3):30
10. Sūrat al-Nisāʾ (4):10
11. *Al-Kāfī* 2/130

81:21 *one who is heard and trustworthy as well.*

81:22 *Your companion is not crazy:*

81:23 *certainly he saw him on the manifest horizon,*

81:24 *and he is not miserly concerning the Unseen.*

81:25 *And it is not the speech of an outcast Satan.*

81:26 *So where are you going?*

81:27 *It is just a reminder for all the nations,*

81:28 *for those of you who wish to be steadfast;*

81:29 *but you do not wish unless it is wished by Allah, the Lord of all the worlds.*

14. Negation of an oath

Verses that contain a negation of an oath, such as "So I swear not..." have been interpreted in a number of ways. The most fitting of these is that Allāh wishes to convey that the matter under discussion is so obvious it does not need someone to swear an oath to establish it as true and that if an oath must be sworn, then one will swear by the things mentioned.

This is something common amongst people. A father might say, "I do not wish to swear by my son, for the matter is such-and-such..." meaning that if I had wanted to swear an oath, I would have sworn it by him. This is much better than swearing a multitude of oaths!

15. Observing the firmament

A number of verses in the Qur'ān refer to planets and stars in a manner that draws attention, whether by invoking an oath or some other method. One such example is found in this *sūrah* when Allāh says, "by the planets that hide." What surrounds this with a degree of ambiguity is that the Qur'ān says they "withdraw" meaning they hide and journey to their place of rest ("planets" (*jawār*)) as an animal returns to its den (which is its home in which it rests ("that withdraw")). So, this verse contains an allusion to something we have yet to discover about the planets of our solar system, classically referred to as "the five stars."

In short, verses like these want servants to turn their attention towards the dominions of the heavens and the signs they contain. Because their creation is greater than that of mankind, observing the firmament allows humankind to enter new realms and discover new horizons in thought, rather than clinging to the earth beneath their feet.

16. Relief at sunrise

When Allāh says "by the dawn as it breathes," this suggests that the day is a new phase of activity after the stillness of the night. It is as though the day was constrained by the night, and as soon as the brightness of the dawn appears, it is released "from the evil of the dark night when it settles"[12] But this meaning only applies to a day that follows night. As for those who make night time their day, they do not experience this relief at sunrise.

17. Gabriel (as)

The oaths repeated in this *sūrah*, whether literal or figurative, are uttered to affirm the trustworthy nature of Gabriel (as) ("heard and trustworthy") which in turn entails the veracity of the Qurʾān and any other revelation brought by the angel. There is no doubting that this principle, the fidelity of revelation's herald, is the foundation for believing in the authenticity of the faith as a whole and in its ascription to Allāh. To doubt this principle means that the revelation given to the Prophet (s) cannot be relied upon because it may be contaminated by errors!

18. Qualities of prophets and messengers

If the messenger represented by Gabriel (as) has the qualities mentioned in this verse—namely, nobility, power, eminence, obedience, and fidelity, then what about those prophets and

12. Sūrat al-Falaq (113):3

messengers whose forefather was Adam, the object of the angels' prostration!

On this basis, we say that the successor, insofar as he is an extension of the messenger, must also be endowed with many of the messenger's qualities in order for a commonality to exist between them. This commonality between them is more fitting than the commonality between the messenger and the herald of revelation!

19. Prophet Muḥammad's (s) character

If we interpret the verse such that the attributes mentioned belong to the Prophet (s), including the quality of obedience as some claim, then this shows that the Prophet (s) is ennobled in the eyes of Allāh to the extent that his own commands are obeyed. The unqualified nature of this statement implies that it encompasses both the physical and moral realms, for he attained the pinnacle of obedience to Allāh, and it has been narrated in some books that his uncle, Abū Ṭālib (as), once said to him, "How obedient your Lord is to you, O Muḥammad!" to which he (s) replied, "And were you to obey him, O Uncle, He would obey you too!"[13]

20. Prophet Muḥammad (s) being called crazy

When Allāh says, "Your companion is not crazy," this shows the foolishness of some people who accuse the most reasonable person on the earth of being crazy! Even though these people are unworthy of a response from the Lord of the Worlds for this grave lie, the Qurʾān answers them and refutes this description of Allāh's messenger. In fact, it goes so far as to call the Prophet (s) the companion of these wicked people ("Your companion is not crazy!").

One could say that describing him as their companion in this manner is not intended to suggest that the Prophet (s) is anything like them but rather to call attention to the fact that they have lived with him and know him as one companion knows another.

13. *Tafsīr rūḥ al-maʿānī* 4/56

They have seen he is perfectly reasonable, so how do they dare to accuse him thus?

21. Nobility

The verse "certainly he saw him on the manifest horizon" shows the nobility of both parties who met:

- Gabriel (as) is honored by seeing the Prophet (s), and this does not mean merely looking at him in passing, it means becoming familiar with him and talking to him.
- From another aspect, the Prophet (s) saw Gabriel on the manifest horizon, and in another verse from Sūrat al-Najm, we read, "while he was on the highest horizon."[14]

What an honor it is for any human being to reach a horizon that no human being could attain by their own nature—a level that is only for those beings not subject to the forces of the material realm like the angels brought near (*malāʾika muqarrabūn*).

22. Generosity

Just as the Prophet (s) was generous in giving material gifts, so too is he generous in bestowing spiritual ones ("and he is not miserly concerning the Unseen"). So those who emulate him, as the religion enjoins us to, must also be generous in both dimensions. Anyone for whom Allāh opens a door to knowledge and wisdom must give thanks for the value of this blessing by sharing it with its people, lest they do an injustice to wisdom. This runs counter to the practice of monastics who hoard the benefits of asceticism for themselves, cloistering themselves away from having an effect on others.

23. Those who have gone astray

Those who wander the wastes of confusion and error are called to with the words "So where are you going?" The likeness of those who stray from the path of guidance are like a people who wander

---

14. Sūrat al-Najm (53):7

confused in the darkness, and it is obvious that no matter how fast they travel, it will only increase their distance from the right path! This is in addition to the fact that a wanderer does not remain on any path but constantly changes route stage by stage. This is the condition of those who have gone astray in their thoughts, as is plain to see!

24. A book for all nations

Even though the Qur'ān contains subtleties and allusions understood only by its people, it is a reminder for all the nations too ("It is just a reminder for all the nations."). So no one can make the excuse that Allāh's book is above most people's level of understanding!

And this is why the Qur'ān is described in various verses as being an explanation for mankind,[15] sent to be contemplated upon,[16] a manifest book,[17] and manifest signs.[18]

25. Determination to receive the Qur'ān's teachings

The Qur'ān is a reminder for anyone who desires to be steadfast ("for those of you who wish to be steadfast"), so its verses are not like water that extinguishes fire by simply being poured over it. Rather this requires the human being's determination to receive its teachings, to act upon them, and to be steadfast in action. But this desire is also connected to the divine will for it is Allāh who, when He desires good for someone, opens their heart first, and then it is the servant who desires to be steadfast, and, thirdly, the Qur'ān becomes a reminder for a servant.

And the essence of the final verse in this *sūrah* is realizing the intermediate affair (*al-amr bayn al-amrayn*) with regards to free will:

---

15. Sūrat Āle ʿImrān (3):138

16. Sūrat al-Nisā' (4):82; Sūrat al-Mu'minūn (23):68; Sūrat Ṣād (38):29; Sūrat Muḥammad (47):24

17. Sūrat al-Mā'idah (5):15; Sūrat Yūsuf (12):1; Sūrat al-Shuʿarā' (26):2; Sūrat al-Naml (27):1; Sūrat al-
Qaṣaṣ (28):2

18. Sūrat al-Ḥajj (22):16

- From one angle, human beings have been given free will lest they excuse themselves by saying they had no choice, as it is unjust to punish someone who was compelled to act in a certain way.
- From another angle, human free will is not completely independent from the divine will lest His authority over the universe be constrained, and this is expressed most eloquently by the Commander of the Faithful (as), when he says, "I knew Allah through thwarted ambitions and dashed hopes."[19]

26. Human will tied to divine will

One could say that in all places where human will is tied to the divine will ("but you do not wish unless it is wished by Allāh, the Lord of all the worlds."), the divine will dominates in the universe by virtue of divine creatorship. However, from another angle it actually follows the will of the human being—meaning that when the servant desires guidance or the like thereof, Allāh acts to fulfil this will and realize its effects. Hence Allāh increases their guidance ("As for those who are [rightly] guided, He enhances their guidance, and invests them with their Godwariness.").[20] He is the one who guides ("Allah guides to His Light whomever He wishes.").[21] He is the one who "gives wisdom to whomever He wishes"[22] "and forgives whomever He wishes."[23]

19. *Nahj al-balāgha*, aphorism no. 250
20. Sūrat Muḥammad (47):17
21. Sūrat al-Nūr (24):35
22. Sūrat al-Baqarah (2):269
23. Sūrat al-Māʾidah (5):40

Sūrat al-Infiṭār (no. 82: The Sundering)

Verses 1–5

82:1 *When the sky is rent asunder,*

82:2 *when the stars are scattered,*

82:3 *when the seas explode,*

82:4 *when the graves are overturned,*

82:5 *then a soul shall know what it has sent ahead and left behind.*

1. Day of Resurrection, signs

This verse, like others dealing with the Day of Resurrection, reminds its audience of the terrors of the resurrection that will alter the face of the heavens and the earth. This includes two signs in the heavens (the sundering (*infiṭār*) and the scattering (*intithār*)) and two signs upon the earth (the cleaving (*tafjīr*) and the overturning (*biʿthara*)). All the terrors of the heavens and the earth are contained in Allāh's words, "The day the earth is transformed into another earth and the heavens...."[1] In all of these places, it is as though Allāh wants to impress upon us the ephemerality of the earth's ornaments and those of the heavens, such as the stars, too. This is so that our hearts do not become attached to any of these transient affairs.

2. Day of Resurrection, beads of a necklace

On the Day of Resurrection, the stars will scatter like the beads of a necklace ("when the stars are scattered"), and it is as though these beads were only held together by virtue of the thread that

1. Sūrat Ibrāhīm (14):48

ran through them—the thread of gravity and other forces. In every new moment, this universe requires something to hold it together, or else it would break apart and fall into oblivion.

In each of these moments, the universe is indebted to Allāh. Hence, we should give thanks to Him at every moment, but who can possibly do that?

3. Exploding seas

This *sūrah* mentions that the sea will be cleaved apart ("when the seas explode") just as the previous *sūrah* said it would be set aflame ("when the seas are set afire").[2] It is possible that one of these two phenomena will lead to the other, but the common meaning of both of these is that a cool liquid used to extinguish flames will become like fuel for fire!

Here, we say that just as the properties of materials will be altered in the hereafter, so too will people's souls transform into something else. For example, arrogance, which is the mark of the affluent, will transform into abasement and humiliation.

4. Treasure

A farmer turns over the soil of his farmland to bring out the desired benefits of the ground. His land is valuable to him because of what it contains. The same applies to the human body, for they, even if only those of the faithful, are the most valuable contents of the earth. The ground must be overturned to bring out these treasures ("when the graves are overturned"), not its material treasures, as some have said,[3] because these have no value on the Day of Judgement!

5. Events that presage the coming of the resurrection

These verses mention awesome events that presage the coming of the resurrection, but in contrast with all of this, there is an important event that the Master wishes to call attention—like the

2. Sūrat al-Takwīr (81):6
3. *Mafātīḥ al-ghayb* 31/73

consequent of multiple conditional statements—and that event of events is revealed when He says, "then a soul shall know what it has sent ahead and left behind." What He wants is for His servant to reach a level where the servant lives this reality, by picturing these events with certainty before they come to pass in the real world. This in turn depends on people reaching the level where an unseen concept can affect them as deeply as something they see and feel directly. This is a level that can only be attained by those with intellects in this life.

6. Sent ahead and left behind

Were we to say that "left behind" in this verse refers to the reward that comes to the servant in his afterlife, as opposed to "what he sent ahead" which means the righteous deeds that he did during his life, then we will understand the importance of everything that falls into the category of "ongoing good deeds" (*sadaqa jāriya*), such as useful knowledge or a righteous child, as the ranks given to the servant after death [as a result of such good deeds] may not be less than what he earned while he was still alive, which is why everyone should aim to achieve something in this domain. It is narrated from Imām al-Ṣādiq (as), "No reward shall reach a man after his death save for three qualities; a charity he set in motion during his life that continues after his death; a rightly-guided practice that he laid down and that is acted upon after his death; and a righteous child that asks for his forgiveness."[4]

"What he has left behind" can also be interpreted as meaning a servant's shortcomings in performing his duties, so it is as if he left righteous conduct behind [in this world, where it does not benefit him], as opposed to "what he sent ahead" where he was made successful in sending righteous deeds ahead for his Day of Recompense. Another interpretation for these two phrases is what he did at the beginning of his life and what he did at the end of it.

4. *Biḥār al-anwār* 71/257

7. Record of deeds

From these verses, we understand that servants' knowledge of their ultimate fate is revealed to them gradually throughout the stages of the resurrection. They know in a general sense that they are destined for paradise or hellfire. Then their record of deeds is opened so that they can read the book hung around their neck, that they might be a witness and a judge against themselves.

8. Bring humankind back to their senses

This *sūrah*, as is the case in the other Makkahan *sūrahs,* wants to shake its audience through different forms of reproach, foretell future calamities, and ultimately bring humankind back to their senses. From this, we might gather that anyone who wants to awaken those who have stayed far from the path of right guidance must first awaken their consciences to hold themselves to account, then detach them from the worldly pleasures that they are most fond of and that they believe will never fade.

Verses 6–12

82:6 *O man! What has deceived you about your generous Lord,*

82:7 *who created you and proportioned you, and gave you an upright nature,*

82:8 *and composed you in any form that He wished?*

82:9 *No indeed! Rather you deny the Retribution.*

82:10 *Indeed, there are over you guardians,*

82:11 *noble writers*

82:12 *who know whatever you do.*

9. Deceiving ourselves

The verse "O man! What has deceived you about your generous Lord" is one of those containing a rebuke that combines both warning and kindness towards Allāh's servants. By mentioning divine attributes such as generosity and kindness, it is as though Allāh means to say in this verse, "When there is someone whose signs on the Day of Resurrection are like this, whose attributes are Lordship and generosity, and who created humankind in the best possible form,[5] no one should be ungrateful towards Him or His blessings, or be deceived by His generosity and forbearance!" The verse does not say whence is the source of this deception but leaves it up to the servant to figure out. Some have said:

- The generosity of the Lord of the Worlds makes some feel safe from His punishment.
- It is the enticement of Satan and the self that prompts to evil.
- It is man's own ignorance of his Lord's station. It has been narrated from the Prophet (s) that when he recited this verse, he said, "He was deceived by his ignorance."[6]

And the change in tone in this verse, from speaking about someone in the third person to addressing them directly ("O man! What has deceived you about your generous Lord") is clearly meant to emphasize that this rebuke is directed towards the human being, while previously the discussion had been about the soul in the third person.

It is very striking that Allāh directs His words towards man six times in just three verses,[7] and this shows the Master's intent to convey this rebuke to man's conscience.

10. Creation of human body

One of the wonders of the universe that is closest to humankind is their own outward creation, as represented by the wonders of the body. The Lord reminds them of the origin of His creation and how He brought them forth from the darkness of non-existence ("who created you"), then formed them by placing every limb and

---

5. Sūrat Ghāfir (40):64: "and He formed you and perfected your forms"
6. *Majmaʿ al-bayān* 10/449
7. Sūrat al-Infiṭār (82):6–8

organ in its proper place ("proportioned you") and then made their different limbs and organs act in harmony with one another ("and gave you an upright nature") before the final composition by which the ultimate form of their creation was made complete ("and composed you"). All of these meanings are encompassed by Allāh's words "We certainly created man in the best of forms."[8]

And it is known that the mention of all this, immediately after having reprimanding humankind for being deceived about their generous Lord, is an even greater cause for humankind to feel shame and embarrassment in front of Him!

11. Rebuke

One interpretation of the verse "O man! What has deceived you about your generous Lord" is that when it describes the Lord as generous in the midst of a powerful rebuke, it is insinuating the excuse for this—so that the servant will say after hearing it, "My Lord! Your generosity deceived me!"

But this interpretation is not valid, for Allāh is also the Vengeful (*muntaqim*) and the Mighty (*jabbār*). This in addition to the fact that the verses under discussion are followed by a forceful rebuke ("No indeed! Rather you deny the Retribution.") So it is as though Allāh means to say, "Rather you and those like you deny the Day of Retribution and Recompense!" Allāh's unassailable Lordship and manifest generosity are by themselves sufficient to prevent someone from being deceived thereby.

12. Angels recording deeds

Our deeds are preserved, first and foremost, with the Lord of the Worlds who encompasses everything from beyond His creation. Then they are preserved with the preserving angels, and they are some of the "noble writers," and then with servants who see their deeds with their own eyes. So a sinner should be ashamed first from his Lord and secondly from the angels brought near because they are spiritual beings who are repelled by evil deeds. Thirdly,

8. Sūrat al-Tīn (95):4

sinners should be ashamed from their own selves when they see it descend from the realm of divine vicegerency to the realm of worshipping desire.

Imām al-Kāḍhim (as) was asked whether the two angels know about a sin or good deed when the servant intends to do it but before they actually do it. He replied, "Are a putrid odor and a pleasant scent the same!?" The questioner replied, "No." Imām al-Kāḍhim (as) continued, "If the servant intends to do a good deed, his soul emerges with a pleasant scent and the angel on the right says to the one on the left, 'Get up! He wants to do a good deed!' And if he does it, then [the angel's] tongue becomes his pen, and his sweat ink, and he records it for him...but if he intends to commit a sin, his soul emerges with a foul stench and the angel on the left says to the one on the right, 'Stop! He intends to commit a sin!' And if he does it then [the angel's] tongue becomes his pen and his sweat ink and he records it against him."[9]

13. Guardian angels

The apparent meaning of "guardians" is that they safeguard deeds by way of being "writers." But it could also be an allusion to the divine grace (*luṭf*) that surrounds all creation such that Allāh has appointed angels as guardians over mankind who protect them from disasters, as is mentioned in Allāh's words, "He has guardian angels, to his front and his rear, who guard him by Allah's command."[10] This interpretation is supported by a narration from Imām al-Bāqir (as), in which he explains the verse thus, "They are two angels who protect him by night, and two angels by day."[11] It has been narrated from the Commander of the Faithful (as), "They are angels who protect him from disasters, until they arrive with him at his determined fates (*maqādīr*), then they leave him to his fates.'[12]

---

9. *Al-Kāfī* 2/429, tradition no. 3
10. Sūrat al-Raʿd (13):11
11. *Biḥār al-anwār* 56/179
12. Ibid. 56/151

14. Bearing witness

It befits us, as human beings, to follow the example of the angels who record our deeds, for they only write what they have come to know of our actions, lest they be a witness for something without certainty ("who know whatever you do"). Servants who truly obey their Master do not say or bear witness to anything that they have no knowledge of, for presumption does not avail anything against the truth.

15. Vigilantly observing our innermost thoughts

It can be said that the apparent meaning of "whatever you do" is that the angels only write the actions of the limbs, because the actions of the heart are hidden and known only to Allāh. But it could also be said that the angels record even these, because Allāh informs the two recording angels of them.

Whatever the case may be, Allāh is aware of the contents of our hearts, whether the angels are informed of them or not, and this should suffice for us to vigilantly observe our innermost thoughts and feelings, as Allāh says, "He knows the treachery of the eyes, and what the breasts hide."[13]

Verses 13–19

82:13 *Indeed the pious shall are amid bliss,*

82:14 *and indeed the vicious shall are in hell*

82:15 *entering it on the Day of Retribution,*

82:16 *and they are not absent from it.*

82:17 *And what will show you what is the Day of Retribution?*

82:18 *Again, what will show you what is the Day of Retribution?*

82:19 *It is a day when no soul will be of any avail to another soul and all command that day will belong to Allah.*

---

13. Sūrat Ghāfir (40):19

16. Bliss

By using the word 'pious' (*abrār*), the verse "Indeed the pious..." highlights the quality of kindness (*birr*) as a basic description of the inhabitants of bliss. It does not, for example, highlight worship (*ʿibāda*). From this expression, it can be understood that the quality of beneficence (*iḥsān*) is foremost in importance for gaining entry to paradise, even if Allāh's acceptance of this beneficence is conditional upon piety (*taqwā*).

And because the pious are said to be in bliss without any qualifications being attached to this statement, this state of bliss could encompass both this world and the next. In other words, they are in a constant state of tranquility. This meaning is especially suited to the verse when we see that bliss is described as a locale (*ḍharf*) to them, and al-Rāzī narrates in his Qurʾān commentary from Imām al-Ṣādiq (as), "Bliss is cognition (*maʿrifa*) and vision (*mushāhida*)."[14] This shows that this kind of bliss is fulfilled for the pious in this world before the hereafter, even if it appears more brilliantly in the latter.

17. Bliss

We should not overlook the subtle meaning in the expression "in bliss" in that it applies to every kind of bliss that the servant enjoys. In opposition to this meaning stand the vicious (*fujjār*), whose name derives from the same origin as the sea that is set aflame. It is said of them, that "they are rent with sins."[15] So it is as though sinners tear themselves apart and lose their properly-proportioned forms, losing in turn their beauty, as would be the case were their body rent apart. This is why daybreak is called *fajr*, as it splits the horizon with light.[16]

18. Punishment in this world

We could even say that the vicious are punished in this world as well as the hereafter as the phrase "are in Hell" implies. As this

14. *Mafātīḥ al-ghayb* 31/80
15. *Al-Mīzān fī tafsīr al-Qurʾān* 20/227
16. *Muʿjam maqāyīs al-lugha* 4/475

expression, which suggests that punishment surrounds its victims, cannot be used to refer to a future punishment, it can only be used in the present to refer to something that has already been effected.

This interpretation is also supported by Allāh's words "entering it on the Day of Retribution" for the fires of hell, even the least degree of them in this world, will flare up on the Day of Resurrection. Or, you might say that the sinner is burnt by their heat on that day. Otherwise we can say the hell of separation from Allāh and a wretched existence in this world is a foreshadowing of hell in the afterlife. The idea that the punishment is realized in this world is also given credence by Allāh's words "and they are not absent from it." We can also understand from His saying "indeed hell besieges the faithless"[17] that hell surrounds the faithless from all dimensions, including the dimension of this world and the hereafter.

19. Prophet Muḥammad (s) and terrifying forms of punishment

The apparent form of address used in "And what will show you what is the Day of Retribution?" suggests that this rhetorical question is directed to the Prophet (s). But this serves to demonstrate how truly terrifying the forms of punishment contained in that day are, to the extent that they are hidden from even the greatest of Allāh's creatures, so what about everyone else? In fact, he had the greatest connection of any person with the unseen realm. He saw the greatest signs of his Lord. The sheer gravity of the punishment of the hereafter is further emphasized when the same question is repeated a second time.

20. The word 'retribution'

It should be noted that the word 'retribution' is used here to allude to the recompense, which is the most important feature of that most terrifying of days. So the verse conveys the sense that this

17. Sūrat al-al-Tawbah (9):49

day is momentous, both because of the terrors it contains and because of the precise accounting that will take place on it.

The Qurʾān frequently uses the rhetorical form "And what will show you...?" to convey the gravity of the resurrection. For example, Allāh says, "What will show you what is the Besieger?!"[18] "And what will show you what is Saqar?"[19] "And what will show you what is the Day of Judgement!"[20] and "And what will show you what is the nightly visitor?"[21]

21. Visibly seeing Allāh's authority

Authority belongs only to Allāh in all creations ("command that day will belong to Allah"), but the greatest manifestation of this shall be during the stages of resurrection when everyone in existence will affirm and actually visibly see this authority. This does not run contrary to intercession as it falls under within purview of this absolute authority. Of course, believers experience this ideal in this world before the hereafter, and this gives them the power of faith, even if they have a humble outward appearance. It has been narrated from Imām al-Bāqir (as), "Command on that day and on this one belongs to Allah in its entirety, O Jābir! But when the Day of Resurrection comes, the rulers will vanish and no ruler will remain except Allah."[22]

18. Sūrat al-Ḥāqqah (69):3
19. Sūrat al-Muddaththir (74):27
20. Sūrat al-Mursalāt (77):14
21. Sūrat al-Ṭāriq (86):2
22. *Majmaʿ al-bayān* 10/450

Sūrat al-Muṭaffifīn (no. 83: The Defrauders)

Verses 1–6

83:1 *Woe to the defrauders who use short measures,*

83:2 *who, when they measure from the people, take the full measure,*

83:3 *but diminish when they measure or weigh for them.*

83:4 *Do they not think that they will be resurrected*

83:5 *on a tremendous day,*

83:6 *a day when mankind will stand before the Lord of all the worlds?*

1. Deviant beliefs

In His scripture, Allāh shows His satisfaction with whomever He desires to reward by saying "Blessed be..."[1] (*ṭūbā*) which conveys the sense of a pleasant life that Allāh has prepared for those who believe and do righteous deeds. This includes happiness in this world and the hereafter. In contrast to this, the Qurʾān uses the expression "Woe to..." for those towards whom Allāh desires to display His anger and threaten them thereby.

Usually, the Qurʾān uses it to threaten polytheists,[2] the faithless,[3] and deniers,[4] namely, those who have deviant beliefs. But it also uses this expression for those whose behavior goes astray, including "the defrauders," scandal-mongers and slanderers,[5] and sinful liars.[6]

1. Sūrat al-Raʿd (13):29
2. Sūrat Fuṣṣilat (41):6: "And woe to the polytheists"
3. Sūrat Ibrāhīm (14):2: "And woe to the faithless for a severe punishment"
4. Sūrat al-Ṭūr (52):11: "Woe to the deniers on that day"
5. Sūrat al-Humazahh (104):1 "Woe to every scandal-monger and slanderer"
6. Sūrat al-Jāthiyah (45):7: "Woe to every sinful liar"

2. Fraud in weights and measures

Some people think that fraud in weights and measures is a trivial thing when compared to the major sins in that this kind of fraud may only involve a small amount of money that no one will miss. But the verses of the Qur'ān that harshly rebuke this fraud contain a severe threat against it that begins with invoking woe. This expression is usually reserved for major sins such as denying the Day of Resurrection ("Woe to the deniers on that day!"[7]).

From this, we know that Allāh places great importance on the rights of people (*ḥaqq al- nās*) to the extent that He made the prohibition of this sin a fundamental part of Prophet Shuʿayb's (as) mission when Prophet Shuʿayb (as) said to his people, "O my people! Observe fully the measure and the balance, with justice, and do not cheat the people of their goods, and do not act wickedly on the earth, causing corruption."[8] Contravening this divine commandment was one of the causes of his people's ruin. This shows us that spreading corruption in the land is a grave offense that is tantamount to disbelieving in Allāh, and this is why both are punishable by death, subject to the proper jurisprudential conditions.

3. Ill-gotten wealth

Those people who cheat others shall suffer the consequences of falsely consuming wealth. One such consequence was mentioned by the Prophet (s) when he was explaining the effects of forbidden acts on nations ("Do not cheat the measures or else you will be denied vegetation and suffer droughts."[9]). Perhaps they are threatened with woe to warn them of the harmful effects of consuming illicit gains, to which many people give little consideration, because their effect is not immediately visible as it is with drinking wine. So there are some people who are very careful when it comes to avoiding alcohol but not when it comes to illicit wealth!

In the same vein, Imām Ḥusayn (as) also rebukes those who consume ill-gotten wealth, which drives them towards this evil

7. Sūrat al-Mursalāt (77):15
8. Sūrat Hūd (11):85
9. *Al-Kāfī* 2/374

outcome, by saying, "They have filled their bellies with ill-gotten gains."[10]

4. Defrauders

Defrauders, as the verse describes them, combine the quality of selfishness and coveting benefits for themselves with that of dishonesty and fraud in business so that when they measure for themselves, they make sure that they receive their full due without any shortfall ("who, when they measure from the people, take the full measure"), but they cause others to lose theirs when they measure for them ("but diminish when they measure or weigh for them"). Both of these qualities are morally repugnant, even if the first does not, in and of itself, necessarily reach the level of prohibition, but the condemnation is on their combination in the form of loving oneself while betraying others.

It is worth noting that the verse calls those harmed by this practice "people" rather than singling out Muslims, for instance, to show that such deceit is immoral with any of Allāh's servants.

5. Other forms of fraud

Even though this verse is addressing those who cheat people through measures and weights, the spirit of the verse can include anyone who violates the rights of others in their dealings such as someone who agrees to perform a task in a certain way but when it comes to it, he does not perform the task as agreed; or someone who wrongly seizes the property of others.

6. The word 'think'

It is as though someone who commits a sin, in practice, does not even think about the Day of Judgement because any reasonable person would consider potential harms and see them as necessary to avoid when they see that they might be exposed to danger!

---

10. *Tuḥuf al-ʿuqūl* 240

The verse alludes to this level of thought, saying, "Do they not think that they will be resurrected," although some have interpreted the word 'think' (*ḍhann*) here to signify "certain knowledge" (*yaqīn*), as in Allāh's saying "those who know (*ḍhann*) that they will encounter their Lord,"[11] about which it has been narrated from ʿAlī (as) in *Tafsīr al- ʿAyyāshī*, "They are certain that they will be resurrected; from them, *ḍhann* is certainty."[12]

7. Sinning in private

The single solution to prevent someone from all sins, even in private, is what the Qurʾān mentions in these verses—remembering that they will one day stand completely exposed before the Lord of the Worlds ("a day when mankind will stand before the Lord of all the worlds") whereat there will be no meaning to doing things in private because there will be no such thing as privacy! Everything that a servant does in private is still visible to Allāh, and that is why this verse exhorts us to remember that we will one day stand before the Lord of the Worlds to dissuade us from defrauding others, as we might believe that the person we are defrauding will not notice.

Verses 7–17

83:7 *No indeed! The record of the vicious is indeed in Sijjīn.*

83:8 *And what will show you what is Sijjīn?*

83:9 *It is a book inscribed.*

83:10 *Woe to the deniers on that day,*

83:11 *who deny the Day of Retribution;*

83:12 *and none denies it except every sinful transgressor.*

83:13 *When Our signs are recited to him, he says, 'Myths of the ancients!'*

---

11. Sūrat al-Baqarah (2):46

12. *Tafsīr al-ʿayyāshī* 1/44

83:14 *No indeed! Rather their hearts have been sullied by what they have been earning.*

83:15 *No indeed! They will be veiled from their Lord on that day.*

83:16 *Then they will indeed enter hell,*

83:17 *then told, 'This is what you used to deny!'*

8. *Sijjīn*

Allāh's devices of accounting are of the utmost precision and scope, so the records of evil deeds are described as:

- a book (*kitāb*) "a book inscribed" and
- the *Sijjīn,* which is a repository that contains all the judgments against the sinners, whether this place refers to the different levels of hell or something else. The name *Sijjīn* is the emphatic conjugation of the word 'prison' (*sijin*) and is the opposite of the place where the book of the righteous resides, the *ʿIliyyīn.* This second meaning applies if Allāh's words "a book inscribed" are not intended as a description for the *Sijjīn.* If they are, however, then the *Sijjīn* is the encompassing book.

9. Sullied heart

These verses draw a connection between denying the resurrection and being absorbed by sin, insofar as amassing sins sullies one's heart and thereby veils you from even the clearest realities, including the resurrection. So sometimes people will deny it and, at others, they will dismiss the signs of Allāh as "myths of the ancients." We can find support for this interpretation in what we read in the verse "Then the fate of those who committed misdeeds was that they denied the signs of Allāh and they used to deride them."[13] So habitual sinners do not enjoy the blessing of sound beliefs because this soundness could fade and "what they have

---

13. Sūrat al-Rūm (30):10

been earning" reaches the extent that the Qur'ān says, "rather their hearts have been sullied."

It is known that when a person's heart, which is the seat of their being, is tainted and sullied, then servants will go to even greater extremes in the sins they commit.

10. Tainted heart

A tainted heart is a stage of level decline that results when servants persist in earning that which does not please their Master, so let those who sin persistently, even if their sins are small, beware a tainted heart. This stage will take hold suddenly, like a stone splitting open on the final strike. It has been narrated in a tradition, "When a servant commits a sin, we inscribe a black mark upon his heart; if he repents, desists and seeks forgiveness, his heart will be wiped clean; but if he returns [to his sin], then the mark will grow until it consumes his entire heart...that is the taint (*rīn*) that Allah mentions in the Qur'ān."[14]

There are other matters connected to people's hearts that fall within the context of a taint or sully. Some say that this taint is the heart blackening from sins. But being impressed (*ṭabʿ*) is worse than being sullied, it means that he heart is closed completely ("They are the ones on whose hearts Allah has set an impressure."[15]). This is also called sealing (*khatm*) the hearts ("Allah has set a seal on their hearts..."[16]).

11. The word *kallā*

When the Qur'ān employs the word *kallā* ("No indeed!"), this has several connotations worthy of attention. It is but a single word, and yet sometimes it implies repudiation (*radʿ*), sometimes negation (*nafī*), and yet other meanings still. It has a unique meaning for every context in which it is used!

---

14. *Tafsīr al-durr al-manthūr* 6/325
15. Sūrat Muḥammad (47):16
16. Sūrat al-Baqarah (2):7

In the verse "No indeed! Rather their hearts have been sullied..." we could say that this implies a repudiation of them for uttering falsehoods—namely, calling Allāh's signs myths, as if it is used in the same way as "hush!" when you wish to silence someone and belittle them. They only utter these things because of the taint that has infected their hearts.

As for in the verse "No indeed! They will be alienated from their Lord on that day," this is a repudiation of that which causes hearts to be sullied, which in turn causes them to deny the truth in this fashion in this world and veil them from their Lord in the next.

Meanwhile, in the verse "No indeed! The record of the vicious is indeed in Sijjīn,"[17] this is a repudiation of their dishonest business practices and their disregard for the Day of Recompense.

12. The veil

Even though people will have the veils removed from them on the Day of Resurrection, and they will visibly see the manifestations of Allāh's majesty and perfection, to the extent that they become desperate to speak to their Master, the Qurʾān describes them as "veiled from their Lord on that day." This is being veiled from proximity to divine mercy, as is clarified by another verse elsewhere, "and Allah will not speak to them nor will He look at them on the Day of Resurrection, nor will He purify them...."[18] So this kind of veiling remains with them throughout the resurrection, just as it was with them in the abode of this world. It remains even when all the other veils have been removed from them in the isthmus (*barzakh*) and during the resurrection.

17. Sūrat al-Muṭaffifīn (83):7
18. Sūrat Āle ʿImrān (3):77

Verses 18–28

83:18 *No indeed! The record of the pious is indeed in Illiyun.*

83:19 *And what will show you what is Illiyun?*

83:20 *It is a written record,*

83:21 *It witnessed by those brought near.*

83:22 *Indeed the pious shall be amid bliss,*

83:23 *observing, on couches.*

83:24 *You will perceive in their faces the freshness of delight*

83:25 *as they are served with a sealed wine,*

83:26 *whose seal is musk—for such let the viers vie—*

83:27 *and whose seasoning is from Tasnim,*

83:28 *a spring where those brought near drink.*

13. *ʿIlliyyīn:* An exalted direction

The record of the pious is in a location that stands in contrast to that which houses the record of the vicious. It is in an exalted direction called *ʿIlliyyīn* that is described in a prophetic tradition, "Elevated (*ʿilliyyūn*) in the seven heavens beneath the Throne."[19] But, like the *Sijjīn*, it is beyond human comprehension which is why Allāh uses the phrase "And what will show you...?" This is in addition to the fact that the determinations written in both are neither open to doubt nor at risk of harm—they are inscribed (*marqūm*) because their author, namely, Allāh and His angels, lacks nothing in wisdom or precision. The same expression is used to describe the *Sijjīn*, but Allāh has described the book of the pious here as being witnessed by a group of "those brought near" (*muqarrabīn*) which has been explained to mean the angels brought near[20] but also as the elite of paradise's inhabitants who have been given the right to view the records of the pious.[21]

19. *Majmaʿ al-bayān* 10/692
20. *Al-Mīzān fī tafsīr al-Qurʾān* 20/235
21. Ibid.

14. Those brought near

It is also possible that the pronoun in "it is witnessed by those brought near" refers to the Almighty Himself [i.e., "He is witnessed by those brought near."] So "those brought near" are a group of people from whom all the veils have been lifted such that they are worthy of witnessing Allāh's divine majesty, and their level is above that of the pious (*abrār*) and the angels. They are the companions of that spring "where those brought near drink." And whose Lord quenches them with "a pure drink."[22]

15. *Tasnīm*

The inhabitants of paradise do not all occupy a single level of divine blessings. The pious are in bliss, but those brought near are in another kind of bliss so that the drink represented by the wine of paradise that is prepared for them is different to the drink of the pious. The drink of the pious is seasoned with *Tasnīm* ("and whose seasoning is from *Tasnīm*") while the drink of those brought near is *Tasnīm* itself ("a spring where those brought near drink"), and their drink is not of such a quantity that it can be measured in cups. It is an abundantly flowing spring from which they drink directly. As for the rest of their special qualities, none can comprehend them save he who has reached the stations of looking at His noble countenance.

16. Bliss

The sensible delight (*naʿīm ḥissī*) enjoyed by the inhabitants of paradise are reflected in their faces in the form of freshness and blissfulness ("You will perceive in their faces the freshness of delight"), and they are in a relaxed state, watching as all the different kinds of bliss unfold around them ("observing, on couches"). This could include looking towards divine beauty (*jamāl ilāhī*). From this, we can know that not every kind of bliss is a delight (*bahja*). After all, worldly people have so much enjoyment, and yet to them apply Allāh's words, "his shall be a wretched life."[23]

22. Sūrat al-Insān (76):21
23. Sūrat Ṭa Ha (20):124

Therefore, the kind of bliss that the Lord of the Worlds unfurls is that which brings familiarity and felicity in both worlds not just the comfort enjoyed by the wealthy inhabitants of this world.

17. A sealed wine

The sealed heavenly wine in paradise is sealed with sweet-scented musk ("whose seal is musk"), which is unlike that which was used to seal the wine vessels of this world, such as clay, in order to keep them pure and unadulterated.

On this basis, we can say that the starting point of this otherworldly bliss is that someone who wants to enjoy the pleasures of union with the divine in this world must protect themselves from contamination by well-known impurities—ostentation (*riyāʾ*), listening to hearsay, neglecting one's duties, vying for superiority, and other such things.

18. Wine and *Tasnīm*

The differing levels of bliss in paradise should motivate its inhabitants to compete with one another in attaining the utmost degree therein ("for such let the viers vie"). This is something they can only do in the life of this world, for today is a day of striving without accounting, while tomorrow is a day of accounting without striving!

So what is the difference between the wine that flows beneath the inhabitants of paradise, which the Qurʾān usually describes as one of the rivers of paradise, and the drink of *Tasnīm*? There are two opinions:

- The first is that it is a special drink found only in the highest reaches of paradise.
- The second is that it is a river that flows through the sky and overflows into the cups of the inhabitants of paradise.[24]

24. *Biḥār al-anwār* 8/115

19. Competition

There is nothing fundamentally wrong with competition. It only becomes blameworthy depending on what it is a competition for. After mentioning some of the bliss found in paradise, the Master calls people to compete in pursuit of those things that will earn it, showing that this kind of competitiveness is a praiseworthy!

Of course, any competition for an infinite prize, like that of paradise, has no winner or loser because the prize of this competition is not limited so as to induce animosity between the competitors. But still, any competition is always a race because each competitor wants to reach the finish line before opponents, and this means people must move quickly along the race route!

Verses 29–36

83:29 *Indeed the transgressors used to laugh at the faithful,*

83:30 *and when they passed them by they would wink at each other,*

83:31 *and when they returned to their folks they would return rejoicing,*

83:32 *and when they saw them they would say, 'Indeed those are the astray!'*

83:33 *Though they were not sent to watch over them.*

83:34 *So today the faithful will laugh at the faithless,*

83:35 *observing from couches:*

83:36 *Have the faithless been requited for what they used to do?*

20. The faithless

Instead of saying "the faithless," the Qur'ān says "the transgressors." This indicates that the reason they harass the faithful is the transgressing disposition that follows from their faithlessness, as a faithless person might only be faithless in matters of belief.

For this reason, we say that if this disposition is present in the personality of someone who professes Islām outwardly, it could lead to the same acts that emanate from the faithless, such as mocking the faithful and other acts mentioned in these verses.

21. Habits of faithless

The faithless have no logic with which to argue. Rather their habit is to mock ("the guilty used to laugh"), make derisive signals ("they would wink at each other"), gather together on the basis of falsehood and ridiculing the faithful ("they would return rejoicing"), and look down upon them without any evidence of their own rightness ("They would say, 'Indeed those are astray!'").

But all of this will be reversed on the Day of Resurrection so that the inhabitants of paradise will have these positions in relation to the inmates of hellfire while they live in the bliss of paradise, reclining on thrones. Their condition shall be as the Qurʾān describes it, "So today the faithful will laugh at the faithless") except that this time the derision will be appropriate and approved by the Lord of the Worlds.

22. Harassment from disbelievers

These verses, which describe how those disbelievers who transgress treat the faithful, prepare the faithful to endure various kinds of harassment—mocking, derisive gestures, false accusations, and others—and leave no room for the faithful to expect any praise or approval from the faithless. The fact that these persons not only hold on to erroneous beliefs but are also of a transgressing disposition leaves no room for these two groups to come together, save that one submits to follow the religion of the other. This is especially true when we see that the verse emphasizes the compound ignorance (*jahl murakkab*) of the transgressors in that the latter describe the faithful as being astray ("Indeed those are astray!") while they are themselves the very epitome of people who have gone astray! But how Allāh refutes them and how harshly He derides them when defending His friends (*awliyāʾ*) saying, "Though they were not sent to watch over them," meaning that you have nothing to do with our rightly-guided servants!

23. Delayed punishment

Some people in this world are hasty to see the wrongdoers receive their just desserts, while the truth is that their affair is in Allāh's hands, and there is no risk of it being forgotten. It is in His hands that the fates of the wrongdoers and their victims rest. It is He who will judge between them about that in which they differed.

And hence, however much their punishment is delayed, there shall be a day in which the Lord of the Worlds cries out, "Have the faithless been requited for what they used to do?" As though Allāh wants to show his faithful *awliyāʾ* the terrible vengeance He has wrought against the wrongdoers, to appease them for what they suffered at the latter's hands during their lives in this world.

Sūrat al-Inshiqāq (no. 84: The Splitting)

Verses 1–6

In the name of Allāh, the All-Beneficent, the All-Merciful

84:1 *When the sky is split open*

84:2 *and gives ear to its Lord as it should.*

84:3 *When the earth is spread out*

84:4 *and throws out what is in it, emptying itself,*

84:5 *and gives ear to its Lord as it should.*

84:6 *O man! You are labouring toward your Lord laboriously, and you will encounter Him.*

1. Condition on the Day of Judgement

This *sūrah* gives a detailed image of the condition of Allāh's servants on the Day of Judgement, whether they are destined for bliss or punishment. This should give humankind occasion to deem insignificant many of the forms of enjoyment and happiness found in this world when they compare them to everything that will come to them on the Day of Resurrection, as Allāh says, "Indeed he used to be joyful among his folk, and indeed he thought he would never return."[1]

2. Fragility of the heavens

The Qur'ān repeatedly mentions events that lay bare the fragility of the heavens on the Day of Resurrection. Sometimes it calls this "sundering" (*infiṭār*) ("When the sky is rent asunder"), and other

1. Sūrat al-Inshiqāq (84):13–14

times "splitting" ("When the sky is split open"). Perhaps this is to show the profound changes being wrought in the realm of existence.

After all, the Earth has been altered markedly by both natural and human agency, whereas the heavens, as if by its very nature, before the hour sets in, appears unchanging. It is a manifestation of power and permanence, and that is why mentioning the changes in the heavens is an even more eloquent expression of the breaking apart of the universe and its transformation!

3. "Splitting open" of the heavens

Some commentators[2] have explained the "splitting open" of the heavens to mean their separating after having been joined. According to this interpretation, they were joined as a temporary measure in this world to ensure that the universe operated in a way that was conducive to human existence, but when the resurrection sets in, this state of being joined is no longer considered necessary for the well-being of the universe.

According to this interpretation, this verse could also be alluding to the condition of the heavens being joined together at the beginning of creation...having been separated before it. There are some cosmological theories that talk about a "big bang" from which the raw stuff of the universe emerged, which later turned into stars and planets.

4. Oaths in Qurʾān

Sometimes the Qurʾān swears oaths by material phenomena that appear permanent in this world such as "By the morning brightness, by the night when it is calm!"[3] But at others, it mentions material phenomena that lose this apparent permanence in the hereafter such as "when the sky is split open." This is so that the servant will reflect upon the outcome embodied in the object of the oath in the

2. *Tafsīr al-Tibyān* 10/307
3. Sūrat al-Ḍuḥā (93):1–2

first instance and the consequence of the conditional clause in the second.[4]

Both expressions invite one and the same conclusion—that we must move from the sensible (*maḥsūs*) to the intelligible (*maʿqūl*), or from knowledge of our immediate circumstances to knowledge of our ultimate fate. In short, we must know that every single being, whether it appears permanent or mutable, is, in fact, completely and utterly under Allāh's control.

5. Submissiveness of the heavens and the earth

Existence in its entirety submits to Allāh as a slave submits to his master, and that is why the verse speaks about the sky as if it has ears like those of humankind ("and gives ear…"). But the verse does not stop there, it says, "as it should," which shows that this obedience and submissiveness is not confined to this tremendous day alone. Rather, it has been thus since the beginning of creation itself, such that the heavens and the earth spake, whether verbally or otherwise, such words as befitted them ("They said, 'We come heartily!'"[5]).

But the submissiveness of the heavens and the earth on the Day of Resurrection is even more profound because the Day of Resurrection is the station of destruction and sundering and not fashioning and joining as was the case at the beginning of creation. So how shameful it is that the human being forsakes such obedient behavior.

6. The spreading out of the earth

The spreading out of the earth on the Day of Resurrection could mean that its surface is expanded to accommodate every creature ever to have existed or it could mean that it is leveled by removing its mountains and their peaks that were placed upon the earth when it was spread out and created the first time, as Allāh says, "It

---

4. Meaning the information that these oaths and conditional clauses introduce
5. Sūrat Fuṣṣilat (41):11

is He who has spread out the earth and set in it firm mountains...."[6] The earth is exactly like the sky in all of this—completely obedient to its Lord, as is its nature to be.

And that is why Allāh repeats the phrase "and gives ear to its Lord as it should" to make us understand that existence in its entirety, the heavens and the earth, is undifferentiated in its submissiveness and obedience.

7. The dead and buried

The Qurʾān frequently discusses the resurrection of the dead on the Day of Recompense in such a way as to imply that the dead are within the earth as if entrusted to its depths, as Allāh says elsewhere, "and the earth discharges her burdens,"[7] and in this *sūrah,* "and throws out what is in it, emptying itself." As though it must bring forth these trusts to be resurrected for accounting, so let no one think that whoever is dead and buried in the ground has been forgotten and at an end when he is decayed to dust! No, rather the earth is obedient to its Lord and will bring them forth for Him at the hour of their resurrection, just as it received them at the hour of their burial. The verse uses hyperbole in describing it as "emptying itself" of whatever it contains to show that no part of these bodies, no matter how small or insignificant, will be left behind.

8. Necessity of paying attention

In Sūrat al-Infiṭār, we saw a multitude of conditional clauses all leading to a single consequent, "When the sky is rent asunder, when the stars are scattered, when the seas explode, when the graves are overturned, then a soul shall know what it has sent ahead and left behind."[8] We see something similar in this *sūrah,* "When the sky is split open, and gives ear to its Lord as it should. When the earth is spread out and throws out what is in it, emptying itself, and gives ear to its Lord as it should. O man! You are labouring toward your

6. Sūrat al-Raʿd (13):3
7. Sūrat al-Zalzalah (99):2
8. Sūrat al-Infiṭār (82):1–5

Lord laboriously, and you will encounter Him." This illustrates the gravity of the ideas that these verses call our attention to. In the first collection, this is represented by the necessity of paying attention to future outcomes, while in the second collection it is represented by the necessity of vigilantly observing our actions, and these are two things that most people are heedless of.

9. Attaining the goal

This *sūrah*, like other Makkan *sūrahs*, reminds human beings of ends while they are focused on beginnings. This is the natural outcome of applying reason, for any rational person must, regardless of their religiosity, direct their efforts towards attaining their goal from the outset. This is nothing other than facing the Real One on the Day of Resurrection, without guilt or rebuke. This, in its entirety, is summed up in Allāh's words, "You are labouring toward your Lord laboriously, and you will encounter Him."

10. Oaths sworn without an explicit object

Oaths sworn without an explicit object (and conditional clauses not followed by an obvious consequence as we sometimes see in the verses of the Qurʾān) should give occasion for human beings to think what has been left implicit. This is a powerful motivation for them to ponder and reflect.

An instance of this principle is the verse under discussion—it does not mention an explicit consequence for its opening conditional clauses, even if it is connected to the words "You are labouring toward your Lord...." This is to give it a more profound effect—to call attention to a meeting that is sure to happen and to which allude other verses such as "and that the terminus is toward your Lord"[9] and "and to Allah is the return."[10]

9. Sūrat al-Najm (53):42
10. Sūrat Fāṭir (35):18

11. Labor

The inhabitants of this world labor and toil for most, if not all, of their lives for the sake of worldly provision. So is it not more fitting that human beings should labor in pursuit of the purpose for which they were created? Add to that the fact that anyone who labors for the hereafter will definitely see the fruits of their toil therein, as is demonstrated by Allāh's words "and you will encounter Him." Compare this to the labors of this world and how people's best laid plans herein come to naught!

12. Moving towards the Highest Source

The verses of the Qurʾān highlight the importance of moving in this world towards the Highest Source. It refers to this variously as:

- fleeing – "So flee toward Allah!"[11]
- hastening – "And hasten towards a forgiveness"[12]
- striving – "And that nothing belongs to man except what he strives for"[13]
- laboring – which combines the meanings of travel and movement with that of effort and toil; we grasp this from the fact that the particle "toward" (*ilā*) is used to denote the utmost goal, as we see in Allāh's words "...towards your Lord." What is most interesting about this is that this verse addresses the human being directly as a human being. This is in marked contrast to those people who think that the greatest struggle (*al-jihād al-akbar*) is only the exclusive purview of the most devout of the faithful.

13. Toil

The expression "...towards your Lord" suggests—keeping in mind that this particle, "towards" (*ilā*) is used to signify the utmost goal of a journey—that the outcome of this labor shall be found

11. Sūrat al-Dhāriyāt (51):50
12. Sūrat Āle ʿImrān (3):133
13. Sūrat al-Najm (53):39

in meeting Allāh, after which there shall be no more toil. In fact, the outcome shall be the opposite of toil—felicity and ease of life. As you might say to a farmer, "You are laboring towards the day of harvest." From this, he would understand that there will be no more toil after the harvest.

Conversely, we also see that the toil of worldly persons will not end with dead. In fact, it will become harsher after they die. This is why we say that this world is the disbeliever's paradise and the believer's prison.

14. Laboring towards Allāh

Laboring towards Allāh must necessarily be in harmony with the divine plan for the creation. It is towards Allāh that is the goal beyond all goals. Therefore, any labor that is not divine will not lead to Him and, as a result, the outcome ("and you will encounter Him") will never materialize. This is true whether we interpret this encounter to mean encountering Allāh in the sense of encountering His recompense; encountering Him in the sense of a spiritual unveiling; encountering Him in the sense of encountering His presence and authority during the stages of the resurrection; or encountering Him in the sense of encountering one's own deeds, as according to the verse "They will find present whatever they had done."[14]

And what a gulf there is between laboring for the hereafter (whose outcome is encountering the One towards whom you labored) and laboring for this world (whose outcome shall be failure and betrayal and bearing the burdens of others, as Allāh says, "But surely they will carry their own burdens and other burdens along with their own burdens, and they will surely be questioned on the Day of Resurrection concerning that which they used to fabricate."[15]).

---

14. Sūrat al-Kahf (18):49

15. Sūrat al-ʿAnkabūt (29):13

15. The encounter

The encounter mentioned in this verse ("and you will encounter Him") is inevitable for everyone who is mustered at the resurrection. But the greatest excellence is that this compulsory meeting should be preceded by a voluntary one brought about by a person's own desire and choice. This is the utmost limit of moral refinement, an encounter that results from a person's labors that can only be realized in the life of this world. Such a voluntary encounter with the divine is like water that flows through a channel to a tree in order to irrigate it.

Whereat we say, "How beautiful this compulsory meeting is if it is preceded by a voluntary one. This explains the deep love Allāh's *awliyāʾ* have for death because it only hastens this meeting that they have been fervently awaiting. We can find all of these ideas in the Commander of the Faithful's (as) description of the pious (*muttaqīn*).[16]

16. Terrors of the resurrection

It is also possible that all of the above sentences concern the terrors of the resurrection and, with regards to grammar, they are collectively in the accusative case (*manṣūb*) as objects of an implicit command "Remember...!" (*udhkhur!*). This implication, in turn, places no small amount of emphasis on the gravity of what these verses are discussing, especially if we assume that the addressee is the Final Prophet (s), as he is at the very highest degree of remembrance.

Clearly, the one who recites the Qurʾān must demonstrate a high level of awareness by enacting the divine command to remember (*tadhakkur*). Otherwise, what is the purpose of recitation divorced from reflection?

---

16. *Nahj al-balāgha,* sermon on the *Muttaqīn*

Verses 7–15

84:7 *Then as for him who is given his record in his right hand,*

84:8 *he shall soon receive an easy reckoning,*

84:9 *and he will return to his folks joyfully.*

84:10 *But as for him who is given his record from behind his back,*

84:11 *he will pray for annihilation,*

84:12 *and he will enter the Blaze.*

84:13 *Indeed he used to be joyful among his folk,*

84:14 *and indeed he thought he would never return.*

84:15 *Yes indeed, his Lord sees him best.*

17. Kind of people resurrected

These verses show that there are two kinds of people who shall be resurrected:

- The faithful—namely, those who will receive their records in their right hands ("who is given his record in his right hand") and
- The faithless who denied the resurrection, who will receive their records from behind their backs ("But as for him who is given his record from behind his back") either because Allāh has blotted out their faces and turned them backwards, as in the verse "...before We blot out the faces and turn them backwards"[17] or because they take their records with their left hands and then hide them behind their backs.

It is also possible to say that there is a third group of people—namely, the sinful believers who receive their records with their left hands and so stand in contrast with both the first and second group here.

17. Sūrat al-Nisā᾽ (4):47

18. Easy reckoning

The easy reckoning mentioned in the verse "he shall soon receive an easy reckoning" could mean that the record of deeds is presented to its owner, including any sins it contains, but without subjecting it to a precise inspection. Hence, from one angle, the owner has a reckoning, it is easy. But it could also easy because Allāh overlooks the owner's sins or turns them into good deeds, whether through the blessing of intercession (*shafāʿa*) or because of a deed that necessitates an easy reckoning. It has been mentioned in a prophetic tradition: "There are three qualities that, if one possesses them, Allāh will give him an easy reckoning and admit him unto Paradise by His mercy...." People asked, "What are these things, O Messenger of Allah?" He said, "Give to one who withholds from you, keep ties with one who cuts you off, and forgive one who wrongs you."[18]

19. Returning to the family

There is a huge difference between the return of the believer to his family on the Day of Resurrection and the return of others to theirs. The believer returns to his family to live with them forever in happiness and joy ("and he will return to his folks joyfully") whether we interpret this as referring to his wives amongst the heavenly maidens who await him, or to his wife and children who are attached to him in paradise, or to his righteous comrades who are like his family because of their common faith.

All of this is juxtaposed with the happiness of the faithful, for it is a happiness that fades with this world and is followed by eternal misery because he is separated from those amongst whom he was joyful when they abandon him to his own devices. So what good did it do him that "he used to be joyful among his folk" and "That is because you used to exult unduly on the earth...."[19] Notice that these verses are in the past tense while his present reality—as indicated by the Qurʾān's use of the present tense—is "he will

18. *Majmaʿ al-bayān* 10/699
19. Sūrat Ghāfir (40):75

enter the Blaze" while crying laments and pleading for his own destruction "he will pray for annihilation."

20. Joy

The joy a believer experiences in this world is really and truly justified because the source of this joy is Allāh's grace and mercy. Joy at the Lord's satisfaction is even greater than what the blessings they receive reveal thereof: "Say, 'In Allah's grace and His mercy - let them rejoice in that! It is better than what they amass.'"[20] As if to say that the cause of their happiness is anything that displays Allāh's satisfaction with them. All of this stands in stark contrast with the happiness of worldly people, for it is more like blissful ignorance. That is why the Qur'ān describes it as undue ("That is because you used to exult unduly on the earth and because you used to walk exultantly."[21]). So what use is falsehood, even if it makes you happy?

21. Mark of sinners

If the division of people according to how they receive their records of deeds—in their right hands, left hands, or behind their backs—applies to everyone who is resurrected, then this inevitably leads to a public humiliation of the sinners, which is something they would have done anything to avoid in this world. Add to this the fact that their faces are visibly transformed and darkened, so as to reveal the terrible fate in store for them,[22] and you have yet another form of public humiliation on the resurrection, which in turn is a form of psychological punishment for the sinners before they enter hellfire.

22. False joy

One of the causes of false joy and exultation in this world is people's disregard for the hereafter and ignorance of the different kinds of recompense that await its inhabitants. This is why the

---

20. Sūrat Yūnus (10):58

21. Sūrat Ghāfir (40):75

22. Sūrat Āle ʿImrān (3):106

first description the Qurʾān gives them is that "he thought he would never return." In other words, they thought they would never go back to Allāh. It is narrated in one saying, "Eid is not for those attired in new garments; rather, Eid is for those saved from punishments!" (*laysa al-ʿīd li man labisa al-jadīd, wa innamā al-ʿīd li man amina al-waʿīd*).

So if something befalls servants that gives them occasion for false joy, then they need only remember first the terror that awaits them and, second, Allāh's watchfulness over them (as Allāh says, "Yes indeed, his Lord sees him best") to return to their senses. Two matters have been mentioned together in these verses in order to remove this blissful ignorance—namely, that people should remember that they will one day return to Allāh and that Allāh sees them, whatever they do.

Verses 16–25

84:16 *So I swear not by the evening glow,*

84:17 *by the night and what it gathers,*

84:18 *by the moon when it blooms full:*

84:19 *you will surely fare from stage to stage.*

84:20 *So what is the matter with them that they will not believe?*

84:21 *And when the Qurʾan is recited to them they will not prostrate?*

84:22 *Rather the faithless deny,*

84:23 *and Allah knows best what they keep to themselves.*

84:24 *So warn them of a painful punishment,*

84:25 *except such as are faithful and do righteous deeds: there will be an everlasting reward for them.*

23. Oaths

Swearing an oath by something—even if it is something inanimate like the evening glow, the night, or the moon—at its core is an oath sworn by the Lord of that thing insofar as one sees it as signifying (*āyatiyya*) its Lord's exaltedness. So there is no reason for us to cling to the notion that no oath can be sworn except an oath sworn by Allāh. Everything in existence is attributed to Him, so by looking at it, we are, in truth, looking at its Originator. That is why believers should feel a genuine and intimate connection with nature, just as a lover feels an intimate connection with the gifts of a beloved.

24. Night

It is a feature of human nature that we do not pay detailed attention to the signs of Allāh's power and mercy that surround us. This is why many verses swear oaths by natural phenomena that are all around us and which we are used to, without paying the slightest attention to the wisdom behind them. Who amongst us gives notice to the night's blessing of gathering things scattered and uniting things divided for every animate being returns to its abode and nests there, preparing itself for the new day. We can glean this idea from Allāh's words "by the night and what it gathers."

25. Full moon

The verse does not swear by the moon itself but only by its becoming full ("by the moon when it blooms full"), in other words, when it is at its most luminous on the night of the full moon, as if it only becomes worthy of being sworn by when it reaches its highest state of excellence (*kamāl*), which is when it is most luminous. Of course, everything has its own individual excellence.

On this basis, we say the fullness of the moon being the proper time to swear an oath by it harks to the completion of Adam's (as) creation, which is when Allāh commanded the angels to prostrate to him. Allāh did not command them to prostrate until He had blown His spirit into him!

26. Change in states

The above verses were revealed to affirm the reality alluded to in the later verse "you will surely fare from stage to stage." But the interpretations of this verse vary. Some say that it refers to the different stages of a human being's life in this world. Others say that it refers to our states in this world, the isthmus and the resurrection, and others still say that it refers to our states in the various stages of the resurrection.

We can reconcile all of these opinions by saying that these verses are discussing the speed and magnitude of change in human existence in a way that shows there is a hidden power behind all that—that it is this hidden power that alters our states and that we must take recourse to this power to change our state to the best one possible! Moreover, these verses encourage us to bring ourselves, through all of these changes, to the perfection for which we were created and to be avaricious for this and not content with our present condition. For verily "One for whom two days are the same has been cheated!"[23]

27. Difficulty to ease

That our state can change from difficulty to ease (which is a corollary of the stratified nature of human existence that we can deduce from this verse) should give hope to people's hearts. The fact that these states are not fixed is in and of itself a kind of blessing. In fact, if we were to suppose that someone's whole life will be consumed only by difficulty, then this gives occasion for God's servant to despair. But so long as a person anticipates the following stages of the isthmus and the resurrection, safe in the knowledge these will compensate us fully for every difficulty we endured in this world, we will have hope.

28. Prostration

Prostration (*sujūd*) has a physical manifestation, which is placing seven parts of the body on the ground, and a spiritual manifestation, which is demonstrating obedience. Perhaps the most appropriate interpretation of the verse "and when the Qur'an is recited to them they will not prostrate" is the second manifestation, as the

---

23. *Ma'ānī al-akhbār* 342

object of this verse is not for people to prostrate every time they hear a verse of the Qurʾān—only a limited number of verses in the Qurʾān require a prostration. So what is meant here is obedience to its ideas and the commands and prohibitions it contains.

This is why we say that whoever prostrates their body without submitting their heart has not attained the essence of prostration that they have been called on to demonstrate.

29. Difference between faithful and faithless

There is an essential difference between the position of the faithful towards Allāh's signs and that of the faithless and the hypocrites:

- Faithful: "When the signs of the All-beneficent were recited to them, they would fall down weeping in prostration."[24] "When His signs are recited to them, they increase their faith...."[25]
- Faithless: "When the Qurʾan is recited to them they will not prostrate." "But as for those in whose heart is a sickness, it only adds defilement to their defilement."[26]

30. Denial

In many of its verses, the Qurʾān affirms that the persistence of the faithless in their disbelief, if only in some circumstances, is not because of any conviction in their own beliefs or because of any failure to explain the revelation properly, rather it is because they are obstinate, following the traditions of their forefathers or pursuing their own interests. This is why the Qurʾān says, "Rather the faithless deny" for denial (*takdhīb*) is the resort of someone who is powerless to argue and has no reasonable proof to support one's claims.

Here, the tone of the verses shift from addressing them directly to speaking about them in the third person ("So what is the matter

---

24. Sūrat Maryam (19):58
25. Sūrat al-Anfāl (8):2
26. Sūrat al-al-Tawbah (9):125

with them that they will not believe?") as if to turn aside from them because they are unworthy of being spoken to face-to-face.

31. The heart

In His scripture, Allāh often alludes to the fact that He is aware of the contents of His servants' hearts. He is the one who knows "to what his soul tempts him."[27] He knows "the secret and what is still more hidden"[28] and "what the breasts hide."[29] This verse mentions that "Allah knows best what they keep to themselves." All of this calls on us to pay attention to the depths of our soul and not only our limbs for the heart is the vessel from which everything else flows as the Commander of the Faithful (as) says in *Nahj al-Balāgha*, "These hearts are vessels; the best of them are the most conscious!"[30]

Of course, the best kind of vessel when it comes to the heart is, first, one that can hold a lot and, second, one that holds good things in it.

32. Glad tidings

Just as Allāh gives "glad tidings" of punishment to the faithless (and this contains no small amount of derision and rebuke insofar as glad tidings are supposed to be happy news!), He also gives glad tidings to the faithful of a noble reward ("he shall have a noble reward"[31]), a magnificent reward ("We shall give him a magnificent reward"[32]), a great reward ("For such there will be...a great reward"[33]), and a reward that is "everlasting"[34] and never ending. Moreover, these verses have no trace of affront (*minna*), which means mentioning things that weigh upon the one receiving the reward. These two

27. Sūrat Qāf (50):16
28. Sūrat Ṭa Ha (20):7
29. Sūrat Ghāfir (40):19
30. *Nahj al-balāgha* 495
31. Sūrat al-Ḥadīd (57):11
32. Sūrat al-Nisā᾽ (4):74
33. Sūrat Hūd (11):11
34. Sūrat Fuṣṣilat (41):8

things, ending or being followed by an affront, are very frequent when it comes to the rewards of people in this world.

33. Happiness

The Qurʾān frequently invokes the duality of faith and righteous deeds with the definite article to signify that these are universals, meaning they encompass all of their instances in the highest possible form! This is because complete happiness obviously can only be attained by following all of Allāh's commands and performing all the righteous deeds required by faith, to the extent that the Qurʾān makes humility in prayer—which refers to supererogatory prayers rather than obligatory ones—one of the pillars of this happiness ("those who are humble in their prayers"[35]). Clearly, the level of this happiness is proportional to a person's level of faith and righteous deeds.

35. Sūrat al-Muʾminūn (23):2

Sūrat al-Burūj (no. 85: The Houses of the Zodiac)

Verses 1–9

85:1 *By the sky with its houses,*

85:2 *by the Promised Day,*

85:3 *by the Witness and the Witnessed:*

85:4 *Slain are the People of the Ditch!*

85:5 *The fire, abounding in fuel,*

85:6 *above which they sat*

85:7 *as they were themselves witnesses to what they did to the faithful.*

85:8 *They were vindictive towards them only because they had faith in Allah, the All-mighty, the All-laudable,*

85:9 *to whom belongs the dominion of the heavens and the earth, and Allah is witness to all things.*

1. Celestial signs

The Qurʾān frequently invokes oaths by Allāh's celestial signs, such as the sun, moon, and stars. We find another example of this in the current *sūrah,* which swears by the "houses" of the zodiac as well as calling to mind the sky itself that contains all of these celestial bodies with His saying "Certainly We have appointed houses in the sky and adorned them for the onlookers."[1]

Perhaps the reason for this focus on the firmament is that it is there and available for everyone to contemplate upon. No matter where they are, a person need only cast their gaze upwards to take

1. Sūrat al-Ḥijr (15):16

it in. Moreover, it is, in its vast expanse, a manifestation of Allāh's greatness as well as being His sole dominion as it is beyond the power of man to corrupt the heavens as he has corrupted the earth.

2. "Houses"

Some say[2] that these "houses" are actually the places of the planets. Of course, the care and wisdom taken in placing them is no less important than the fact of their existence, for if they moved from their positions, the running of the world would be altered, from the progression of the seasons to the rhythm of the tides. This makes clear to us that this act, like all other acts of creation, have been executed according to Allāh's utmost wisdom.

It is most interesting that Allāh, after mentioning His creation of the houses of the zodiac, mentions the resurrection and the vengeance He will enact therein against the wrongdoers after all the corruption they have caused. From this we can understand that the same wisdom behind placing the celestial bodies in their proper places requires Allāh to requite the wrongdoers as well, in order that everything be in its proper place in both the physical world and the moral one.

3. The promised day

Specifically referring to the resurrection as "the Promised Day" after mentioning some features of the first creation ("By the sky with its houses") suggests that every kind of persecution faced by the faithful in this world should actually be seen from the perspective of the One in whose hands is all existence. Whatever hardships they suffer for the sake of Allāh will not be in vain, for Allāh may grant respite to the oppressors but He will never ignore the oppression they commit. It is narrated that the Commander of the Faithful (as) described what happens to the people of the ditch: "A woman came with her child of one month, and when she was seized she feared for her child. But the child called out, "Fear not! But cast me into the fire with you, for by Allah, this is but a trifle

2. *Tafsīr al-Tibyān* 8/460

for Allah's sake! So she cast herself into the fire with her child, and her child was one of those who spoke while a babe."[3]

Referring to it as "the Promised Day" suggests that it will gladden the spirits of those who await it, as if Allāh has made that day a promised day that His friends (*awliyā'*) await expectantly, in order to placate them because of their prayers for the punishment of their oppressors to be hastened.

4. Witness and witnessed

One of the astonishing things about the Qur'ān is that a single one of its words is open to many meanings, so concerning the verse of Solomon's (as) kingdom, some commentators identify as many as 1.26 million possibilities! Another verse like this is "by the Witness and the Witnessed" which has as many as thirty possible interpretations. We rarely find words that can be so widely applied except in the Qur'ān.

One of the most appropriate interpretations mentioned for this verse is that the witness (*shāhid*) is the Prophet (s), based on Allāh's saying "O Prophet! Indeed We have sent you as a witness, as a bearer of good news and as a warner."[4] The witnessed (*mashhūd*) is the Day of Recompense, based on Allāh's saying "That is a day on which all mankind will be gathered, and it is a day witnessed."[5]

5. The witness

The witnessing of "the Witness" has been interpreted[6] sometimes to mean being present and seeing something with your own eyes but at others to mean bearing witness, declaring the truth, and acting upon the consequences of this witnessing. Whichever meaning is adopted, they both demonstrate the lofty station of the Final Prophet (s) who sees our deeds whether we are alive or dead and then bears witness over us, which in turn is a threat to those obstinately refuse to believe and a source of embarrassment

3. *Majma' al-bayān* 10/707
4. Sūrat al-Aḥzāb (33):45
5. Sūrat Hūd (11):103
6. *Tafsīr al-mīzān* 20/249

to those who love him (s) as whatever bad actions we undertake ultimately reach him and cause him distress.

This should be sufficient to keep anyone with the slightest amount of love in their hearts for the Prophet (s) away from sinning. How can a lover be happy when he harms his beloved, if he is truthful in his professions of love?!

6. People of the ditch

If the expression "people of the ditch" in Allāh's saying "Slain are the People of the Ditch!" refers to the faithful who have been slain, then these verses are informing the audience about what has happened to them. On the other hand, if they are referring to the faithless murderers, then this is an invocation against them.[7] The Qur'ān has also used this style of invocation elsewhere; for example, "Perish man! How ungrateful is he!"[8] and also, "Perish the liars...!"[9] As though Allāh, who originated them with His hand of providence, sees them as unworthy of living any longer upon His earth that He created for His vicegerents, because they have forsaken the very purpose of creation. So Allāh invokes death upon them, which is the opposite of life. What a difference there is between invoking death upon them and promising to give a good life to the faithful ("We shall revive him with a good life...."[10]

And this, to some extent, can apply to many other people, insofar as their lives do not embody the reason for which humankind was created—to be Allāh's vicegerent upon the earth.

7. Crime of the ditch

The crime perpetrated by the men of the ditch was one of the most terrible atrocities the faithful endured. There are several reasons for this:

---

7. In which case, this can be translated, as Qara'i does, as "Perish the Men of the Ditch!"
8. Sūrat ʿAbasa (80):17
9. Sūrat al-Dhāriyāt (51):10
10. Sūrat al-Naḥl (16):97

- Their killers dug a ditch for them in the ground so that they could not run away.
- They threw them into the ditch while they stood and sat around it, watching what happened to their victims ("above which they sat") both deriding them and tormenting them.
- They went to extremes in kindling a fire that Allāh described as "abounding in fuel" which indicates that it was a fire that was continuously burning because it had all the fuel it needed.
- They took revenge on the faithful for something that had nothing to do with their persons—they had only defied them for the sake of Allāh ("They were vindictive towards them only because they had faith in Allah, the All-mighty, the All-laudable."). This is similar to what befell another ground of the faithful, "Are you vindictive toward us for any reason except that we have faith in Allah...?"[11]
- Not to mention the fact that burning someone alive is the most repulsive form of murder because it is a slow, agonizing death, and anyone who sits watching it idly must be truly repulsive themselves.

Verses 10–22

85:10 *Indeed those who persecute the faithful men and women, and then do not repent, for them there is the punishment of hell, and for them there is the punishment of burning.*

85:11 *Indeed those who have faith and do righteous deeds, - for them will be gardens with streams running in them. That is the supreme success.*

85:12 *Indeed your Lord's violence is severe.*

85:13 *It is indeed He who originates and brings back again,*

85:14 *and He is the All-forgiving, the All-affectionate,*

11. Sūrat al-Māʾidah (5):59

85:15 *Lord of the Throne, the All-glorious,*

85:16 *enactor of whatever He desires.*

85:17 *Did you receive the story of the hosts*

85:18 *of Pharaoh and Thamud?*

85:19 *Rather the faithless dwell in denial,*

85:20 *and Allah besieges them from all around.*

85:21 *Rather it is a glorious Qurʾan,*

85:22 *in a preserved tablet.*

8. Pharaoh and Thamud

After the first verses of this *sūrah* mention a merciless confrontation between the faithful and their killers, whose cruelty was such that they burnt their victims to death, Allāh reminds the Prophet (s) in the verses that follow of two other kinds of confrontations the faithful faced (as represented by the violence of Pharaoh and Thamud through their display of military might—"the story of the hosts"). Of all the manifestations of their strength, the Qurʾān specifically chooses their military power, which was on display through the violence of their soldiers towards Allāh's servants, and yet Allāh destroyed them in the most unexpected ways, represented by water for Pharaoh's men and air for Thamud's.

And yet the faithless of the Quraysh do not take a lesson from this, rather they "dwell in denial." It is as though denial contains them and encompasses them as a vessel surrounds its contents, and this suggests that, as the reality suggested, they will never believe.

9. Men of the ditch

Qurʾānic oaths are there to affirm whatever object follows them. But sometimes the Qurʾān leaves ambiguous what the object of its oaths is as a way of encouraging its audience to ponder on what its object could be and to impel people to think and reflect on Allāh's revelation.

We can find an example of this device in the present *sūrah*. The object of the oath is not explicitly mentioned, but it is hinted at by Allāh's words "Indeed those who persecute the faithful men and women, and then do not repent, for them there is the punishment of hell, and for them there is the punishment of burning." So it is as though the object of the oath is that divine retribution will be taken on the Day of Resurrection in its most severe form and in a way that is appropriate to the crime that warrants it. In this case it is punishing the men of the ditch with burning ("punishment of burning") meaning with a fire like the one they set ablaze in this world.

10. Encouragement

Mentioning repentance in a way to offer encouragement, as Allāh does in this one: "and then do not repent" is in the middle of the verse. Immediately before it, Allāh mentions the persecution of the faithful by the faithless "who persecute the faithful men and women." Then after, it mentions a form of divine punishment for them "for them there is the punishment of hell, and for them there is the punishment of burning." This reflects the extent of Allāh's mercy towards His servants. He leaves open the door of repentance to even the most vicious of His creatures. It is as though this verse wants to bring the faithless of the Quraysh back from their transgression and promise them forgiveness if only they will desist from persecuting the Prophet (s) and his companions.

So how can anyone despair of Allāh's mercy and forgiveness when their sins do not come close to the persecution and murder of the faithful!?

11. Punishments

That the Qur'ān mentions "the punishment of burning" as a kind of punishment in hell shows that the punishment of hell is not restricted to fire. In fact there is:

- a drink that a person will "gulp it down, but hardly swallowing it: death will assail him from every side...."[12]
- foodstuff represented by "Indeed the tree of Zaqqum will be the food of the sinful."[13]
- psychological torment in that they will be told: "Begone in it, and do not speak to Me!"[14]

And there are still other forms of punishment besides burning that suffice to terrify the sinners. So how terrible will it be if on top of all that they are subjected to the punishment of burning, wherein their bodies will be eternally incinerated and restored, only to be incinerated again, as Allāh says, "as often as their skins become scorched, We shall replace them with other skins, so that they may taste the punishment."[15] It is possible that when Allāh says, "It is indeed He who originates and brings back again,"' after mentioning His severe violence, that this alludes to the condition of having their skins replenished. So He originates the creation of new skins and then brings them back again to perpetuate their punishment for as long as He wishes.

12. Fear and hope

The Qurʾān demonstrates Allāh's wisdom by juxtaposing the bliss of paradise with the torments of hell, for the human being must forever be between fear (*khawf*) and hope (*rajāʾ*). Hence the verse about paradise ("Indeed those who have faith and do righteous deeds, for them will be gardens with streams running in them. That is the supreme success") immediately follows the verse about punishment in order to balance intimidation with encouragement. This is the general strategy the Qurʾān follows in educating Allāh's servants, and we should follow its example in driving them towards their Lord.

---

12. Sūrat Ibrāhīm (14):17
13. Sūrat al-Dukhkhān (44):43–44
14. Sūrat al-Muʾminūn (23):108
15. Sūrat al-Nisāʾ (4):56

13. Righteous deeds

The expression "righteous deeds" in the plural, which appears in so many verses, requires us not to be content with only a single kind of righteous deed, as some do, just as righteous deeds will not intercede for their doer unless they are also accompanied by faith! Add to this the fact that the categorical usage of the word 'faith' necessitates faith in all the necessary doctrines if a believer is to truly be considered a believer. The faith of someone who only believes in some things but disbelieves in others is not accepted.

Of course, faith (*īmān*) is an idea distinct from that of Islām, as is clear from the verse "The Bedouins say, 'We have faith.' Say, 'You do not have faith yet; rather say, "We have embraced Islam," for faith has not yet entered into your hearts.'"[16] So if partial faith is not rewarded, then what about partial Islām?

14. Violence

The expression "violence" (*baṭsh*)—an expression that is appropriate in response to the behavior of tyrants—means to seize someone forcefully and assault them. Allāh uses it here to give composure to the heart of the Prophet (s) and those around him in the sense that the bearer of violence against the faithless is also the bearer of love for His faithful friends ("all-affectionate" (*wadūd*)), and the "enactor" (*faʿāl*) against whose will (*irāda*) nothing can stand. We could say that this expression is connected to other ideas that appear in this *sūrah*:

- He is the bearer of violence against His enemies ("Indeed your Lord's striking is severe").
- He is the bearer of love and forgiveness towards His friends ("He is the All-forgiving, the All-affectionate").
- He is the innate master of majesty and supremacy because He is "the enactor of whatever He wills."
- His being "Lord of the Throne" shows that He has complete authority over existence.

16. Sūrat al-Ḥujurāt (49):14

These ideas, taken altogether, affirm the fact that Allāh executes His rule by showing His satisfaction with the faithful from one angle, repelling the faithless from another, and manifesting the grandeur of His essence from another still. For how firmly has He wrought His signs, and how wondrous they are in conveying His promise and His threat!

15. Actions of His enemies

If we ponder the similarity between Allāh's description of His own acts and what His enemies do, we see:

- They witnessed the murder of the faithful ("as they were themselves witnesses to what they did to the faithful") while Allāh "is witness to all things."
- They ignited "a fire, abounding in fuel" to torture the righteous while Allāh is the Lord of "the punishment of burning."
- They took revenge on the faithful in this transitory world "only because they had faith in Allah, the All-mighty, the All-laudable," but Allāh will take revenge against them with His severe violence in the eternal abode ("Indeed your Lord's violence is severe.").
- They are the ones whose rebuke Allāh has recorded in a book that will be recited until the Day of Resurrection while He lauds the fate of his friends by promising them that He will admit them to His everlasting gardens ("Indeed those who have faith and do righteous deeds, for them will be gardens with streams running in them. That is the supreme success.").

16. Allāh's attributes

Allāh mentions His magnificent names and the attributes that apply to Him in the context of discussing this event, and it should be clear that there is a correspondence of sorts between these names and what the *sūrah* recounts about the challenge to the authority of the Lord of the Worlds that torturing His friends represents. For Allāh is:

- "All-Mighty" (*al-ʿazīz*) with whom nothing in existence can compete.
- "the enactor of whatever He wills" when exacting vengeance from the murderers of the faithful, or rather in everything that His boundless wisdom demands.
- "All-Laudable" who deserves every form of praise, which means that His friends should be honored rather than persecuted.
- the possessor of "the dominion" (*al-mulk*), so no one should challenge Him in His authority by killing His friends.
- a "witness" from whom not so much as an atom in the heavens and the earth is hidden. So how can He be unaware of the oppression wrought by the faithless against the faithful.
- "The All-Affectionate, the All-Forgiving" towards all of His servants but especially those who have been persecuted for His sake—amongst whom the victims of the ditch are counted.

17. Awareness of reality

The Qurʾān repeatedly says that Allāh encompasses things, people and deeds. In this *sūrah,* for example, we read: "and Allah besieges them from all around," while in another *sūrah:* "Is it not sufficient that your Lord is witness to all things?"[17] Obviously, if a person is aware of this reality throughout all the vicissitudes of life, they can achieve the lowest level of infallibility, or the highest level of moral probity, such that they will never commit a sin so long as they sense this divine presence.

To draw an analogy, we cannot conceive of a person exposing their private parts in polite company. So, by the same token, a servant

---

17. Sūrat Fuṣṣilat (41):53

who is vigilant of his Lord sees sinning almost like spiritually disrobing in Allāh's presence! This is what happened to our forefather, Adam (as): "So they both ate of it, and their nakedness became evident to them, and they began to stitch over themselves with the leaves of paradise."[18]

18. Sūrat Ṭa Ha (20):121

Sūrat al-Tāriq (no. 86: The Morning Star)

Verses 1–8

In the name of Allāh, the All-Beneficent, the All-Merciful

86:1 *By the sky, by the Morning Star,*

86:2 *(and what will show you what is the Morning Star?*

86:3 *It is the brilliant star):*

86:4 *there is a watcher over every soul.*

86:5 *So let man consider from what he was created.*

86:6 *He was created from an effusing fluid*

86:7 *which issues from between the loins and the breast-bones.*

86:8 *Indeed He is able to bring him back [after death],*

1. The morning star

The Qurʾān frequently invites humankind to cast their eyes upwards and gaze at the sky and the stars. This is to take their attention away from the familiarity of the earth to the wonder of the heavens!

It is in this vein that these verses mention that star which pierces the darkness of the night, and the Qurʾān magnifies it by saying, "and what will show you what is the Morning Star?" This is the only time in the whole Qurʾān that this expression ("And what will show you...") is used not for the events of the resurrection or the night of power but for a material component of existence. This demonstrates the greatness of this star!

2. Piercing star

And what is there to prevent the One who splits the darkness of the night with that "piercing star" from splitting the darkness of the soul and illuminating its depths? It is the same divine power in both cases, so how can we despair of Allāh's providence even in our darkest and most difficult times while He can banish the night's darkness with a single piercing star!

3. The watching

The watching (*hifḍh*) mentioned in this verse could allude to either:

- the angels watching over a person's deeds, as in Allāh's saying "Indeed, there are over you watchers, noble writers who know whatever you do"[1] or
- the angels watching over people and protecting them from calamities and disasters, as in Allāh's saying "He has guardian angels, to his front and his rear, who guard him by Allah's command."[2]

But both of these interpretations show that the human being is connected to another kind of creation—the angels who act as intermediaries between them and their Lord...sometimes by witnessing and recording their deeds and at other times by protecting them and keeping them safe from harm.

4. Pondering

This *sūrah* moves from talking about something in the highest reaches of the firmament ("the 'piercing star") to one of the lowest aspects of man's physical existence–the semen he ejaculates. This is so a person ponders and reflects on every aspect of this wondrous existence, acknowledging the magnificence of its creator in everything, comprehending that everything is the result of His all-encompassing wisdom, epitomized by the fact that everything will return to Him just as He created it in the first place.

1. Sūrat al-Infiṭār (82):10–12
2. Sūrat al-Raʿd (13):11

5. The process of creating a human being

The Qurʾān reminds its listeners of one of the most complex processes in this universe—the process of creating a human being that Allāh made in the best form. It begins by mentioning our origin–that we were created from "a gushing fluid" emitted from "the loins" as if it this substance was neither liquid nor ejected forcefully, then conception would not happen! It mentions the place where the fertilized egg settles, which is a chamber protected by the bones of the chest "ribs" and back. This is so that, firstly, we remain amazed by the greatness of our creator and, secondly, so that we remain convinced of His power to create us again.

6. Outcome of the affair

The Qurʾān frequently connects the beginning of creation with its end, as when Allāh says, "He will revive them who produced them the first time,"[3] and the power to originate with the power to bring back, as this *sūrah* mentions ("Lo! He verily is Able to return him."). This keeps servants mindful of the outcome of the affair, while they are usually preoccupied with its beginning!

So the nature of this world, and the mixture of joys and tribulations it contains, is a cause for us to remain unaware and be distracted from our purpose therein.

Verses 9–17

86:9 *On the day when the secrets are examined,*

86:10 *and he shall have neither power nor helper.*

86:11 *By the skies which give returning rain,*

86:12 *by the earth which splits:*

86:13 *it is indeed a decisive word,*

86:14 *and it is not a jest.*

86:15 *Indeed they are devising a stratagem,*

---

3. Sūrat Yā Sīn (36):79

86:16 *and I [too] am devising a plan.*

86:17 *So respite the faithless; give them a gentle respite.*

7. Accounting

Corrupt people can conceal their true nature by putting on an outward appearance that will cause others to speak well of them and that will benefit them in this life, but that will not help them "on the day when secrets are examined." Therefore, servants who are vigilant must reform their innermost character and not suffice themselves by merely changing their outward behavior. This is something that even the most dedicated people will sometimes forget!

But Allāh will hold people to account for their inner character just as readily as He holds them to account for their outward behavior. In fact, He will even punish them for it, as in the case of holding deviant beliefs or those things which cause them to sin outwardly ("and whether you disclose what is in your hearts or hide it, Allah will bring you to account for it. Then He will forgive whomever He wishes and punish whomever He wishes..."[4]).

8. No other helper except Allāh

Someone whose shameful secrets are disclosed (and this causes outrage amongst people) will do everything in their power to protect themselves, whether by relying on their own abilities or the abilities of others. But on the Day of Resurrection, we know that people will be completely equal before their Lord, so no one can help them against Allāh's absolute power.

How much better it is for a person to apprehend reality while they live in the abode of this world—namely, that there is no power nor recourse save with Allāh and that there is no helper except Him ("and he shall have neither power nor helper"). In reality, there is never any helper or might besides Allāh, whether in this world or the hereafter, even if a person only sees this on the Last Day.

---

4. Sūrat al-Baqarah (2):284

9. Revival

As a rule, the oaths of the Qur'ān display a relation between the oath and its object. There is, without doubt, wisdom behind every instance an oath in the Qur'ān. Here, for example, Allāh swears by:

- the skies "which give returning rain"—which is the rain that returns to the earth after having evaporated from it[5] and
- then the earth "which splits"—meaning it has openings from which plants emerge.[6]

So, taken together, both of these oaths reveal that there is a power that revives the earth after its death, by way of various intermediate causes in the heavens and the earth!

And, of course, the one who has the power to give life in this creation is able to give it in the next too. This is what Allāh means when He says, "Indeed He is able to bring him back."

10. Divide guidance

This relation is also clear between the phenomena of rain falling from the heavens and the plants springing from the earth and between the sending down of the Qur'ān (which is another manifestation of divine mercy that descends upon hearts that are ready) and the fruits of knowledge that then spring forth.

Therefore, anyone who wishes divide guidance to have an effect on them must have the capacity to receive these divine effusions, just as the earth must be ready to receive the rain of mercy in order for "delightful gardens"[7] to grow from it. The Qur'ān has described itself as "decisive word" which separates truth from falsehood, so anyone who does not adhere to it will inevitably fall into falsehood ("So what is there after the truth except error?"[8]).

---

5. *Mufradāt alfāḍh al-Qur'ān* 343
6. *Majma' al-baḥrayn* 4/358
7. Sūrat al-Naml (27):60
8. Sūrat Yūnus (10):32

11. The plotting of the wrongdoers

Those who treat the Qurʾān in a manner that can be described as "jest" (than which there is nothing more serious) put themselves in the position of challenging the Lord Almighty. This is why Allāh puts Himself in the position of plotting against them—which is a form of revenge that will creep up and seize them by surprise ("Indeed they are devising a stratagem, and I too and devising a stratagem."). It is utmost foolishness for a servant to vie with the Lord of the Worlds!

Based on this logic we also should not fear the plotting of the wrongdoers so long as we believe that Allāh has laid an ambush for them.

12. Responding in kind

Plotting, even if it is something usually considered improper, when done in response to the plotting of others, falls within the bounds of responding in kind, for example "the requital of a misdeed shall be its like...."[9]

This is in addition to the fact that Allāh, who is the utmost sovereign, has the right to require the wrongdoers in a hidden manner, which is implicit in calling this a "stratagem" (*kayd*). So Allāh will seal their hearts, their hearing, and their eyes to drive them toward a painful punishment without their realizing it.

13. Respite

Allāh asks His prophet not to be hasty to witness Allāh's revenge against the faithless and not to be preoccupied with them. Rather, He asks Prophet Muḥammad (s) to grant them "a gentle respite"—a brief respite so that Allāh may show them the recompense for their stratagem! This is exactly what happened for the Prophet (s) during his blessed life. He experienced amazing victories against the polytheists beginning with the Battle of Badr and ending with the defeat of his enemies who had driven him out of his homeland

9. Sūrat Yūnus (10):27

and captured Makkah. The punishment they have in store for them on the Day of Resurrection is even more severe—this too is near at hand for those who are certain that it will come to pass!

Sūrat al-Aʿlā (no. 87: The Most High)

Verses 1–5

In the name of Allāh, the All-Beneficent, the All-Merciful

87:1 *Celebrate the Name of your Lord, the Most High,*

87:2 *who created and proportioned,*

87:3 *who determined and guided,*

87:4 *who brought forth the pasture,*

87:5 *then turned it into a black scum.*

1. Allāh's sanctity

Just as the Qurʾān commands us to venerate Allāh Himself ("Whatever there is in the heavens and the earth celebrates Allah"[1]), it also commands us to venerate His name ("celebrate the Name of your Lord"). In the same vein, it sometimes assigns blessings to the divine essence as in "Blessed is Allah,"[2] and sometimes assigns them to His name ("Blessed is the Name of your Lord..."[3]). Together, these show that those words that refer to Allāh are endowed with a special status, and, therefore, we must venerate them as well as venerating His essence.

The practical lesson from this is that anything attributed to Him outside of His essence is also imbued with sanctity, as His sanctity overflows from Him to everything else so long as it is ready to receive this sacred effusion.

1. Sūrat al-Ḥadīd (57):1
2. Sūrat al-Aʿrāf (7):54
3. Sūrat al-Raḥman (55):78

2. Glorifying Allāh's name

Commentators differ about what it means to glorify Allāh's name in the verse "celebrate the Name of your Lord." The first thing that comes to mind is to celebrate the divine essence. So some say[4] that there is no problem in celebrating His names in the following senses:

- Not mentioning His name alongside those entities that people associate with Him, such as Lat and Uzza
- Not disrespecting the gods of the faithless in such a way as to draw the ire of their worshipers, who will respond by disrespecting Allāh in turn ("Do not abuse those whom they invoke besides Allah, lest they should abuse Allah out of hostility, without any knowledge."[5])
- Not taking Allāh's name in vain, as when people utter His name heedlessly

The practical lesson, according to the final meaning, is that servants must be mindful of their duty to revere both the name and the One it names. This is why there are special rules concerning the appearance of the name, such as not touching it without ritual purity and not uttering it except with an attentive heart.

3. Celebrating His name

Some say[6] that the meaning of celebrating His name is celebrating the One whom it names in His essence, attributes, acts, names, and rules. As for revering (*tanzīh*) Him, then this applies:

- To His essence by believing that it is neither a substance (*jawhar*) nor an accident (*ʿaraḍ*)[7]
- To His attributes by believing that they are neither originated (*muḥdath*), limited, nor deficient

---

4. *Tafsīr al-mīzān* 20/264
5. Sūrat al-Anʿām (6):108
6. *Mafātīḥ al-ghayb* 31/125
7. These are two terms taken from Islamic philosophy, negating them from the divine essence means that it is not a something in which other things inhere (i.e., a substance), nor does it exist within anything else (i.e., as an accident). [Translator]

- To His acts by believing that He is the absolute sovereign, so no one can object to anything He does
- To His names by believing He should only be mentioned using the names He has given Himself
- To His laws by knowing that whatever He has imposed upon us returns to Him

The practical lesson behind all of this is that however much the scope of divine sanctity extends for servants, they should exalt it for the sake of their Lord and strive to revere His essence, acts, and attributes too by divesting them of any association with others, whether explicit or subtle.

4. The expression "the Most High"

The expression "the Most High" is similar to the meaning of magnification (*takbīr*), which means elevating Allāh above all descriptions. The meaning of "the Most High" means to elevate Him above being encompassed by human intuition or imagination, for no matter, how lofty anything else may be, is possible for the human mind to encompass it. So this verse is a partner to the other: "and magnify Him with a magnification."[8]

It is narrated from Imām al-Bāqir (as), "When you recite: 'Celebrate the Name of your Lord the Most High' then say: 'Glory to my Lord the Most High!' (*subḥāna rabbī al- aʿlā!*), even if you only say it in your heart."[9] It is interesting that this tradition mentions saying it in your heart, so it is not appropriate to restrict Allāh's remembrance (*dhikr*) only to what we say aloud. This is supported by Allāh's words "And remember your Lord within your heart beseechingly and reverentially, without being loud, morning and evening...."[10]

---

8. Sūrat al-Isrāʾ (17):111

9. *Majmaʿ al-bayān* 10/719

10. Sūrat al-Aʿrāf (7):205

5. Creatorship and lordship

The Qur᾿ān regularly connects creatorship (*khāliqiyya*) to lordship (*rubūbiyya*) so that we move from the first to the second. The station of lordship is an abstract concept that a person's mind must be prepared to grasp while the station of creatorship has a connection with sensible realities near at hand and the creation as a whole.

This is why we see that the call of the prophets focused on the principle of creatorship, whose effects can be seen throughout the universe with the slightest thought, and that then takes someone to the idea of lordship. So Allāh's prophet, Abraham (as), mentions the station of creatorship saying, "who created me, it is He who guides me,"[11] and Moses (as) says, "Our Lord is He who gave everything its creation and then guided it."[12] In the case of Muḥammad (s), the first revelation he received was Allāh's words "Read in the Name of your Lord who created, created man from a clinging mass."[13]

Of course, even only paying attention to the magnificence of creatorship should inspire the depths of humility in worship and an abundance of thanksgiving for the many blessings that this universe contains.

6. Creation

After introducing the principle of creation, the Qur᾿ān mentions some of its instantiations—this is a form of firmly establishing a principle by mentioning its subsidiaries to acquaint servants with looking at the heavens and their own selves. So it mentions:

- a spiritual affair as represented by His saying "who determined and guided" as determination (*taqdīr*) takes place in the unseen realm and is something hidden, while guidance, like determination, is a subtle process that takes place in the creation.

11. Sūrat al-Shuʿarā᾿ (26):78
12. Sūrat Ṭa Ha (20):50
13. Sūrat al-ʿAlaq (96):1–2

- a material affair represented by His saying "who brought forth the pasture" so the feed of livestock and the dung it ultimately becomes, "a black scum," is something plainly visible to human eyes.

7. Pondering

When looking at the created world, it is important to be aware of the wise power that lies behind it, otherwise what value is there in discovering the great unknowns of the universe if we do not connect them to their source in a way that inspires us with faith and reverence? This is why the verse "who created and proportioned" highlights the fact that the creation is proportioned after discussing the principle of creation itself, and the verse "who determined and guided" follows determination with guidance. This too is something that people with intelligence need to ponder!

In contrast to this, the disbeliever ascribes the fact that every being is guided to the goal for which it was created to blind natural processes, while in fact Allāh ascribes both forms of guidance to Himself together:

- Physical guidance ("Our Lord is He who gave everything its creation and then guided it."[14])
- Moral guidance ("and shown him the two paths [of good and evil]"[15])

8. Provisions of this worldly life

In multiple verses, the Qurʾān warns people against being beguiled by the thriving vegetation that sprouts from the earth. We find one such verse in this *sūrah* when Allāh says, "then turned it into a black scum." This is reinforced by other verses with a similar meaning, such as His sayings, "Then with it He brings forth crops of diverse hues. Then they wither and you see them turn yellow. Then He turns them into chaff..."[16] and "like the rain whose vegetation

14. Sūrat Ṭa Ha (20):50
15. Sūrat al-Balad (90):10
16. Sūrat al-Zumar (39):21

impresses the farmer; then it withers and you see it turn yellow, then it becomes chaff...."[17]

In all of this there is a lesson not to allow ourselves to become conceited because of the provisions of this worldly life, for it does not take long to see that even the most lush vegetation is fleeting. It is enough for a single spring to pass and we should draw an analogy between that and everything decorous on this earth.

Verses 6–13

87:6 *We shall make you recite, then you will not forget*

87:7 *except what Allah may wish. Indeed He knows the overt and what is hidden.*

87:8 *We shall smooth your way to the easiest.*

87:9 *So admonish, if admonition is indeed beneficial:*

87:10 *he who fears will take admonition,*

87:11 *and the most wretched will shun it*

87:12 *—he who will enter the Great Fire,*

87:13 *then neither live in it, nor die.*

9. Recite and never forget

There is an obvious connection between the command to celebrate Allāh and the promise to make recitation and never forget ("We shall make you recite, then you will never forget."). These two things, which caused the Qurʾān to become deeply rooted in the heart of the Final Prophet (s), show us that being aware of the Master and celebrating Him as described in the verse "Celebrate the name of your Lord the Most High" is a prelude to a singular form of divine assistance—never being allowed to forget.

Moreover, undertaking the mission to preach is also a cause for going aright. This divine grace is connected (as in the following

17. Sūrat al-Ḥadīd (57):20

verse: "Indeed He knows the overt and what is hidden.") from one aspect to the fact that Allāh knows everything that happens in the Prophet's heart, such as his ardent desire to convey the Qurʾān just as it was revealed to him. This is alluded to in the verse "Do not move your tongue with it to hasten it."[18]

10. Divine grace

However great it may be for a servant, there must first be means for safeguarding divine grace, and, secondly, these means must be continuous or else what is the point of making someone recite if the one who receives it cannot be protected from forgetfulness? What is the point of protecting someone from forgetfulness if this is not a permanent state of affairs?

Allāh, in spite of His promise to His chosen messenger (s), still makes this promise contingent upon the divine will (*mashīʾa*). This produces a state of fear and hope even for the Final Prophet (s)! This is something explicitly stated in another verse, "If We wish, We would take away what We have revealed to you."[19]

This principle applies even to those whom Allāh has blessed with eternal life in paradise. Allāh says, "They shall remain in it for as long as the heavens and the earth endure — except what your Lord may wish...."[20] So what we notice in both verses is an affirmation of Allāh's absolute authority over the entirety of existence and in all situations. All the threads of bounties are in His hands, and there is nothing that can compel Him, not even in the bounties He has promised.

11. "The overt"

Part of "the overt" mentioned in this *sūrah* are those things that are obvious in the sensible realm—things that can be seen and heard. This is in contrast to "what is hidden" in that realm as well such as sights and sounds that cannot be apprehended without using

18. Sūrat al-Qiyāmah (75):16
19. Sūrat al-Isrāʾ (17):86
20. Sūrat Hūd (11):107

special equipment. Our Master's greatness is manifested by the fact that He apprehends them without needing anything to do so. This can even apply to those things that cannot be apprehended at all by human beings because they lack the faculties necessary to uncover those hidden realities in the existent realm, such as Allāh's greatest name. So again, Allāh's greatness is made manifest by the fact that there are some realities known only to Him that He has not chosen to share with anyone else.

12. Everything hidden

If one believes that their Master watches over everything that is hidden, even over the person themselves, even over their unconscious thoughts that come to mind from time to time without being aware, not to mention over those hidden things they are conscious of ("He knows the treachery of the eyes, and what the breasts hide."[21]), then they will vigilantly observe their thoughts, not to mention their limbs! This means that they will not even think of anything that would displease their Master, because, even if that will not cause them to suffer punishment, it will invite their Master's rebuke, which is something that any servant who loves the Lord would be embarrassed of! This shows us the greatness of the infallible (*maʿṣūm*) who even directs his imagination in accordance with the pleasure of his Lord in all circumstances.

13. Divine success (*tawfīq*)

The verse "We shall smooth your way to the easiest" contains a subtle allusion to:

- Allāh's program to save His friends (*awliyāʾ*), for He does not only smooth their way, He also prepares their persons for the way according to the implication of the address, which is directed to the person. So the assistance Allāh gives to His friends is really for their sake and not for the sake of their actions. This is exactly like Allāh's words "and paradise will

21. Sūrat Ghāfir (40):19

be brought near for the Godwary."[22] So just as paradise is brought near to them, Allāh makes ease close at hand for them in the same fashion.

- The source of this ease is the person themselves. It is because of the habits (*malakāt*) they possess that they have become attached to this divine assistance. When a person becomes ready to receive this assistance, the path is made smooth for them! So divine success (*tawfīq*) does not come from any source save the person themselves!

It is fitting to say here that Allāh can also ordain potential assistance for His servants, rather than actual assistance, because people themselves have fallen short in practically preparing for this assistance. It has been narrated from the Prophet (s), "Strive, for everyone is assisted in obtaining that which has been created for him!"[23]

14. Allāh's assistance

Allāh's most elect graces are accompanied by the majestic plural,[24] so He says, "Indeed We sent it down on the Night of Ordainment."[25] "Indeed We have sent down the Reminder"[26] and "Indeed We have given you abundance."[27] The assistance He bestows upon His servants by granting them success in calling others towards Him is no exception. He says, "We shall smooth your way to the easiest." Because this is one of the most magnificent spiritual blessings compared to the material ones.

15. Qualities of those persons who call others towards Allāh

The above verses all outline the qualities that those persons who call others towards Allāh must possess:

22. Sūrat al-Shuʿarāʾ (26):90
23. Ṣadūq, *Tawḥīd* 356
24. This is when an individual holding high office refers to themselves in the first person plural (i.e., "we") to denote their excellence, power, and dignity. [Translator]
25. Sūrat al-Qadr (97):1
26. Sūrat al-Ḥijr (15):9
27. Sūrat al-Kawthar (108):1

- Being prepared by turning towards Allāh with praise and celebration
- Having their character set right, as represented by being inspired to recite and then protected from forgetting
- Having their actions set right and the way smoothed for them, whether through acting upon objects, as was the case with the miracles of the prophets (as), or upon persons, by softening people's hearts.

16. Accepting guidance

The Prophet (s) was commanded to preach to those who had the potential to accept his message and be guided, or else his efforts would be in vain: "So admonish, if admonition is indeed beneficial." The life and energies of the Prophet (s) were far too important to be squandered on those unworthy of either. But we can say that it is still worthwhile to preach even if there is no hope of it yielding any benefit because the Prophet (s) adopted Allāh's manners in warning everyone, as when He commanded Moses (as) to preach to the most disobedient of His creatures saying, "Speak to him in a soft manner; maybe he will take admonition or fear."[28] Whether this was to offer Pharaoh Allāh's all-encompassing grace (*luṭf*) or simply to leave him with no excuse for his actions.

This verse could also be conveying the reason that some people will never take admonition—because they lack the basic ability in their hearts to accept guidance.

17. Divine guidance

Before someone can accept divine guidance, they must have traversed a prior stage represented by the existence of some level of fear towards Allāh in the person being admonished: "he who fears will take admonition." So this fear, whether in the sense of being afraid of Allāh's punishment or feeling unworthy of His blessings, motivates a person to search for that which will spare

28. Sūrat Ṭa Ha (20):44

them punishment or embarrassment. So someone who is guided should not expect their guide, whoever they are, to bring about some kind of miraculous transformation for them. Rather, they must be themselves in the position of the soil ready to receive the seed and then nurture that seed in themselves with the receptiveness that Allāh has bestowed upon them.

Therefore, those who call others towards Allāh must prepare this foundation in the hearts of the people, before burdening them with admonitions!

18. The wretched

The most-wretched (*ashqā*) here refers to the wretched (*shaqī*) in general, but it is the habit of the Qurʾān to use the superlative for normal traits, as in His words "On that day the inhabitants of paradise will be in the best abode and most excellent resting place."[29] On the other hand, we can also say that there are different levels of wretchedness, and the most-wretched is the intractable disbeliever who will be taken to the greatest blaze in the lowest levels of hell, whether this is in comparison to the fires of this world or the lesser punishments of hellfire.

However, the wretched (*shaqī*) is the opposite of the felicitous (*saʿīd*), but they are still in a better position than the most-wretched (*ashqā*)—namely, the ones who did not seize the opportunities they were given in life and so spent all of their days in a state of loss, which is sadly the case for the majority of mankind.

19. Severity of punishment

A manifestation of the severity of punishment in the hereafter, even for those who will not be punished forever, is the fact that the punishment in hellfire is continuous, without interruption or respite. This will be eternal for the faithless and a long (but finite) period of time for sinners. The Qurʾān describes this condition thus: "he will neither live nor die."[30] This means they will neither

29. Sūrat al-Furqān (25):24
30. Sūrat Ṭa Ha (20):74

die nor live a good life therein. At least the tribulations of this world, even in the worst circumstances imaginable, are broken by moments of relief and respite.

Worse still than the punishment of hellfire is Allāh's continuous wrath towards the inmates of Hell: "As for the faithless there is for them the fire of hell: they will neither be done away with so that they may die, nor shall its punishment be lightened for them. Thus do We requite every ingrate."[31] Otherwise, Allāh's mercy would sometimes interrupt their punishment, the upshot of which would be, as is the case for sinners in this world, it would become bearable for them, and a person would be able to plead for salvation in those times that Allāh turned towards him with His mercy.

Verses 14–19

87:14 *Felicitous is he who refines himself,*

87:15 *remembers the Name of his Lord, and prays.*

87:16 *Rather you prefer the life of this world,*

87:17 *while the Hereafter is better and more lasting.*

87:18 *This is indeed in the former scriptures,*

87:19 *the scriptures of Abraham and Moses.*

20. Self-refinement

The categorical use of "self-refinement" (*tazakkā*) in Allāh's words "Felicitous is he who refines himself" entails an act of purification that encompasses all aspects of a person's being, beginning with emptying the heart from everything that occupies them besides Allāh and ending with the limbs by using them for everything that pleases the Master. This is a preliminary to remembrance ("remembers"), which is again used categorically to mean living as if in the presence of Allāh at every moment and also a preliminary to the outward humility embodied by prayer, as the most important connection between servants and their Lord ("and prays").

31. Sūrat Fāṭir (35):36

To sum up, these verses look to emptying the heart of impurities ("refines"), adorning it with remembrance ("remembers the name of his Lord"), and garbing it thereafter in actual obedience ("and prays"). Altogether, this will bring people to the level of perfection that they were created to attain.

21. Enjoyments of this world

It is a kind of stupidity to give this world more importance than the hereafter because:

- the enjoyments of this world are connected to the physical realm and the pleasures of the body, while the bliss of the hereafter is connected to the pleasures of the spirit and body together, whether gazing upon His noble countenance, or living with the maidens of paradise.
- the enjoyments of this world, even the sensory ones, are interrupted by pains and difficulties, as is plain for all to see, and they are transient, which should also be obvious. On the other hand, the hereafter contains enjoyments unsullied by difficulty ("In it we are untouched by toil, and untouched therein by fatigue."[32]) nor contaminated by transience ("There will be an everlasting reward for them."[33]).

The verses here allude to two qualities of these enjoyments—being superior to those in this world and also everlasting with the words "better and more lasting." But obviously, to grasp these meanings requires a special level of spiritual maturity or else everyone in this world would become people living for the hereafter!

22. Various divine scriptures

The various divine scriptures, despite their different levels and the different levels of those prophets to whom they were revealed, are unanimous in their agreement upon the principles of moral refinement that the verses in this *sūrah* discuss: "This is indeed in the former scriptures." So there is no nation exempt from the rules

32. Sūrat Fāṭir (35):35
33. Sūrat al-Tīn (95):6

of wayfaring towards Allāh and worshipping Him. So if the nations of Abraham and Moses (as) were enjoined to follow the teachings of this *sūrah* on the basis of their own scriptures ("the scriptures of Abraham and Moses"), then the nation that bears witness, namely, the nation of the Final Prophet (s) is enjoined to excel further in everything mentioned here because Allāh's authority over them is more complete, their scripture is more comprehensive, and their Prophet (s) is at the greatest level of all the prophets!

Sūrat al-Ghāshiyah (no. 88: The Enveloper)

Verses 1–16

In the name of Allāh, the All-Beneficent, the All-Merciful

88:1 *Did you receive the account of the Enveloper?*

88:2 *Some faces on that day will be humbled,*

88:3 *toiling and weary:*

88:4 *they will enter a scorching fire,*

88:5 *and made to drink from a boiling spring.*

88:6 *They will have no food except cactus,*

88:7 *neither nourishing, nor availing against hunger.*

88:8 *Some faces on that day will be joyous,*

88:9 *pleased with their endeavor;*

88:10 *in a lofty paradise,*

88:11 *wherein they will not hear any vain talk.*

88:12 *In it there is a flowing spring*

88:13 *and in it there are raised couches,*

88:14 *and goblets set,*

88:15 *and cushions laid out in an array,*

88:16 *and carpets spread out.*

1. Rhetorical devices

When preparing people's minds for discussions about their ultimate destiny, the Qur'ān employs a number of methods to grab the attention of its audience. Sometimes, it uses oaths ("By the Dawn"[1]). At other times, it uses rhetorical questions ("Did you receive...?"), and at other times still, expressions of ineffability that emphasize magnificence ("And what will make you understand...?"[2]). There is a lesson in this, for anyone who wishes to give their words weight with people must use rhetorical devices to capture the audience's attention rather than immediately speaking about things to which they give no importance.

It is interesting to note that this question, and others like it in the Qur'ān, are first and foremost addressed to the Prophet (s). It is as though he is the very core of mankind and, as a result, he alone is worthy of being addressed by Allāh before all others. We can also say that addresses such as these in the Qur'ān are actually addressed to everyone, even if their appearance might suggest they are directed specifically towards the Prophet (s).

2. "The Enveloper"

Referring to the Day of Resurrection as "the Enveloper" (*al-Ghāshiyah*) highlights the horror of the event because:

- it is either taken from the Arabic word *ghishyān*, which means to envelop everyone so no one will escape the accounting, as Allāh says, "We shall muster them, and We will not leave out anyone of them"[3] or
- it means that it will envelop people with different kinds of distress ("on the day when the punishment envelopes them, from above them and from under their feet..."[4]) as Allāh says in another verse, "a day whose ill will be widespread."[5]

1. Sūrat al-Fajr (89):1
2. Sūrat al-Qāriʿah (101):3
3. Sūrat al-Kahf (18):47
4. Sūrat al-ʿAnkabūt (29):55
5. Sūrat al-Insān (76):7

Of course, considering this terrifying fate should cause us to keep back from forbidden lusts in this world, and that is for someone who has reached the level where they have complete certainty about this divine foretelling that shall surely come to pass.

3. Facial expressions

A person's innermost feelings are usually expressed by their facial expression, whether in this world or the hereafter. That is why we see a touch of darkness, which can be perceived by those able , in the faces of wrongdoers in this world. In the hereafter, this will be clearly visible to all creatures because the veil will have been removed from them.

This is why the verse describes the faces of the sinners as being humbled. In other verses it describes them as "Were you to see when the guilty hang their heads before their Lord..."[6] and "humbled by abasement, looking askance secretly"[7] while the faces of the obedient are called "joyous" and elsewhere "fresh."[8] In this act of revealing there is a kind of public disgrace for some people and a kind of ennobling of others in the mustering of the resurrection.

4. Achieving humility

Everyone is ultimately traveling to the realm of all-encompassing humility and fear that is the Day of Resurrection because, on that tremendous day, everyone will have the veil pulled from their eyes. So we say that reason dictates that a person should strive to reach this position of their own volition before being brought to it forcibly. They can achieve this by observing those practices that instill them with humility, foremost amongst which is prayer, which is the utmost expression of humility.

6. Sūrat al-Sajdah (32):12
7. Sūrat al-Shūrā (42):45
8. Sūrat al-Qiyāmah (75):22

So why is it, then, that people will come in abasement on the Day of Resurrection without thinking how they can obtain the means of dignity therein while they are in this world!?

5. Works

One of the greatest causes for regret on the Day of Resurrection is mentioned in two verses: one is "Then We shall attend to the works they have done and then turn them into scattered dust."[9] The other is in this *sūrah* where Allāh says, "toiling and weary" for the sinners have spent their entire lives for the sake of this world that is filled with fatigue and suffering, as a confirmation of Allāh's words "If you are suffering, they are also suffering like you...."[10] In fact, they may have suffered more, for the sake of their falsehoods, than some of the faithful! But their true affliction begins when all their efforts are shown to have come to naught in the abode of recompense. Their toil and weariness continues while the inhabitants of paradise are described with Allāh's words as being "pleased with their endeavor."

6. Food and drink of hellfire

The life of the inmates of hellfire cannot be conceived of by the inhabitants of this world. The verses merely give us a broad overview and details that everyone can understand, for the truth is more terrible than anything that can be put into words! For example, imagine someone pleading and asking for water, and then boiling water is their drink ("If they cry out for help, they will be helped with a water like molten copper which will scald the faces. What an evil drink, and how ill a resting place!"[11]). Imagine, when they ask for food, they are fed thorns and fill their stomachs with them ("Its spathes are as if they were devils' heads. Indeed they will eat from it and gorge with it their bellies."[12]). When their bodies are wounded and covered in sores, they will eat their fluids,

---

9. Sūrat al-Furqān (25):23
10. Sūrat al-Nisā᾽ (4):104
11. Sūrat al-Kahf (18):29
12. Sūrat al-Ṣāffāt (37):65–66

which are called pus ("nor any food except pus"[13]). This is all after these people have enjoyed all kind of good things in this world.

This verse also alludes to the food and drink of the inmates of hellfire. Their food is cactus (*ḍarīʿ*), which is a plant in this world[14] and, according to some, the most detestable sort of food that even beasts will not eat. There is no doubt that however terrible cactus may be in this world, it cannot compare to what the hereafter contains. As for the drink in the hereafter, it is a spring of the utmost heat ("made to drink from a boiling spring"). The expression "made to drink" might allude to the fact that they are forced to drink it, in which case this combines the elements of humiliation and punishment.

7. Faces of the inhabitants of paradise

The faces of the inhabitants of paradise are described as joyful ("Some faces on that day will be joyous") and fresh ("You will perceive in their faces the freshness of bliss"[15]). This sign on their faces is similar to the light that will shine in the hereafter because of what they did in this world in that nothing enters the hereafter save that it originated in this world, as can be understood from Allāh's words "Go back and grope for light!"[16] Going back in this verse is interpreted as returning to this world.

And there is no doubt that whoever is destined to receive such blessings in the hereafter will attain a degree, however lo, of freshness in this worldly life also, as the people of discernment (*firāsa*) and insight (*baṣīra*) can attest.

8. The condition of being pleased

The condition of being pleased and at ease that the believer experiences in paradise, as Allāh says, "Pleased with their endeavor" is really in contrast to the anger the sinners feel towards themselves. So the state of the faithful is either:

13. Sūrat al-Ḥāqqah (69):36
14. *Mufradāt alfāḍh al-Qurʾān* 1/506
15. Sūrat al-Muṭaffifīn (83):24
16. Sūrat al-Ḥadīd (57):13

- with regards to the satisfaction they felt with their endeavors in this worldly life as a result of self-accounting (*muḥāsiba*) and vigilant self-observation (*murāqaba*) or
- with regards to the bliss they find themselves in, as the inner reality of this bliss is Allāh's satisfaction with them, so they are satisfied with themselves because Allāh is satisfied with them.

This form is the state of the contented soul (*al-nafs al-mutma'inna*) that Allāh describes as "pleased, pleasing!"[17]

9. Blessings of paradise

In this *sūrah,* the Qur'ān enumerates the particular blessings of paradise in seven places, and all of them are in the indefinite article (*nakira*) to convey their magnificence. For instance: a lofty paradise, a flowing spring, raised couches, goblets set, cushions laid out, and carpets spread. To these sensible (*maḥsūs*) blessings, Allāh adds a blessing that cannot be directly sensed at the very beginning of this list—His saying "wherein they will not hear any vain talk." In another verse, He says, "They will not hear therein any vain talk or sinful speech."[18] These verses indicate that vanity and pointless speech are a form of punishment that contradicts the bliss of paradise.

This is why a believer avoids those environments in this world that are not compatible with paradise, which is, as it has been described, the station of being Allāh's neighbor.

Verses 17–26

88:17 *Do they not observe the camel, how she has been created?*

88:18 *and the sky, how it has been raised?*

88:19 *and the mountains, how they have been set?*

88:20 *and the earth, how it has been surfaced?*

17. Sūrat al-Fajr (89):28
18. Sūrat al-Wāqiʿah (56):25

88:21 *So admonish—for you are only an admonisher,*

88:23 *except him who turns back and disbelieves.*

88:24 *Him Allah will punish with the greatest punishment.*

88:25 *Indeed to Us will be their return.*

88:26 *Then, indeed, their reckoning will lie with Us.*

10. Styles found in the Qurʾān

One of the styles found in the Qurʾān is transitioning from the apparent goal that Allāh desires to the hidden cause that occasions it. The previous verses called on their audience to remember the resurrection and give heed to the condition of the people blessed and punished therein. But this description by itself is not sufficient to constitute a call for servants to do what Allāh desires of them. So it is accompanied by a call for people to seek knowledge that will inspire them with awe towards their Lord—looking to the heavens and whatever manifestations of divine power surround the human being. So it is only natural that at the time the revelation was sent down that the inhabitants of the desert who lived then would look to the camel, because it was one of the main means of their subsistence. If they raised their gaze, they would see the beauty of the heavens, and if they looked in front of them they would see the mountains sticking out of the earth.

All of these indications, taken together, cause our minds to conclude first that there is a creator, second that He is powerful, and third that He is wise. From these three things, we must also believe in the enveloper with whose mention this *sūrah* began.

11. Rousing hearts

It is only suitable that those calling others towards Allāh should rouse the hearts of their listeners by asking them questions to motivate them to search for answers that will, ultimately, give them inner conviction.

So these verses use the word 'how' (*kayf*) four times—beginning with something visible close at hand, like the camel, then something that cannot be reached, like the heavens, another far-off phenomenon, like the mountains, and then the earth, that everyone with eyes can see and that has been flattened so that mankind may subsist upon it. All of this is mentioned so that the listener will ultimately arrive at an intelligible concept—that there must be someone there who created the camel, made the stars, placed the mountains, and flattened the earth!

12. No authority over people's hearts

Many times, the Qurʾān mentions that the Prophet (s), like the rest of the prophets, has no authority over people's hearts. Otherwise this would invalidate free will that is the cause of divine reward and punishment:

> *So admonish for you are only an admonisher, and not a taskmaster over them*[19]
>
> *Would you then force people until they become faithful?*[20]
>
> *And you are not to be a tyrant over them.*[21]
>
> *You are liable to imperil your life for their sake, if they should not believe this discourse, out of grief.*[22]
>
> *So do not fret yourself to death regretting for them.*[23]

This, in turn, curtails the expectations of those who call others towards Allāh lest they become discouraged when they see people turning away. In fact, the practice of the prophets was to

19. Sūrat al-Ghāshiyah (88):21–22
20. Sūrat Yūnus (10):99
21. Sūrat Qāf (50):45
22. Sūrat al-Kahf (18):6
23. Sūrat Fāṭir (35):8

constantly admonish others without trying to control their hearts or else there would not have remained anyone who denied their teachings.

13. "Except him who turns back and disbelieves"

Some scholars have understood the verse "except him who turns back and disbelieves" to indicate that Islām is both a religion of reality and compassion. Its primary basis is simple admonition, but when faced with "him who turns back and disbelieves" and who opposes the call to faith, then it becomes a matter of struggling against them and completely removing all pockets of persecution (*fitna*) from the earth, as according to Allāh's words "Fight them until persecution is no more."[24] This is completely different from the approach of someone who limits calling others towards Allāh to verbal exhortations in order to avoid a confrontation that requires people to sacrifice their lives and property.

14. Verses describing hell

Everything is lowly compared to the magnificence of the Exalted Lord, so if He describes something as great or severe, then the thing thus described must be something truly grave. This is what we see when Allāh describes the punishments of hell variously as "a severe punishment,"[25] "a painful punishment,"[26] "a humiliating punishment,"[27] "an everlasting punishment,"[28] "the punishment of the blaze,"[29] "a grave punishment,"[30] "the punishment of burning,"[31] "an eternal punishment,"[32] "a harsh punishment,"[33] "the punishment of Hell,"[34] and "more severe and more enduring."[35]

24. Sūrat al-Baqarah (2):193
25. Sūrat Āle ʿImrān (3):4; Sūrat al-Anʿām (6):124; Sūrat Ibrāhīm (14):2
26. Sūrat al-Baqarah (2):10, 104, 174
27. Sūrat al-Baqarah (2):90; Sūrat Āle ʿImrān (3):178; Sūrat al-Nisāʾ (4):14
28. Sūrat al-Māʾidah (5):37; Sūrat al-al-Tawbah (9):68; Sūrat Hūd (11):39
29. Sūrat al-Ḥajj (22):4; Sūrat Luqmān (31):21; Sūrat Sabaʾ (34):12
30. Sūrat al-Baqarah (2):7, 114; Sūrat Āle ʿImrān (3):105
31. Sūrat Āle ʿImrān (3):171; Sūrat al-Anfāl (8):50
32. Sūrat Yūnus (10):52; Sūrat al-Sajdah (32):14
33. Sūrat Hūd (11):58; Sūrat Ibrāhīm (14):17
34. Sūrat al-Zukhruf (43):74; Sūrat al-Mulk (67):6
35. Sūrat Ṭa Ha (20):27

In this *sūrah,* Allāh threatens the faithless with a punishment called "the greatest punishment." So someone who believes in their creation and resurrection, and is aware of these descriptions, must, without a doubt, relinquish their falsehood unless there is some doubt in their faith or in their understanding of what is in their own best interests!

15. "Indeed to Us will be their return..."

The verse "Indeed to Us will be their return. Then, indeed, their reckoning will lie with Us" has two dimensions to it:

- First, it consoles the heart of the Prophet (s) after mentioning the faithless at the beginning of this *sūrah.* Their return to Allāh, in the position of Him exacting retribution from them, makes whatever dominance they enjoy or persecution they perpetrate in this world seem trivial.
- Second, it inspires terror in the hearts of the obstinate, for Allāh makes the task of holding them to account His personal business, and He is the one from whom nothing can be hidden. Whoever believes in the reality of going back to Allāh will never so much as incline towards sinning in their heart, let alone actually commit a sin.

Sūrat al-Fajr (no. 89: The Daybreak)

Verses 1–14

In the name of Allāh, the All-Beneficent, the All-Merciful

89:1 *By the Daybreak,*

89:2 *by the ten nights,*

89:3 *by the Even and the Odd,*

89:4 *by the night when it departs!*

89:5 *Is there an oath in that for one possessed of intellect?*

89:6 *Have you not regarded how your Lord dealt with ʿAd,*

89:7 *[and] Iram, [the city] of the pillars,*

89:8 *the like of which was not created among cities,*

89:9 *and Thamud, who hollowed out the rocks in the valley,*

89:10 *and Pharaoh, the impaler,*

89:11 *—those who rebelled [against Allah] in their cities*

89:12 *and caused much corruption in them,*

89:13 *so your Lord poured on them lashes of punishment.*

89:14 *Indeed your Lord is in ambush.*

1. The way in which Allāh treats different individuals and nations

This *sūrah* is set out in such a way as to convey the way in which Allāh treats different individuals and nations. His precedent (*sunna*) and these precedents, like all other creational precedents (*sunan takwīniyya*), are never invalidated. The *sūrah* mentions:

- The nature of rebellious nations and what became of earlier peoples; how their rebelliousness destroyed them completely
- The nature of rebellious persons who embezzle the property of orphans and love amassing wealth, who become restless in times of difficulty and wanton in those of ease
- The nature of contented persons—the servants who are pleased with their Lord while their Lord is pleased with them

2. Verses without an agreed upon interpretation

There are few instances where there is as much disagreement about the interpretation of the objects of Qur'ānic oaths as there is in this *sūrah*. Some scholars have counted as many as forty different possible meanings for "the daybreak" and "the even and the odd!"

Based on what we have already said similar places, we can only confess that there must be someone who accompanies the book of Allāh and who knows the intended meaning between all of these possibilities. This person can be none other than the second of the Two Weighty Things (*thaqalayn*)—the Household of the Prophet to whom were entrusted the realities of the Qur'ān, as it was to them that these were addressed.

3. Possible interpretations of "daybreak," "the ten nights"...

The basic issue of the controversy about the different meanings of the words "daybreak," "the ten nights," "the even and the odd," and "the night" revolves around two possibilities:

- First, that these are connected to the time of Ḥajj, so the meaning of "daybreak" is the daybreak of Eid. "The ten nights" are the first ten nights of the Islamic month of Dhū al-Ḥijjah. "The even and the odd" are the days of Tarwiya and ʿArafa. "The night" is the night of Muzdalifa.

- Second, that these are connected to prayer (*ṣalāh*), so the meaning of "daybreak" is the time of the true daybreak that is connected to the obligatory dawn prayer. "The ten nights" are the last ten nights of Ramaḍān in which a person devotes themselves to following the example of the final messenger (s) in worshipping their Lord. "The even and the odd" are the parts of the night prayer (*shafʿ* and *witr*) offered in the pre-dawn hours. "The night when it departs" is simply the end parts of the night when most of it has passed.

Looking at these two opinions, the importance of these two pillars of worship—prayer and Ḥajj—becomes apparent.

4. Objects of oaths in Qurʾan

It is the convention of the Qurʾan to mention the object of an oath immediately after the oath itself, but in this *sūrah* it is interesting to note that:

- the object of the oath is left implicit (according to one opinion), although the context suggests its import.
- after invoking these oaths, Allāh poses a rhetorical question—Are these oaths sufficient for someone possessed of intellect? ("Is there an oath in that for one possessing intellect?")

5. Objects of oaths in Qurʾan

The object of the oath (*jawab al-qasam*) can be either:

- Allāh's words ("Indeed your Lord is in ambush.") or
- implicit. It is either an implicit warning of divine punishment and retribution for the rebels in this world and the hereafter or an implicit tiding of wonderful rewards for those persons with souls that are satisfied and satisfying, who are happy because of their inner peace (*itmiʾnān*) in this world and shall

enter the paradise of their Lord on the Day of Resurrection. This, like all other situations where the object of an oath is left unsaid, calls us to ponder and reflect on the verses of the Qur᾿an.

6. *Ḥijr*

There is a connection between the linguistic meaning of the Arabic root *ḥ-j-r* and the "intellect" (*ʿaql*) in the words "possessed of intellect" (*dhū al-ḥijr*). In every derivation of *ḥijr*, such as "compartment" (*hujra*), "ward" (*maḥjūr ʿalayh*), "a mother's care" (*hijr al-umm*), we find a common element that joins them together—protection and restraint. So someone who is a "ward" is prevented from disposing of his property, and both a compartment and care prevent others from entering while protecting the thing they contain.

In this sense, when a person's intellect (*ʿaql*) is complete, it protects them from deviation and inclinations and prevents them from acting against their own nature, according to the intellectual laws planted in their heart.

7. Human power

This *sūrah* paints an image of human power as represented sometimes by:

- engineering prowess and urban development, such as in building the city of Iram that we are told is without peer, filled with lofty palaces and tall pillars, as we can understand from Allāh's words "Iram, of pillars, the like of which was not created amongst cities."
- progress in industry, as represented by cutting boulders to use them in construction. This is something not without skill, especially in times past that lacked advanced tools for cutting and shaping stone. This is alluded to by Allāh's words "and Thamud, who hollowed out the rocks in the valley."

- military might, as represented by the power of Pharaoh and his ruthlessness in dealing with his enemies, to the extent that even his wife Asiya was not safe from him. He impaled her as he did all his opponents, as alluded to by the words "and Pharaoh, the impaler."

All of these tyrants are united under a single banner—rebellion (*ṭughyān*), transgressing Allāh's bounds and causing corruption on the earth.

8. Corruption of the whole human species

Allāh grants respite to some of those who disobey Him on a personal level and whose disobedience does not cause the corruption of the whole human species. In fact, He is eager to forgive them when they turn to Him in repentance. But He seizes with severity anyone who becomes a source of corruption for the whole human species, as He says in another verse: "And if he were to wield authority, he would try to cause corruption in the land, and to ruin the crop and the stock...."[1] This is why one of the causes of Allāh's most severe retribution that is mentioned in this *sūrah* are the deeds of those rebels who "caused much corruption," and now there is no trace of them left on the face of the earth.

It should be clear that this verse gives reassurance to the mind of the final messenger (s) who was facing the rebels of his own time. We can see this because Allāh refers to Himself as "your Lord" and connects Himself to His prophet to show that the one who dealt out retribution in previous generations is the one who will exact it upon present ones as a natural consequence of His unrivalled Lordship. This is what happened when He sent flocks of birds against them, and other forms of retribution as well.

9. Divine punishments

Divine punishments are always appropriate to the nature of the sin, so for those mentioned in the verse who caused much corruption upon the earth (such as the peoples of 'Ad, Thamud, and Pharaoh)

1. Sūrat al-Baqarah (2):205

the punishment they received was always fitting for their rebellion in which they violated Allāh's bounds. It is described as:

- continuous, as alluded to by Allāh's words "poured upon them" because when water is poured it flows continuously. This also alludes to its vigor and force. This Qur'ānic expression has been used to describe rain elsewhere: "We poured down water plenteously."[2]
- severe, as we can glean from the words "lashes of punishment" because a lash is a common device of corporal punishment.
- sudden ("Indeed your Lord is in ambush") because unexpected punishment is more painful for its victim because they have not been able to prepare themselves psychologically to receive or protect themselves from it.

10. The expression "in ambush"

The expression "in ambush" suggests two things:

- The ambusher wishes to exact retribution from his victim at an appropriate time for it to be more effective.
- The victim has no idea that the attacker is lying in wait or else it would not be an ambush!

It is obvious that if someone is aware that the Lord is watching over them, and this fact inspires them with a sense of fear and awe towards Him, then they will not fall victim to this kind of retribution that is manifested in the fires of hell by Allāh's words "Verily hell is an ambush."[3]

---

2. Sūrat ʿAbasa (80):25
3. Sūrat al-Nabaʾ (78):21

Verses 15–20

89:15 *As for man, whenever his Lord tests him and grants him honor and blesses him, he says, 'My Lord has honored me.'*

89:16 *But when He tests him and tightens for him his provision, he says, 'My Lord has humiliated me.'*

89:17 *No indeed! Rather you do not honor the orphan,*

89:18 *and do not urge the feeding of the needy,*

89:19 *and you eat the inheritance rapaciously,*

89:20 *and you love wealth with much fondness.*

11. The way that we see blessings and tribulations

These verses want to produce an essential change in the way that we see blessings and tribulations. Blessings are not always an honor that should occasion happiness: "...nor exult for what comes your way."[4] Nor is tribulation always a humiliation that should occasion fear and sadness: "so that you may not grieve for what escapes you...."[5] Of course, it is only natural for a human being to experience these feelings in the soul, but it is the mission of the prophets to take people's hands and bring them out of the confines of their nature, both in this and other situations, as the Qur'ān repeatedly affirms.

It is interesting to note that Allāh has repeated the word 'tests' (*ibtalā*) for both blessings and tribulations, as if to affirm that they both occupy the same level as a test of a servant's commitment and obedience to the Lord!

12. Human nature

The verses criticizing this aspect of human nature ("As for man, whenever his Lord tests him...") are connected to those before and after them:

4. Sūrat al-Ḥadīd (57):23
5. Sūrat al-Ḥadīd (57):23

- As for their connection to the previous verses, it is as though they are saying that the fact Allāh is watching over mankind and waiting in ambush for the rebels means that a person should make pleasing the Lord and avoiding His displeasure a concern—and not just look at their own short-term gratification, thinking that having means is an honor while lacking them is an humiliation.
- As for their connection to the verses that follow them, it is as though they wish to say that the sources of honor and humiliation are not as human beings imagine them. The real source of humiliation is some of the sins mentioned in the verse, such as failing to honor the orphan and consuming the property of others, while the real source of honor is feeding the needy and detaching one's heart from one's property.

13. Benchmark of honor and humiliation

It is natural for a believer, when conversing with the Lord, to keep in mind the community of the faithful as a whole, which is why Allāh uses the expression "our Lord" in more than sixty places throughout the Qurʾān. This means that when believers turn towards the Lord and sees all the faithful with Him, they include them all in their supplications. But someone who is not a believer will put themselves at the center of a dialogue with the Lord without paying attention to anyone else, even if this is only because they are absorbed by terror at something they see. But this is the reason why, when Allāh relates their words, He uses the individual pronouns 'my' and 'me' ("my Lord has honoured me" and "my Lord has humiliated me").

Here we should note that the benchmark of honor and humiliation in their eyes are sensible blessings (*mahsūsāt*). Their level of thought does not reach the level where they consider the standard of honor and humiliation to be their degree of proximity to their Master. This is something the later verses (discussing the contented soul (*al-nafs al-muṭma'inna*)—"pleased, pleasing"[6]) are alluding to. This is how people should see their behavior in day-to-day life.

14. Blessings and tribulations

When a person reaches the level where they can understand how Allāh organizes this existence and that it is connected to His unparalleled wisdom, then both blessings and tribulations become as one to them because a true servant:

- loves whatever their Master loves, in whatever form this love takes, so a tribulation could actually demonstrate more love for His servant than ease.
- does not see any privilege in blessings or indignation in tribulations, so long as both of these fall upon the path towards self-development and spiritual ascent. In fact, they may even reach the level where they see themselves inclining towards tribulation because it will grant them patience (*ṣabr*) in the form of entreating and taking refuge with the Lord in this world and additional rewards in the hereafter.

15. Helping orphans

What Allāh intends by the verse "No indeed! Rather you do not honour the orphan" is not what most people understand—namely, helping the orphan by giving food, clothing, and the like. In fact, what is meant here is much more general—honor in its broadest sense. This means more than merely feeding. It includes doing things to make the orphan feel respected and held in high esteem rather than feeling insignificant—a feeling that usually accompanies being an orphan. Equally, Allāh does not mean that you should only feed the needy but that you should encourage others to do likewise too. If only some people spend, this will not meet the needs of all the needy persons because of how many needy persons there are in every age. No, rather all the faithful must strive to encourage one another, especially when it comes

6. Sūrat al-Fajr (89):28

to providing food. Lacking a basic means of subsistence, as we are told by the Commander of the Faithful (as), causes "the poor to be perturbed by their poverty."[7]

It is interesting that the Qurʾān singles out this iniquity—failing to encourage others to feed the needy—out of all others for harsh rebuke and categorizes it as one of the qualities of the faithless ("Indeed he had no faith in Allāh, the All-supreme, and he did not urge the feeding of the needy..."[8]).

16. Usurping the property of an orphan

The fact that an orphan lacks a guardian is one of the reasons why some people dare to usurp their property and treat it as their own ("and you eat the inheritance rapaciously") only to ultimately ingest fire into their belly. This is the spiritual reality (*malakūt*) of wrongfully consuming the property of orphans.

And the verses encouraging friendliness towards orphans are indeed abundant, whether with regards to their selves or their property. For example, Allāh says:

> *...you should maintain the orphans with justice...*[9]
>
> *And when the division is attended by relatives, the orphans and the needy, provide for them out of it, and speak to them honourable words.*[10]
>
> *...and do not eat up their property, mingling it with your own...*[11]

In this *sūrah*, we read: "No indeed! Rather you do not honour the orphan." The shift in address that this verse contains, whereby it moves from the third person ('he') to the second person ("you"),

7. *Nahj al-balāgha*, sermon no. 209
8. Sūrat al-Ḥāqqah (69):33–34
9. Sūrat al-Nisāʾ (4):127
10. Sūrat al-Nisāʾ (4):8
11. Sūrat al-Nisāʾ (4):2

serves to make the prohibition of the sin more effective and the reprimand of its perpetrator more forceful!

17. Struggle

When the Qurʾān attributes something to human nature, such as greed, anxiety, or parsimony (as in Allāh's words "Indeed man has been created covetous, anxious when an ill befalls him and grudging when good comes his way"[12]) and such as love of wealth ("and you love wealth with much fondness!"), this highlights an important fact—uprooting these vices from the soul and restraining oneself from following this baser nature requires that a person struggle and overcome low self (*nafs*) or else the human being will be pulled along by this nature just as objects are pulled to the ground by gravity.

It is worth noting here that this *sūrah* warns against some specific consequences of loving wealth—failing to honor the orphan, to feed the needy, devouring the inheritance of others, and loving to amass wealth by any means possible, whether moral or otherwise.

Verses 21–30

89:21 *No indeed! When the earth is levelled to a plain,*

89:22 *and your Lord and the angels arrive in ranks,*

89:23 *the day when hell is brought [near], on that day man will take admonition but what will the admonition avail him?*

89:24 *He will say, 'Alas, had I sent ahead for my life!'*

89:25 *On that day none shall punish as He punishes,*

89:26 *and none shall bind as He binds.*

89:27 *'O contented soul!*

89:28 *Return to your Lord, pleased, pleasing!*

89:29 *Then enter among My servants!*

89:30 *And enter My paradise!'*

12. Sūrat al-Maʿārij (70):19–21

18. Magnificent sights

When Allāh says "No indeed! When the earth is levelled to a plain" this prevents human beings from attaching too much importance to the magnificent sights their eyes perceive in this world, whether these are manmade, like the towering buildings, or natural, like the firm mountains. This is because their hearts perceive that these lofty and imposing edifices will ultimately be reduced to scattered dust ("They question you concerning the mountains. Say, 'My Lord will scatter them like dust.' Then He will leave it a level plain. You will not see any crookedness or unevenness in it."[13]). Clearly, when these towering manmade and natural landmarks on the earth are leveled and a new stage begins ("and your Lord and the angels arrive in ranks") then the awe of being in the divine presence at that terrifying moment will be clearly visible. How fortunate someone is to have a friendly relationship with the Master of this grandeur while they are in this world, before they see what will become of its towering landmarks!

19. "No, indeed!"

The words "No, indeed!" (*kallā*), which is repeated twice in this *sūrah* (even though it is not visibly connected to anything), have a very deep meaning, represented by a rejection of a previous idea in preparation for receiving a new one:

- In the first instance, "No indeed! Rather you do not honour the orphan" is a rejection of their false belief that being blessed is a mark of honor, while a tightening of provision is a mark of humiliation. This is a preliminary step to adopting an alternative belief—that honoring the orphan is a mark of honor and withholding sustenance from the needy and not encouraging others to feed them is a mark of humiliation.
- The second instance, "No indeed! When the earth is levelled to a plain" prepares the audience to receive the belief that a person's real honor or humiliation begins with what is made manifest on the Day of Resurrection as a result

13. Sūrat Ṭa Ha (20):105–107

of their efforts in this world, when Allāh levels the earth completely and the human being stands before the Lord as a meek servant.

20. Physical form of Allāh

The Qurʾān wants those who recite its verses to be people of intelligence. This requires them to think and ponder. So there are verses that would appear to indicate that the Creator has a physical form, for example:

- "the All-beneficent settled on the Throne."[14]
- "the hand of Allah is above their hands."[15]
- "Do they await anything but that Allah should come to them in the shades of the clouds..."[16]
- In addition to the phrase contained in this *sūrah*: "and your Lord and the angels arrive..."

However, when a person opens the locks upon their heart and realizes it is impossible for the Creator to have a physical form (because "Nothing is like unto Him"[17] and because He said of Himself, "You shall not see Me..."[18]), there is no other explanation except that there is an implicit meaning to the aforementioned verses, such as Allāh's command, dominance, or magnificent signs etc.

21. Hell being brought near

When we talk about hell being brought near on the Day of Resurrection, we can explain it either:

- metaphorically—meaning that it came into view for its inmates, as in Allāh's saying "and hell is brought into view

---

14. Sūrat Ṭa Ha (20):5
15. Sūrat al-Fatḥ (48):10
16. Sūrat al-Baqarah (2):210
17. Sūrat al-Shūrā (42):11
18. Sūrat al-Aʿrāf (7):143

for one who sees"[19] so it is as though it came to them after being absent or

- literally—meaning that hell moves from its place and heads towards them. This appears to be even more terrifying because it makes hell seem eager to devour them saying, "Is there any more?"[20] This interpretation is supported by a narration from the Prophet (s) when he was asked about hell being brought near ("When the first and the last are gathered, Hell is driven forth."[21]).

It is narrated that the Prophet (s) was so distressed by this that his face changed visibly and it was difficult for his companions to see him like this. That is when this verse came down because of the severity of its contents. It is only to be expected that a person will remember their efforts in this world, but without this reminder what use is it, for on that day they will have no time left to work!

22. What resurrected people will wish for themselves

There are a number of things that the resurrected people will wish for themselves when they see the divine punishment, including:

- That they had not taken as a friend one who barred their way towards Allāh in this world ("Woe to me! I wish I had not taken so and so as a friend!"[22])
- That they had not been given their record of deeds because of the humiliating details it contains ("But as for him who is given his book in his left hand, he will say, 'I wish I had not been given my book.'"[23])
- That they were reduced to dust so that they would never have known an accounting nor a record of deeds ("Indeed We have warned you of a punishment near at hand — the

19. Sūrat al-Nāziʿāt (79):36
20. Sūrat Qāf (50):30
21. *Biḥār al-anwār* 7/125
22. Sūrat al-Furqān (25):28
23. Sūrat al-Ḥāqqah (69):25

day when a person will observe what his hands have sent ahead and the faithless one will say, 'I wish I were dust!'"[24])

- And what this *sūrah* records—that they wish they had sent something ahead for their life ("Alas, had I sent ahead for my life!")

It is interesting that the one speaking in this verse "Alas, had I sent ahead for my life" does not say "for my Hereafter," as if everything that came before that moment was not really life. This is made clear in another verse: "The life of this world is nothing but diversion and play, but the abode of the Hereafter is indeed Life, had they known!"[25]

23. Allāh's threats

It is the habit of Allāh, the Most-Generous and Most-Forbearing, to avoid threats and warnings except where necessary, so what about actually carrying out a threat? What if a threat was more appropriate than a warning? You see, mankind's insolence towards their Lord reaches such a level that it causes Him, the One whose mercy precedes His wrath, to threaten them with the very highest level of threat. He says, "On that day none shall punish as He punishes, and none shall bind as He binds." He places Himself in the position of the greatest force, whether we attribute "punishes" or "binds" to the divine essence, as according to the common recitation, or to the servant, according to the alternate recitation whereby "punishes" and "binds" are read in the passive voice (i.e., "On that day none shall be punished as he [the servant] is punished, and none shall be bound as he [the servant] is bound"). Of course, when we ponder this terrifying description of punishment and binding, it makes the persecution of the faithful by the disbelievers seem trivial in comparison, as what awaits the oppressors is so terrible it cannot even be conceived of!

24. Sūrat al-Naba' (78):40
25. Sūrat al-ʿAnkabūt (29):64

24. The "contented soul"

The "contented soul" (*al-nafs al-mutmaʾinna*) is ennobled here by being the object of Allāh's direct address ("O contented soul!") even if the possessor of this soul is not a recipient of revelations!

Let it be known that the way to this state of inner peace is made clear in the Qurʾan, and it is represented by remembrance (*dhikr*), as in Allāh's saying "Lo! Verily in the remembrance of Allāh do the hearts find rest!"[26] This is achieved through two means:

- Prayer (*salāt*): Allāh says, "Maintain the prayer for My remembrance."[27]
- The Qurʾan: For He refers to His scripture, "Indeed We have sent down the Reminder..."[28]

So the combination of ascent, represented by prayer, and descent, represented by the Qurʾān, can convey us to this level. This is why Imām al-Sajjād (as) says, "Even if everyone between the East and the West were to die, [and I was the last man alive,] I would not fear so long as I had the Qurʾān with me."[29]

25. "Enter My Paradise!"

Allāh speaks about paradise and attaches it to Himself with the words "enter My Paradise!" We do not find this expression anywhere except in this *sūrah*. This is to convey the exceptional honor of this paradise that has been prepared for a group of servants whom Allāh has attached to Himself. The same applies to His words "enter among my Servants!" as Allāh makes entering within the ranks of His servants who have been singled out for His providence the recompense of the contented soul. This is only because they dedicated the most sacred part of their being to Him alone—and, of course, it is their heart—which means that He poured out contentedness upon them, causing them to become pleased with Him and pleasing to Him.

---

26. Sūrat al-Raʿd (13):28
27. Sūrat Ṭa Ha (20):14
28. Sūrat al-Ḥijr (15):9
29. *Al-Kāfī* 2/602

It is interesting to note here that Allāh mentions, as a recompense, entering the ranks of His servants first, at whose head is, according to a narration from Imām al-Ṣādiq (as), "Muhammad and his Household"[30] and, second, entering paradise, for verily the nobility of paradise comes from its inhabitants, just as any place becomes noble because of the one who is in it!

26. Entering paradise

Entering paradise, whether this is paradise in general or the paradise reserved for Allāh's friends (*awliyāʾ*), depends on fearing standing before one's Lord, as Allāh says, "But as for him who fears standing before his Lord and forbids the soul from desire, his refuge will indeed be paradise."[31] This fear accompanies or is accompanied by a person resisting their own desires themselves, as there is no fatalism meanwhile.

Here we must distinguish between the fear of standing before one's Lord and the fear of His punishment, for what radiates from Allāh's closest servants is the former rather than the latter, because they would not do anything that would bring down His punishment upon them!

30. *Al-Kāfī* 3/127

31. Sūrat al-Nāziʿāt (79):40–41

Sūrat al-Balad (no. 90: The Town)

Verses 1–7

90:1 *I swear not by this town,*

90:2 *as you reside in this town;*

90:3 *by a father and what he begot:*

90:4 *certainly We created man in travail.*

90:5 *Does he suppose that no one will ever have power over him?*

90:6 *He says, 'I have squandered immense wealth.'*

90:7 *Does he suppose that no one sees him?*

1. Oath by negation

The oath that opens this *sūrah* is accompanied by the negation "not." This can be explained in a number of ways, and these apply to all other instances of this ambiguity. Some of these interpretations are:

- The negation of the oath at the beginning of this *sūrah* is a real negation, meaning that Allāh does not swear by a town like Makkah, while the Prophet's life, property, and family are denied protection therein. For Makkah, despite its nobility, will not be made the subject of an oath while the Prophet (s) is treated thus therein. According to this interpretation, the negation of the oath serves to extol the Prophet's exalted rank in the eyes of Allāh.
- So the oath's object, assuming the negation is real, is already so obvious that it does not need an oath to support it.

- Or, if we assume that the oath is genuine, then the negation can be understood as an affirmation of it, as we see in eight other places throughout the Qur'ān. According to this interpretation, the oath means "I am swearing by this town while you live and reside therein." In other words, this spot of ground is worthy of an oath being sworn by it, not because of its own innate nobility, but because of the nobility of another, namely, the Prophet (s) who resides in it. So this also serves to extol the rank of the Prophet!

2. "By a father and what he begot"

If we say that the words "by a father and what he begot" refer to Abraham and his son, Ishmael (as), to accord with the mention of Makkah at the beginning of the *sūrah,* then this *sūrah* contains the human paragons of divine unity, namely, Abraham ("a father"), Ishmael ("what he begot"), and the Final Prophet ("as you reside in this town") alongside the geographical center of divine unity, namely, Makkah ("I swear not by this town"). It is well-known that the Qur'ān contains a great deal of praise for the one who built the Kaʿba, his son, and his wife, for Allāh is indeed grateful to the one who established His divine unity upon the earth!

It should be noted here that Allāh mentions "a father" here in the indefinite in order to magnify Abraham, and the son is referred to as "what he begot" instead of "who" to signify amazement. This, in turn, demonstrates their exalted station. The same is true of His words about the birth of Maryam: "and Allah knew better what she had borne."[1]

3. Level of discomfort

The Qur'ān prepares people to endure a level of discomfort during their existence in this worldly life, so a person should not be surprised by the difficulties they encounter because they will reap their fruits later, as Allāh says, "O man! You are labouring toward

1. Sūrat Āle ʿImrān (3):36

your Lord laboriously, and you will encounter Him."[2] When this *sūrah* discusses humankind, it speaks as though they were created in difficulty and hardship—as hyperbole in describing their condition—and this difficulty accompanies the very fact of their existence, even from the time when they were in their mother's womb until they were borne into this world, as "his mother has carried him in travail"[3] and then "bore him in travail."[4]

So this difficulty follows them throughout the different stages of life—whether it is in earning a living or being harmed by others, until the time of death.

Of course, knowing that this difficulty will follow us everywhere will help us to rely only upon Allāh, in whose hand is relief from sufferings and the lightening of our burden.

4. Travail

Some interpreters think that the "travail" (*kabd*) referred to in the verse "certainly we created man in travail" actually means in a proportioned and upright manner, in which case the verse is similar to Allāh's words "We certainly created man in the best of forms."[5] This meaning is appropriate to what we will encounter in the following verses that elucidate the different ways in which humankind's creation has been proportioned, such as the creation of the eye, tongue, lip.

This is also in harmony with the call for people:

- to vigilantly observe themselves (*murāqaba*), after seeing this amazing creation ("Does he suppose that no one sees him?" and
- to spend in Allāh's way out of gratitude for these blessings ("the freeing of a slave or feeding on a day of starvation").

---

2. Sūrat al-Inshiqāq (84):6
3. Sūrat al-Aḥqāf (46):15
4. Ibid.
5. Sūrat al-Tīn (95):4

5. Difficulty and ease

One dimension of contrast between this world and the hereafter is that, in the former, Allāh created the human being caught up in difficulty and hardship, while He placed safety and ease in the hereafter, with the crucial distinction between the two being that the hardship of this world is transient and ends with death while the ease of the hereafter is everlasting and endures with eternity. So what sane person would not purchase eternal comfort at the price of temporary hardship!?

In fact, we can say that even if this world were made of fleeting gold, while the abode of the hereafter were made of everlasting clay, the hereafter would still be superior to this world. So what about when this world is made of fleeting clay and the hereafter is made of everlasting gold!

6. Spending wealth

In this *sūrah,* the Qur᾿ān mentions someone who has spent a large quantity of wealth ("He says, "I have squandered immense wealth."). These people fall into a number of divisions:

- Those who spend their wealth to show off, of whom it must be said that Allāh sees them and their deeds and knows that the intention behind their deeds is ostentation ("Does he suppose that no one sees him?")
- Those who spend their wealth to oppose the divine mission and persecute the Prophet (s), of whom it must be said Allāh is able to seize them and obliterate their wealth ("Does he suppose that no one will ever have power over him?")
- Those who spend their wealth and begrudge the fact that Allāh has ordained their wealth for the poor and needy. This is like the person who said at the time of the Prophet, "All my wealth has been squandered on expiations and donations since I adopted the religion of Muḥammad!"[6] About these people it must be said that Allāh has more right to begrudge

6. *Biḥār al-anwār* 18/174

them the fact that He made for them "two eyes, a tongue and two lips."

7. Attention to the unseen world

The Qur'ān is replete with verses that invite people to look at themselves by calling their attention to the unseen world, which in turn causes them to cleave to Allāh inwardly and vigilantly observe their own behavior outwardly. Some of these verses are Allāh's sayings:

- "...does he not know that Allah sees?"[7]
- "Is it not sufficient that your Lord is witness to all things?"[8]
- And in this *sūrah*: "Does he suppose that no one sees him?"

The upshot of all these verses us that Allāh sees His servant in all of the vicissitudes of life, not to mention the fact that the servant is forever in Allāh's grasp ("Does he suppose that no one will ever have power over him?"). So the fact that the human being experiences hardship and toil should nurture inner reverence, just as it occasions, even if it is not always accompanied by, outward reverence and humility.

8. Belief in higher realities

The problem with every person who strays from the path of guidance is that they see reality only through the lens of themselves. They do not believe in higher realities save to the extent that they can imagine them, and they deny some of them out of arrogant disdain, without any solid reason for doing so. This is why these two verses rebuke them with the refrain "Does he suppose...?"

Therefore, the only way to free themselves from this state is by altering this supposition so that it conforms to desires of the Master who not only sees the servants but also has complete power over them. What is particularly noteworthy here is that these people, through their mistaken suppositions, deny two things that are

7. Sūrat al-ʿAlaq (96):14
8. Sūrat Fuṣṣilat (41):53

clear to any person of intelligence: First, that anyone can see them; and second, that anyone has power over them. And what foolish suppositions these are!

Verses 8–16

90:8 *Have We not made for him two eyes,*

90:9 *a tongue, and two lips,*

90:10 *and shown him the two paths [of good and evil]?*

90:11 *Yet he has not embarked upon the uphill task.*

90:12 *And what will show you what is the uphill task?*

90:13 *[It is] the freeing of a slave,*

90:14 *or feeding on a day of starvation,*

90:15 *or an orphan among relatives,*

90:16 *or a needy man in desolation,*

9. "Making"

The verses of the Qurʾān allude to more than seventy instances of "making" (*jaʿl*) in both the sensible world and others. We find one such instance in this sūrah where Allāh says, "Did we not make...?" This extends to more than one manifestation of His power. But what matters here is not the act of making or the thing made itself, for that is the province of lordship (*rububiyya*), but rather that the person comprehends this act of making and turns it into a means for reflection and sensing the generosity and power of the Maker. This goal is what is sought from the province of servanthood (*ʿubudiyya*).

10. Pondering the body

A person does not need, in order to realize the magnitude of Allāh's generosity, to travel to faraway lands or plumb the depths of their soul. It is sufficient that they consider the contents of their body, especially those incredible signs that Allāh has deposited in their heads ("two eyes") and their wonders. Not only are they organs of perception, but they are also a medium through which we can convey feelings and emotions, or even spiritual influence: "a tongue" that serves amazing purposes, whether in chewing, speaking, or swallowing; "two lips" that are essential for speech, for they are the final instrument for forming sounds after the throat and mouth cavity. It should be obvious that the act of speaking with one's tongue and lips is one of the most complex processes in existence, as it involves taking thought, which exists beyond the senses, and expressing it in a sensible format. It is through these two processes of thought and expression that all forms of human learning and knowledge are ultimately transmitted.

In short, pondering the human being, in body and spirit, is equivalent to the acts of traveling to faraway places and delving into the depths of the soul put together!

11. Inner guidance

Allāh frequently affirms the reality of inner guidance (*hidāya bāṭiniyya*) for the human being. For example, He says, "and inspired it with its virtues and vices."[9] In this *sūrah*, He says "and shown him the two paths" and the word *najdayn* ("two paths") contains a subtle meaning in that a *najd* originally refers to a raised road. When you consider that every road exists to facilitate the travel of wayfarers upon it, then what about one that is raised up high with clear landmarks?!

The reason Allāh's places so much emphasis upon this reality is so no one can claim that there was nothing to remind them of their moral duties when they were committing sins that are innately known (*bil-fiṭra*), such as lying, oppression, and the like. This is because the rebuke of the conscience is one of the most effective arguments against committing sins, and it is something that exists in each and every human being!

---

9. Sūrat al-Shams (91):8

12. Outer faculties of judgement

There is a clear relation between two eyes and two lips on the one hand and two paths on the other. Just as Allāh has represented a person's inner faculties of judgement through one's innate knowledge of good and evil, He has also made their outer faculties of judgement two eyes that can easily lower the gaze and two lips that easily can restrain the tongue.

This means there is no excuse for anyone who misuses sight or speech, whether for something forbidden or for the purposes of prying.

13. Overpowering desires

What is desired from a person in this life is to boldly overcome the obstacles that stand in their way. This is achieved by overpowering the desires (*hawā*) and appetites (*mushtahiyāt*) of the low self (*nafs*). So just as piety (*birr*) cannot be attained without a person spending from that which they love, neither can the barriers on a person's journey towards Allāh be stormed except by them undertaking things that are difficult for them, such as "the freeing of a slave" which is something that might require a lot of wealth or spending on others in a time of shortage "feeding on a day of starvation"—the difference being that the first involves freeing a person in his entirety from the ties of bondage while the second involves freeing him from hunger in particular. These are of such importance that the Qurʾān introduces them with the refrain "And what will show you...?" which is only used for concepts whose reality it is difficult for people to grasp. This shows that the recompense for these deeds, which is hidden from them in this world, is something that cannot even be conceived of!

14. Spending wealth or feeding others

When believers want to spend their wealth in the way of Allāh or feed others for the sake of His love, they will look to the nearest means to obtain His pleasure in the details of that act of devotion.

In other words, they will be keen to choose the best examples of that general category of action. So these verses contain some indications of other preferred groups after having established the general prerogative of action, these groups are:

- "an orphan" because of the pains they suffer as a result of having no one to look after them
- a relative ("amongst relatives")
- someone who is destitute ("in desolation")
- And it is best on days in which their needs are most pronounced, such as a day of deprivation ("on a day of starvation")

15. Freeing slaves and feeding the hungry

The apparent meaning of these verses is concerned with freeing slaves and feeding the hungry in the physical realm and counts this as overcoming an obstacle, noting that the verses do not specify that the recipients of this kindness must be pious or even Muslims. So what about in the spiritual realm? Meaning someone who frees a Muslim slave from hellfire or looks after an orphan of Muḥammad's Household (as). What sort of recompense could a person who does this expect on the Day of Resurrection?

This interpretation is supported by tradition: "Allah revealed to Moses, 'Endear me to my creation, and endear my creation to me.' Moses asked, 'My Lord, how should I do that?' He said, 'Remind them of by blessings and gifts so that they will love me, for if you return a fugitive to my door, or save one who has strayed from ruin, this is better for you than a hundred wears of worship – fasting by day and keeping vigil by night!' Moses said, 'And who is this fugitive of whom you speak?' Allāh said, 'A rebellious sinner'"[10]

10. *Biḥār al-anwār* 2/4

Verses 17–20

90:17 *then being one of those who have faith and who enjoin one another to patience, and enjoin one another to compassion.*

90:18 *They are the people of good fortune.*

90:19 *But those who defy Our signs, they are the people of ill-omen.*

90:20 *[Imposed] upon them will be a closed Fire.*

16. Overcoming obstacles

Spending wealth on others, especially in times of difficulty, is a manifestation of overcoming obstacles that is connected to a person's limbs in the realm of action. But there is also another manifestation for this that is connected to the appendages of the soul, as represented by Allāh's words "then being one of those who have faith and who enjoin one another to patience, and enjoin one another to compassion." This spiritual level is higher than the physical level we have just mentioned because the actions of the body stem from the activities of the soul. Perhaps this is why this clause is introduced with the conjunction "then" (*thumma*) to indicate that there is a gap between different levels rather than a gap in time.

Therefore, we must always develop our spirituality in parallel with our outward activities as follows:

- Faith (*īmān*) ("those who have faith") because without being grounded in a foundation of correct belief, there is no possibility of self-development.
- Adopting a mentality of being keen to see other people develop and grow ("who enjoin one another to patience") as represented by advising one another to be steadfast, whether this is patience in times of difficulty, to be steadfast in obedience, or to be steadfast in avoiding forbidden things.
- Kindness to others represented by nurturing compassing between themselves: They "enjoin one another to

compassion," which includes observing the rights of the Creator and the creation, as we read in Sūrat al-ʿAṣr: "and enjoin one another to truth, and enjoin one another to patience."[11] One instance of this truth is enjoining one another to compassion.

17. Patience and compassion

When the Qurʾān mentions righteous deeds, it usually does so in conjunction with faith, but this *sūrah* mentions patience and compassion instead. But there is nothing strange about this because together these two things result in righteous deeds, whether obligatory or supererogatory, in addition to the presence of two other distinguishing factors in the phrase about enjoining one another to patience and compassion:

- By this enjoining of one another (*tawāṣī*), righteous action will spread throughout society.
- That this mutual enjoinment lays the foundations of righteous deeds. Someone who practices patience and makes themselves feel compassion towards others will be motivated to do righteous deeds.

18. Enjoining each other

In a believing society, development cannot be achieved through just one group of people enjoining others to good deeds such that people are divided into those who preach and those who listen to the preaching. Instead, what is desired here is that everyone enjoins one another ("and enjoin one another") meaning that everyone is simultaneously a preacher and a listener because all human beings are affected by moments of heedlessness and lapses, save those whom Allāh has protected.

The effect of this mutual enjoinment is that actions will become states of being (*ḥālāt*) that will in turn become customs (*ʿādāt*) and finally habits (*malakāt*), which is the ultimate goal.

---

11. Sūrat al-ʿAṣr (103):3

19. Calling others

Through the Qur'ān, Allāh teaches His servants the right methods of calling others towards His way: even though He is the sovereign of everything and its possessor, and—if He wanted to—He has the right to demand that His servants blindly obey His commands and prohibitions, He does not do this. Instead, He tries to persuade them through various kinds of speech. This *sūrah* contains a number of ways in which He influences His servants, for example by mentioning:

- specific instances of good deeds instead of a general and ambiguous call. He mentions freeing a slave and spending wealth on others on a day of hunger, especially on orphan relatives and needy persons in abject poverty.
- things that inspire them to offer the thanks that they owe to their Creator, by mentioning the creation of the eyes, the tongue, and the lips.
- activities that cause non-believers to take note of them by making a general call to do good deeds that includes non-Muslims as well, such as freeing them from slavery or giving alms to them.
- avoiding creating a special class of preachers a degree above everyone else—the command comes to enjoin one another to patience.
- the guarantee of prosperity in their worldly lives as well. So that their only goals will not be otherworldly, the command comes to enjoin one another to compassion.

20. Final outcomes in the hereafter

The majority of people see good and bad omens in baseless things, like seeing a crow and other things like this, but the last verses of this *sūrah* want to firmly establish this on the basis of final outcomes in the hereafter: "the people of good fortune" are those who cross the bridge (*ṣirāṭ*) safely while the "people of ill-omen" are those who did not, and both of these groups are determined by their brief existence in this world.

Being wicked and of ill-omen entail one another, as does being noble and of good fortune. We can glean this from the discourse of Salmān when he was asked, "Who are you, and what worth are you!" He replied, "As for my beginning and yours, it was a lowly drop. As for my end and yours, it is a rotting corpse. But when the Day of Judgement comes and the scales are set up, then whosoever's scales weigh heavy is noble, and whosoever's scales weigh light is wicked."[12]

21. Punishment

The verse of punishment in this *sūrah* does not offer any details about its different forms, but it suffices to deter people because it says "a fire" in the indefinite to convey its magnitude! Add to this the fact that it mentions something that intensifies the punishment—namely, that this fire is brought down upon them from above as well, because of the words "over them" (*ʿalayhim*) that belong to the same category as the verse "a Fire whose curtains will surround them."[13]

But how does this intensify the punishment? Well, if someone who is being punished feels that they have no way to escape it, this makes it all the more painful. Not to mention the fact that they will dwell therein forever, something always mentioned as a recompense for the faithless and those who deny Allāh's signs.

12. *Biḥār al-anwār* 22/355
13. Sūrat al-Kahf (18):29

Sūrat al-Shams (no. 91: The Sun)

Verses 1–10

In the name of Allāh, the All-Beneficent, the All-Merciful

91:1 *By the sun and her forenoon splendour,*

91:2 *by the moon when he follows her,*

91:3 *by the day when it revealed her,*

91:4 *by the night when it covers her,*

91:5 *by the sky and that which built it,*

91:6 *by the earth and that which spread it,*

91:7 *by a soul and that which fashioned it,*

91:8 *and inspired it with its vices and virtues:*

91:9 *felicitous is he who refines it,*

91:10 *failed is he who buries it.*

1. Oaths of the Qurʾān

There is definitely a connection between the oaths of the Qurʾān and the object of these oaths, but someone must ponder the Qurʾān in order to discover that. This is one aspect of the wisdom behind Allāh invoking such oaths, for He is too exalted to need an oath in order to dispel any doubts about what He says, as people sometimes need in courts of law, for instance!

Accordingly, we can say that the association between these oaths, as represented by that between the wonders of creation and human self-refinement, is that Allāh has placed everything in existence at a person's disposal in order that they might reach this level of perfection, by which I mean self-refinement. Without this fruit, a person's own existence is thrown into discord with the rest of existence, because all mute beings attain the purpose of their existence. It is only this rational being that does not! This idea is affirmed in a *ḥadīth qudsī:* "O son of Adam! I created everything for you, and I created you for Me."[1]

2. Quantity and quality and oaths

Oaths in the *sūrahs* of the Qur'ān differ in quantity and quality. With regards to quality, they differ according to their relatum, whether this is celestial phenomena ("By the sky, by the nightly visitor..."[2]), terrestrial ones ("And the earth and Him Who spread it..."), wonders of the soul ("And a soul and Him Who perfected it..."), or those of the hereafter ("by the Promised Day"[3]) From the perspective of quantity, these groups of oaths vary between one ("By Time...!"[4]), two ("By the morning brightness, by the night when it is calm...!"[5]), three ("By the night when it covers, by the day when it brightened, by Him who created the male and the female..."[6]), four ("By the fig and the olive, by Mount Sinai, by this secure town"[7]), and five oaths ("By the Dawn, by the ten nights, by the Even and the Odd, by the night when it departs!"[8]). But the number in this *sūrah* reaches eleven oaths, and all of these are directed towards a single object—the soul (*nafs*) (Successful is he who refines it."). This indicates that the basis of all excellence in this world and the hereafter is nothing other than this or else it would not deserve these repeated oaths to be sworn upon it.

At this point, it is interesting to note that we do not find, anywhere in the Qur'ān, a build-up such as this for any other branch of the religion. This shows that what Allāh desires from His servants is

1. *Biḥār al-anwār* 22/355
2. Sūrat al-Ṭāriq (86):1
3. Sūrat al-Burūj (85):2
4. Sūrat al-ʿAṣr (103):1
5. Sūrat al-Ḍuḥā (93):1–2
6. Sūrat al-Layl (92):1–3
7. Sūrat al-Tīn (95):1–3
8. Sūrat al-Fajr (89):1–4

that affair that lies beyond outward worship—namely, that they free themselves from immoral qualities and habits in their inner realm, whose effects are usually felt in the external realm as a matter of necessity.

3. "Reveals her"

Some scholars connect the pronoun in "reveals her" to the earth, in which case there is no ambiguity, but some others connect to the sun in the sense that the day, which is caused by the sun, reveals the sun, and this contains an obvious ambiguity. In order to resolve this, we say that because the sun is too far away for people to reach, the way it appears to people is not the same as the way other things on the earth do, while the fact is that the day, in whose light people live and whose blessings they benefit from, is something obvious because of how immediate it is to their senses. This is exactly the same as the image in a mirror that merely reflects the original object but, in doing so, also reveals it.

In this sense it can be said that the servant who calls towards Allāh is like the day that reveals the shining sun—he is a guide towards Allāh. This is exactly the situation with regards to reviving the remembrance of the Prophet and his Household (as)—mercy has been promised to those who revive their cause while the truth is that those who revive their cause are on a lower level than the ones who they are reviving!

4. "That which" *(mā)*

Something that has caught the eye of Qur'ān commentators is using the pronoun "that which" (*mā*) rather than "He who" (*man*) to refer to the Creator in these verses. This is to allude to the wondrous and mysterious force—at least, according to our limited perception—by which the heavens, the earth, and the soul all inhere. The verse refers to instances of inanimate beings such as the sun and earth and also complex ones such as the soul, that, unlike the former two entities, is referred to in the indefinite ("a soul") to indicate its greatness.

Hence it is necessary to move conceptually from the manifestation of greatness to the source of greatness. This is a problem that scientists have when they study the natural world. They are amazed by the creation, without moving from that to the Creator, and so their studies do not help them become closer to Him. Nor do we see that fear promised to Allāh's servants with knowledge...finally, the joining of the divine essence to His creations, in the context of the oaths, obviously signifies the greatness of the creation mentioned in conjunction with its creator!

5. "That which" *(mā)*

It is also possible to interpret "that which" (*mā*) in the aforementioned verse to refer to the divine laws that govern the universe and that are responsible for raising the heavens "by the sky and that which built it" and leveling the earth "by the earth and that which spread it," (e.g., the law of gravity that provides all heavenly bodies with their courses of travel). From this we understand that we can place the creation of all the fixed elements of the universe in one hand and the laws that govern these fixed elements in the other.

Of course, the one who comprehends these laws is the human being, or else animals would have perception equal to that of humans, or even better than them, as we know that the physical senses of many animals are superior to those of humans. But animals are not able to logically reason from an effect back to its cause.

6. "Soul"

Just as the "soul" (*nafs*) can refer to the spirit (*rūḥ*), as in "Allah takes the souls at the time of their death...,"[9] it can also refer to something that includes the body as well (e.g., in Allāh's saying "Indeed I have killed one of their persons, so I fear they will kill me."[10]). In this *sūrah*, the fashioning mentioned in the verse "by a soul and that which fashioned it" could refer to either the spirit

9. Sūrat al-Zumar (39):42
10. Sūrat al-Qaṣaṣ (28):33

or the body, for Allāh has employed His power of creation in both of them together, as He has extolled Himself by saying, "Blessed is Allah, Lord of all the worlds!"[11] after creating the body and infusing it with the spirit. This is alluded to by His saying "Then We produced him another creation."[12]

7. Conscience

The verse that attributes inspiration (*ilhām*) to Allāh, saying "and inspired it with its virtues and vices," is one of the means by which Allāh's servants will be left without any excuse on the Day of Resurrection. They cannot make the plea that they had no external reminder because the Lord of the Worlds has inspired them with a conscience that acts as an internal messenger (*rasūl bāṭinī*) that no one is without.

8. Divine inspiration

It is interesting to note that in this verse, Allāh has said that the recipient of divine inspiration is the human soul and that He has said this categorically without stipulating that this soul must have faith. In the same vein, He has made the subject of the verses "Rather man is a witness to himself, though he should offer his excuses,"[13] categorically the human being as well, and He states that all mankind, as opposed to a particular group, are recipients of *fiṭra* (original humanity) ("the origination of Allah according to which He originated mankind"[14]). All of this shows us that staying true to one's original humanity and moral probity does not require anything extraneous to the human being himself.

But to this we must add that the mission of the prophets is reminding people of the call of their own original humanity, preventing this from being snuffed out by obstinacy, and then guiding people to the particular forms of obedience that cannot be apprehended by reason. But in spite of that, the responsibility for self-refinement

11. Sūrat Ghāfir (40):64
12. Sūrat al-Muʾminūn (23):14
13. Sūrat al-Qiyāmah (75):14–15
14. Sūrat al-Rūm (30):30

ultimately falls to the person himself, which is why Allāh attributes it to the person saying, "felicitous is He who refines it."

9. Inspiration

Inspiration here refers to Allāh effusing that which will aid the human being in conceptualizing (*taṣawwur*) and verifying (*taṣdīq*) in the realm of moral good and evil (or theoretical wisdom). This represents the lowest degree of inspired guidance for the human soul.

But we can also ask what is there, after the gate of Allāh's mercy has been opened through judicious self-refinement, to prevent the gate of Allāh's effusion opening with regards to those things that will aid the person in discerning what is right and wrong in personal behavior (namely, practical wisdom) so that their practice in each particular issue they face will be on the straight path, as well as their general outlook in life. This is something we seek through every unit of prayer, whether obligatory or supererogatory, by reciting Sūrat al-Fātiḥah.

10. Vice and virtue

Etymologically, vice (*fujūr*) means to rend the curtain of religiosity just as daybreak (*fajr*) means to rend the darkness of the night, while virtue (*taqwā*) means to protect the soul from harm. This means that whomsoever Allāh has inspired with these two affairs, as necessitated by His words "and inspired it with its vices and virtues," has been granted the means to obtain this protective veil and also to remove the barriers to those things that tear it. This is the basis of moral excellence, unlike:

- those who tear this veil by perpetrating vices. Do they imagine they can stitch it after ripping it like this?
- those who remove protection from themselves by forgoing virtue. Do they believe that the devils will not take charge of their affairs?

11. Vice and virtue

Perhaps the reason why vices are mentioned before virtues in the realm of inspiration ("and inspired it with its vices and virtues") is that a person must shed their iniquities before adorning themselves with virtues. Another reason may be that our original humanity (*fiṭra*) is instinctively repelled by the wrongness of vice. Hence, the culpability of one who engages in vices is greater than that of one who forgoes virtue because they have gone against their own conscience!

This is what happened to the one who hamstrung the she-camel,[15] for he had challenged divine lordship as represented by this miraculous camel and thereby violated it. This was not simply a case of practically disobeying Allāh because of giving preference to some inclination or desire. Hence, the divine punishment came down upon him and his people—a punishment unique in its severity and scope!

12. Felicity

Everyone in existence is striving for felicity (*falāḥ*) according to their own viewpoint, but the problem arises when putting this into practice and identifying those things that will bring them this felicity. So some think it will result from:

- worldly enjoyments—like the people of Korah (*Qārūn*) ("We wish we had like what Korah has been given! Indeed he is greatly fortunate."[16])
- knowledge familiar to themselves, as in Allāh's saying of those who used their knowledge for worldly gain ("they exulted in the knowledge they possessed"[17])
- amassing wealth and children ("I have more wealth than you, and am stronger with respect to numbers."[18])

---

15. Referring to the story of Ṣāliḥ, see below and also Sūrat Hūd (11):64–65
16. Sūrat al-Qaṣaṣ (28):79
17. Sūrat Ghāfir (40):83
18. Sūrat Kahf (18):34

- power and authority over others ("Today he who has the upper hand will be joyful!"[19])

But the Qur'ān settles this argument by saying that felicity belongs only to "he who refines it" not "he who has the upper hand"!

13. Felicity

When the Qur'ān mentions felicity resulting from doing good deeds, it mentions it in the form of anticipation ("and do good, so that you may be felicitous"[20]), while felicity resulting from self-refinement is mentioned as if it has already been achieved ("felicitous is he who refines it").

In this we can discern the distinction between the actions of the soul and the actions of the limbs: The relation of the first to the second is like the relation between roots and branches. In other words, if there are healthy roots, a lush tree will grow. This is supported by the prophetic tradition "A believer's intention is better than his deeds!"[21]

14. Felicity

When the Qur'ān speaks categorically, it intends an all-inclusive meaning, so long as there is no qualifier to the contrary. For example, when the Qur'ān uses the words "faith" (*īmān*) and "righteous deeds" (*'amal sāliḥ*) in a multitude of verses, this denotes faith and righteous deeds in their most comprehensive and complete sense. The same applies in this verse, "felicitous is he who refines it" as this also denotes self-refinement in its broadest sense, whether this is to do with beliefs, senses, or actions. These are the three dimensions of our existence.

This meaning is supported by the fact that the felicity referred to here is also mentioned in another verse "Certainly, the faithful have attained salvation"[22] which is followed by verses detailing

19. Sūrat Ṭa Ha (20):64
20. Sūrat al-Ḥajj (22):77
21. *Biḥār al-anwār* 74/178
22. Sūrat al-Mu'minūn (23):1

the qualities of the faithful, including avoiding idle talk, which some people might see as unnecessary for self-development. This indicates that the scope in which one must pursue self-refinement if one desires felicity.

15. Self-refinement

Self-refinement (*tazkiya*) is a voluntary action that a person undertakes of their own accord. Otherwise this would be a matter of determinism (*jabr*), and there would be no point in divine reward and punishment. It has been narrated from Imām al-Ṣādiq (as): "You have been made the physician of your own soul; you have been shown the illness, taught the meaning of health and instructed in its proper treatment; so look to how you take care of yourself!"[23] But in spite of this, a person should supplicate wholeheartedly for Allāh to assist them with themselves for their own sake, and against their enemy for their own sake, for it has been narrated that when Allāh's messenger recited this verse, "felicitous is he who refines it," he stopped and said, "O Allah! Grant my soul its virtue and purify it above its purification, You are its keeper and its master!" (*allāhumma aat nafsī taqwāhā, wa zakhā anta khayra min zakāhā, anta waliyuhā wa mawlāha!*).[24]

This meaning is supported by Allāh's words "Were it not for Allah's grace and His mercy upon you, not one of you would ever be pure. But Allah purifies whomever He wishes...."[25] There is no contradiction between a person refining their own soul and Allāh purifying them, just as there is no contradiction in bringing about an action between the one who helps and the one who is being helped!

16. Self-refinement

Calling self-refinement *tazkiya*, literally "nurturing," contains a kind of encouragement and motivation for those who struggle against themselves, for the fruit of this struggle is growth and

23. *Jāmiʿ aḥādīth al-shīʿa* 13/246
24. *Biḥār al-anwār* 92/220
25. Sūrat al-Nūr (24):21

development and not merely purification from one's faults. In the words of the Commander of the Faithful (as) concerning the connection between knowledge and its increase, we read, "Knowledge grows as it is spent."[26]

In other words, someone who refines themselves is granting themselves an excellence that will please them, not denying themselves an enjoyment that will satisfy them! For what causes some people to abandon this path is a fear of deprivation, while the truth is that if they encounter such deprivation on this path, it is a stage in their development. It is worthwhile for them to forgo some short-term enjoyment for the sake of eternal perfection...how interesting it is that worldly people will endure the deprivation of one thing to secure something better, so why don't we learn from them in this matter?

17. Self-refinement

There is a considerable distance between a sprouting seed whose planter watches as it grows day by day until it yields its harvest and a seed whose owner buries it in the ground, only for it to die before it sprouts.

This is the condition of someone who does not take the path of self-refinement, as expressed by the words "failed is he who buries it" for they have buried the soul entrusted to their care in the grave of their desires and lusts, just as the pre-Islamic Arabs would bury the daughters entrusted to their care beneath the ground ("or bury it in the ground!"[27]). So the expression "bury" (*dass*) is the same in both verses, as if the person who buries their soul and the one who buries their child alive are on a similar level in the essence of their sin, even if this is not apparent at first glance.

It is interesting that the Arabic word *qad* (signifying emphasis) is repeated for both felicity and failure to show that the oaths sworn above apply equally to both of these realities.

---

26. *Biḥār al-anwār* 1/188
27. Sūrat al-Naḥl (16):59

18. 'Failed'

The one who realizes the meaning of "burying" (*dass*) in themselves instead of "refinement" (*tazkiya*) has actually grown in a way contrary to what is natural and healthy. Hence, why they are afflicted by failure and frustration! So Allāh's word 'failed' shows this failure with a view to the effect this burial will have on the Day of Resurrection. This could be the group of people the Qur'ān was describing with the words "Those whose endeavour goes awry in the life of the world, while they suppose they are doing good."[28]

And what a difference there is between the person who will be surprised by their failure on the Day of Resurrection and the person who senses felicity in this world before reaching the hereafter!

Verses 11–15

91:11 *Thamud denied out of their rebellion,*

91:12 *when the most wretched of them rose up.*

91:13 *But then the Messenger of Allah said to them, 'Let Allah's she-camel drink!'*

91:14 *But they impugned him and then they hamstrung her, so their Lord took them unawares by night because of their sin, and levelled it.*

91:15 *And he does not fear its outcome.*

19. Disbelief

The greatest sin that causes someone to be imprisoned in hellfire forever is disbelief (*kufr*). This sin might not emerge from a person all at once. History is replete with examples of apostasy by people from whom it was never thought possible! The source of this disbelief is the outward sins that build up until they blind a person to the very foundation of their faith in the Exalted Creator! So the one who hamstrung the she-camel was already "wretched" (*shaqī*) by virtue of having committed sins, but he became "most-

28. Sūrat al-Kahf (18):104

wretched" (*al-ashqā*) by challenging the gift of the heavens and the message of the prophets. His rebellion became a cause of his denial, as we understand from the causal relationship implied by the Arabic particle *bā'* (translated as "out of" above) in His words "Thamud denied out of their rebellion." We can also apply the verse "Then the fate of those who committed misdeeds was that they denied the signs of Allāh and they used to deride them"[29] to this context as well. Sins begin with misdeeds and ultimately lead to disbelief and denial.

20. Rebellion

A failed person is someone who buries themselves in the darkness of the soil like the infant girls buried during the Ignorance, but the matter does not end here—if only they were a thing undone! No, because rebellion (*ṭughyān*) is like planting the seed from which a wicked tree will grow. Allāh expresses this crime with His words "when the most wretched of them rose up" showing that the source of His wretchedness was in plain sight and not buried.

And the words "rose up" (*inbiʿāth*) could imply some degree of obstinacy or resolve to confront the messenger who had warned them against harassing Allāh's she-camel.

21. She-camel of Ṣāliḥ

All creatures in this universe belong to Allāh insofar as they are created—and this includes all the she-camels upon the earth—but Allāh honors the she-camel of Ṣāliḥ (as) in particular by claiming her as His own (just as applies to the Black Stone, Joseph's shirt, and Moses' ark), and this is why daring to hamstring her invited such a painful punishment.

This all applies to an animal that Allāh singles out for concern, so what about a righteous person who is called Allāh's monument upon the earth (*bunyān allāhu fī al- arḍ*)!?

29. Sūrat al-Rūm (30):10

22. Approving deeds

The one who actually undertook to kill the she-camel reached the apex of wretchedness, as Allāh says, "when the most wretched of them rose up." This shows that when amassed sins reach their peak in the realm of actions, so too does their felony reach its peak in the realm of consequences. This is something we see clearly in the cases of history's greatest tyrants!

But we should also take stock of the fact that other members of his people approved of his action, even if they did not do the deed themselves, and that is why they were encompassed by its tribulation. Even though only one person actually hamstrung the camel, the verse attributes the crime to all of them ("they hamstrung her"). This is as the Commander of the Faithful (as) describes them, "Allah enveloped all of them with punishment, because all of them had approved [of the crime.]"[30] By the same token, approving the deeds of a righteous people means that you have a share in their reward. This means we must first be careful of mixing with tyrants, second of approving of their deeds, and third of emulating their attributes.

23. Sensory similitudes

The Qurʾān makes a habit of offering sensory similitudes of things, such as a lantern, to explain its light and sending down water from the heavens to the earth to explain the nature of worldly life, to analogize the concepts that it aims to convey to mankind.

One such similitude mentioned in this *sūrah* is that someone who abandons virtue (*taqwā*) and actually takes the path of vice is the same as the people of Thamūd. That is because they abandoned self-refinement and thus fell into the sin of hamstringing the she-camel, which represents a challenge to one of Allāh's signs—the she-camel that He sent— which in turn brought down upon them a divine punishment so terrible it leveled their homes to the ground ("so their Lord took them unawares by night because of their sin, and levelled it.").

---

30. *Biḥār al-anwār* 97/95

24. Pondering the consequences of actions

One of the ways in which people are prevented from committing evil is pondering the consequences of their actions, namely, that, whether good or evil, they are in the sight of Allāh, and it is up to Him whether or not He grants respite! It is indeed strange that people do not take a lesson from peoples past and so condemn themselves to repeat the very sins that brought about their ruin. Had the one who hamstrung the she-camel thought about the punishment that befell those whom Allāh annihilated before them, he would not have dared to challenge the prophet of his own time!

This is the meaning we glean if we say that the subject of the words "And he does not fear its outcome" is the one who hamstrung the camel, but we can also say that 'he' here refers to Allāh, meaning that He does not fear sending down His punishment upon the obstinate, unlike the kings of this world who sometimes fear the consequences of taking revenge on others because they know that one day the tables might be turned against them, as often is the case!

Sūrat al-Layl (no. 92: The Night)

Verses 1–11

In the name of Allāh, the All-Beneficent, the All-Merciful

92:1 *By the night when it covers,*

92:2 *by the day when it brightened,*

92:3 *by that which created the male and the female:*

92:4 *your endeavors are indeed unlike.*

92:5 *As for him who gives and is Godwary*

92:6 *and confirms the best promise,*

92:7 *We shall surely facilitate him into ease.*

92:8 *But as for him who is stingy and self-complacent,*

92:9 *and denies the best promise,*

92:10 *We shall surely ease him into hardship.*

92:11 *His wealth shall not avail him when he perishes.*

1. "The night"

"The night" (*al-layl*) is mentioned in three successive *sūrahs* of the Qurʾān: Sūrat al-Shams, Sūrat al-Layl, and Sūrat al-Ḍuḥā, each time using similar language ("By the night when it covers her,"[1] "By the night when it covers," "by the night when it is calm!"[2]). In the first two instances, the night is associated with envelopment (*ghashyān*), but what it is that the night covers is open to dispute:

1. Sūrat al-Shams (91):4
2. Sūrat al-Ḍuḥā (93):2

- Some say that it covers the day, drawing support from Allāh's saying "He draws the night's cover over the day."[3]
- Others say that it covers the sun, with reference to Allāh's words "By the night when it covers her."[4]
- Others say that it covers everything concealed by darkness, based on Allāh's words "and from the evil of the dark night...."[5]

Perhaps the reason for this emphasis on the night, in the context of oaths sworn by these recurring dimensions, is to highlight the magnificence of the way in which it has been fashioned—the cycle of night and day is the result of massive celestial bodies, such as the earth and moon, rotating on their axes while they orbit an even greater body like the sun.

The goal here is to call attention to the power that keeps these planets turning, and Allāh refers to this with His words "It is He who made the night and the day alternate for one who desires to take admonition, or desires to give thanks."[6] The result of this day-night cycle is the changing nature of time—movement during the day and rest during the night. That rest sometimes allows people to relax, but it also provides an opportunity to be alone with Allāh, especially in the last watches of the night ("and at dawns they would plead for forgiveness"[7]).

2. "Covers"

Some scholars have suggested that the present tense is used for the verb "covers" in the verses "by the night when it covers" and "by the night when it covers her"[8] to indicate continuity. However, the Qurʾān uses past tense verbs for the day in the same locations

3. Sūrat al-Raʿd (13):3; Sūrat al-Aʿrāf (7):54
4. Sūrat al-Shams (91):4
5. Sūrat al-Falaq (113):3
6. Sūrat al-Furqān (25):62
7. Sūrat al-Dhāriyāt (51):18
8. Sūrat al-Shams (91):4

("by the day when it brightened" and "by the day when it revealed her"[9]). So, it is suggested that:

- the disparity between past tense and present tense for day and night is an allusion to the time of prophecy in that the darkness of the Ignorance still enveloped the land. This obviously contains an element of *taʾwīl.*
- that a past tense verb following the conditional particle "when" (*idhā*) yields the meaning of present tense.
- that the original meaning intended was "when it reveals."
- that the default state of being is that of night—the absence of a light source to bring about the day. So it is as though the night is something pervasive and ongoing. This is supported by Allāh's words "He draws the night's cover over the day, which pursues it swiftly…."[10] This suggests that the night is the stronger of the two, because it pursues the day and chases it swiftly.

The lesson we learn from these verses and others like them is that the Qurʾān is deliberately vague in some issues, despite it being a scripture sent to inspire remembrance, because it wants to awaken the human mind to the level where even the greatest commentators become perplexed!

3. An oath by Himself as the Creator

After Allāh invokes oaths by the night and day in this *sūrah,* He invokes an oath by Himself as the Creator ("by that which created…") assuming the intended meaning of the pronoun "that which" is none other than the divine essence, or His creative power. As was the case in Sūrat al-Shams, we see Allāh using "that which" (*mā*) instead of "He who" (*man*) to refer to the reality itself "by the soul and Him who fashioned it."[11] So in more than one place in the Qurʾān, we see an oath sworn upon the Creator invoked in

9. Sūrat al-Shams (91):3
10. Sūrat al-Aʿrāf (7):54
11. Sūrat al-Shams (91):7

conjunction with one sworn upon the creation to demonstrate that pondering the creation is one way in which we can reach its creator.

Herein we see the fulfilment of Allāh's promise to show people His signs on the horizons and in their souls ("Soon We shall show them Our signs in the horizons and in their own souls..."[12]), and this is what is technically known as an a posteriori demonstration (*burhān innī*).[13]

Concerning the oaths that open this *sūrah*, it is clear that they point to the signs on the horizons in the form of night and day and signs in the souls in the form of the soul itself.

4. Male-female pairs

When an oath is invoked upon the Creator, after oaths having been invoked upon the phenomena of night and day, Allāh connects the male and female to the ingenuity of His creation. Whether He means by this the creation of all the male-female pairs in existence, just the human male and female, or just the very first human pair (Adam and Eve), this ultimately points to the creation of male and female, which is one of the most complex phenomena in existence insofar as:

- the divine arrangement of the two coming together, both by way of instinct and through other amazing physical means.
- the wondrous stages of creation, for it seems impossible to imagine that there is a relation between the matter of the first stage, semen, and the perfectly proportioned creation that ultimately emerges!

What we have said here applies to all male-female pairs in existence, whether in different kinds of animals or in plants.

---

12. Sūrat Fuṣṣilat (41):53

13. Meaning an argument that rests upon experience of the external world, as opposed to an a priori demonstration (*burhān lammī*), which means an argument that is independent of experience. [Translator]

5. "Endeavors"

Human activity on the earth is described as "endeavors" (*saʿī*) which literally means to walk with haste. This word contains a suggestion of someone expending their efforts, whether for good or for ill. This is why multiple verses use the expression of "endeavors" for human activity in this world. But these endeavors are also described as being numerous and varied in their nature. Allāh says, "your endeavors are indeed unlike." This verse is the object of the three oaths at the opening of this *sūrah,* and we can find the same reality being discussed in another: "Is someone who is faithful like someone who is a transgressor? They are not equal."[14] Pondering these two realities, by which I mean human endeavor and its varied forms, teaches us that a sensible person—because they know they are expending effort, whether they like it or not, must direct these efforts towards pleasing the Creator, according to the verse "him who gives and is God wary," rather than angering Him, as in the verse "him who is stingy and self-complacent," or else they will be truly "wrought-up and weary."[15]

Of course, the paths of goodness are as numerous as there are souls of human beings. Everyone is predisposed to their purpose in life, so does wisdom not then demand that a sensible person direct their endeavors towards the most direct route to it? Is this not the Straight Path that represents the shortest distance between two points?

6. Giving

The giving mentioned in these verses applies to anyone who gives, but it is joined to virtue (*taqwā*), and, therefore, we can explain "giving" to mean more than just monetary giving. It can mean one's soul giving its due in obedience to Allāh. We have this expression in everyday language too: "So-and-so gave his obedience to so-and-so." Although some commentators restrict its meaning to monetary giving because money and stinginess are mentioned in the same context below.

14. Sūrat al-Sajdah (32):18
15. Sūrat al-Ghāshiyah (88):3

It is noteworthy that the verse joins giving to virtue, because fruitful giving is that which takes place in the atmosphere of virtue. This is supported by Allāh's words "Allah accepts only from the Godwary."[16]

7. Giving

This *sūrah* affirms a fact that must be realized in the practical realm—the act of making monetary donations ("him who gives and is God wary") or more general still, as it affirms yet another fact that must be realized in theoretical realm—believing in the Last Day, as indicated by the words "and confirms the best promise" meaning the best promise that will be fulfilled on the Day of Resurrection. In another verse, we read, "to each Allah has promised the best"[17] and "and in case I am returned to my Lord, I will indeed have the best"[18] and "he shall have the best."[19]

Of course, this belief, taken together with acting upon its practical demands, such as spending from one's wealth and other things, is one of the factors that makes a person's endeavors praiseworthy in a world in which people's endeavors are indeed unalike.

8. Divine grace

It is well-known that this world of ours is subject to the laws of cause and effect, but this does not mean that divine grace (*tawfīq*) cannot operate within these causes. It ultimately depends on there being a suitable foundation in the person themselves. This grace is what Allāh promises with His words "We shall surely facilitate him into ease," and the word 'to facilitate' (*tayassur*) means to prepare and equip someone. As for 'ease' (*yusrā*) this is explained as:

- a quality in which there is ease without hardship—in which case being granted divine grace for righteous deeds means that these righteous deeds are made easy for you.

16. Sūrat al-Māʾidah (5):27
17. Sūrat al-Nisāʾ (4):95, Sūrat al-Ḥadīd (57):10
18. Sūrat Fuṣṣilat (41):50
19. Sūrat al-Kahf (18):88

- making it a provision for a happy life with one's Lord in paradise because of the righteous deeds one has brought. This is most appropriate if we interpret "the best" to mean paradise.

9. Deeds

The nature of being facilitated into ease is something directly experienced by anyone who has taken the path of nearness to the Lord of the Worlds because they see good as something to which their own soul is endeared, as Allāh says, "But Allah has endeared faith to you and made it appealing in your hearts...."[20] Moreover, they are determined to do good without hesitation, as Allāh says, "Allah fortifies those who have faith with an immutable word in the life of this world...."[21] This removes all fear and grief from them ("Look! The friends of Allah will indeed have no fear nor will they grieve."[22]). To the extent that the angels descend to assist them, as happened in the Battle of Badr ("your Lord will aid you with five thousand marked angels"[23]).

Conversely, good deeds are difficult for someone who denies Allāh's promise. They find it difficult to stand for prayer ("and it is indeed hard except for the humble."[24]). In fact, they are even lazy during it ("when they stand up for prayer, they stand up lazily..."[25]). They are averse to struggling for the sake of Allāh ("What is the matter with you that when you are told: 'Go forth in the way of Allah,' you sink heavily to the ground?"[26]).

Therefore believers should not rely solely on their own efforts, because it is divine assistance that ultimately determines their success or failure, even if the servants do not realize this. Special notice should be given to the fact that Allāh has connected His facilitation to the person himself, not his deeds, so it is the

20. Sūrat al-Ḥujurāt (49):7
21. Sūrat Ibrāhīm (14):27
22. Sūrat Yūnus (10):62
23. Sūrat Āle ʿImrān (3):125
24. Sūrat al-Baqarah (2):45
25. Sūrat al-Nisāʾ (4):142
26. Sūrat al-al-Tawbah (9):38

person in his entirety for whom all good deeds become easy ("we shall surely facilitate him") to the extent that Imām al-Bāqir (as) describes it saying, "He wants no good thing save that Allah makes it easy for him."[27]

10. Giving charity

There is a clear relation between "As for him who gives and is Godwary" and "We shall surely facilitate him into ease" insofar as "facilitate" here means to open the path to good for the servant. This is because someone who makes easy the affairs of Allāh's servants by spending on them, their immediate recompense for that shall belong to the same category as their deeds in this world—in other words, divine assistance and facilitation. As it is often said, "Show mercy and you shall receive it!" There are abundant narrations indicating that the effects of giving charity include: avoiding an evil death, longevity, an expanse in sustenance, and blessings in one's property and children, in addition to the well-known rewards that await the giver in the hereafter!

11. Visible traits for the people of falsehood

The visible traits for the people of falsehood after their denial and disbelief include love of this world, seeking wealth therein, then stinginess by amassing wealth and hoarding it.

This means that anyone who displays these traits shares some of the most important vices of the faithless, in spite of whatever faith they may personally have. Now the nature of believing in Allāh and the Last Day requires a person to display abstinence in worldly matters and a love of spending wealth so that Allāh will facilitate them into ease.

It's interesting that Allāh describes a wealthy person as tumbling down the path to perdition, or specifically through the levels of hell ("His wealth shall not avail him when he falls."). This represents complete humiliation for them—it describes them as though they

---

27. *Majmaʿ al-bayān* 10/376

are an animal that has slipped from above a mountain. In fact, they are more astray than such an animal, as we find in another verse!

Verses 12–21

92:12 *Indeed upon Us rests guidance,*

92:13 *and indeed to Us belong the world and the Hereafter.*

92:14 *So I warn you of a blazing fire,*

92:15 *which none shall enter except the most wretched*

92:16 *— he who denies and turns back.*

92:17 *The Godwary shall be spared it*

92:18 *—he who gives his wealth to refine himself*

92:19 *and none has any favour with him for reward,*

92:20 *but seeks only the countenance of his Lord, the Most Exalted,*

92:21 *and, surely, soon he will be well-pleased.*

12. Guidance

Allāh has decreed for Himself, out of courtesy and without compulsion, that He must guide His creation just as He has decreed He must provide for them. The expression "upon" (*ʿalā*) is used to signify this, as though Allāh has made this His own responsibility, just as a person makes it their responsibility to fulfil their own promises. Allāh says, "Indeed upon Us rests guidance" and "There is no animal on the earth, but that its sustenance is upon Allah...."[28]

We can also explain the guidance mentioned in this *sūrah* and elsewhere as follows:

- Showing people the way, while leaving the decision up to them, as we understand from Allāh's words "With Allah rests guidance to the straight path, and some of them stray,"[29] "Indeed We have guided him to the way, be he grateful or

28. Sūrat Hūd (11):6
29. Sūrat al-Naḥl (16):9

ungrateful."[30] Of course the prophets, by His leave, are made to share in this duty of moral guidance, based on His saying "And indeed you guide to a straight path."[31]

- Conveying people to the destination: In this world, they are conveyed to a good life, and in the hereafter, to the best recompense, as in Allāh's saying "Whoever acts righteously, male or female, should he be faithful, - We shall revive him with a good life and pay them their reward by the best of what they used to do."[32] Allāh only treats the chosen of His creation in this manner (i.e., conveying people to their destination), while He treats everyone else as above (i.e., showing them the path) in that "gave everything its creation and then guided it."[33]

Of course, attributing this fully realized guidance to Allāh—whether in the sense of showing people the right path or conveying them to their destination—does not prevent us from also attributing it to people, as in all other areas where there is a chain of cause and effect between the Maker and His creatures.

13. "And indeed to Us belong the world and the Hereafter"

The verse "and indeed to Us belong the world and the Hereafter," which demonstrates Allāh's sovereignty and His ownership of existence, suggests:

- His might (*ʿizza*), if we take this verse to mean that Allāh possesses this world and the hereafter. So their denial of the Day of Recompense and their stinginess with what He has given them does not harm Him in the least. He is the sovereign and master of everything that exists.
- an encouragement to the faithful to obey Him and spend their wealth in His way, if we take this verse to mean that Allāh possesses both worlds, and thus He gives whatever

30. Sūrat al-Insān (76):3
31. Sūrat al-Shūrā (42):52
32. Sūrat al-Naḥl (16):97
33. Sūrat Ṭa Hā (20):50

He wants from them to whomsoever He wills. So whoever wants this world should turn to Allāh and whoever wants the next world should turn to Him as well. This is why we seek the best of both worlds from Allāh ("Our Lord, give us good in this world and good in the Hereafter..."[34]).

14. Disbelievers and the God-fearing

The exclusivity (*ḥaṣr*) in the verse "which none shall enter except the most wretched" is qualified exclusivity, not absolute; and the fire is qualified by being perpetual (*istimrārī*). Only the one who lies and turns away will enter it—namely, the one who combines doctrinal disbelief with practically turning away from Allāh's *sharīʿa.* This does not mean that the punishment of hellfire, without the quality of being eternal, cannot be directed towards sinful believers, as we can glean from many indicators in the Qurʾān and *sunna.*

In other words, this verse is discussing the contrast between one group that denies and another that is God-fearing and spends its wealth. This is not the right place to mention a group in between these two—the believers who are not God-fearing.

15. "The most wretched"

The expression "the most wretched" invites people to ask what the qualities of the wretched or, in fact, the most wretched of the wretched are. What are the different kinds of wretchedness? Some see it in poverty, sickness, and the loss of loved ones, but the Qurʾān says that the most wretched person is one whose final abode is the blazing fire!

Imām ʿAlī (as) has mentioned this fact saying, "No good is good when it is followed by Hellfire, and no bad is bad when it is followed by Paradise! Every joy beneath Paradise is a trifle, and every tribulation less than Hellfire is a boon."[35]

---

34. Sūrat al-Baqarah (2):201
35. *Nahj al-balāgha,* aphorism no. 387

16. Definition of wretchedness

Allāh's criteria for distinguishing the wretched (*shaqī*) from the God-fearing (*taqī*) differ from those of human beings. In fact, they differ in their very definition of wretchedness. We have already said that the greatest wretch is one who enters hellfire, while the most God-fearing person is described in this *sūrah* as "the most God-wary shall be spared it." This is not someone who fears the terrors of this world but someone who protects themselves from Allāh's wrath!

It should not escape notice that using the superlative ("most God-wary") opens a discussion of vying in good deeds, for a sensible person will not be satisfied with reaching a particular ceiling of virtue. No, they will race to be the best, or at least as close to the best as one can be.

17. Deeds

Salvation from hellfire depends upon the deeds of the person, especially spending from one's wealth as is mentioned in these verses, but one should not rely on their own efforts alone because in a momentary lapse they might sin without excuse in which case they must enter hellfire. That is why Allāh does not say that the servant will avoid it, but that they will be spared it (in the passive voice), as it is Allāh who spares them! Also, notice that hell is described in the indefinite "a blazing fire" to signify its magnitude, and the word 'blazing' appears in the present tense to show that this fire continues to burn uninterrupted!

18. Giving from one's wealth

The act of giving from one's wealth in this *sūrah* is at one point joined with *taqwā* (being wary of God) and at another qualified by self-refinement ("to refine himself"). This qualifier could be to explain:

- the state of self-refinement—meaning that one undertakes this deed intending to purify themselves, from love of this world for example.
- the outcome of spending one's wealth in Allāh's way, for self-refinement is necessarily achieved by the one who is God-fearing and gives from their wealth. This is something we can glean from the verse "Take charity from their possessions to refine them and purify them thereby...."[36]

Here, it is appropriate to pay attention to the expression "his wealth" in "who gives his wealth" for the basic criterion for struggling with the self and raising oneself above wealth is spending from one's own property, not for someone to encourage another to do so and ask them for permission to spend from the latter's property, as often happens in good projects and programs to feed the poor.

19. Countenance

The tone of the Qurʾanic address follows a profound wisdom. So every time it switches from the third person to the second person or vice versa, this is only because the Wise Speaker has a particular goal in mind. So when the verse "So I warn you of a blazing fire" switches from speaking in the third person to the second person, this is appropriate to its being a warning—a threat only becomes serious when it is directly addressed to its target. But in the verse "but seeks only the countenance of his Lord, the Most Exalted" we see that it switches to the third person as this better befits the magnificence of the station of Lordship. Extolling the divine essence does not need anyone to be present or listening, for He praises Himself for Himself by Himself, especially when He mentions the attribute of being exalted!

The only thing that turns a person's face away from others, not seeing any favor with them to reward, is seeing that countenance whose beauty enshrouds every transient countenance beneath it, after which one does not find it difficult to turn their face away

36. Sūrat al-al-Tawbah (9):103

from others, nor see any effective cause in existence except Him. These ideas are contained in Allāh's words "...but seeks only the countenance of his Lord..." and the mention of Allāh's countenance (*wajh*) is repeated in numerous verses, including the one in this *sūrah* and others. We can explain this concept in one of two ways:

- First, the countenance of every being is that aspect of it that faces others, and this countenance befits the nature of that thing. So the human being's countenance is the frontal portion of the face, but for Allāh who is neither seen nor exists in a specific location, His countenance is that which manifests from Him through His interactions with His servants, such as the effects of His attributes of essence, such as hearing and sight, or His attributes of act, such as creation and sustenance.
- Second, what is meant by "countenance" is something external to the essence but attributed to it in some way, shape, or form. In this case, seeking the divine countenance means seeking the divine essence by the latter's leave, and this countenance is represented by the prophets, legatees, and *awliyāʾ*.

20. Spending of wealth

When the God-wary spend, they do so free from contamination, even from the hidden forms of associating partners with Allāh (*shirk khafī*), as one might show kindness to another in return for a previous kindness, in which case this is not considered as being for God but rather to remove oneself from their debt of kindness to another. But this kind of spending [i.e., that of the God-wary] sees only the Lord's countenance first and foremost and with its description as exalted second. These are both motivations for a person to devote their efforts to His noble countenance alone.

But one might ask: The verse indicates that the God-wary person who spends of his wealth does not see any blessings coming from other people in order that he reward them for it ("And none has any favour with him for reward") while the fact is that no one is free from the debt of kindness to another, so how can we reconcile this with what the Lord is demanding here?

The answer is that this class of people has attained a level of insight whereby they see no efficient cause in existence except Allāh, so whatever good reaches them from other people, they see it issuing from the hand of their master. As Allāh says, "All good is in Your hand...."[37]

What is meant here is when someone does not act kindly towards the God-fearing person, but he still treats them kindly for the sake of his Lord's countenance, not because he sees any benefit with them that he needs. Of course, this does not mean there is no benefit from people who the God-fearing person does not show kindness to.

21. Recompense

The greatest recompense that the Lord of the Worlds will grant the God-fearing is His words "and, surely, soon he will be well-pleased." This is the same kind of recompense as that which He gave to His beloved prophet, Muḥammad (s), as Allāh promised him a gift that would please him, interpreted to mean the power of intercession (*shafāʿa*). This is the greatest gift, for it is the power to save people from hellfire through the blessing of the person whom Allāh has singled out for this gift. This kind of gift is available to those mentioned in the verse in the sense that they might be given a degree of this power that will please the believing person also. This is supported by narrations that indicate that the faithful will fall within the scope of this intercessory power on the Day of Resurrection.

---

37. Sūrat Āle ʿImrān (3):26

Sūrat al-Ḍuḥā (no. 93: The Morning Brightness)

Verses 1–5

In the name of Allāh, the All-Beneficent, the All-Merciful

93:1 *By the morning brightness,*

93:2 *by the night when it is calm!*

93:3 *Your Lord has neither forsaken you nor is He displeased with you,*

93:4 *and the Hereafter shall be better for you than the world.*

93:5 *Soon your Lord will give you [that with which] you will be pleased.*

1. Oaths

A significant portion of the oaths contained in the Qurʾān are concerned with the times of day: daybreak (*fajr*),[1] dawn (*ṣubḥ*),[2] morning, afternoon (*ʿaṣr*)[3], and night (*layl*).[4] More still invoke the sun and the moon that are the symbols of night and day. All of this serves to demonstrate the importance of time:

- From one angle, time is the receptacle in which the deeds that grow a person's hereafter are performed. So the more time a person has and the longer one lives, the more magnificent one's hereafter becomes.
- From another angle, the cycle of night and day, which gives form to time, drives a person towards the magnificence of the force that governs these times. Their continuous cycle draws attention to their Master.

1. Sūrat al-Fajr (89):1: "By the daybreak"
2. Sūrat al-Takwīr (81):18: "By the dawn as it breathes"
3. Sūrat al-ʿAṣr (103):1: "By the afternoon!"
4. Sūrat al-Layl (92):1: "By the night when it covers"

2. Out of darkness

The oaths contained in the Qurʾān are joined to objects that they are sworn to affirm, or else the things chosen to be sworn upon would be random and haphazard. This *sūrah* is no exception. Allāh swears by "the morning brightness" which is the time when the day rises and "the night when it is calm" which is the time darkness covers the land. In these oaths is a subtle allusion to the fact that the same force that alternates night and day is the same force that alternates people's states and conditions. After all, is not the One who brings the land out of night's darkness into day's brightness also able to transform the heart of His chosen servant, Muḥammad (s), from a state of fear because he has not received any revelation from Him "forsaken you" to the realm of pleasing gifts "will give you"? It is as though the brightness of the day has come after the darkness of the night!

Is He not also able to bring the hearts of all His servants out of the darkness of turning away (*idbār*) from Him to the light of turning toward Him (*iqbāl*)? The same hand that moves the heavens also moves the hearts! Anyone with a heart or who is willing to listen can understand this and witness it.

3. Day for livelihood

The contrast between night and day is used here for a profound reason—that Allāh is the one who made the night for rest and the day for livelihood. He also made the night calm in order that people could rest therein, while making the morning brightness the time when things begin to move and come out from this rest that the night produced.

How contradictory it is, then, when these days we see that people invert this wisdom and take the night as a time for activity and turmoil and the day as a time for sleep and rest, contrary to what the Lord intended, as He said, "and make your sleep for rest"[5] and "make the day for livelihood."[6]

---

5. Sūrat al-Nabaʾ (78):9
6. Sūrat al-Nabaʾ (78):11

4. "Forsaken you"

Concerning the verse "Your Lord has neither forsaken you nor is He displeased with you" scholars have taken two views:

- When the Prophet (s) did not receive any revelation for a while, this delay made him fear that his Lord had turned away from him or become displeased. This caused him to devote himself even more to his Lord.
- That this was the claim of his enemies, who wasted no opportunity to revile the Prophet (s), so these verses came to reassure his noble heart. The extent of Allāh's affection for His chosen prophet is plain to see when we consider that the singular "you" (*anta/ka*) is repeated close to fifteen times in this *sūrah*, even though the revelation had only been absent, according to the differing accounts, for between two nights and four days.

5. Gap in revelation

This *sūrah*, assuming it is even possible for Allāh forsaking or being displeased with His prophet, was revealed after a gap in revelation that distressed the heart of Prophet Muḥammad (s), and also the verse "Had he faked any sayings in Our name."[7] There are a multitude of verses praising the prophets, especially those with followers at the time of our prophet (s), such as Jesus (as) and Moses (as), and countless other indications in the Qur᾿ān that make it clear to all—except to perhaps the most obstinate of disbelievers—that the Qur᾿ān is a revelation from Allāh and that had the Prophet (s) the capacity to produce anything like its contents, it would be inconceivable that he should be distressed by any gap in revelation if it was in anyone's hand save Allāh's, just as it would be far-fetched to praise past generations if this was not a divine call!

---

7. Sūrat al-Ḥāqqah (69):44

6. Gap in revelation

Allāh guaranteed His prophet that the revelation would continue, as this is something necessary for the divine mission, especially when there was something to occasion revelation or a question from someone, but despite that, Allāh stopped sending revelation to His prophet (s) to the extent that his enemies began to mock him, or that even the Prophet (s) himself became perplexed, according to whichever interpretation we choose. This shows that this special kindness (*luṭf*), like all other divine gifts, was in the hands of the Lord and He could bestow it whenever He willed. It has been narrated that the Prophet (s) said to Gabriel (as), "You kept away until I missed you." Gabriel (as) said, "I missed you more desperately, but I am a servant at His bidding and I cannot descend save by your Lord's command!"[8] So verses do not come down according to pleasure, just as they are not withheld out of displeasure. That is why the believer must always act in a manner that is appropriate to the guise of servitude (*ʿubūdiyya*) and leave the question of divine effusions, their frequency, quantity, and form to the One who bestows all graces.

7. Guiding others

Those who call others towards Allāh must not want to succeed in their preaching more than their Lord desires them to! This is because there is a danger that their determination to have an effect may cause their ego to become invested in this, meaning that their desire to guide others will turn into a desire to validate and aggrandize themselves, though this may be done in the guise of holiness.

Hence Allāh does not disdain stopping the revelation to His prophet (s), whatever the consequences, even if people begin to claim that Allāh is displeased with him and has forsaken him, for Allāh is He who "had your Lord wished, all those who are on earth would have believed."[9] But He did not do this, in order to test

---

8. *Majmaʿ al-bayān* 10/764
9. Sūrat Yūnus (10):99

them "that He may test which of you is best in conduct."[10] So when conducting oneself in the presence of divine lordship, the eye of the preacher must be fixed on the call itself and not those to whom he preaches, for Allāh tells His prophet (s), despite all the miracles and amazing qualities He endowed him with, "You cannot guide whomever you wish...."[11]

8. Intercession

The abode of this world is far too small for Allāh to make visible all the honors He has bestowed upon His faithful servants because it cannot possibly contain them, not because they are lacking...and that is why Allāh says, "and the Hereafter shall be better for you than the world." However, Allāh was not stingy with His prophet in this world. He granted him all manner of honors. He taught him what he knew not. Allāh's grace upon him was magnificent, and He raised up his remembrance...but He saved His greatest gifts for the Day of Resurrection, and that is what will truly please him. About these gifts, we have traditions from the Prophet's Household (as), including one in which Imām al-Sādiq (as) is narrated to have said, "My grandfather's being pleased is that not a single monotheist will enter hellfire."[12] From Imām al-Bāqir (as) it is narrated: "The People of the Qurʾān say: 'The most hopeful verse is Allah's saying "Say O My servants who have committed excesses against their own souls, do not despair of the mercy of Allah."'[13] But we, the People of the House say: 'The most hopeful verse is Allah's saying "Soon your Lord will give you [that with which] you will be pleased."' For by Allah, this is the power of intercession (*shafāʿa*), which he will be granted for the people of *la ilāha ill allāh* until he says: 'I am pleased.'"[14]

---

10. Sūrat Hūd (11):7
11. Sūrat al-Qaṣaṣ (28):56
12. *Majmaʿ al-bayān* 10/765
13. Sūrat al-Zumar (39):53
14. *Shawāhid al-tanzīl* 2/447

9. *Umma*

It is truly striking that the divine gift that pleases the Prophet (s) is not something for himself but something for his *umma,* namely, that his intercession will extend to even its major sinners! This contains a lesson for all the faithful—that they should place their concern in the wellbeing of the *umma* because seeking personal advantage is a subtle kind of idolatry (*shirk khafī*) from which the most elect worshipers purify themselves. However, seeking advantages for the human race as a whole is not a kind of idolatry. It is actually a corollary of *tawḥīd* and divine love because it flows from the fact that the servant loves to see Allāh's authority extended over the earth.

10. Mercy

If the Prophet's eagerness for his *umma* was at such a level that he would not be satisfied without the power of intercession, while he endured the persecution of his enemies throughout his mission, unceasing in his struggle, then what about Allāh's overflowing mercy from which is drawn not only the Prophet's mercy but all the mercy in existence? The magnitude of this mercy is so great that we are told when it spreads out in the hereafter, it will reach the throat of *Iblīs*. So what a mercy this is!

11. Intercession

It is possible to establish the power of intercession on the basis of these verses without needing any recourse to narrations. This is because Allāh commanded His prophet (s) to seek forgiveness in this world saying, "and plead forgiveness for your sin and for the faithful, men and women."[15] Pleading forgiveness (*istighfār*) means asking for Allāh's pardon, and there is no doubt that if someone is asks for something they will not be satisfied with a rejection, they will only be satisfied by the granting of their request. So when it is established that the only thing that will please the Prophet (s) is the granting of his request, and from another angle that Allāh will

15. Sūrat Muḥammad (47):19

give him whatever it is that will please him, we can conclude that this verse establishes his power of intercession for the sinners, for the intercession is nothing other than Allāh granting the request of the one who intercedes.

12. What pleases the Prophet (s)

It should be pointed out here that what pleases the Prophet (s) is in accord with what pleases Allāh:

- He was pleased with the Makkahan *qibla,* hence why Allāh says of Himself, "We will surely turn you to a *qiblah* of your liking...."[16]
- He was pleased with the full power of intercession, which is why Allāh says, "Soon your Lord will give you [that with which] you will be pleased.'

To sum up, when the Prophet (s) is pleased with something, even if this is a state that exists within the soul of the Prophet (s) himself, it also corresponds in the unseen realm with that which pleases Allāh. Putting the two above verses together clearly shows that Allāh desires to please His prophet (s) in ways that cannot even be conceived of. This how a lover customarily treats his beloved, and what a level this is!

Verses 6–11

93:6 *Did He not find you an orphan, and shelter you?*

93:7 *Did He not find you astray, and guide you?*

93:8 *Did He not find you needy, and enrich you?*

93:9 *So, as for the orphan, do not tyrannize him;*

93:10 *and as for the beggar, do not drive him away;*

93:11 *and as for your Lord's blessing, proclaim it!*

---

16. Sūrat al-Baqarah (2):144

13. Tribulation

When we study the lives of the prophets (as) generally, we see that every last one of them was tested with trials and tribulations throughout the different stages of their lives. In fact, Allāh burdened them with things that clashed with their duties as prophets, as a basic category, so they would experience the pain that others felt and sympathize with them. It has been narrated from Imām al-Ṣādiq (as), "Allah never sent a prophet without first making him a shepherd of cattle to teach him how to be a shepherd of people."[17] This is in addition to the fact that hardship causes a person to turn towards Allāh. This is why the best people are always tested the most. In fact, it is proportional to their level of faith, like the two sides of a scale. This offers consolation and healing to the hearts of those suffering in hardship, because if tribulation was not a kindness from Allāh, He would have not subjected His greatest prophets to it.

14. Tribulation

People thus afflicted with the various kinds of weakness that a person experiences—financial (such as poverty) or psychological (such as being an orphan)—could also suffer inwardly from a lack of self-worth, depression, or dissatisfaction with the state of their life. But some people might have reason to still feel the pain of one who falls into that condition even after they have left it behind. This is what Allāh wanted for His greatest prophets (as). It is said that Joseph (as) would not eat until he was full so that he would not forget hunger, and it is obvious that the poverty of our Prophet (s) and his experience of being an orphan both fall into this category.

This means that there is no cause for grief when a believer experiences some times of tribulation, perhaps Allāh wishes to educate him just as He did for His prophets (as).

---

17. *ʿIlal al-Sharāʾiʿ* 1/32

15. The Prophet's orphanhood

It is said that the Prophet's orphanhood was a blessing for him from a number of angles, even if it cannot be compared to his other blessings, like being chosen by Allāh. Some of these angles are as follows:

- Directly experiencing the condition of being an orphan, which equipped him to live with the kind of challenges they face.
- Being an orphan meant that he learned to rely only on his Lord from a young age; and though he was deprived the care of his parents, he was compensated for this with the care of the Lord of the Worlds, from whom all the care in existence flows.
- It also shows that being an orphan is not a barrier to any kind of advancement, whether in the eyes of the creation or the eyes of the Creator.
- Allāh wanted no one else to be responsible for his care, even when he was young, save to the extent that was necessary for him to live.

16. Guidance

The Lord of the Worlds demonstrates a special concern for explaining His kindness to His servants and making it apparent to them. In fact, if it were not for this kindness, not a single person in the whole of creation would be pure, as Allāh says, "Were it not for Allah's grace and His mercy upon you, not one of you would ever be pure."[18] It is in this context that He mentions His care for His beloved chosen prophet, Muḥammad (s), saying, "Did He not find you astray, and guide you?" So even you would not have had the blessing of guidance were it not for the care of your Lord. In other words, you were astray, not considering this continuous guidance from your youth, and so Allāh's words apply here: "You did not

---

18. Sūrat al-Nūr (24):21

know what the Book is, nor what is faith."[19] As does His saying "and indeed prior to it you were among those who are unaware."[20] So do the words of Moses (as): "I did that when I was astray."[21] Being astray (*ḍalāla*) here refers to lacking guidance in the matter of exigency when he killed that Egyptian.

17. Need of others

Allāh was the one who enriched His prophet through the Mother of the Faithful, Khadīja (as), and He was the one who looked after him after he lost his father while he was still in his mother's womb through his grandfather, ʿAbd al-Muṭṭalib, first, and then He looked after him after he lost his mother at the age of six through his uncle Abū Ṭālib, second. It is clear that this world operates according to cause and effect, even if Allāh is free to do as He likes. So someone shouldn't think that they will receive their sustenance without effort or relying on someone else.

This shows that there is no sense in offering supplications to be without need towards other people when what is desired is to be needless towards evil persons! The same applies when it comes to meeting one's needs; or else, why did not Allāh bring out all the hidden treasures of the earth for His prophet (s) instead of the wealth of Khadīja (as)?

18. Petitioner

In order to follow the Prophet's example properly, one must never refuse a petitioner ("and as for the beggar, do not drive him away") whether they ask for money or knowledge, and whether they are truthful or not. Narrations tell us that we must only respond to petitioners with either a pleasant refusal or giving a little. The verse indicates that we must not treat the orphan harshly ("So, as for the orphan, do not tyrannize him"), and the word 'tyrannize' (*qahr*) here alludes to a kind of disdain combined with power—a person who has power over his enemy tyrannizes him. So kindness

19. Sūrat al-Shūrā (42):52
20. Sūrat Yūsuf (12):3
21. Sūrat al-Shuʿarāʾ (26):20

to orphans is not restricted to mere material generosity but also looking after their psychological and spiritual wellbeing, as the inner hurt they feel cannot be healed with money. It is poignant that the Prophet (s) lived in a state of both neediness and orphanhood, and so he gave thanks for the care and wealth he received by working to look after others and provide for those in a similar condition.

19. Responding to a petitioner

One can respond to a petitioner after he has requested something, but honoring the orphan does not come after a request because of their youth and inexperience, and this is why it has a more powerful effect! Narrations that discuss honoring the orphan are truly amazing. For example, to show the place of someone who honors the orphan in relation to him in paradise, the Prophet crossed his fingers together.[22] Let it be known here that honoring the orphan properly means not waiting for him to ask, because what dignity the petitioner loses by asking is worth more than whatever the one he asks will give him. So what about when the act of giving is accompanied by reproaches and affronts? It is obvious that what ʿAbd al-Muṭṭalib and Abū Ṭālib (as) undertook with regards to the Prophet is certainly worthy of this great reward because in doing so, they cared for the greatest man who ever lived without him ever having to ask them. This is especially true considering the great distress this care caused for the Prophet's uncle, Abū Ṭālib.

It is in this context that we say that Allāh is most deserving to be given credit for what this *sūrah* describes. It was He who found His servant a lost and needy orphan, and His mere awareness of this was sufficient to enrich, guide, and care for him, even if without his ever asking for it.

20. Remembering blessings

Allāh's blessings are proclaimed either:

---

22. *Majmaʿ al-bayān* 10/740

- through speech, by making these blessings clear to people to endear them to the Source of all blessings. It has been narrated that Allāh said to Moses (as), "Endear me to my creation, and endear my creation to me." Moses asked, "My Lord, how should I do that?" He said, "Remind them of by blessings and gifts so that they will love me...." This is because reminding people of this makes them more aware of the blessings and benefits Allāh has conferred on them (for reasons of which only He is aware) and encourages them to remember the blessings. This is because forgetting blessings can sometimes lead people to be upset in times of ill fortune, which brings them dangerously close to ingratitude (*kufr*). This is in addition to encouraging people to follow the example of the righteous, for it has been narrated from Imām Ḥusayn (as), "When you do something good, tell your brothers about it so they can follow your example."[23]
- through action. It has been narrated that the Prophet (s) said, "Verily when Allah blesses a person, He loves to see the effect of His blessing upon him."[24] For when someone displays this blessing in their soul, it is as though they are saying implicitly, "Look at what Allah blesses His servants with," without conceit (*ʿujub*), of course! This in turn nurtures devotion which produces this visible blessing.

But something else, entirely different to the aforementioned meaning, might be intended here—to proclaim anything that will bring people closer to Allāh. Of course, one must seek help from the blessings Allāh has bestowed upon them in order to achieve that, and two of these blessings must be an open breast (*sharḥ al-ṣadr*) and beautiful speech (*ḥusn al-bayān*).

23. *Mafātīḥ al-ghayb* 31/201
24. *Al-Kāfī* 13/22

Sūrat al-Sharḥ (no. 94: The Opening-Up)

Verses 1–4

In the name of Allāh, the All-Beneficent, the All-Merciful

94:1 *Did We not open your breast for you*

94:2 *and relieve you of your burden*

94:3 *which [almost] broke your back?*

94:4 *Did We not exalt your name?*

1. Blessings for Prophet Muḥammad (s)

Assuming that this *sūrah* is connected to Sūrat al-Ḍuḥā, above, as we can understand from the fact that we can only recite them together in prayer and never separately, it draws attention to the many ways in which Allāh has been generous to the Final Prophet (s). It is as though this is meant to stand in sharp contrast to the erroneous idea that Allāh is displeased with him because of the break in revelation. This is connected to the different kinds of divine generosity detailed in the previous *sūrah* that begins by stating that Allāh is not displeased—explaining that it is in the hereafter that Allāh's full esteem for him will become clear and that He will give him something that will surely please him, before turning to mention Allāh's special care for His prophet from his childhood when he was an orphan and He cared for him, then when he was a grown man without special guidance and He guided him, and then when he was poor and Allāh enriched Him. As for this *sūrah,* it continues enumerating the blessings that Allāh has bestowed upon His beloved prophet, Muḥammad, the

Chosen One (s), as represented by opening his breast, relieving his burden, exalting his name, and making easy his hardship.

These two *sūrahs* mention the blessings directed towards him a total of ten times. Add to this the number of pronouns referring to the Prophet (s), whether visible or implicit (to complete this special affection) and these number eleven. So between these two *sūrahs* we see the Prophet (s) being addressed a total of twenty-one times, which is also the total number of verses in both of them.

2. Opening of the breast *(sharḥ al-ṣadr)*

Expounding the blessings of Allāh causes a person to feel lowly and humble before the One who is the source of these blessings. Even if they do not, generous people do not reproach people for their gifts for they see no wisdom in that. So what about the Most Generous One? So when we see the Lord, at the beginning of the *sūrah,* mentioning the different kind of blessings bestowed upon His chosen prophet (s), it should be understood in the same way.

Hence it is very appropriate for people to remind themselves of the blessings their Lord has given them, to deepen their sense of devotion towards Allāh whenever they find their connection with the Lord lacking.

The opening of the breast (*sharḥ al-ṣadr*) is a station that every seeker (*murīd*) of the Master should seek, just as Moses (as) sought it, saying, "My Lord! Open my breast for me."[1] This is not only to endure the persecution of other persons but to also receive the divine wisdom of the elect, which is not given to the majority of people, let alone borne by them!

It is possible for this state to be achieved by people who are not messengers, as happened to Luqmān the Wise, who received special wisdom from the Lord of the Worlds.[2] The value of this privilege is expressed in a tradition from the Prophet (s) in which he is narrated to have said, "I asked my Lord something which I wish I had not asked him. I said, 'My Lord, there have been prophets before me—

1. Sūrat Ṭa Ha (20):25
2. Sūrat Luqmān (31):12: "Certainly We gave Luqman wisdom"

for some you disposed the winds, others revived the dead.' He said, 'Did I not find you an orphan and care for you?' I said, 'Of course!' Then He said, 'Did I not find you astray and guide you?' I said, 'Of course, my Lord!' He said, 'Did I not open your breast for you and relieve you of your burden?' I said, 'Of course, my Lord!'"[3]

3. Opening of the breast *(sharḥ al-ṣadr)*

If a person is placed in charge of the prophetic mission and bears the responsibility of calling Allāh's servants towards Him and transforming the corrupted lands, then Allāh must grant him an open breast to bear the consequences of this mission. The enmity of the people of falsehood, not to mention the instigations of the devils, is a source of great distress that cannot be suffered except by one whose breast has been expanded by Allāh for that purpose.

4. Effects of the opening of the breast

Some of the effects that opening the breast has on the recipient are:

- receiving special divine guidance that will show him the correct path when all paths seem alike.
- being given special illumination from his Lord that removes confusion from his decisions.
- empowering him to guide others towards Allāh and bring them out of darkness and into light, having himself been brought out thereof.

All of these traits are only attained by the grace of having one's breast opened to divine illumination.

5. Degrees of superiority between different prophets

Moses (as) asked Allāh to open his breast with the words "My Lord! Open my breast for me."[4] But Allāh granted our prophet (s) this blessing directly, as we can discern from the words "Did We not

3. *Majmaʿ al-bayān* 10/770
4. Sūrat Ṭa Ha (20):25

open your breast for you?" which shows that there are degrees of superiority even between different prophets. It is only natural that the bearer of the final message is also endowed with the most opened breast.

6. Opening in the heart for servants

The opening of the breast is a great gift from Allāh, and it is for those who take the path of calling others towards Him. But is possible for a servant who pays attention to the divine gifts to detect signs of this. The Prophet (s) has alluded to these with his words "Turning towards the abode of everlasting life, shunning the abode of deceit, and preparing for death before it draws near."[5] So someone who does not find these qualities in themselves should not imagine they have attained this level, even if they find some degree of opening in their heart.

7. Deep affection between Allāh and His most beloved messenger (s)

It could be said that when Allāh says, "Did We not open your breast for you?" this serves to clarify and affirm His words "Your Lord has neither forsaken you nor is He displeased with you."[6] After all, how can Allāh forsake someone whose breast He has opened and whose name He has exalted? This demonstrates the deep affection between Allāh and His most beloved messenger (s). The Qurʾān is full of words that allude to Allāh's extreme kindness (*luṭf*) towards him:

- Sometimes He swears an oath by his noble life: "By your life..."[7]
- Sometimes He expresses sympathy for what he suffers for the sake of Allāh: "We did not send down to you the Qurʾan that you should be miserable."[8]

---

5. *Amālī* 532
6. Sūrat al-Ḍuḥā (93):3
7. Sūrat al-Ḥijr (15):72
8. Sūrat Ṭa Ha (20):2

- And sometimes He even places the matter of his marriage and divorce in His hand: "It may be that if he divorces you...."[9]

8. Effects of the open breast

One of the effects of the open breast that Allāh bestowed upon His chosen prophet (s) is him behaving peerlessly with the people who persecuted him and exiled him from his homeland, when he (s) said, "O Allah! Guide my people...for they do not know!"[10] If he had asked his Lord for vengeance, not only would he have been granted it, but there would have been no blame on him either! Here is a valuable lesson for anyone who wants to follow his example, and that is to look upon those astray from Allāh's path with kindness. So what about the obedient?

9. The nature of Allāh's relationship with His prophets

The first four verses highlight the nature of Allāh's relationship with His prophets and the gifts He gives them, especially His final prophet (s), namely, the level of having an open breast, being relieved of one's burdens, having one's name exalted, and being granted ease after hardship. But all these great qualities are connected to the last two verses of this *sūrah,* namely, "So when you are done, toil and turn eagerly to your Lord." This means either:

- a connection between a cause and its effect, namely, that these qualities are the result of putting one's soul to work, causing it to toil in worship, and desiring nothing from Allāh except Himself.
- a connection between an effect and its cause, namely, that whoever has been given these qualities should putting themselves to work in worship and turn eagerly towards the Lord.

---

9. Sūrat al-Taḥrīm (66):5
10. *Al-Iḥtijāj* 1/212

10. Calling others towards Allāh

The great burden of which Allāh relieved His prophet (s) is embodied by his confrontation with the thugs of pre-Islamic Ignorance who brutally resisted the rise of Islām. This reveals that one of a person's most difficult duties is to face Allāh's enemies, but of course the harder the duty, the closer it brings one to the divine!

Hence, those who forewent the difficulty of calling others towards Allāh and enjoyed the pleasures of worship in private, like monks and ascetics, are only pursuing their own comfort and avoiding the hardships in which lies their Lord's pleasure.

11. Obstacles

The best solution to a problem is never to flee from obstacles and seek relief from sources of anxiety and concern. Rather the only solution is to seek the strength to bear these things, and this is the opening of the breast. When a person is granted this blessing, they become like a deep ocean that takes whatever is thrown at it without any effect, unlike a bowl that overflows at the first opportunity.

12. Success in calling others towards Allāh

Exalting the name of those who call to Allāh, and at their head stands the Prophet (s) and his Household (as), is caused by one thing and in turn causes another ("And exalted your name." So from one aspect it is a gift and a blessing that comes from Allāh's effusions in the firmament and the souls, as Allāh bestowed on Abraham (as) by causing people's hearts to incline towards him, as well as creating a special affection between him and his Lord. So in this way, exalting his name was caused by this divine kindness.

From another aspect it is a special quality that makes the prophetic mission a success, for anyone whose name is exalted amongst people is in turn better able to have an effect on them. It is the nature of people's hearts to accept something from a person whom they love. This explains why the companions of the *imāms* (as) threw themselves into struggling for Allāh's sake and other causes. So it is in this way that this divine kindness brings about a person's success in calling others towards Allāh.

13. Allāh exalting someone

There is a significant difference between someone who strives to promote their own reputation through their endeavors for short-term gain and someone whose name Allāh wishes to exalt. The first may not be successful in this, and even if they are, the fame they win may be short-lived, for Allāh rotates fortune amongst different people while the second's reputation shall endure with Allāh. This is what has happened in the case of the final messenger (s), in that his name is mentioned in the declaration of faith (*shahada*), the call to prayer, the *iqama,* and the *tashahhud* of every single prayer, whether obligatory or supererogatory. This idea will remain until the final hour. It has been narrated from the Prophet (s) as an explanation of this verse: "Gabriel (as) told me, Allah says, 'When I am mentioned, you will be mentioned with me.'"[11]

Verses 5–8

94:5 *Indeed ease accompanies hardship.*

94:6 *Indeed ease accompanies hardship.*

94:7 *So when you are done, toil,*

94:8 *and turn eagerly to your Lord.*

14. Ease

Certainly ease (*yusr*) is the general principle that accords with Allāh's overflowing mercy. It is as if to say that hardship does not befall anyone except to bring them closer to perfection. Hence it is possible to say that a single hardship is accompanied by two eases, because here in the Arabic, "hardship" takes the definite

11. *Manāqib* 1/302

article and is repeated. Whenever a definite noun is repeated in speech, the thing intended by the second instance is always the same as that intended by the first. It has been narrated from the Prophet (s), "No difficulty shall overcome two eases."[12]

15. Hardship

Hardship accompanies ease concomitantly (*maʿiyya*), as is mentioned in the verse. It does not precede ease in the sense of being before it. This offers solace to the faithful who have fallen into hardship because they know that ease actually accompanies their hardship rather than merely coming at some future time. Of course, they are aware that all of this is in the hands of the All-Aware and Most-Wise, who governs all the sources of hardship and ease together. It has been narrated from the Prophet (s), "Know that with assistance (*naṣr*) comes patience (*ṣabr*), with grief (*karb*) comes relief (*faraj*), and with hardship (*ʿusr*) comes ease (*yusr*).[13]

16. "Indeed ease accompanies hardship"

We can treat the verse "Indeed ease accompanies hardship" as either:

- the cause for opening the breast (*sharḥ al-ṣadr*), above, for one of the instances of being granted ease is to open the breast of one who is afflicted by grievous woe.
- the result of opening the breast from another angle, in that we take the experience of ease to be a consequence of this opening. So whosoever's breast Allāh opens, and whosoever's burden He relieves, He has also made easy their hardship.

17. The path of obedience

Mention of the divine blessings, especially spiritual blessings such as the opening of the breast, gives occasion for the servant to turn to the Lord and be eager for Him, as shown by the verse "...and

12. *Majmaʿ al-bayān* 10/771
13. *Mishkāt al-anwār* 20

turn eagerly to your Lord." This encourages servants to urge themselves onwards upon the path of obedience ("So when you are done, toil...") as the final two verses of this *sūrah* suggest.

18. Toil

Those who strive to attain proximity to the truth know no weariness or boredom in their devotions. After they are finished with their duties to spread the message, they put themselves to toil in worship and supplication before their Lord—to prepare themselves to endure further hardships to free Allāh's servants and purify His lands.

There is a powerful lesson in this for those who call to Allāh, namely, that their preoccupation with confronting Allāh's enemies does not excuse them from devoting themselves to worship and seeking recourse with Allāh to the extent that they put themselves to toil, as we understand from the word 'toil' seeking additional steadfastness and divine grace.

19. Being eager for Allāh

Some verses of the Qurʾān mention material forms of reward in paradise (such as young men (*ghulmān*) and maidens (*hūr*)[14]) and bids the faithful to hasten towards a paradise whose breadth is the heavens and the earth.[15] Others encourage the elect (*khawāṣṣ*) to attain degrees that cannot be compared to those blessings, such as the bliss of divine satisfaction (*riḍwān*), which is greater than every other bliss in paradise, or the bliss of proximity and connectedness to the divine.

It is possible that Allāh's words "and turn eagerly to your Lord" allude to the level of being eager for Allāh, not for His recompense, because in these verses it is to Allāh that eagerness is directly fastened. There is a clear distinction between desiring the real Himself and merely desiring His reward.

14. For instance, Sūrat al- Dukhkhān (44):54: "So shall it be, and We shall wed them to black-eyed houris."

15. Sūrat Āle ʿImrān (3):133: "And hasten towards your Lord's forgiveness and a paradise as vast as the heavens and the earth, prepared for the Godwary"

Sūrat al-Tīn (no. 95: The Fig)

Verses 1–5

95:1 *By the fig and the olive,*

95:2 *by Mount Sinai,*

95:3 *by this secure town:*

95:4 *We certainly created man in the best of forms;*

95:5 *then We relegated him to the lowest of the low,*

1. Oaths

It is truly amazing how the Qurʾān varies its oaths; moving from swearing oaths by fruits ("By the fig and the olive") to two sacred places ("by Mount Sinai, by this secure town"), but there is nothing strange about this because everything that belongs to Allāh in some way, whether it is a fruit or a piece of blessed ground, is sacred and can be sworn upon, for the nobility of a superior extends to those beneath him if we consider them as part of his affairs. Why should this be strange when both of these things emanate from the realm of His command and creation?

2. Sanctity of a place

Mount Sinai was not a home for Moses (as) but a place where he conversed privately with his Lord, unlike the other holy places mentioned in this *sūrah*. This shows that a person's ennoblement by invoking the Lord, even if only for a short time, like forty nights, imbues the place in which he invokes Him with sanctity—sanctity sufficient enough to warrant it being it being invoked in an oath.

3. Makkah

Using the adjective "secure" categorically for Makkah in the verse "by this secure town" alludes to the sanctity of this place, whether we interpret "secure" here:

- in the active sense—meaning it protects everyone who enters its protective circle, as if to say this place puts all of its inhabitants and visitors under its guard. This is an integral part of the religion, even if people violate it. It is a safe place, where it is not permitted to hunt game or harm its pilgrims, even if the person in question is a criminal.
- in the passive sense, as Allāh says, "Have they not seen that We have appointed a safe sanctuary...?"[1]—meaning that Allāh has decreed it so that anyone who violates its security has challenged Allāh's authority directly. This is why we see a painful punishment directed to the Army of the Elephant who tried to assail this sanctity.

4. Blessings

We should be attentive to the abundant variety of divine blessings in our lives that, in turn, require us to offer an abundant variety of thanks, whether in word or deed, for each and every one of those blessings. Some people enjoy worldly blessings and thus forget heavenly ones, such as the blessing of being a Muslim and having faith while others experience spiritual blessings but forget to give thanks for the food and drink they consume, for example. A true believer regards everything that comes from their Lord, whether material or spiritual.

This is why this *sūrah* combines the mention of material blessings (such as foodstuffs like the two fruits) with intelligible blessings (such as faith), just as it combines those things that preserve the body's health (in the form of beneficial fruits like figs and olives which we are told have many amazing properties) with those

1. Sūrat al-ʿAnkabūt (29):67

things that preserve the health of nations (like security ("by this secure town")).

5. The honor of a location

The first verses of this *sūrah* have been explained as referring to the lands of different prophets (as), namely:

- Syria, which is famous for its figs. This was to whence Abraham (as) emigrated.
- Palestine, which is famous for its olives, which is where Jesus (as) was born and raised.
- Mount Sinai, which is the place where Moses (as) conversed privately with his Lord.
- The secure town, which is the land of our prophet, the Final Messenger (s).

Taken together, these verses show that spots of ground acquire nobility from the people in them. So a person should not be proud of a home because of the ground it rests upon—because the honor of a location derives from the one who resides in it, not the other way around!

6. The supplication of Abraham (as)

The legal safety decreed for the secure town is only in response to the supplication of Abraham (as) who asked Allāh for safety saying, "My Lord! Make this city a sanctuary..."[2] and His response was, "Have they not seen that We have appointed a safe sanctuary...?"[3] What a great thing it is for Allāh to guarantee the security of a land until the Day of Resurrection in response to the supplication of one of His ennobled servants!

---

2. Sūrat Ibrāhīm (14):35
3. Sūrat al-ʿAnkabūt (29):67

7. Material and spiritual excellence

Allāh created the human being with the best capacity to attain material and spiritual excellence (*kamāl*) ("Surely We created man of the best stature.").

- So the human body, with all its abilities and innate faculties, can do some truly astounding things, as we are learning at the moment through our advancing scientific knowledge in all areas.
- But the human spirit, insofar as Allāh has shown it the paths of good and evil ("and shown him the two paths"[4]) also has the ability to attain the highest levels of excellence.

So what a waste it is when a person does not attain this excellence despite being endowed with everything they need to reach it. Truly it can be said of such a person: "They are just like cattle; rather they are further astray from the way."[5]

8. "The best stature"

Allāh attributes creation in "the best stature" to Himself, but He also attributes reducing man to the lowest of the low to Himself ("Then we reduced him to the lowest of the low") with the key distinction that:

- the first is a unilateral divine act, for Allāh was with a person the moment he was created, when he was not "anything worthy of mention"[6] and
- the second is a divine act that follows from the actions of the person. This belongs to the category of being forsaken and punished, like any law in the realm of cause and effect. Allāh is the one who burns, but this is only when a person has ignited the fire himself!

---

4. Sūrat al-Balad (90):10

5. Sūrat al-Furqān (25):44

6. Sūrat al-Insān (76):1

9. Two arcs of ascent and descent

What a difference there is between the ascending arc (referred to in Allāh's words "Surely We created man of the best stature," the verse "To Him ascends the good word, and He elevates righteous conduct,"[7] and the narration from Him, "Were it not for you, I would not have created the firmament"[8]) and the descending arc referred to in His words "Then we reduced him to the lowest of the low" and the verse "Indeed the hypocrites will be in the lowest reach of the Fire...."[9] It is interesting to note that a person moves between the two arcs of ascent and descent in this world that, despite its limitations, determines all of that.

Verses 6–8

95:6 *except those who have faith and do righteous deeds. There will be an unrestrained reward for them.*

95:7 *So what makes you deny the Retribution?*

95:8 *Is not Allah the fairest of all judges?*

10. Faith and righteous deeds

The Qurʾān connects faith (*īmān*) to righteous deeds (*ʿamal ṣāliḥ*) in approximately fifty places, which shows us that salvation can only be achieved through both of them. So those who seek a religion other than Islām, or even a path other than that of the Prophet and his Household (as) have lost the first pillar, while those who swerve from the upright way and do not do righteous deeds, or contaminate their righteous deeds with evil ones, have lost the second one.

Notice that the tone of the verses that demonstrate this reality vary between:

---

7. Sūrat Fāṭir (35):10
8. *Manāqib* 1/217
9. Sūrat al-Nisāʾ (4):145

- mentioning righteous deeds in the past tense ("those who have believed and done righteous deeds,"[10] which indicates steadfastness (*thubāt*)),
- mentioning righteous deeds in the present tense (indicating continuity, and faith is used as an attribute of a person, not of an act, as in Allāh's words "Whoever does righteous deeds, should he be faithful..."[11]), and
- mentioning righteous deeds as a prelude to glad tidings, whether these are directed to an individual believer, such as His words "But whoever comes to Him with faith and he has done righteous deeds,"[12] or to a group of them, as in "and gives the good news to the faithful who do righteous deeds that there is a great reward for them."[13]

11. The most excellent gift

The most excellent gift:

- is that which is uninterrupted, for the sadness the recipient experiences for the moment that it is absent cannot be compensated by the past moments when it was present. It is obvious that fleeting happiness cannot make up for real and present sadness. This is why Allāh describes His reward in this *sūrah* as being "unrestrained" (*ghayru mamnūn*), meaning that it never ends.
- is that which is not accompanied by affronts (*mann*) as this distresses the recipient of the gift. We can also understand this from the words *ghayru mamnūn.*
- is that for which it is understood that the recipient is worthy of this recompense, and the verse says that this reward is fixed for them ("they shall have an everlasting reward") as if to say this reward is due to them. In fact, the truth is that Allāh is being gracious not only in giving them a reward,

10. Sūrat Ṭa Ha (20):75
11. Sūrat al-Anbiyāʾ (21):94
12. Sūrat Ṭa Ha (20):75
13. Sūrat al-Isrāʾ (17):9

because what they did was nothing more than what their station as His servants demanded, but also in the quantity of the reward that they receive because an eternal and everlasting reward cannot be compared to some fleeting obedience in this world!

12. Rhetorical questions

The Qurʾān teaches us how to interact with people and convince them theoretically. After mentioning the wonders of His creation in the material world and His sending of great prophets, He poses a rhetorical question about what motivates people to deny the Day of Recompense ("So what makes you deny the Retribution?") as if to suggest that such a denial is something strange indeed. This is one of the ways in which Allāh reanimates the ossified intellects.

We can also understand this address as being directed to the Prophet (s) to put his noble mind at ease, in which case the meaning is: "So what is it that could make you deny the recompense, O Messenger, after these unshakable proofs have been put forth!?"

13. Summary in one verse

Sometimes, Allāh summarizes all the goals of a *sūrah* in a single sentence. We can identify a possible instance of this in the verse "Is not Allah the fairest of all judges?"—as if to say that the only conclusion to be drawn from everything that has been said in this *sūrah,* namely,

- the magnificence of the material realm,
- choosing some persons as prophets while reducing others to the lowest states,
- the promise of never-ending rewards, and
- the threat of retribution for the denier

is that all of that springs from Allāh's absolute authority over everything in existence.

14. Loss

The context of this *sūrah* resembles that of Sūrat al-ʿAṣr in that it affirms the fact that everyone who exists is on a journey, as represented by its exposition of the principle of loss (*khasrān*), which is the default state for the life of every individual and from which no one can escape, except by combining faith with righteous deeds.

This means that if a person excuses themselves from ascending to the realm of "the best of forms," then the unavoidable outcome of this will be their descent to "the lowest of the low" just as all bodies with mass ultimately fall to the ground because of gravity if they do not expend energy to rise.

Sūrat al-ʿAlaq (no. 96: The Clinging Mass)

Verses 1–5

96:1 *Read in the Name of your Lord who created;*

96:2 *created man from a clinging mass.*

96:3 *Read, and your Lord is the most generous,*

96:4 *who taught by the pen,*

96:5 *taught man what he did not know.*

1. "Read"

There is a difference between ordering someone to read (*qirāʾa*) and ordering someone to speak (*ḥadīth*). The first requires that there be something to read from. In other words, for every reader there is a text. So from the command "Read..." (*iqraʾ*), we understand that there is something that the Prophet (s) must read from, and that is the Qurʾān, as we see in Allāh's words "We have sent the Qurʾan in parts so that you may read it to the people..."[1] as if his heart stands in the place of the divine throne from which the revelation descends. This alludes to the fact that the Prophet (s) never forgot any part of the Qurʾān. What a heart he must have had to receive the entire divine scripture in a single burst on a single night!

2. *Basmala*

It is well-known that any action not connected to Allāh is without issue (*abtar*), which is why we are bid to recite the *basmala* before every significant act we undertake. It is even said, based on the fact that any action in which Allāh's name has not been invoked

1. Sūrat al-Isrāʾ (17):106

is without issue, that the command “Read in the Name of your Lord...” means to begin reading by reciting the *basmala*. It is even more necessary to connect matters of preaching to Allāh, for He is not satisfied for people to spread His guidance except through people with whom He is satisfied and in ways that satisfy Him so that His religion owes nothing to anyone.

This is why Allāh commands His chosen prophet (s) to read in the name of his Lord, that same Lord whose mention is repeated more than once in these verses. Add to this the fact that Allāh instructs His prophet to seek assistance from Him through prostration and to draw near to Him in confronting those who bar His worship, and it is clear that success in the beginning of the mission and its continuation is predicated on its being connected to the Absolute.

3. Creatorship

The Qurʾān frequently connects creatorship (*khāliqiyya*) to lordship (*rubūbiyya*). We see this in the verse here: “your Lord who created,” before it turns specifically to the creation of the human being (“created man from a clinging mass”). This intimates that Allāh’s creation of the human species is superior to all other creatures in this vast universe, as He says elsewhere, “We certainly created man in the best of forms.”[2]

4. A clinging mass

The Qurʾān mentions that the creation of the human being began with a clinging mass (*ʿalaq*), which literally means a mass of congealed blood, in order to remind its audience of their lowly origins. In another verse, it refers to this as a base fluid (“Then He made his progeny from an extract of a base fluid.”[3]). Allāh could have mentioned the intermediate and final stages of the human beings creation as a fetus, but He chose the weakest and lowliest stage, as this clinging mass does not exhibit any features of the body. This highlights Allāh’s absolute power in the realm of the

2. Sūrat al-Tīn (95):4
3. Sūrat al-Sajdah (32):8

body, in that He created the human being "in the best of forms"[4] from these lowly beginnings that could not be called complete.

But Allāh also exercises this creative power in the realm of the spirit, for He "taught man what he did not know." The means He uses for this is also something very simple, namely, the pen, which is made from the matter of trees that grow from the soil ("who taught by the pen"). So from the base matter of blood and wood come human beings and human knowledge that, in turn, are the constituents of all the civilizations ever to have existed on the face of the earth.

5. Attachment of the Prophet (s) to Allāh

Repeating the word 'Lord' (*rabb*) in this *sūrah,* and attaching it to the Final Prophet (s), is a kind of magnification of the Prophet, as in "your Lord." But elsewhere, we also see the Prophet mentioned and attached to his Lord such as in the verse "who carried His servant."[5] It is said that this attachment of the Prophet to Allāh is an even greater honor than attaching Allāh to His prophet because when you say "You are mine," this is more noble than saying "I am yours."

It is worth pondering the fact that "Lord" mentioned in the first instance of "your Lord", which is unqualified by any attributes, follows the mention of Allāh's creation, which is His creative manifestation (*tajallī takwīnī*) "who created" but the "Lord" mentioned in the second instance, qualified by the quality of being most-generous ("your Lord is the most generous"), follows the mention of Allāh's teaching, which is His moral manifestation (*tajallī tashrīʿī*), for He is the One "who taught by the pen."

6. Most generous

When the discussion revolves around creation, Allāh describes Himself as generous. He says, "O man! What has deceived you about your generous Lord, who created you and proportioned you,

4. Sūrat al-Tīn (95):4
5. Sūrat al-Isrāʾ (17):1

and gave you an upright nature..."[6] but when the discussion turns to knowledge and teaching, He describes Himself as most generous saying, "Recite and your Lord is most generous" as if creation in its entirety is in one hand, while teaching the human being what he did not know is in the other above it. This should not be seen as strange because it is this knowledge that opens the way to know the creation that rests in the first hand, and, in fact, to know its creator as well.

It should be clear that using the attribute of generosity, out of all the divine attributes, in these two places alludes to the fact that the divine effusion in both of them is pure kindness, offered without expecting anything in return, so this does not fall into the category of rewards but into the realm of grace and benevolence.

7. Knowledge

Some biased parties accuse Islām of being a religion of the sword when it is actually the religion of the pen, as we understand from these very first verses revealed of the Qurʾān, which was sent to open people's hearts with the slogan "There is no compulsion in religion."[7] This is the real reason why Islām has spread to the furthest reaches of the world.

The level of reverence that the Qurʾān displays towards knowledge is so high that it even invokes oaths upon the implements of writing, namely, the pen, and that which is written on, the book. Both of these appear at the beginning Sūrat al-Qalam ("By the Pen and what they write"[8]). Notice that it does not mention any specific kind of knowledge being written, out of respect for any kind of knowledge that flows from a person's pen, even if this is only for worldly benefit.

8. Teaching

Allāh frequently attaches the act of teaching to Himself. He says:

---

6. Sūrat al-Infiṭār (82):6–7
7. Sūrat al-Baqarah (2):256
8. Sūrat al-Qalam (68):1

> *He "taught man what he did not know."*[9]
>
> *...has taught the Qurʾan. He created man, taught him articulate speech.*[10]
>
> *And He taught Adam the Names, all of them...*[11]
>
> *...and when I taught you the Book and wisdom, the Torah and the Evangel...*[12]
>
> *Indeed he had the knowledge of what We had taught him...*[13]
>
> *...it is just a revelation that is revealed, taught him by One of great powers...*[14]

This means that anyone who chooses the path of teaching people knowledge that is useful to them is not just following in the footsteps of the great prophets, they are actually following in the footsteps of Allāh and adopting His manners. So it is a must that Allāh should furnish them with the same kind of assistance that He bestowed upon all His prophets (as)! This also reveals the clear distinction between the actions of scholars who have adopted this divine attribute and worshipers whose interest is their own salvation.

9. Acquired knowledge and inspired knowledge

In this *sūrah,* teaching is sometimes mentioned without being qualified, as in "taught man what he did not know" and sometimes it is qualified by the pen, "who taught by the pen." Perhaps this alludes to the two different kinds of knowledge—one being acquired knowledge (*ʿilm iktisābī*) (which is received from the physical sources of reading, writing, and the minds of men) and inspired knowledge (*ʿilm ilhāmī*) (which is something bestowed

9. Sūrat al-ʿAlaq (96):5
10. Sūrat al-Raḥman (55):2–4
11. Sūrat al-Baqarah (2):31
12. Sūrat al-Māʾidah (5):110
13. Sūrat Yūsuf (12):68
14. Sūrat al-Najm (53):4–5

only upon the elect of Allāh's servants). Inspired knowledge was bestowed on Khiḍr (as) as Allāh's says He "taught him a knowledge from Our own"[15] and on Luqmān—Allāh says, "Certainly We gave Luqman wisdom...."[16]

10. Lordship

The problem of the polytheists was not in acknowledging Allāh as the creator of the universe ("If you ask them, 'Who created the heavens and the earth, and disposed the sun and the moon?' They will surely say, 'Allah.'"[17]). Their problem was that they refused to submit to Allāh's lordship, and that's because they submitted to other manmade deities and idols.

Therefore, a Muslim who professes to accept Allāh's lordship while obeying another, at the level of action, is tainted by an attribute of this group, even if they are not really like them. This is why our Master bids us in Sūrat al-Fātiḥah to praise Him by His lordship first, before acknowledging that our obedience and worship belong to Him second. This *sūrah* also mentions lordship first ("your Lord") and creation ("who created") as a description of Him second.

Verses 6–8

96:6 *No indeed! Surely man becomes rebellious*

96:7 *when he considers himself without need.*

96:8 *Indeed to your Lord is the return.*

11. Rebellion

After talking about knowledge and the pen, this *sūrah* turns to rebuke the person who sees themselves without need because of their wealth. Allāh says, "No indeed! Surely man becomes rebellious...." It is as though it is drawing a contrast between wealth and knowledge or between this world and the hereafter in general,

15. Sūrat al-Kahf (18):65

16. Sūrat Luqmān (31):12

17. Sūrat al-ʿAnkabūt (29):61

for as the narration says, they are opposites. If someone absorbed by their love of this world occupies themselves with things that distract them from Allāh, they cannot enjoy the blessings of knowledge which would avail them, just as the warnings of the prophets will not avail them ("You can only warn someone who follows the Reminder and fears the All-beneficent in secret..."[18]). The Qurʾān has mentioned clear examples of those who become rebellious because they feel needless. The prime example of these people is Pharaoh, about whom Allāh says, "Let the two of you go to Pharaoh. Indeed he has rebelled."[19] His destruction will be a lesson to anyone else who becomes rebellious because they see themselves without need!

12. Rebellion

The basis of all rebellion is that the human being sees themselves as being without need, even if this is illusory, and so cuts ties to the real and absolute source of every kind of wealth. Otherwise, wealth, as an external state, is actually a form of divine grace and assistance, insofar as this world is the farm in which we grow our hereafter. However, external wealth could motivate someone to become rebellious inwardly if they fail to vigilantly observe themselves. This is why the subject of this verse is the human being generally, not specifically those who believe, and, therefore, it is proper for a person to satisfy themselves with the amount of sustenance that suffices them, lest they be driven to self-destructive rebellion.

13. Humiliators

The Qurʾān frequently mentions those groups who confronted the message of the prophets (as) to humiliate them and warn others like them, for example:

- Kings ("Indeed when kings enter a town, they devastate it, and reduce the mightiest of its people to the most abased. That is how they act."[20])

18. Sūrat Yā Sīn (36):11
19. Sūrat Ṭa Ha (20):43
20. Sūrat al-Naml (27):34

- The affluent ("And when We desire to destroy a town We command its affluent ones [to obey Allāh]. But they commit transgression in it, and so the word becomes due against it, and We destroy it utterly."[21])
- Major sinners ("Thus have We installed in every town its major criminals that they may plot therein."[22])
- The arrogant ("The elite of his people who were arrogant said, 'O Shuʾayb, we will surely expel you...'"[23])

This *sūrah,* which was one of the first to be sent down, also contains a warning at the very beginning of this mission to the wealthy and rebellious, who are those who have invested their wealth in opposing the prophets (as), such as Korah of ancient times and the arrogant leaders of the Quraysh at the advent of Islām.

14. Wealth and knowledge combined

Wealth, when combined with knowledge, becomes a means for human society to grow and develop. This is what happened in the case of Joseph (as) ("My Lord! You have granted me a share in the kingdom, and taught me the interpretation of omens."[24]). So his reign, which was a kind of wealth, and his knowledge became two means by which people were saved from worshipping false gods from one angle and the hardships of famine from another.

When these two elements are combined in any ruler and at any time, the result is always the same. This is the justice and ease of living that the human race will witness in the time when our *imām,* the Mahdī (ajfs), returns.

15. "Without need"

The word for 'without need' (*istaghnā*), insofar as its verbal form signifies seeking the meaning of the root letters (*gh-n-y,* or "wealth"), suggests that those whom wealth has made rebellious

21. Sūrat al-Isrāʾ (17):16
22. Sūrat al-Anʿām (6):123
23. Sūrat al-Aʿrāf (7):88
24. Sūrat Yūsuf (12):101

see that the wealth they possess—if it is, in fact, real wealth—is the sole result of their own efforts and labors in this world. They are unaware of the fact that whatever wealth anyone has, even the rebellious, is only by Allāh's facilitation because the world and everything in it ultimately returns to Him. It is He that says, "Do you not see that Allāh has disposed for you whatever there is in the heavens and whatever there is in the earth...?"[25] In the present *sūrah,* He follows with the words "Indeed to your Lord is the return." It is as if to show that remembering the resurrection and judgement before Allāh is one of the ways in which this feeling of needlessness can be broken in those people who still have hearts!

16. Spiritual excellence

At the root of every spiritual excellence is being attentive to two facts:

- Believing that the return is to Allāh ("Indeed to your Lord is the return.")
- People seeing themselves standing before Allāh ("...does he not know that Allah sees?"[26]). For this will endow them with humility in their physical existence and submission in their spiritual one. Together these engender self-accounting (*muḥāsiba*) because they will remember their accounting in the hereafter and also self-observation (*murāqaba*) because they will remember that Allāh is watching them in this world. Without this, no one will ever attain excellence! It has been narrated in a tradition, "Worship Allah as though you see Him, for if you do not see Him, He surely sees you."[27]

It is interesting to note that this source of self-development in the spiritual realm has been mentioned in the Qurʾān at the very beginning of the prophetic mission before Gabriel had brought down any particulars of the *sharīʿa.* So we should not accept the claim of some people that there is nothing beyond the exterior of

25. Sūrat Luqmān (31):20
26. Sūrat al-ʿAlaq (96):14
27. Ṭūsī, *Amālī* 526

the *sharīʿa,* namely, performing obligations and avoiding forbidden things.

Verses 9–19

96:9 *Tell me, he who forbids*

96:10 *a servant when he prays,*

96:11 *tell me, should he be on guidance,*

96:12 *or bid to Godwariness,*

96:13 *tell me, should he call him a liar and turn away*

96:14 *—does he not know that Allah sees?*

96:15 *No indeed! If he does not stop, We shall seize him by the forelock,*

96:16 *a lying, sinful forelock!*

96:17 *Then let him call out his gang!*

96:18 *We [too] shall call the keepers of hell.*

96:19 *No indeed! Do not obey him, but prostrate and draw near!*

17. A principle to deter

The three verses beginning with the words "Tell me..." (*a raʾayta,* lit. "Have you seen...") display astonishment at the actions of one who forbids a person who prays, who is upon guidance, and bids others to beware of Allāh. This is to say that this action is so evil, even the Exalted Lord is shocked, and to show the terrible punishment that awaits as a result!

Note that Allāh mentions a principle to deter others like them, namely, the fact that all of this is witnessed by Allāh in this world. So the apparent meaning of the words is directed to the polytheists who do not deny the existence of their creator. This verse wants to produce the consequence of this belief, namely, the fear that He could be watching them. As such, there is no need to threaten them with hellfire on the Day of Recompense, and, therefore, the warning that He is watching extends even to those, just as the invitation to refine oneself was directed to Pharaoh when Allāh said, "...maybe he will take admonition or fear."[28]

18. Repentance

It is the habit of the Qurʾān to allude to the fact that the doors of repentance are still open, even for the worst cases of disobedience, in order to give hope to the hearts of those consumed by sins and who are immoderate with themselves. One example of this can be found in Sūrat al-Burūj where Allāh says, "Indeed those who persecute the faithful men and women, and then do not repent, for them there is the punishment of hell, and for them there is the punishment of burning."[29] In this verse, as we have discussed already, He predicates the execution of the punishment on the absence of repentance, even in the case of this terrible crime.

Another example can be found in this *sūrah,* in that Allāh also hints at repentance here, despite the fact that this is in the context of a threat to the one who has a lying sinful forelock and who persists in forbidding others from prayer, as indicated by the use of the present tense in the verse "Tell me, he who forbids...." Nevertheless, Allāh says, "No indeed! If he does not stop..." and this leaves him the option of desisting. What clemency this is from the Most Generous of the generous! He even leaves the opportunity to repent and be pardoned in His threats!

19. Rebuke and threat

The rebuke and threat contained by this *sūrah* (even if they are specifically directed to someone who forbade the Prophet (s) from praying, as indicated by the injunction to him (s) at the end of the *sūrah* not to heed his enemy but to prostrate and draw near to his Lord) still imply, fundamentally, that displaying enmity towards a believer because of their faith (and especially because they perform their prayers) arouses Allāh's wrath. This is because such behavior

28. Sūrat Ṭa Ha (20):44
29. Sūrat al-Burūj (85):10

constitutes a challenge to the most noble of His creatures while he is engaged with His most noble act of obedience. This challenge ultimately returns to Allāh, who is the most severe in avenging His servants and making examples of their persecutors!

20. The greatness of the Prophet (s) before his mission

Assuming that this *sūrah* in its entirety was the first revelation received by the Prophet (s), it serves to show the greatness of the Prophet (s) before his mission even began. This is because it describes him as being upon guidance and bidding others to piety and that he would pray even if he had not yet been instructed in the particular rulings of prayer, or else why bother issuing rebukes and threats in these verses, if what is being discussed has not yet come to pass!?

It is obvious here that people's obstinacy towards the Prophet (s), and their persecution of him, before his mission began and after, was not directed to him personally but to what he represented. This is why the verse describes him as "a servant when he prays" rather than mentioning him by name. This is another mark of distinction bestowed by Allāh upon His beloved prophet (s), for He describes him as "a servant," in the indefinite, to show the gravity of this situation!

21. The outcome of worshipping

Allāh connects the fact that the Prophet (s) bade others to piety to his being upon guidance in the verse "Tell me, should he be upon guidance or bid to godwariness." It is clear that only those who adopt piety themselves are fit to bid others to it, for how can one person who is naked clothe another?

Here, we should pay attention to the fact that the verse makes the object of the Prophet's bidding something that is the outcome of worshipping, namely, Godwariness (*taqwā*), not worship itself. So, for example, the desired outcome of fasting is not the act of avoiding food and drink itself but the state of piety and being wary of Allāh that results from that. This is why Allāh says the goal of fasting is "so that you may be Godwary."[30] This should also be the goal of those people who call others towards Allāh—to bring about the result, not to simply mention the preliminaries to that result by themselves.

22. Rebels

Allāh intends to humiliate the rebels on the Day of Resurrection, so they will be brought back on the Day of Resurrection like dust, trampled underfoot until Allāh has finished account the rest of creation. This *sūrah* provides us with another form of humiliation for them, namely, to be grabbed by their forelocks, which is the hair at the front of the head, and pulled forcefully ("We shall seize him by the forelock."). So the wicked person will be put in the charge of the one who drives him forward in a state of utter abasement, and this will cause his head to be pulled low, while raising it would usually be a sign of pride and haughtiness. Note that these forelocks are described as "lying" and "sinful" which means that this verse specifically mentions lying before other sin because lying is the source of many evil things and it is one of the worst sins!

Therefore, when the believer who is dispossessed looks at this world and sees the heads of the rebels held high in this abode, which is one filled with spurious ranks, he should remember what will soon become of them, and this in turn should lend him a sense of dignity inwardly and degree of patience outwardly.

23. Warnings and glad tidings

Divine warnings and threats of punishment are essential for the success of the prophetic mission, as are glad tidings and promises of reward. Several styles of threat appear in this *sūrah* that are directed to the affluent rebels—for example, "Tell me...," "We shall seize him by the forelock," "We shall call the keepers of Hell." It is necessary to employ these threats to remove obstacles from the path of calling others towards Allāh, so those who lack resolve or

30. Sūrat al-Baqarah (2):183

decisiveness in calling towards Him are not following the path of the Prophet (s) who based his mission on both the elements of loyalty and disassociation (*tawallī wa tabarrī*), which are understood from:

- the two-part testimony of faith that consists of both a negation and an affirmation ("There is no god / except Allah").
- the concept of prohibition and command in Allāh's words "No indeed! Do not obey him, but prostrate and draw near!"

24. Facing the ranks of the people of falsehood

Throughout the ages, the faithless have been eager to gather together, whether in public or in private, to confront the faithful who placed their hopes in Allāh, in that they did not wait to form a band of people before confronting the faithless as the faithless do to confront them. But the Qurʾān derides these gatherings that will be thwarted in the hereafter, saying, "Then let him call out his gang." This derision functions as follows:

- They will be gathered together again in the fires of hell but under the power of an avenging tyrant.
- Then how will they confront the host of hell's keepers, the angels who are entrusted to watch over the hellfire, for then there will be no comparison between the gang of faithlessness and the host of faith.

Therefore, the believer must remember this outcome while they live in this world, to give themselves resolve and steadfastness in facing the ranks of the people of falsehood who are forever plotting and scheming, as we see even today.

25. The gangs and parties of the faithless

The gangs and parties of the faithless, as numerous and varied as they have been throughout the ages, are all cut from the same cloth. The gang assembled by Abū Lahab and Abū Jahl as a council for Makkah, at its core, resembled the leaders of faithlessness and error in every age. So the law that applies to those gangs, namely, that they will be wiped out and obliterated, will apply to every gang like them as well, for Allāh is the one who annihilates kings and causes others to succeed them.

The same is true of the verse "Perish the hands of Abu Lahab, and perish he!"[31] It shows that the forces of falsehood will fail in every age, whoever their leader is. Allāh uses a similar expression with regards to Pharaoh's destruction, "and Pharaoh's stratagems only led him into ruin."[32] The words 'perish' (*tabbat*) and 'ruin' (*tabāb*) both contain a single meaning that applies to two of the foremost disbelievers in history.

26. Prostration

It is said that prostration in the verse "but prostrate and draw near" refers to prayer (*ṣalāt*) because it stands in contrast to the forbiddance against praying, as an affront to this forbiddance and to show that he should pay no heed to it ("No indeed! Do not obey him, but prostrate and draw near!") But "prostration" here could also mean prostration (*sujūd*) itself, based on the fact that prostration is always a desired action, even outside of prayer, whether as prostration or in general, or the prostration upon reciting this *sūrah* that contains a verse of obligatory prostration.

Narrations stressing the importance of prostration overflow in abundance. They say that the closest a servant will ever be to the Lord is when they are in prostration. This verse links drawing near to the Lord ("...draw near!") to prostration ("...prostrate...") because it is one of the most important ways in which a person can seek nearness to the Lord.

---

31. Sūrat al-Masad (111):1

32. Sūrat Ghāfir (40):37

27. Taking recourse with Allāh

Taking recourse with Allāh is a characteristic of all the prophets when calling people towards Him because of the many difficulties they face in this path. This *sūrah* also bids that reading, which is a feature of calling towards Him, be initiated by invoking the name of the Lord, the Creator and the One who taught with the pen. Therefore, the call to Allāh must begin by turning towards Him, but Sūrat al-Sharḥ says that the call must end with turning towards Him as well ("So when you are done, toil and turn eagerly to your Lord."[33]). So turning eagerly towards Him, and putting oneself to toil in His worship, is something necessary before, during, and after calling others towards Him. This is the secret behind the success of the Prophet Muḥammad's (s) mission and that of those members of his household who followed him right down to the present day.

28. Affirmations of this *sūrah*

One of the distinguishing features of this *sūrah,* which was the first to be sent down to the Prophet (s), is that it affirms:

- a doctrinal reality in that it affirms Allāh's lordship over the universe after His creating it, paying attention to the logical corollaries of this, namely, obedience and submission to Him.
- an educational reality as embodied in the call for the human being to acquire knowledge and learning, whether from the pen or directly from Allāh, such as His exclusive knowledge (*ʿilm ladinī*).
- a moral reality embodied by sensing Allāh's immanent presence throughout existence, namely, that He sees everything, good or evil, that comes from a person.
- a practical reality embodied by the command to pray, specifically to prostrate, as the most important branch of the religion.

33. Sūrat al-Sharḥ (94):7–8

Sūrat al-Qadr (no. 97: The Ordainment)

Verses 1–3

In the name of Allāh, the All-Beneficent, the All-Merciful

97:1 *Indeed We sent it down on the Night of Ordainment!*

97:2 *And what will show you what is the Night of Ordainment?*

97:3 *The Night of Ordainment is better than a thousand months.*

1. Qurʾān's magnificence

This *sūrah* affirms the Qurʾān's magnificence in several forms:

- The Qurʾān is referred to [in the first verse] using the pronoun 'it' rather than by its name, as if what is being referred to is so self-evident that it need not be named.
- The time in which Allāh chose to send it down is one of the noblest times, embodied by the Night of Ordainment.
- In the same manner, Allāh chose the heart of His noblest creation as the receptacle into which He revealed it all at once, based on His saying, "Indeed We sent it down...."
- So just as the Qurʾānic revelation is honored by its chosen recipient, namely, the Final Prophet (s), so too is its chosen recipient honored by receiving the Qurʾān.
- Allāh refers to Himself using the plural "We" which signifies grandeur ("Indeed We have sent down..."[1] "Indeed We have given you abundance."[2]).

1. Sūrat al-Insān (76):23
2. Sūrat al-Kawthar (108):1

2. Importance of Night of Ordainment

There is a striking reality to be witnessed in this *sūrah* in that it begins by mentioning the revelation of the Qurʾān, and one would assume that the natural course would be to continue discussing it. Instead, however, the discussion turns abruptly to the Night of Ordainment. It is as if someone said, "I lodged an important guest in such-and-such a place." But then, instead of mentioning the importance of the guest, they begin describing the place in which the guest is lodged! If such words were uttered by a competent speaker, we would understand that their primary intent was to inform us of the importance of the place, as demonstrated by the fact that they chose to put such an important guest in it. This is what has happened in this *sūrah*. The *sūrah* wants to say, "One of the reasons why the Night of Ordainment is so important is because it was the time in which the Qurʾān was revealed."

3. Nighttime

It is no secret that the night has a special place above all other times. This is why the night was chosen for such blessed occasion rather than the day. For it is by night that Allāh turns towards His saints (*awliyāʾ*) to envelop them in the lights of His majesty. The Qurʾān swears an oath by daybreak (*fajr*) and another by late afternoon (*ʿaṣr*) just once, but it swears oaths by the night in seven places including: "By the night as it approaches,"[3] "By the night when it recedes!"[4] and "By the night when it departs!"[5] The qualities of the believers are mentioned in connection with the night, for example: "...And at dawns they would plead for forgiveness."[6] "And keep vigil for a part of the night...."[7] They "recite Allah's signs in the watches of the night"[8] "...and glorify Him the night long"[9] and "Stand vigil through the night, except a little."[10] Allāh set a tryst for Moses of

3. Sūrat al-Takwīr (81):17
4. Sūrat al-Muddaththir (74):33
5. Sūrat al-Fajr (89):4
6. Sūrat al-Dhāriyāt (51):18
7. Sūrat al-Isrāʾ (17):79
8. Sūrat Āle ʿImrān (3):113
9. Sūrat al-Insān (76):26
10. Sūrat al-Muzzammil (73):2

"forty nights"[11] just as He took His beloved, Muḥammad(s), to the heavens by night. All of these facts demonstrate that the night is a time uniquely suited to convey spiritual blessings therein.

4. World of the unseen

The Qurʾān usually uses the formula "And what will show you..." for metaphysical realities that are beyond the reach of man's physical senses, such as some phenomena on the Day of Resurrection, including the *saqar*,[12] the Day of Judgement (*yawm al-faṣl*),[13] the Day of Recompense (*yawm al-dīn*),[14] the crusher (*ḥuṭama*),[15] and the scorching fire (*nār ḥāmiya*).[16] Therefore, mentioning the Night of Ordainment in this manner shows that it too is connected to the world of the unseen, even though it actually occurs in the visible realm. This is because mankind can no more comprehend the reality of this night than they can comprehend the realities of the isthmus (*barzakh*) and the resurrection, which are hidden from their physical senses.

5. Magnificence of the Night of Ordainment

This *sūrah* demonstrates the Night of Ordainment's magnificence in a number of ways:

- It says that this night was the occasion on which the Qurʾān was sent down, and the night itself occurs in the best of months, namely the month of Ramaḍān.
- Laylat al-Qadr is referred to by name three times in this single *sūrah* rather than simply using a pronoun to refer to it.
- Allāh directly addresses the Final Prophet (s) with the words "And what will show you...?" meaning if you (the messenger) cannot fully grasp the importance of this night

11. Sūrat al-Baqarah (2):51
12. Sūrat al-Muddaththir (74):27
13. Sūrat al-Mursalāt (77):14
14. Sūrat al-Infiṭār (82):17
15. Sūrat al-Humazahh (104):5
16. Sūrat al-Qāriʿah (101):11

and its exalted stature, then how can the intellects of the ordinary people possibly hope to do so?

6. A thousand months

Allāh wished, in His abundant kindness, to compensate the final *umma* for the shortness of their lives and singled out some of its members for a magnificent kind of compensation. He gave them a single night that was worth more than a thousand months. It is narrated that when Allāh showed His messenger (s) the length of people's lives, the messenger saw that the lives of his *umma* were shorter [than those of people who had come before them], and he feared that they would not be able to accomplish the same good deeds as their predecessors. As a result, Allāh gave him the Night of Ordainment, which is better than a thousand months of these other nations! Note that the verse does not only say that this night is equal to a thousand months but rather that it surpasses them. Allāh says that this night is "better" (*khayr*) without telling us how much better it is! Instead, He mentions only the least amount of its value, which is a thousand months. This is similar to what the Prophet (s) said about the striking of ʿAlī (as) when the latter dueled with ʿAmr b. ʿAbdu Wadd: "ʿAlī's duel with ʿAmr b. ʿAbdu Wadd at the Battle of the Trench will have a reward better than all the deeds of my *umma* until the Day of Resurrection!"

7. *Qadr*

Here we must understand the word *qadr* [in Laylat al-Qadr] to mean:

- regard for someone, as in "They do not regard Allah with the regard due to Him..."[17]
- the ordainment of affairs, as in "Then you turned up as ordained, O Moses!"[18]

17. Sūrat al-Zumar (39):67
18. Sūrat Ṭa Ha (20):40

- narrowness in that the earth becomes crowded by the angels from the heavens, in the sense of "...and let he whose provision has been tightened..."[19]

So, in a general sense, all of the above meanings signify the greatness of this night, whether this is because of its own essence, because of the angels who descend to earth therein, or because of the ordainments set in motion during it. Of course, from all of this we can also understand the greatness and the nobility of the creator Himself who blesses us with such a gift in but a few hours of a single night of the year.

8. "A blessed night"

When Allāh calls the Night of Ordainment a "blessed night,"[20] this suggests that He sends down blessings for the spiritual lives of His servants on this night in the same manner as He grants physical life to dead lands when He says, "And We send down from the sky blessed water."[21] Someone who is not exposed to these abundant blessings and does not make use of them is truly a deprived person. Perhaps it is these divine blessings that grant all of Allāh's servants the energy to stay awake on that night, despite their lack of energy on others, even those in the holy month itself. Of course, blessings have different degrees for different people, so it is inconceivable that the blessing that the Imām of our Age (ajfs) receives would be given to anyone else. This means we should never be satisfied with the level of divine favor we have obtained in this blessed night and always be striving for more.

9. Receiving Qur᾿ān

One of the reasons that the Night of Ordainment has acquired this nobility is that Allāh, who decided to send down the Qur᾿ān gradually over the course of the prophetic mission, sent down the entirety of the Qur᾿ān's lofty spiritual truths to the heart of His own chosen prophet (s) in a single night. What an amazing heart

19. Sūrat al-Ṭalaq (65):7
20. Sūrat al-Dukhkhān (44):3
21. Sūrat Qāf (50):9

the Prophet (s) must have to endure receiving the Qurʾān in its totality all at once, when the revelation of just a single verse to him on other occasions was so taxing that the strain of it could sometimes be seen on his blessed face!

10. Spreading of a blessing

The nature of a genuine blessing is that it spreads to everything around it. Allāh says about His prophet, Jesus (as), "He has made me blessed, wherever I may be...."[22] About Moses (as), "Blessed is He who is in the fire and who is around it...."[23] The blessed month of Ramaḍān, in addition to those blessings it possesses as a month that belongs to Allāh, has been blessed further still by the Night of Ordainment. Because this night has become a part of it, this night's blessings extend throughout the entire holy month. Based on this, we can say that the Night of Ordainment's blessings also extend to the faithful themselves, meaning that anyone who is worthy will partake of this magnificent overflowing of the divine.

11. The superiority of the Night of Ordainment

The superiority of the Night of Ordainment compared to a thousand months could either be with regards to the deeds performed therein (as people usually say) or it could be with regards to the souls of the worshipers. The latter is actually more significant because it is the person performing these deeds who receives their blessings, not the deeds themselves! In other words, a person might get closer spiritually to truth and perfection on this night than they would have done in a thousand other months, even if they did their utmost. This is the perfect motivation for those worthy persons who are striving to perfect their souls and not just their deeds.

---

22. Sūrat Maryam (19):31
23. Sūrat al-Naml (27):8

12. Ordained affairs

The fact that all affairs are ordained in a single night (as we understand from another verse, namely, "Every definitive matter is resolved in it"[24]) can be a source of confusion for one of God's servants who wants to secure their wellbeing in religious and worldly matters. But this confusion, in turn, serves to whet one's appetite to strive for the best ordainments for oneself before the ink of destiny dries at the time of *fajr*, especially in those last moments before the end of the greatest Night of Ordainment. Hence, with regards to divine ordainments, we say that even if they emanate from the unseen, the servant still has a role to play in shaping and changing them to safeguard their moral and material success. This rule applies to any area in which the Qurʾān uses the words "whomsoever He wills," as He could mean that the one who determines this is the servant, as when He says, "Allah guides to His Light whomever He wishes."[25]

13. Increased reward

When we consider that the reward for good deeds is increased on the Night of Ordainment, it leads us to ponder: How can we reconcile this verse with the fact that the reward (*ajr*) of a good deed depends on the difficulty (*mashaqqa*) involved in performing it? How can the worship of a single night compare to the worship of a thousand months? The answer to this question is the same answer we give when explaining the great blessings that come from any little thing that becomes attached to Allāh—Moses' ark (*tābūt*), Joseph's shirt, the stone of the Kaʿba, and the blessed month of Ramaḍān, to name just a few! When an object or an action becomes attached to Allāh, its very essence changes, and when we realize that Allāh, the One who endows things with their qualities, bestowed this wondrous quality on a single night of the year out of His grace, then it is hardly surprising that it carries such rewards, for He does as He wills.

---

24. Sūrat al-Dukhkhān (44):4
25. Sūrat al-Nūr (24):35

14. Crucial for all existent beings

The Night of Ordainment is not only crucial for mankind but for all existent beings, as it is said that Allāh ordains everything that will happen in the coming year on that night, including rains, sustenance, life, and death. Therefore, the ordainment that takes place on this night affects events in creation as the divine ordainment (*qadr ilāhī*) encompasses everything that Allāh has created. This is demonstrated by His saying, "Indeed We have created everything in an ordained measure."[26] Therefore, one can say that whoever supplicates earnestly in this night, their supplication might have an effect on worldly events such as earthquakes and other natural disasters, not to mention the lives of other creatures, such as their believing brethren and even non-Muslims!

15. Hidden things

Allāh could have, had He willed it, been kind to us, told us which night was the Night of Ordainment, and spared us this confusion every year! Instead, He chose to hide it by virtue of His perfect wisdom, as a motivation for His servants to strive hard for many nights with their hearts caught between the fear of missing it and the hope of attaining it. This way, the one who attains it will not suffer smugness or pride any more than the one who misses it will suffer dejection and despair. Moreover, by keeping it hidden, He adds to its nobility. After all, something truly precious is rarely left in plain sight so that anyone could come and take it! Therefore, we should always remember that there is wisdom behind Allāh's decisions to hiding this and other things:

- He hides His satisfaction with our acts of obedience so that we continue to seek it in all our righteous deeds.
- He hides His anger with our sins so that we will avoid all lapses.

26. Sūrat al-Qamar (54):49

- He hides His representative (*walī*) amongst the people so that we will show respect to all of His servants.
- He hides His answer to our prayers so that we strive harder in all our supplications.
- He hides His greatest name (*al-ism al-aʿzam*) so that we will venerate all of His names.
- He hides the identity of the middle prayer (*al-ṣalāt alwusṭā*) so that we will focus on all of our prayers.
- He hides His acceptance of our repentance so that we will seek His forgiveness through all kinds of repentance.
- He hides our time of death so that we will always be wary of a sudden, unexpected death.

Verses 4–5

97:4 *In it angels and spirit descend, by the leave of their lord, with every command.*

97:5 *It is peaceful until the rising of the dawn.*

16. Angels descending

The apparent meaning of His words "The angels...descend" is that all of the angels in existence descend as this is the implication of using a plural with the definite article (*al-malāʾika*). As a result, some commentators on the Qurʾān have wondered how this great host of angels can possibly gather together on earth in a single night. There are those that say that they do not descend to earth but remain in the heaven of this world. Others say that they come down to the earth in successive waves, so it can still be said that they all come down in a single night. What is clear, however, is that being aware of this massing of angels will amaze God's servant and motivate him to try his utmost to be the best worshiper on this night so that he can win peace from this vast host by virtue of their supplications for him.

17. The Spirit

Mentioning the Spirit (rūḥ) alongside the angels suggests that there is a hierarchy that permeates the entirety of creation. Just as Allāh has favored some messengers over others, He has made some inhabitants of the throne superior to others. Hence He has made the Spirit an entity separate from the rest of the angels. This is a source of disagreement amongst commentators.

- Some say that it is a great angel without any other like it.
- Others say that it is a special group of angels who only descend on the Night of Ordainment.
- Some say that it is Gabriel about whom Allāh says, "the Holy Spirit has brought it down duly from your Lord...."[27]
- Others say that it refers to Jesus (as) about whom Allāh says, "The Messiah, Jesus son of Mary, was only an Messenger of Allah, and His Word that He cast toward Mary and a spirit from Him."[28] He comes down to oversee the deeds of the *umma* of the final messenger (s) and to see the great worship being performed by his followers. At the head of this great worship is the worship of the Final Successor (ajfs).

18. *Wilāya*

There is a strong connection between this *sūrah* and the principle of *wilāya*. The Night of Ordainment occurs, without fail, in all eras, and the angels descend in it with divine ordainments as a result. Now, we know for every angel that descends there must be a person to whom it descends. But who could this be besides the one without whom the earth would have been swallowed up with its inhabitants? The Night of Ordainment corresponds symbolically to the existence of an infallible *imām* in every age, and, hence, we can say that this *sūrah* is one of the *sūrahs* of *wilāya*. At its core, it subtly turns the *umma's* attention to the other weighty thing (*thaqal*) that the Prophet (s) left behind alongside the Qur'ān.

---

27. Sūrat al-Naḥl (16):102
28. Sūrat al-Nisā' (4):171

19. Divine permission

Even though the descent of the angels to earth is something very normal, it still requires divine permission. This is the nature of the angels who do not even venture to speak ahead of Him ("They do not venture to speak ahead of Him, and they act by His command."[29]). This verse contains some indication that the angels act as though they ardently desire to visit the righteous members of this *umma*, at whose head is the Imām of the Age (ajfs), just as they desire to visit them in paradise saying, "'Peace be to you, for your patience.' How excellent is the reward of the [ultimate] abode!"[30] It is only natural that one who goes to visit someone experiences some desire to meet the object of his visitation (*ziyāra*), even if that is by virtue of a divine command that he cannot disobey.

20. Honor of the Night of Ordainment

All of the fundamental elements of the Night of Ordainment are connected to Allāh in some way, shape, or form: It falls in the month of Allāh, and the one who sent down the book in it is Allāh, and it was sent to Allāh's messenger in the hands of one of Allāh's angels to guide Allāh's servants. So the elements of this night are all dyed in the colors of the divine. This this is why it has been singled out and honored above all other nights.

21. The word 'with'

It is part of the Qur'ān's greatness that its words, or even its letters, can carry multiple distinct meanings. For example, scholars have differed in their interpretations of the word 'with' (*min*) in His saying "with every command." It is said:

- that it implies concomitance (*mulābisa*) as it explains what it is that descends in that night with the angels.
- that it implies causation (*sababiyya*) meaning that this descent is the cause for every divine command in this world

29. Sūrat al-Anbiyā' (21):27
30. Sūrat al-Ra'd (13):24

as indicated by His saying "All His command, when He wills something, is to say to it 'Be,' and it is."[31]

- that it implies motivation (*taʿlīl*) meaning that it happened in order to arrange every future affair in creation.

22. Peace

There are two directions from which one of God's servants loses peace and well-being in his life. The first is the commanding self (*al-nafs al-ammāra*), and the other is Satan, the accursed outcast, and it is known that their role is circumscribed in the Night of Ordainment:

- All the devils are chained up in the holy month, especially on the Night of Ordainment so there is no room for Satan to exercise his authority while the authority of the angels permeates the heavens completely on that night.
- As for the self, it has been tamed by fasting for the duration of the month and especially for the Night of Ordainment. This special night is surrounded by a halo of divine sanctity of which all creatures are aware in their own selves. This is why this night is peace until the rising of the dawn.

23. Peace

The peace (*salām*) on the Night of Ordainment could be with regards to:

- the night itself—it is described as peace insofar as it provides safety from those harmful things that obstruct the acceptance of good deeds. And [when we say "It is peace" rather than "it is peaceful"] we must bear in mind that this is a kind of emphasis, as when we say, "So-and-so is justice (*ʿadl*)" by which we emphasize that he is just (*ʿādil*).
- the greetings of peace given by the angels to one another or to the faithful, or that they come and invoke peace upon the

31. Sūrat Yā Sīn (36):82

Prophet (s) and his infallible successor. It is narrated from ʿAlī (as), "They descend to give greetings of peace to us and to intercede on our behalf, for whoever receives [such] a greeting of peace shall have all his sins forgiven."

Sūrat al-Bayyinah (no. 98: The Manifest Proof)

Verses 1–5

98:1 *The faithless from among the People of the Book and the polytheists were not set apart until the manifest proof had come to them*

98:2 *an Messenger from Allah reciting impeccable scriptures,*

98:3 *wherein are upright writings.*

98:4 *And those who were given the Book did not divide, except after the manifest proof had come to them.*

98:5 *Yet they were not commanded except to worship Allah, dedicating their faith to Him as men of pure faith, and to maintain the prayer and pay the zakat. That is the upright religion.*

1. The word for 'from among'

The word for 'from among' (*min*) in the verse "The faithless from among the People of the Book and the polytheists were not set apart until the manifest proof had come to them" could mean:

- distinction (*tabyīn*)—meaning distinguishing the group of the faithless, in which case the verse is referring to their condition before the prophetic mission. They were all faithless, whether they accepted a divine scripture outwardly while it had really been distorted or they did not accept any scripture, like the idol- worshipers.
- division (*tabʿīḍ*)—in which case the verse is referring to their condition after the prophetic mission had begun, in which case the verse is rebuking that group of them that persisted in their faithlessness and error.

2. "People of the Book"

Those people who have received a divine scripture are referred to in various ways. So sometimes they are "People of the Book" (*ahl al-kitāb*), and sometimes they are "Those who were given the Book." The difference between these two expressions is as follows:

- "People of the Book" means the followers of divine religions, hence they are mentioned separately from polytheists who are idol worshipers.
- Whereas "Those who were given the Book" refers to those to whom the book has been sent down, meaning that the address is directed to them as in Allāh's saying "Mankind were a single community; then Allah sent the prophets as bearers of good news and as warners, and He sent down with them the Book with the truth, that it may judge between the people concerning that about which they differed, and none differed in it except those who had been given it, after the manifest proofs had come to them, out of envy among themselves."[1] The discussion in this verse is actually about everyone to whom messengers were sent.

But whoever the people, when they reject divine guidance, the outcome is one and the same—they differ about guidance, whether this disagreement is:

- within a single divine religion as in Allāh's words "When Jesus brought the manifest proofs, he said, 'I have certainly brought you wisdom, and [I have come] to make clear to you some of the things that you differ about. So be wary of Allah and obey me. Indeed Allah is my Lord and your Lord; so worship Him. This is a straight path.' But the factions differed among themselves. So woe to the wrongdoers for the punishment of a painful day."[2] or
- not within a single religion as in "Had Allah wished, those who succeeded them would not have fought each other after

1. Sūrat al-Baqarah (2):213
2. Sūrat al-Zukhruf (43):63–65

the manifest proofs had come to them. But they differed. So there were among them those who had faith and there were among them those who were faithless...."[3]

3. The word for 'set apart'

One of the areas in which there is a great deal of disagreement between commentators is the first verse of this *sūrah,* to the extent that it is considered one of the hardest verses of the Qur'ān in its arrangement and explanation! So anyone who ponders the Qur'ān must have a certain level of intelligence and discernment to solve its puzzles.

The word for 'set apart' (*munfakkīn*) is the source of this ambiguity. This is firstly because the verse does not mention what they were set apart from. If we say from faithlessness (*kufr*), which is the apparent meaning, then the verse means that they will be set apart from their faithlessness after clear proofs come to them, but the fact is that they remained faithless even after this. In fact, they increased in obstinacy and opposition to the prophetic mission as Allāh says in the following verse: "And those who were given the Book did not divide, except after the proof had come to them." So two other answers are offered:

- First, what it means is that they were not set apart from the general principle that applies to all nations as expounded in Allāh's words "Allah does not lead any people astray after He has guided them until He has made clear to them what they should beware of."[4] and "We do not punish until We have sent an Messenger."[5] In this context, the clear proof in this verse is the sending of a messenger, which is mentioned in the following one. So by sending a "clear proof," they have been left without any excuse. But even after this, they continue to differ, with some accepting it and some rejecting it ("And when there came to them a Book from Allah, confirming that which is with them - and earlier they would pray for

3. Sūrat al-Baqarah (2):253
4. Sūrat al-al-Tawbah (9):115
5. Sūrat al-Isrā' (17):15

victory over the pagans - so when there came to them what they recognized, they defied it. So may the curse of Allah be on the faithless!"[6]).

- Second, they claimed that they would not turn aside from what they were following without a clear proof coming to them that would set them onto a new path. But after this clear proof came to them, they did not believe as promised. In other words, after "the manifest proof had come to them" and after they had made their belief conditional upon it coming ("until the manifest proof had come to them"), they did not keep their promise to follow this manifest proof, rather they fled from it.

4. Traits of Prophet Muḥammad (s)

When the discussion turns to the subject of the Prophet (s), it is a discussion about someone who bears two traits:

- First, he is the bearer of the clear and "manifest proof" which is necessary for them to be left without excuse, so all of his words and deeds occurred in this context.
- Second, he recited "impeccable scriptures" which no falsehood, whether in the form of distortions by men or the corruption of devils, could reach and which contained teachings prescribed for Allāh's servants such as His words "Prescribed for you is fasting as it was prescribed for those who were before you,"[7] "Warfare has been prescribed for you,"[8] "Prescribed for you, when death approaches any of you and he leaves behind any property,"[9] and "Retribution is prescribed for you regarding the slain"[10] and that looks after their wellbeing in the best and most holistic manner possible (as we understand from the use of the *tā'* of

6. Sūrat al-Baqarah (2):89
7. Sūrat al-Baqarah (2):183
8. Sūrat al-Baqarah (2):216
9. Sūrat al-Baqarah (2):180
10. Sūrat al-Baqarah (2):178

hyperbole in "upright writings" (*kutubun qayyima-t-un*)) just as a guarding looks after the affairs of an orphan.

5. Avoiding mention

The verse avoids mentioning the People of the Book as Jews and Christians, instead referring to them with the description of having been given the book, to increase their culpability, so that they would have no excuse after Allāh's proof was completed through their uncorrupted divine scriptures, all of which promise a prophet of the end times ("...and to give the good news of a Messenger who will come after me, whose name is Ahmad."[11]).

Here, we cannot help but notice the greatness of the Prophet (s) revealed to us in these verses as they show that whoever does not believe in him (s) is counted amongst those who do not believe in Allāh at all or who associate partners with Him. Their destination altogether shall be hellfire ("Indeed the faithless from among the People of the Book and the polytheists will be in the fire of hell.").

This is also the reason why the name of the Prophet (s) is not mentioned explicitly. Instead, he is described as a messenger ("an apostle from Allah"). This also aggrandizes him, just as describing others as having been given the book increases their culpability.

6. Not mentioning polytheists

One could ask why the polytheists are not mentioned alongside "those who were given the book" in the fourth verse of this *sūrah,* while they are mentioned at its beginning. A possible explanation of this is that, in the fourth verse, the discussion is about dividing into different parties and sects (which is only conceivable for a people of learning, religion, and literature, even if this is, at its core, false) whereas the polytheists have not reached a level where they can divide into various groups and tendencies because of the simplicity of their beliefs or, in fact, the foolishness thereof. After all, we cannot speak of them being divided on something that has no stability in the first place!

11. Sūrat al-Ṣaff (61):6

7. Worshipping Allāh

There is a difference between those who worship Allāh seeking paradise or fearing hell and those who worship Allāh out of dedication to Him, seeking His satisfaction in spite of their knowledge that their reward with their Lord shall be "Their reward, near their Lord, is the Gardens of Eden, with streams running in them." The similitude of this is someone who washes themselves for Allāh, even though they are aware that the effect of this is to remove dirt from the body. So just because someone knows the effect of their actions, this does not contradict their deeds being solely dedicated to Allāh. It is only if they perform these actions seeking such effects that a contradiction arises. But few people attain this level whose occupants Allāh describes as "dedicating" (*mukhliṣīn*) in their faith. He refers to them with an adjective rather than a verb (e.g., "who dedicate...") [to indicate their steadfastness in this level].

8. Monasticism

All of the revealed religions share a single spirit, represented, after believing in Allāh and the prophet He has sent in any given age, by worship described with two qualifications:

- Dedication ("dedicating their faith to Him") for whatever is done for anyone besides Allāh is not truly worship, even if it is mixed with proper worship in its outward form.
- Avoiding the extremes of excess and deficiency (*ifrāṭ wa tafrīṭ*). This is the meaning of "people of pure faith" (*ḥunafā'*) or at least one of its implications if we interpret it to mean "uprightness." So Christian monastics have forsaken this balance for the sake of presumptuous worship for their own sake, neglecting their duties towards others, such as confronting the oppressors and serving the needy.

It is fitting to mention here a tradition from the Prophet (s) that forbids this kind of monasticism: "For every nation there is a monasticism; the monasticism of my nation is in congregational and Friday prayers, and instructing one another in the teachings of the religion."[12]

9. Prayer and charity

There is no doubt that the particular teachings of one religion differ from those of another, but according to the Qur'ān, what is shared between them is prayer (*ṣalāt*) and charity (*zakāh*). Allāh says, "and to maintain the prayer and pay the zakat" and "He has enjoined me to prayer and to zakat as long as I live."[13] Of course, there are differences between the different religions in the particular elements of these acts of worship.

But perhaps the reason for these shared features is that prayer governs the relationship between a servant and the Lord while charity governs the relationship between a servant and His creation. Prayer encompasses an inner struggle to turn one's heart towards Allāh while charity contains an outward struggle to remove one's attachments to wealth. Both of them involve relying on Him alone in everything He has commanded so that the servant becomes like a level road leading to the Lord that is easy to travel upon. The sum of these religions' contents fall under the rubric of Allāh's words "the upright religion" whether this means:

- the religion of upright books—alluding to all the revealed scriptures.
- specifically the religion of the Final Prophet (s) because its teachings look after the wellbeing of Allāh's servants.
- a religion of upright values as it contains lofty teachings.

10. Final message

The spirit of the verses that appear in this *sūrah* testifies to the universality of the Islamic mission and indicates that even if earlier religions were authoritative for their people before the advent of

---

12. *Biḥār al-anwār* 67/115
13. Sūrat Maryam (19):31

Islām, now that the Final Prophet (s) has been sent with Allāh's final message, there is no need for any other religion except Islām.

Hence we should not flaunt any religious or humanitarian project that falls outside the framework of the pure religion of Islām. Allāh says, "Indeed, with Allah religion is Islam..."[14] and the acceptance of good deeds depends on a person's piety (*taqwā*). There is no meaning to piety if the activities in question are not done in accordance with Allāh's desire, even if the act in of itself is a virtuous one.

11. Ignorance

We must adopt Allāh's manners mentioned in this *sūrah,* namely, that He does not chastise anyone without good reason. So, first of all, we should not chastise someone who is ignorant, unless of course they are willfully ignorant, in which case we are relieving them of their ignorance.

We learn this from the fact that Allāh does not punish His servants except after providing them with clear and irrefutable proof from impeccable scriptures sent down with valuable teachings, whether this means teachings that look after the well-being of Allāh's servants or teachings that are upright and without crookedness, unlike manmade laws and ways of living, many of which are contrary to healthy human nature (*fiṭra*) and also neglect essential human needs!

Verses 6–8

98:6 *Indeed the faithless from among the People of the Book and the polytheists will be in the fire of hell, to remain in it [forever]. It is they who are the worst of creatures.*

98:7 *Indeed those who have faith and do righteous deeds—it is they who are the best of creatures.*

---

14. Sūrat Āle ʿImrān (3):19

98:8 *Their reward, near their Lord, is the Gardens of Eden, with streams running in them, to remain in them forever. Allah is pleased with them, and they are pleased with Him. That is for those who fear their Lord.*

12. Punishment and reward

In this *sūrah,* Allāh places the threat of punishment (*waʿīd*) before His promise of reward (*waʿd*), mentioning the recompense of "the worst of creatures" then following them with the recompense of "the best of creatures." Perhaps the reason for this is that the flow of the first verses of the *sūrah* concerned the false beliefs of the People of the Book and the polytheists, meaning that when it came to the matter of recompense, it was more appropriate to begin with that connected to the beginning of the *sūrah.* There is also the fact that the relation of the threat of punishment to the promise of reward is like that of medicine to food—one must dissuade a person from harmful things before directing them to that which benefits them.

13. Best and worst of creatures

A person who combines, through the school of the prophets, faith with righteous deeds becomes someone about whom it can be truly said they are amongst the best creations Allāh has placed on the face of His earth, based on the fact that the term 'creatures' (*bariyya*) includes every creation, even the angels, because they too have been created by Allāh. From the scriptures we understand that some creatures are better than angels as Allāh has revealed by commanding them to prostrate before Adam, who had not yet been sent with any message. That was because of the capacity he had to move towards perfection and ascend to a level above even that of the angels!

We can also treat the verse referring to the best and worst of creatures as an allusion to the two arcs of ascent and descent in creation, which we have already seen in Sūrat al-Tīn ("We certainly created man in the best of forms. Then We relegated him to the lowest of the low."[15]).

14. The word 'near'

It should be clear that the word 'near' (*ʿind*) in the phrase "near their Lord" suggests kindness (*luṭf*) because "the best of creatures" are those who placed their desires solely in He who possesses anything like this kind of recompense. They did not care about the fleeting rewards of others! We can also understand this to mean that their recompense is like a deposit with someone trustworthy, a deposit that will be returned to them at a time when its owner will need it most!

This sense of the reward's "nearness" with Allāh should place the believer's mind at ease and not make them hasty to see the fruits of their labor in this world, even in the form of some kind of spiritual attainment, because knowledge that their fruits are stowed for them with the Lord should avail them of any need for any immediate advantage.

15. Eternal paradise

Some of the most important constituents of paradise are its attributes, embodied in "Eden" which signifies permanence and stability ("remaining in them forever" which signifies everlasting life therein). There are other verses that confirm this fact, namely, "nor will they be expelled from it"[16] and "from where they will not seek to shift."[17] In fact, it has even been said that eternal life is better still than paradise. The Prophet (s) has been narrated to say, "Verily eternal life (*khulūd*) in Paradise is even better than Paradise... and Allāh's pleasure is even better than Paradise!"[18] That is because were it not for this eternal life, people could not fully enjoy paradise as this enjoyment would be tainted by the

15. Sūrat al-Tīn (95):4–5
16. Sūrat al-Ḥijr (15):48
17. Sūrat al-Kahf (18):108
18. *Mafātīḥ al-ghayb* (32):252

pain of knowing this would one day come to an end, and there is nothing that can possibly replace its magnificent pleasure!

16. Body and spirit

Just as a person is created from both a body and spirit, and each of these have a share in this world, each of these also have a share in the hereafter. The body's share of the hereafter is the paradise described in this *sūrah* and others as containing various kinds of sensory bliss—maidens and palaces. As for the spirit's share, it is Allāh's satisfaction ("Allah is pleased with them and they are pleased with Him"). This is embodied in the paradise of nearness to the divine.

It is interesting that Allāh does not mention the attribute of lordship when He mentions His satisfaction with them being "the best of creatures" but rather mentions the majestic name ("Allah") which is considered to be the greatest of all the divine names in signification of awe and majesty. It is the name that signifies the divine essence and the divine attributes in their entirety, namely, the attributes of both majesty and generosity.

17. Contented soul

The utmost perfection is represented by attaining the level at which the servant becomes pleased with the Lord and also the servant becomes pleasing to the Lord. This is the level of the contented soul (*al-nafs al-mutmaʾinna*) that Allāh refers to in His words "O soul at peace! Return to your Lord, pleased, pleasing! Then enter among My servants! And enter My paradise!" This verse also mentions "For those who fear their Lord" which shows that the way to attaining Allāh's pleasure is reciprocated between the servant and the Lord, namely, the servant fears the Lord with a fear joined to magnification as Allāh says of the angels, "...and they are apprehensive for the fear of Him."[19] An identical expression appears for the faithful servants elsewhere: "Indeed

19. Sūrat al-Anbiyāʾ (21):28

those who are apprehensive for the fear of their Lord"[20] and this fear springs from their knowledge as Allāh says, "Only those of Allah's servants having knowledge fear Him."[21] For it is the sense of Allāh's magnificence and the fact He is watching everything that dissuades people from misdeeds and serves to motivate them to every good act.

It should be known that this state of divine pleasure is the greatest bliss in paradise. It is, in fact, its nectar, and it is a separate recompense in its own right compared to the gardens of paradise. We know this because it is mentioned separately from them in the verse "with streams running in them, to remain in them forever. Allāh is pleased with them, and they are pleased with Him." Obviously, anyone who possesses this trait in this world is already blessed in this world with the most precious treasures of paradise—even if it takes on a lower form here.

18. Lordship

When the Qur'ān attributes fear to those with knowledge (*al-ʿulamāʾ*) in the verse "Only those of Allah's servants having knowledge fear Him,"[22] it uses the majestic name, "Allah," which signifies the level of the divine essence in all of its perfection and beauty. This is appropriate for the rank of that knowledge by which is grasped the features and levels of lordship. But when the Qur'ān attributes fear to the faithful in general ("those who have faith and do righteous deeds") as in this *sūrah,* it refers to Him as their Lord ("That is for those who fear their Lord."). This is because it is His lordship, unmatched and sovereign, that has a role in conveying them to "the Gardens of Eden, with streams running in them" and hence their fear of Allāh is connected to the level of His lordship.

20. Sūrat al-Mu'minūn (23):57

21. Sūrat Fāṭir (35):28

22. Sūrat Fāṭir (35):28

Sūrat al-Zalzalah (no. 99: The Quaking)

Verses 1–5

In the name of Allāh, the All-Beneficent, the All-Merciful

99:1 *When the earth is rocked with its terrible quake*

99:2 *and the earth discharges her burdens,*

99:3 *and man says, 'What is the matter with her?'*

99:4 *On that day she will relate her chronicles*

99:5 *for her Lord will have inspired her.*

1. Resurrection and its terrifying events

One of the distinguishing features of the Qurʾān is its focus on the resurrection and the terrifying events it contains. This is because its goal is to motivate a person to do righteous deeds, and so it shows us the connection between our deeds in this world and their outcomes in the next. It is within this context that we must understand this *sūrah* as it begins by mentioning the resurrection and its terrors, then closes by mentioning the physical manifestation of a person's deeds in that new creation so that a person will be on guard at the beginning of their journey, lest they be surprised by its outcomes.

The ultimate goal of this *sūrah* is to motivate a person to strive continuously—not to think of any good deed as too small, even if it is an atom's weight, for perhaps it is that deed that will save them, nor to underestimate any wicked deed, for perhaps it is that deed that will destroy them as it might be just enough tip the scales against him, as can happen in weights and scales.

2. Resurrection

An earthquake, as anyone will tell you, is one of the most destructive and terrifying natural disasters and one that can last a mere matter of seconds. This is why the Qurʾān specifically invokes this phenomenon to expound what will happen on the Day of Resurrection as the first event of people coming out of their graves ("as if they were scattered locusts"[1] and "like scattered moths"[2])!

But this earthquake is called "its terrible quake" which tells us that it is a special quaking of the earth that Allāh has reserved for that day—one that is not confined to any particular spot or locale like the earthquakes of this world. Rather this quake is attributed to the earth as a whole and, as such, is an even more powerful description of the terror and shock of that day!

3. The word 'burdens'

Whatever the depths of the earth contain, whether bodies, treasures, or more still (depending on the different interpretations of the word 'burdens'), all of these are nothing more than burdens in the depths of the earth no matter whether they are silent treasures or bodies that were a means of dominating this earth in days gone by. What a relief it is for any bearer of burdens to set down their load or to unpack it as Allāh says, "and the earth discharges her burdens"!

It should be clear from this expression that the resurrection is a physical affair—it does not only apply to people's souls, as some have suggested.

4. Shock

Some commentators have said that the amazement expressed in Allāh's words "And man says, 'What is the matter with her?'" is only for people who are not believers, similar to the verse "Who raised us from our place of sleep?"[3] In fact, the events of that day

1. Sūrat al-Qamar (54):7
2. Sūrat al-Qāriʿah (101):4
3. Sūrat Yā Sīn (36):52

will shock everyone, believers and disbelievers alike, who emerge suddenly from their graves in the place of mustering with all the terrors it contains. This is why Allāh says "man" (*al-insān*) asks about the quaking of the earth.

But this in no way precludes some of the elect being spared this shock altogether or at least in some stages of the resurrection, as Allāh says of them, "and they shall be secure from terror on that day."[4]

5. "Chronicles"

The verse "On that day she will relate her chronicles" has been interpreted in a number of ways. Some say that this is conveyed by her state (*bi lisān al-ḥāl*). Others say that a voice will be created for her, and others still say that she will speak as a living creature, which is the apparent meaning of this verse and supported by other verses too, for example, "There is not a thing but celebrates His praise, but you do not understand their glorification."[5] and "They will say, 'We were given speech by Allah, who gave speech to all things....'"[6]

Of course, whichever interpretation you choose, the earth bearing witness is like nothing else—one cannot imagine the earth seeking benefit or avoiding harm for its own self as can sometimes happen when testimony is given in this world. Add to this the fact that the earth's testimony follows that of the One whose knowledge encompasses everything. But here we should wonder that if the earth can be divinely inspired and receive revelation to the level that it can describe events in detail, then what can human beings do should Allāh desire it?

6. Praying in different spots

The words "she will relate her chronicles" suggests that she will relate these accounts in detail, not merely testify to them in a

4. Sūrat al-Naml (27):89
5. Sūrat al-Isrā' (17):44
6. Sūrat Fuṣṣilat (41):21

general sense. So the earth will not testify to the mere fact that a worshiper offered prayers upon her surface but rather how many times, where and how! This is why we are bid to pray in a number of places. It has been narrated from Imām ʿAlī (as), "Pray in different spots in mosques, because every spot will testify in favour of the one who worships upon her on the Day of Resurrection."[7] It is narrated that when he finished allotting funds from the treasury, he would offer two rakʿats of prayer and say, "Bear witness that I filled you rightfully, and I emptied you rightfully!"[8] It is also narrated that the Prophet (s) one day recited the verse "On that day she will relate her chronicles" and said, "Do you know what are her chronicles?" The people replied, "Allah and His Messenger know best!" He said, "Her chronicles are that the earth shall testify what each servant and nation wrought upon her surface. She will say, 'My Lord! They did such-and-such on this day and that!'"[9]

Taken together, these traditions should give cause for sinners to feel ashamed on the Day of Resurrection because something that they thought was inanimate has become a witness against the one who was supposed to be Allāh's deputy upon the earth.

Verses 6–8

99:6 *On that day, mankind will issue forth in various groups to be shown their deeds.*

99:7 *So whoever does an atom's weight of good will see it,*

99:8 *and whoever does an atom's weight of evil will see it.*

7. Issue forth in various groups

The fact that mankind will issue forth in various groups on the Day of Judgement follows from what another verse says: "your endeavours are indeed unalike."[10] Obviously the separation of mankind of the Day of Judgement does not mean that they are all

7. *Wasāʾil al-Shīʿa* 5/188
8. *Laʾālī al-akhbār* 5/79
9. *Majmaʿ al-bayān* 10/798
10. Sūrat al-Layl (92):4

in the same condition because it is clearly stated that "The day We shall summon every group of people with their imam..."[11] so there is nothing that precludes them from emerging in different groups but under different banners according to what they followed in the life of this world. If someone followed a rock, Allāh will resurrect them with it.

It should be noted that the verb "issue forth" (*yaṣdur*) contains a subtle point. It is normally used to refer to the departure of a camel from water having approached it. This is as if to say that in this world, it was as though mankind were at an oasis but now they have left it behind to suggest that whoever drank from that oasis is one of those who remained thirsty beside it. This is supported by the words narrated from the Commander of the Faithful (as): "O people! Today there are deeds with no accounting, but tomorrow there shall be accounting with no deeds."[12]

8. Expounding a consequent

When a conditional sentence is used in exposition, it serves to expound the consequent (*jawāb al-sharṭ*) and emphasize it in some circumstances, in which case its import is that of an oath. Of course, both the consequent and an oath can sometimes be left implicit in order to encourage people to reflect and search for their meaning because of the special concern the speaker has for the place of oaths and conditionals. This is something we can see in this *sūrah* of the Qur'ān as well.

So there are those who say that the consequent of the sentence "When the earth is rocked..." is left implicit, but the context alludes to it such as "When the imminent event befalls."[13] But also there are others who say that its consequent is "On that day, mankind will issue forth in various groups...." Others still say it is "On that day she will relate her chronicles...."

---

11. Sūrat al-Isrā' (17):71

12. *Al-Kāfī* 8/58

13. Sūrat al-Wāqi'ah (56):1

9. The comprehensive verse

The verses "So whoever does a mote's weight of good will see it, and whoever does a mote's weight of evil will see it" contain a form of warning and deterrence that is clear to anyone who reflects on them. It has been narrated from the Prophet (s) that this verse is referred to as the "comprehensive verse" because:

- it refers to every person endowed with moral agency, even the prophets, because its subject is the pronoun 'whoever' which applies to everybody.
- it makes the subject of a person's deeds something of the utmost precision, namely the dust mote (*dharra*) which can be seen in bright sunlight, and this word is also used for tiny ants as well.
- this precision is applied to both good and evil together. Allāh's generosity and clemency do not run contrary to this precision. This is to ensure that brazen persons do not dare to sin.
- the outcome, namely, seeing one's deeds, either refers to their essence, on the basis of one's deeds taking on a physical reality, or their reward. Allāh says "seeing" rather than "knowing" in this verse just as He says "finding" rather than "knowing" in His words "The day when every soul will find present whatever good it has done...."[14]

10. The recompense fitting the deed

There is no contradiction between this verse which speaks of the recompense fitting the deed (even if it weighs no more than a mote of dust) and those verses which indicate that deeds will fail in the sense of good deeds being effaced ("If you ascribe a partner to Allah your works shall fail..."[15]) and equally those verses which talk about wicked deeds being erased ("Indeed good deeds efface misdeeds."[16]). That is because the verse we are presently discussing

14. Sūrat Āle ʿImrān (3):30
15. Sūrat al-Zumar (39):65
16. Sūrat Hūd (11):114

lays out the general law of humanity's accounting. There is nothing to preclude another set of laws to apply in exceptional cases, for He "is not questioned concerning what He does, but they are questioned."[17] Another explanation we could offer in this case is that for anyone whose works Allāh causes to fail in the hereafter, this failure reveals that they had not actually done anything good in the first place because truly good things are those whose value inheres until the Day of Recompense, not merely those things that took on a pleasant form in people's short-sighted gaze!

11. Awareness of death

For someone who has absolute certainty about the reality of the hereafter, it is sufficient for them to recall the horrors that await on the Day of Resurrection to discourage themselves from sinning. Death is called "the destroyer of pleasures" (*hādim al-ladhdhāt*)[18] so what about something even greater than death? It has been narrated that a man came to the Prophet (s) and said, "Teach me what Allah has taught you." So he sent him to a man to teach him. He taught him "When the earth is rocked..." until he reached the verse "...So whoever does a mote's weight of good will see it, and whoever does a mote's weight of evil will see it." Then he said, "That is enough for me!" The Prophet (s) was informed of this whereat he said, "Leave him be, for he has understood."[19]

17. Sūrat al-Anbiyā᾽ (21):23

18. The Commander of the Faithful (as): "Remember death abundantly, for it is the destroyer of pleasures." – *Al-Amālī*, 264

19. *Biḥār al-anwār* 92/107

Sūrat al-ʿĀdiyāt (no. 100: The Chargers)

Verses 1–11

100:1 *By the snorting chargers,*

100:2 *by the strikers of sparks,*

100:3 *by the raiders at dawn,*

100:4 *raising therein a trail of dust,*

100:5 *and cleaving therein a host!*

100:6 *Indeed man is ungrateful to his Lord,*

100:7 *and indeed he is witness to that!*

100:8 *He is indeed avid in the love of wealth.*

100:9 *Does he not know, when what is in the graves is turned over,*

100:10 *and what is in the breasts is divulged,*

100:11 *indeed their Lord will be best aware of them on that day?*

1. Oaths

The oaths in this *sūrah* revolve around the states and movements of a band of fighters in Allāh's way, specifically their charging horses. Their sounds as they approach the enemy, the sparks that their hooves strike, their surprise attack against their enemies at dawn, the dust they kick up as they gallop, and how they plunge into the midst of their foes as they attack.

Now if the horses of those who fight in Allāh's way are worthy of such oaths, then what about the fighters themselves? Is there any implication more powerful than this? Than to swear by the mounts of those who you desire to exalt!?

2. Greatness being transferred from a great person

In the Qur'ān, we find many instances of greatness being transferred from a great person to some of those things connected to him, which would lack greatness in of their own selves without this connection, for example:

- The shirt of Joseph (as): "When the bearer of good news arrived, he cast it on his face, and he regained his sight."[1]
- The ark of Moses (as): "Their prophet said to them, 'Indeed the sign of his kingship shall be that the Ark will come to you, bearing tranquility from your Lord...'"[2]
- The she-camel of Ṣāliḥ (as): "But then the Messenger of Allah said to them, 'Let Allah's she-camel drink!'"[3]

Of this we can find a further instance in the present verse—the horses of the fighters are so exalted that Allāh swears oaths by the hooves of these mounts, which strike sparks as they charge ("By the strikers of sparks.").

3. Defeating the enemy

Praising a dawn raid by invoking it in the context of an oath demonstrates that it is desirable to launch surprise attacks on the enemy, for war is guile. One form of surprise attack is the dawn raid, for it is neither in the gloom of the night, such that a person cannot see his enemy, nor in the brightness of the morning, such that the enemy is prepared.

But this principle is not confined to the above instance of taking measures to overwhelm the enemy. Every effort must be made to obtain the means of defeating the enemy, including amassing force ("Prepare against them whatever you can of power and

1. Sūrat Yūsuf (12):96
2. Sūrat al-Baqarah (2):248
3. Sūrat al-Shams (91):13

war-horses..."[4]). It should be obvious that the present verse is not restricted to horses specifically but means any kind of power that allows you to confront the enemy, even if it is not horses. It is also clear, hopefully, that the verse we have just quoted about military preparations does not only refer to war horses!

4. Pilgrims

Some take the opinion that the meaning of these oaths are the camels of the pilgrims moving between ʿArafāt, Minā, and Muzdalifa which has been narrated from the Commander of the Faithful (as).[5] According to this interpretation, the verses expound the greatness of the pilgrims from one angle and the greatness of this spot of ground from another. In this case, the oath is about a mount carrying a noble rider in a noble spot. From this and other similar instances, we can see that the Qurʾān is multifaceted in its meanings.

5. Being ungrateful

The connection between this oath and its object ("Indeed man is ungrateful to his Lord") is somewhat subtle. It could be said that the relationship between man's ingratitude and the horses of the fighters is:

- the contrast between a group who offer the most valuable thing in their possession—their lives—in the service of the religion and those who prefer the wealth with which Allāh has entrusted them over returning to Him, while being ungrateful towards Him and heedless of His blessings. So the honoring of the mounts of these fighters is a hint to them that Allāh considers them beneath these horses in merit!
- The ordinance of *jihād* was given to confront these ungrateful and recalcitrant persons, so the above verses are intended to belittle them, in that they will be abased by those who are

4. Sūrat al-Anfāl (8):60
5. *Tafsīr nūr al-thaqalayn* 5/656

granted victory over them on account of their own iniquity and misguidance.

6. Ingratitude

There is a collection of traits gathered in the human soul mentioned by the Qurʾān, such as:

- Injustice and foolishness ("...Indeed he is most unfair and senseless"[6])
- Greed ("Indeed man has been created covetous"[7])
- Anxiety ("...anxious when an ill befalls him"[8])
- Despair and ingratitude ("He becomes despondent, ungrateful."[9])
- Rebelliousness ("Indeed man becomes rebellious"[10])
- Weakness ("...man was created weak."[11])

And this *sūrah* mentions another one of these inner traits, making its subject the human being as a human being, that does not apply to the prophets (as). This trait is ingratitude (*kufrān*) which is preceded in the Arabic by the particle of emphasis "indeed" (*inna*) as well as the *lām* of emphasis (*al-lām al-mu'akkada*).

It is obvious that such traits can be found in people's hearts as surely as can be found seeds in the earth waiting for the right conditions to sprout. So without struggling with oneself, probing the depths of the human soul and cleansing it of whatever it contains, it is only natural that these traits will remain seeds for evil deeds.

7. Aware of our own evil

Something that will mean a person is punished severely on the Day of Resurrection is the fact that he is already aware of the evil in

6. Sūrat al-Aḥzāb (33):72
7. Sūrat al-Maʿārij (70):19
8. Sūrat al-Maʿārij (70):20
9. Sūrat Hūd (11):9
10. Sūrat al-ʿAlaq (96):6
11. Sūrat al-Nisāʾ (4):28

himself ("and indeed he is a witness to that!"). Assuming, of course, that 'he' refers to the person and not Allāh. It is as if to say that this ingratitude is actually man's willful refusal to acknowledge his own flaws, which run parallel to his carnal self. That is because going against the nature of these traits, like miserliness for instance, requires effort that they are not willing to expend. Hence, they are truly left without any excuse! Another verse that, like this one, expounds the fact that man is well aware of his own self reads, "Rather man is a witness to himself, though he should offer his excuses."[12]

8. Oath

This *sūrah* contains realities that touch upon the inner realm, such as the human being's ingratitude, his avid love of wealth, and the fact that he is aware of what is within his own soul, even if he is too proud to admit to it. So too does this *sūrah* touch upon the unseen realm from another angle—namely, that Allāh will reveal He is best-aware of His servants on the Day of Resurrection.

Hence it is only appropriate for there to be a clear oath in order that people accept these realities that the senses cannot apprehend, and an affirmation in all of these points, using the particle "indeed" (*inna*) and a nominal sentence in conjunction with the *lām* of emphasis.

9. Wealth

The verse uses the word *khayr* (lit. "good") to refer to wealth, as is the case elsewhere in the Qurʾān. For example, "...he leaves behind any wealth..."[13] and "...and grudging when wealth comes his way."[14] It is possible that this word is used because of:

- their own claims that such wealth is good for them, as all the enjoyments of this world can only be obtained with this wealth.

12. Sūrat al-Qiyāmah (75):14–15
13. Sūrat al-Baqarah (2):180
14. Sūrat al-Maʿārij (70):21

- reality itself—namely, that wealth in and of itself and, in fact, this world in its entirety, is faultless. In fact it is the very stuff of goodness; evil only comes out of loving it ("...and you love wealth with much fondness."[15]) which distracts one from Allāh whereat it becomes a tribulation ("Know that your possessions and children are only a test..."[16]) and an enemy ("O you who have faith! Indeed among your spouses and children you have enemies; so beware of them."[17]).

And if we want proof that there is nothing innate in wealth that distracts people from Allāh, we need only look to His prophet, Solomon (as), who was given great wealth without it sapping his determination to serve Allāh in the slightest. The promised Mahdī (ajfs) will also have unimaginable wealth when he brings forth from the earth its treasures and from the heavens their rains.

10. Earth brings forth

This *sūrah*'s discussion of mankind's bodies in the realm of the graves is similar to the discussion of inanimate things therein. In the verse "and the earth discharges her burdens"[18] we sense that the bodies of human beings are in the same condition as everything else buried in the ground. The earth brings them forth and it as though she is relieved to be rid of them. In this *sūrah* we find the expression "turned over" which refers to the earth being disturbed to bring out whatever is within it, just as a ploughman labors to bring out what grows in it.

Therefore, we can say that these bodies have no value in of themselves—rather their value depends upon the spirits to which they belong. They are like a grain of wheat that is desired in and of itself, and once the wheat has been harvested from the field, the chaff is cast aside to be taken by the winds or consumed by fire.

15. Sūrat al-Fajr (89):20
16. Sūrat al-Anfāl (8):28
17. Sūrat al-Taghābun (64):14
18. Sūrat al-Zalzalah (99):2

11. "What is in the breasts is divulged"

In the verse "and what is in the breasts is divulged," Allāh singles out "breasts" (*ṣudūr*) rather than the other limbs because the latter's relation to the breast is like that of an effect to its cause, and therefore the breast is more worthy of mention. So on the Day of Judgement, the real source of a person's salvation, and the axis around which his accounting will revolve, is a sound heart, as Allāh says, "...except him who comes to Allah with a sound heart."[19]

So someone who adorns his limbs with acts of obedience but does not reform his soul with righteous traits will see that the contents of his breast are not something he will be pleased with on the Day of Resurrection!

A verse that supports the centrality of the soul to our deeds is "...anyone who conceals it, his heart will indeed be sinful"[20] because it describes the heart as the locus of sin. There is also the verse "...lest he in whose heart is a sickness should aspire..."[21] that makes the sickness of the heart a cause for a person's desires to be aroused when he interacts with women, and the verse "It is not their flesh or their blood that reaches Allah. Rather it is your Godwariness that reaches Him."[22] For what is the value of their blood being spilled in Minā if this does not spring from Godwariness?

Next is the verse "And whoever venerates the sacraments of Allah — indeed that arises from the Godwariness of hearts"[23] for it is from a Godwary heart that outward piety emanates. This includes venerating Allāh's sacraments in all their forms. Finally comes the verse "O you who have faith! Prescribed for you is fasting as it was prescribed for those who were before you, so that you may be Godwary."[24] This verse makes the anticipated outcome of fasting that a person should become Godwary, and it is well-known that Godwariness (*taqwā*) is a condition of the heart.

19. Sūrat al-Shuʿarāʾ (26):89
20. Sūrat al-Baqarah (2):283
21. Sūrat al-Aḥzāb (33):32
22. Sūrat al-Ḥajj (22):37
23. Sūrat al-Ḥajj (22):32
24. Sūrat al-Baqarah (2):183

12. Divine knowledge

Allāh is fully aware of all our actions as they emanate from us. In fact, He is fully aware of them even before that because of His knowledge of the unseen. Our awareness of this divine knowledge should cause us to ensure whatever we do is done to the best of our ability. However, when we read the verse "indeed their Lord will be best aware of them on that day," it appears to restrict this divine knowledge to the context of the Day of Resurrection while His knowledge is timeless. So how can we reconcile this verse to reality?

The answer to this question—after affirming that this verse does not preclude His knowledge at other times—is that the resurrection is not the time of this knowledge itself but rather the time at which the effect of this knowledge appears in the form of recompense. Obviously, the connection between this knowledge in the abode of this world and the effect it will have in the abode of the hereafter serves as a deterrent against sinning if someone finds that their faith in the hereafter is deeply rooted!

Similar to this is the verse "To whom does the sovereignty belong today?"[25] We know that His sovereignty is actually eternal and without end, so what connects it to that day in particular? Again, the meaning of this is that His sovereignty will be fully realized and affirmed by all of His subjects. We should also note that the object of the divine knowledge are people's souls themselves ("their Lord will be best aware of them on that day") and not merely their deeds. This is a more eloquent way of expressing Allāh's immanence because someone who encompasses a person's soul necessarily encompasses their deeds as well, but the opposite it is not so.

25. Sūrat Ghāfir (40):16

Sūrat al-Qāriʿah (no. 101: The Catastrophe)

Verses 1–11

101:1 *The Catastrophe!*

101:2 *What is the Catastrophe?*

101:3 *What will show you what is the Catastrophe?*

101:4 *The day mankind will be like scattered moths,*

101:5 *and the mountains will be like carded wool.*

101:6 *As for him whose scales are heavy,*

101:7 *he will have a pleasing life.*

101:8 *But as for him whose scales are light,*

101:9 *his mother will be the Abyss.*

101:10 *And what will show you what it is?*

101:11 *It is a burning fire!*

1. Catastrophe

The flow of the discussion about the catastrophe (*qāriʿa*) that will shake the hearts and deafen the hearing on the Day of Resurrection resembles that of the besieger (*ḥāqqa*): ("The Besieger! What is the Besieger?! What will show you what is the Besieger?!"[1]). In both of these discourses there are two questions: one is simple in its form—it asks about the nature of the subject initially mentioned to grab the audience's attention, but the second question is more complete with the addition of the phrase "...show you..." (*adrāka*), meaning: "What is there that could possibly convey to you the

1. Sūrat al-Ḥāqqahh (69):1–3

nature of this subject!" This is a very eloquent way of providing emphasis, as if the contents of this *sūrah* and others like it cannot possibly convey the real essence of the things they are discussing!

2. Rhetoric and emotions

The phrase "...and what will show you...?" (*wa mā adrāka*) appears in more than ten locations throughout the Qurʾān, while the phrase "...and what do you know...?" (*wa mā yudrīka*) appears in three. It is said the difference between these two phrases is that the first is used in contexts where Allāh wants to show His prophet (s) topics that raise questions for people while the second is used in situations where Allāh turns away and avoids answering the question. So it states explicitly that this is something the audience does not know and something that human minds are not capable of knowing. For example, when discussing the resurrection, Allāh says, "What do you know — maybe the Hour is near!"[2]

It is very interesting that throughout the Qurʾān, Allāh never addresses people's intellects in a way that is detached from rhetoric and emotions. This is a lesson for us as well—that we should never rely merely on speaking directly about an issue without using any devices or styles to rouse people's consciousness.

3. Like moths

The verse "The day mankind will be like scattered moths" describes people on the Day of Resurrection like moths or locusts for two reasons:

- either because these creatures, being insects, are weak and so people are rarely concerned by them, even if they are widespread ("as if they were scattered locusts")[3] meaning they are a mass, crawling over one another or
- because these insects appear haphazard in their movements, just as moths become confused by fire, for when they fly towards it, they do not intend to fly into it!

2. Sūrat al-Shūrā (42):17
3. Sūrat al-Qamar (54):7

So on the Day of Resurrection, people will be like a mass of locusts in their weakness, surging forward without a particular goal. The real disaster of this verse is that the creatures people are being compared to in this verse—insects that no one cares about—are in a better condition than those people who do not attain the goal for which they were created!

4. Instability

The verses that describe people as scattered moths, and mountains as wool of various colors which has been carded, allude to the fact that the things we see as constant and fixed in this life will lose their stability. But as well as a physical reality, this alludes to a social reality as well:

- The former is represented by the towering mountains of various hues ("and in the mountains are stripes white and red, of diverse hues, and pitch black."[4]). Their stability will vanish and they will become like carded wool.
- The latter is represented by human society that has settled and extended its dominion all over the earth, but there will come a catastrophe that shatters this stability and scatters them like moths that have been disturbed.

There is a lesson in this for everyone—that they should not become attached to ephemeral things, but this is especially so for believers because they do not rely on anything except Allāh, who will return it to such a state. This is summed up best in Allāh's words "Everyone on it is ephemeral."[5]

5. Remembering the resurrection

The resurrection is discussed, both in the context of an oath and other ways, in seventy different places in the Qurʾān. This clearly shows first that coming to believe in it is one of the fundamentals of the religion and, second, that paying detailed attention to it in one's day life constitutes a reminder of our meeting with Allāh.

---

4. Sūrat Fāṭir (35):27
5. Sūrat al-Raḥman (55):26

That is because the main obstacle to seeking nearness to Allāh is represented sometimes by heedlessness (*ghafla*) and sometimes by being overcome by one's desires. Both of these conditions are removed or limited by remembering the ultimate end that awaits all mankind, whereat all transient pleasures will fade away and all that will remain will be their consequences. The emphasis contained in this *sūrah* is one form that this remembrance can take.

6. Heaviness

It is not only scales and the things they weigh that can be described as heavy and light. In fact, anything that has importance or consequence can be given a measure in the realm of scales. One scale is that of truth (*ḥaqq*), as Allāh says, "The weighing on that Day is a truth. As for those whose deeds weigh heavy in the scales — it is they who are the felicitous."[6] Whereat the truth becomes a unit by which deeds can be measured. Therefore, when this *sūrah* mentions heaviness ("As for him whose scales are heavy"), this suggests that those people who have pleasing lives are those who expend their efforts in the arena of truth. So a person should avoid anything that can be called "falsehood" (*bāṭil*), whether in his treatment of himself, such as singing for example, or in his interactions with others, such as falsely consuming their wealth. In short, the truth is anything that is connected to Allāh, and falsehood is whatever is connected to other things ("That is because Allah is the Truth, and what they invoke besides Him is falsehood..."[7]).

7. Sending blessings on Muḥammad and his Household (as)

In the narrations of the Prophet's Household (as), we are told that one of those things that weighs heavy in the scales on the Day of Resurrection is sending blessings on Muḥammad and his Household (as) (*al-ṣalāt ʿalā muḥammad wa āle muḥammad*), which falls under the general rubric of loving the Prophet's near relatives (*mawaddat dhuwī al- qurbā*). But is also an instance of a supplication guaranteed to receive an answer, for which supplication is nearer

6. Sūrat al-Aʿrāf (7):8
7. Sūrat al-Ḥajj (22):62

to being answered than asking Allāh to send down blessing on the most noble of His creation?

It should be known that the word 'scales' (*mawāzīn*) in this verse can refer to either the deeds themselves (i.e., the thing weighed (sing. *mawzūn*)) rather than the measure (i.e., thing that does the weighing (sing. *mīzān*)), hence why it is appropriate to refer to them in the plural here.

8. Weighing deeds

Islām is a religion of realism, not idealism, so none of us are expected to dedicate all our actions purely to goodness, for this can only be achieved by an infallible (as), for the fact that the human being is composed of a carnal soul (*al-nafs al-ammāra*), a reproaching soul (*al-nafs al-lawwāma*) means it is only natural that he will sometimes be morally upright and, at other times, suffer lapses. That is why the recompense on the Day of Resurrection is described as a measure (*mīzān*), whether heavy or light ("But as for him whose scales are light...") with two scales, one weighing down and lifting the other. What matters at the end of the day is that the scale of good deeds should outweigh the bad, as the verse says, "But as for him whose scales are heavy...."

9. Satisfaction with life

A person's life is wholesome when they are truly satisfied with it, which is why Allāh describes the inhabitants of paradise as having "a pleasing life" because a person's displeasure with themselves or their life is one of the most difficult forms of punishment for them to endure as it is an endless source of guilt and shame. Of course, this condition in the hereafter is the direct result of a person's behavior in this world. Therefore, the pleasing life enjoyed by the inhabitants of paradise in the next world is what the believer is actually already living in this one, as they do not do anything to invite the displeasure of their Lord therein. Hence, they are truly living a "pleasing life" in this world and the hereafter.

10. "The Abyss"

The description of hell in the verse "his mother will be the Abyss" suggests that it will be like a mother to its inmates, insofar as:

- the deep connection between hell and its inmates, for it is as if they are the children of hellfire who came out of its womb and have now returned to it.
- a child in times of hardship turns to his mother, and these people shall have no refuge left on that day save hellfire.

This assumes that we interpret "the Abyss" (*al-hāwiya*) to be a name of hellfire, so-called because people tumble headfirst into it (*yahwī fīhā*), but we can also interpret it to be an adjective describing the top of a person's head as they are cast into hellfire, in which case it means that a person will fall with the crown of their head into the fires of hell. This is a powerful description of humiliation because they will fall with the most noble part of their body. This is in addition to the fact that the Arabic word *hāwiya* can also imply falling into ruin. We can also draw a connection between the crown of the head and the lying forelock mentioned in a previous *sūrah,* meaning that lying and sinfulness are what cause someone to be hurled headlong into hellfire.

11. Burning

The opening verses of this *sūrah* begin with the phrase "...and what will show you..." about the terrors of the resurrection. This same expression is repeated again with particular regard to hell ("And what will show you what it is?"). So this is a terror upon terrors, because it magnifies the terror of hell over and above all the other terrifying events of the resurrection!

It is interesting that this verse describes hellfire as burning (*ḥāmiya*). This would seem obvious to everyone, as that is what fire normally does. But it is as if the verse means to say that this is the real fire. Compared to this otherworldly fire, you cannot say that the fires of this world truly burn!

Sūrat al-Takāthur (no. 102: Rivalry)

Verses 1–8

In the name of Allāh, the All-Beneficent, the All-Merciful

102:1 *Rivalry distracted you*

102:2 *until you visited the graves.*

102:3 *No indeed! Soon you will know!*

102:4 *Again, no indeed! Soon you will know!*

102:5 *No indeed! Were you to know with certain knowledge,*

102:6 *you would surely see hell.*

102:7 *Then you will surely see it with the eye of certainty.*

102:8 *Then, that day, you will surely be questioned concerning the blessing.*

1. False illusions

The Qurʾān makes rivalry the cause of distraction, as if rivalry has taken control of human existence. Instead of the human being taking himself wherever he wants, matters of convention (*umūr iʿtibāriyya*) (which lack any reality in themselves, such as delusions of status acquired by wealth and children) drive him forward.

Therefore, the only complete solution for this problem is for the person to struggle with his self (*nafs*) to extricate it from the grip of false illusions and take it to a state of temperance (*zuhd*) towards external things, something that engenders inner nobility, rather than abandoning them altogether, for it has been narrated, "No man becomes arrogant or tyrannical save for some weakness he finds in himself."[1]

2. Rivalry

Pursuing gains and then feeling pride in what one has gathered in rivalry is usually with regards to wealth and children, but the low self (*nafs*), which is never satisfied, can also attach its love of gain to other things such as age ("Each of them is eager to live a thousand years"[2]), houses ("Do you futilely build a sign on every prominence?"[3]), and food ("O Moses, We will not put up with one kind of food. So invoke your Lord for us, that He may bring forth for us of that which the earth grows — its greens and its cucumbers, its garlic, its lentils, and its onions..."[4]).

To sum up, the first verse "Rivalry distracted you" leaves the object of rivalry ambiguous so as to encompass all forms of being distracted by this world, including those we have mentioned and others. The second verse, "until you visited the graves," alludes particularly to rivalry in having sons.

3. Distractions

Someone who believes in the Day of Recompense must avoid anything that distracts them from preparing for the hereafter, for the essence of a distraction is that which takes you away from that which is more important. The consequence of this definition is that being taken away from that which is most important by another important thing also falls into the category of a distraction, even if a person is not aware of that because the latter is still important and is not clearly a distraction.

How many common worldly activities that people engage this definition applies to, even if they are not aware of it, because these efforts of theirs are not connected to eternity and everlasting life!

---

1. *Al-Kāfī* 2/312
2. Sūrat al-Baqarah (2):96
3. Sūrat al-Shuʿarāʾ (26):128
4. Sūrat al-Baqarah (2):61

4. Rivalry

The kind of rivalry being reproached by this *sūrah* could be with regards to:

- rivalry in the accumulation of wealth and sons, in which it is the accumulation that is blameworthy because it is an instance of being distracted by worldly enjoyments themselves. Of course, anyone whom this does not distract from the remembrance of Allāh is excluded from this reproach in accordance with His words "by men whom neither trading nor bargaining distracts from the remembrance of Allah...."[5]
- vainglory and boasting with claims of accumulation, even if these are not accurate, in which case the rebuke is directed towards that psychological state in which such a deluded people lives, for this too distracts them from the hereafter.

So the criteria for distraction in both these cases are one and the same, whether the person has actually achieved something externally or not.

5. "Until you visited the graves"

One explanation[6] offered for the verse "until you visited the graves" is that the central concept of this divine address is that you were distracted by rivalry in this world until your time of death, when you visited the graves (i.e., when you were buried in them). But a better explanation is that some people were preoccupied with rivalry and pride amongst men to the extent that they would even go to the graves to add the numbers of the dead to those of the living, to augment their numbers when they were boasting to someone else!

How foolish it is for people to take something illusionary as the measure of one person's superiority over another! The excellence of one living person has nothing to do with the excellence of

5. Sūrat al-Nūr (24):37
6. *Tafsīr al-mīzān* 20/351

another, so what about the excellence of a dead person!? And what about if there isn't really any excellence there to begin with, as was the case with people's boasting during the Ignorance, as it has been suggested that this verse refers to.[7]

6. Recompense

By not explicitly mentioning the object of knowledge in the verse "No indeed! Soon you will know!" and leaving it ambiguous, Allāh demonstrates the magnitude of the recompense awaiting those distracted by rivalry on the Day of Resurrection. This is a terrible threat to its audience, especially because Allāh repeats the denunciation, "No indeed!" more than once in this *sūrah*!

Take note that this verse mentions a recompense but in a vague sense saying, "you would surely see hell" without detailing the different kinds of punishment awaiting therein as we see in other *sūrahs* . This is a more eloquent form of threat, as we see in Allāh's words "Were you to see when they are stationed before their Lord. He will say, 'Is this not a fact?'"[8] Insofar as this verse does not mention what will happen to them as they stand before Allāh.

7. Knowledge with complete certitude

This *sūrah* makes the deterrent against being distracted by vainglory the knowledge with complete certitude that is uncontaminated by doubt. It has been said in definition of this knowledge that it is "Firm, justified and unchanging conviction that cannot be lost; in truth it is a combination of two kinds of knowledge: Knowing something, and knowing that the opposite of that knowledge is utterly impossible."[9]

Therefore, anything short of this knowledge is not sufficient to deter people from rivalry, such as worship during the Ignorance, because this contains neither knowledge nor fear, and this is why the rank of the learned is above that of the worshipers and ascetics!

---

7. Ibid. 20/353
8. Sūrat al-Anʿām (6):30
9. *Tafsīr al-mīzān* 20/351

8. Missing opportunities for good deeds

Knowledge, especially when it has attained a high level of certitude, is authoritative (*ḥujja*) for its possessor. This is one of the most important motivations for a person to free themselves of spiritual impurities. This is why at the end of this *sūrah*, the Lord has counted it as a means of breaking out of this state of rivalry and vainglory that is mentioned at its beginning. If such knowledge does not produce an outcome like this, then it will become a cause for woe and regret on the morrow, which is why Allāh describes the Day of Resurrection as "the Day of Regret."[10]

Let it be known that one who strives in this world and one who does not are equal when it comes to regret. The similitude of this is that of those who entered a dark cave with Dhūl-Qarnayn and found beads on the floor. Some of those who were with him picked up these beads, and when they came out of the darkness, they saw that they were gems. So those who took them were grieved that they had not taken more of them, and those who did not take any were also grieved that they had taken none at all! This is exactly how people will be on the Day of Resurrection when they see all the opportunities they missed for good deeds during the days of their worldly lives!

9. "You would surely see hell"

When Allāh says "you would surely see hell," we can say that this means seeing it with the heart that is able to witness the realities of this existence:

- either in a general sense, as with the believers as a whole, who are described by the Commander of the Faithful (as) when talking about their certainty in Allāh, "The eyes do not see him with their sights, but the hearts apprehend him through the realities of faith."[11] or
- in detail, as was the case with Abraham (as), about whom Allāh says, "Thus did We show Abraham the dominions of

10. Sūrat Maryam (19):39
11. *Nahj al-balāgha* 258

> the heavens and the earth, that he might be of those who possess certitude."[12]

This interpretation is supported by the fact that Allāh joins the act of seeing ("...you would surely see hell") to another act of seeing on the Day of Resurrection ("then you will surely see it with the eye of certainty"). This means sighting it with one's eyes after having seen it with one's heart.

10. Certainty

Certainty (*yaqīn*) shifts between different levels. Certain knowledge (*ʿilm al-yaqīn*), the eye of certainty (*ʿayn al-yaqīn*), and true certainty (*ḥaqq al-yaqīn*). These are analogous to seeing the smoke, then seeing the fire, then touching it. A kind of certainty results in all three cases, but there is still a clear difference between them. These different degrees of certainty also apply to certainty about the hereafter, so there is a difference between being certain of it in this world "No indeed! Were you to know with certain knowledge...") and certain in the next ("Then you will surely see it with the eye of certainty.").

The people of certainty must elevate their certainty to a level close to the eye of certainty. This is as the Godwary (*muttaqīn*) have been described by the Commander of the Faithful (as): "So they are to Paradise as one who hath seen it; they are [already] enjoying its blessings... and they are to Hellfire as one who hath seen it; they are [already] suffering its punishments!"[13]

11. Questioning

The address "Then, that day, you will surely be questioned concerning the blessing," (even though it appears in the midst of a discussion about people of rivalry and vainglory) encompasses everything with which Allāh blesses His servants. This verse does not mean that Allāh (swt) will ask us about food and drink. Rather it refers to what Imām al-Ṣādiq (as) says, "Allah is too generous

12. Sūrat al-Anʿām (6):75
13. *Nahj al-balāgha* 303

and too magnificent to nourish you with food and allow you to consume it, only to then question you about it! Rather, He will ask you about the blessing He gave you in Muḥammad and the Household of Muḥammad (s)."[14]

We can find evidence for this in the question asked by the keepers of hellfire from its inmates on the Day of Resurrection, for it is only about a spiritual matter—namely, being sent a warner ("Whenever a group is thrown in it, its keepers will ask them, 'Did there not come to you any warner?'"[15]

12. Giving thanks

Some people look at the provisions they have been given as a pure blessing, without paying attention to the fact that a blessing is only truly blessed if it is used to obey Allāh or else it becomes a tribulation for its possessor because this will be a cause of rebuke or punishment when they are questioned about it on the Day of Resurrection ("Then, that day, you will surely be questioned concerning the blessing.").

It is well-known that the best way to give thanks for these blessings is laid down in the *sharīʿa* through its ordinances regarding one's body (such as fasting), one's wealth (such as charity), one's spirit (such as the prayers that cause the believer to ascend (*salāt al-miʿrājiyya*)), or people's rights (such as maintaining ties of family). Not paying attention to the laws enshrined in the *sharīʿa* could result in a person ending up doing the opposite of what is mentioned, which is why those who give thanks for Allāh's blessings are in the minority ("Little do you give thanks!"[16]).

13. Proclaim blessings

Some people erroneously suppose that there is some kind of contradiction between those verses that forbid vainglory in wealth, sons and the like thereof, and the verse that enjoins the Prophet (s)

14. *Al-Kāfī* 6/270
15. Sūrat al-Mulk (67):8
16. Sūrat al-Aʿrāf (7):10

to proclaim the blessings of his Lord ("and as for your Lord's blessing, proclaim it!"[17]). In fact, proclaiming Allāh's blessings, whether by displaying them outwardly or speaking about them, should be done with a higher goal—either by practically displaying gratitude for them or by encouraging others to imitate him in the things Allāh has blessed him with. This is completely different from pride and boasting which ultimately stem from following one's lusts rather than obeying the guidance of one's Lord!

17. Sūrat al-Ḍuḥā (93):11

Sūrat al-ʿAṣr (no. 103: Time)

Verses 1–3

103:1 *By Time!*

103:2 *Indeed man is in loss,*

103:3 *except those who have faith and do righteous deeds, and enjoin one another to what is right, and enjoin one another to patience.*

1. Loss

Despite its brevity, this *sūrah* contains many powerful affirmations. It begins with an oath, which is the clearest form of affirmation, not to mention using the particle of affirmation, "indeed" (*inna*), followed by the *lām* of emphasis and a nominal sentence.

Perhaps the reason for this is that the object of the oath is completely unknown to the majority of people, namely, the true nature of loss (*khusr*) which applies to all mankind, save those who exclude themselves from it through a particular reason.

Therefore, anyone who does not find in his heart any faith or any truly righteous deeds with certainty and conviction, falls into the general category of loss. In other words, you do not need a reason to be in a state of loss, unlike the opposite state of affairs. So anyone who doubts whether he is excluded from this category must necessarily be subject to continuous loss. And what a frightening thing this is to anyone who has a heart!

2. *Al-ʿaṣr*

There are divergent opinions about the meaning of the word 'time' (*al-ʿaṣr*) in this *sūrah*:

- There are those who say this refers to the time of *ʿaṣr,* which is the late afternoon, making this oath part of a series of oaths that includes all the hours of a full day: daybreak (*fajr*), dawn (*ṣubḥ*), day (*nahār*), night (*layl*), and mid-morning (*ḍuḥā*).
- It refers to a particular time in human history, as represented by the time of the Prophet (s) and the time of Imām al-Mahdī (ajfs). The prophetic mission began in the former, and in the latter, the religion will be revived after having disappeared.
- It alludes to the *ʿaṣr* prayer because this is the middle prayer that is singled out for mention amongst all others in Allāh's saying "Be watchful of your prayers, and the middle prayer...."[1]
- It refers to time as a whole, which is the receptacle in which all deeds transpire, which in turn makes it the source of all good and evil. This is just as "By your life..."[2] refers particularly to the time of the Prophet's life.

3. Loss

We cannot rightly apply the category of "loss" (*khusr*) to anything besides the human being. All other creatures, beasts or otherwise, are disposed to whatever command their creator wills for them and follow their guidance, as per His words "Our Lord is He who gave everything its creation and then guided it."[3] Even an adder's bite or a lion's strike.

But the category of loss applies only to the human being who can turn aside from the path of servanthood (*ʿubūdiyya*) sketched out before him and, thus, fall into a state of loss as this verse indicates. When this happens, he sinks even lower than the beasts whose efforts are never lost on any occasion.

1. Sūrat al-Baqarah (2):238
2. Sūrat al-Ḥijr (15):72
3. Sūrat Ṭa Ha (20):50

4. Man in loss

The way in which particles of meaning (*ḥurūf*) are used in the Qurʾān is in accordance with the goals of the Qurʾān , in the same way as nouns and verbs, as represented by the divine education of the human being. This can only be achieved through warnings, intimidation, promises, and threats—all in the proper context, of course!

What we notice in this *sūrah,* based on this general rule of how the Qurʾān uses particles, is that Allāh refers to man as being "in loss" as if man is a thing completely encapsulated within a vessel called "loss" such that loss surrounds him from all sides, as a vessel surrounds the water it contains. This is a way most eloquent to express the severity of man's loss!

5. Loss

Loss, literally speaking, means a reduction in capital, and it is obvious that a person's true capital is represented by their life that is continuously draining away from the moment they are born. This is a self-evident truth! So whatever of this capital is invested in provisions for the hereafter becomes a kind of capital that can be moved from this world to another, in which case there is no loss whatsoever!

On the other hand, if the days and hours of a person's life are spent in that which displeases Allāh, which includes not only the hours in which they disobeyed Allāh and forsook their duties but even the hours of heedlessness and diversion, then they have squandered them for they give them nothing they can take with them. What an obvious kind of loss it is to which this verse refers!

6. Belief and righteous deeds

There are visible indicators of belief and righteous deeds, all of which can be summed up under the heading of "avoiding loss." These include a person being given:

- a pleasant life in both worlds, as Allāh says, "Whoever acts righteously, male or female, should he be faithful, — We shall revive him with a good life...,"[4]
- affection with the Creator and the creation ("Indeed those who have faith and do righteous deeds — the All-beneficent will endear them..."[5]), and
- entering Allāh's mercy ("As for those who have faith and do righteous deeds, their Lord will admit them into His mercy."[6]).

7. Elements for success

Effects in the physical realm do not occur except once all their prerequisites are met. For example, for something to burn there must be heat, fuel, and an absence of impediments to burning. The same is true in the spiritual realm, for success (*fawz*) also cannot be attained without first attaining all of its constituent elements, namely to "have faith and do righteous deeds, and enjoin one another..." so if any of these elements are missing, this causes loss.

Therefore, someone who believes and acts righteously in the true sense of the word, but fails to enjoin others to what is right and patience, is missing a fundamental element of avoiding loss. Hence those who worship in private and do not enjoin others to reform themselves should not feel pleased with their deeds. If any element is missing, it does not matter which, from that combination, the effect will not be achieved, just as is the case with burning.

8. Attaining full success

Just as there is profit and loss in worldly business, whereby one person is said to have gained relative to another's loss, or loss relative to another's greater gain, the same applies to otherworldly business. Anyone who does some righteous deeds while neglecting others, like sinful believers, will not achieve full success, rather

4. Sūrat al-Naḥl (16):97
5. Sūrat Maryam (19):96
6. Sūrat al-Jāthiyah (45):30

they will suffer a relative loss compared to one who has forgone all sinful deeds. Perhaps believing this will motivate some to perform the rest of the righteous deeds so that they may escape this relative loss and attain full success!

Clearly this relativity does not exist in matters of belief. Anyone who suffers from deficiencies in fundamental , such as someone who denies prophethood, for example, even if they accept divine unity (*tawḥīd*), will never be considered truly successful. This is supported by Allāh's words "Those who disbelieve in Allah and His Messengers and seek to separate Allah from His Messengers, and say, 'We believe in some and disbelieve in some' and seek to take a way in between — it is they who are truly faithless, and We have prepared for the faithless a humiliating punishment."[7]

9. Enjoining

There is a difference between the act of enjoining good and forbidding evil (*al-amr bi al- maʿrūf wa al-nahī ʿan al-munkar*) and between that of enjoining others to what is right (*tawāṣī bi al-ḥaqq*) as this verse instructs. The former could occur between a believer and a sinner, and it could be from a single direction as well. For example, one person enjoins and forbids while the other is enjoined and forbidden, but enjoining one another (*al- tawāṣī*) could exist between the believers themselves or, in fact, between the very best of them because each one of them enjoins and is enjoined at the same time because however excellent any person might be, they will always need someone to remind them. It is, after all, Allāh who says, "And admonish, for admonition indeed benefits the faithful."[8] In this regard, we can say that enjoining one another (*al-tawāṣī*) has two branches:

- One branch relates to those things concerned with one's connection to the Creator, which is appropriate to enjoining one another to patience (*al-tawāṣī bi al-ṣabr*) both in obeying

7. Sūrat al-Nisāʾ (4):150–151
8. Sūrat al-Dhāriyāt (51):55

Allāh's commands, avoiding His prohibitions, and enduring tribulations.

- While the other relates to one's connection with the creation, which is appropriate to enjoining one another to what is right (*al-tawāṣī bi al-ḥaqq*) so that no one's right is ever lost!

10. Avoiding loss

Avoiding loss requires special assistance from Allāh. Every moment of our lives is a unit that can be described as either a success or a loss, and however accomplished a person becomes in self-observation (*murāqaba*) and self-accounting (*muḥāsaba*), they cannot escape heedlessness in all of these moments, especially considering the devils that lie in ambush for a person's heart, lay siege to it, pounce upon it at the slightest moment of heedlessness, and withdraw when they remember the Lord as we can understand from some narrations. Hence, in order to efface the traces of these moments of heedlessness, Allāh must grant special favor to His servants, for the existence of even a few moments of heedlessness places man in a state of loss, even if only for those fleeting instances. Which is why Allāh says in some verses, affirming this fact:

- "And were it not for Allah's grace upon you and His mercy, you would have all surely followed Satan, except a few."[9]
- "Were it not for Allah's grace and His mercy upon you, not one of you would ever be pure."[10]
- "...and were it not for Allah's grace on you and His mercy, you would surely have been among the losers."[11]

Of course, in parallel to this divine favor in repelling loss, there are servants of Allāh who enjoin one another to repel that also, and this what we read in this *sūrah*.

---

9. Sūrat al-Nisā' (4):83
10. Sūrat al-Nūr (24):21
11. Sūrat al-Baqarah (2):64

11. Enjoining one another

There is no doubt that enjoining one another to what is right and enjoining one another to patience falls within the category of righteous deeds (*ʿamal sāliḥ*), but it is singled out for mention in this *sūrah* because it causes a reduction of loss in people's lives, which is more arduous than people's loss of wealth! Just as enjoining one another to patience also falls within enjoining one another to what is right but it is singled out for mentioning because patience guarantees that people will accept being enjoined to what is right. Why? Because admonitions and preaching can be difficult for people to bear because they often run contrary to the selfishness of the ego and because sometimes it is hard to give credence to the views of others.

12. Moving humanity towards perfection

This short *sūrah* provides a complete philosophy of existence. This is done by highlighting the following:

- Humankind's movement in life is in a continuous state of loss despite the fact that outwardly they appear to be developing and growing.
- Escape from this default mode of loss can only be achieved by joining belief to righteous deeds in a person's relation with their own self.
- Enjoining one another to what is right must be accompanied by enjoining one another to patience so that humankind, in addition to the call of the prophets to their nations, also call to themselves, and members of society call to one another. This is how humanity can move towards perfection.

Sūrat al-Humazah (no. 104: The Scandal-Monger)

Verses 1–9

In the name of Allāh, the All-Beneficent, the All-Merciful

104:1 *Woe to every scandal-monger and slanderer,*

104:2 *who amasses wealth and counts it over.*

104:3 *He supposes his wealth will make him immortal!*

104:4 *No indeed! He will surely be cast into the Crusher.*

104:5 *And what will show you what is the Crusher?*

104:6 *[It is] the fire of Allah, set ablaze,*

104:7 *which will overspread the hearts.*

104:8 *Indeed it will close in upon them*

104:9 *in outstretched columns.*

1. The word 'woe'

The Qurʾān uses the word 'woe' (*wayl*) many times as an indefinite noun in order to magnify the force of the threat and rebuke. It occurs in seventeen different places in the Qurʾān. However, what unites all of the objects of woe found in these seventeen places is associating partners with Allāh (*shirk*) and disbelief (*kufr*) (for instance, Allāh says, "...and woe to the faithless for a severe punishment..."[1]) or moral degradation such as lying, scandal-mongering, and slandering as we find in this *sūrah*. The lesson in

1. Sūrat Ibrāhīm (14):2

this is that Allāh uses the word 'woe'(*wayl*), which denounces the most foul inner vices such as disbelief, for outer vices, represented by the sins mentioned in this *sūrah*, which sinners find easy to perform because they consist of nothing more than uttering words—scandals and lies!

This shows that we should not feel at ease with ourselves just because we have avoided inner vices when such outer vices persist. In short, adopting the morals of the *sharīʿa* is as fundamental a part of it as adhering to its doctrines. This is why the threat of "woe" is applied to both!

2. Scandal-monger and slanderer

Several explanations are offered for distinguishing the scandal-monger (*humaza*) from the slanderer (*lumaza*), but both generally involve mentioning the faults of others. This applies to all instances thereof, whether done in earnest or in jest, whether in religious affairs or worldly ones, whether in word or deed, whether the object of such derision is present or absent.

What is generally understood from this verse and the verse of backbiting[2] is that the intent of the Lord is to condemn those who mention the faults of others without good reason because it causes others to weaken, encourages feelings of enmity in a person's soul, and diverts them from setting right its affairs.

3. Scandal-monger and slanderer

There is no sin on the outside save that it emanates from roots on a person's inside. An arrogant person is not arrogant, as we read in a tradition, save for a weakness they find in themselves; and the one who defrauds others, who is also rebuked with woe in the Qurʾān, does not consume the wealth of others save for the fact they love to amass wealth and enjoyments. The same is true of the scandal-monger and the slanderer who do not besmirch the honor of others save for a baseness and lowness in their own selves for

2. Sūrat al- Ḥujurāt (49):12: "Will any of you love to eat the flesh of his dead brother? You would hate it."

even if neither they nor the backbiter benefit from their actions in this world, they still expose themselves to the retribution of the Lord of the Worlds.

Perhaps we can deduce that the punishment of the backbiter will also be that of the slanderer and the scandal-monger and vice versa because their sins are all of the same type—pursuing the faults of others and mentioning them. There is no doubt that mentioning hellfire and its terrors should cause people to desist from such behavior, assuming they are accustomed to desisting from other sins, and it is with a description of such horrors that this *sūrah* ends.

4. Slandering Prophet Muḥammad (s)

In addition to the censure of all slanderers, as we find in this *sūrah*, Allāh also condemns those who slander the personality of the most noble of mankind, particularly in his quality best-known to people—trustworthiness. For some dared to slander the Prophet (s) and thus about them Allāh said, "There are some of them who slander you regarding the charities: if they are given from them, they are pleased, but if they are not given from them, behold, they are displeased."[3] In fact, the Lord also defends those who believe and volunteer charities saying, "Those who blame the voluntary donors from among the faithful concerning the charities"[4] Let it be known that this quality, clearly visible in the hypocrites, when it is found in other people amongst the faithful, is the self-same moral iniquity, especially because the verse explicitly makes its rebuke general with the words "Woe to every scandal-monger and slanderer." How terrible it is to think that a believer could possess the quality of a hypocrite such as mentioning the faults of others or getting up for prayer lazily!

3. Sūrat al-al-Tawbah (9):58
4. Sūrat al-al-Tawbah (9):79

5. Amassing wealth

Amassing wealth without using it and spending it in the proper way is immoral in and of itself. Although this does not necessarily prohibit in the jurisprudential sense, it does mean it could lead to other sins, and it suffices to demonstrate that it is mentioned in the context of slandering and scandal-mongering! It is obvious that if a person's heart is polluted with the love of this world, they will forget the Creator or the Creator will cause them to forget His remembrance ("And do not be like those who forget Allah, so He makes them forget their own souls."[5]) whereat it becomes easy for a person to drown in all manner of falsehoods as they see themselves higher than others so it is easy for them to disparage them. Indeed "the love of this world is the source of every iniquity."[6] It has been narrated from Imām al-Riḍā (as), "Wealth is not gathered except with five qualities: Extreme stinginess, far-fetched hopes, overwhelming greed, severing family ties, and preferring this world over the hereafter."[7]

6. Wealth earned after remembering Allāh

Wealth that is earned after remembering Allāh is full of goodness and blessings. In fact, the Qurʾān encourages people to gather it ("And when the prayer is finished disperse through the land and seek Allah's grace, and remember Allah greatly so that you may be felicitous."[8]). But if wealth is earned before remembering Allāh, then it remains ill-gotten, as in His saying "When they sight a deal or a diversion, they scatter off towards it and leave you standing! Say, 'What is with Allah is better than diversion and dealing, and Allah is the best of providers.'"[9]

The amassing of wealth censured in this *sūrah* is, of course, of the latter kind, as no one gathers wealth and counts it over and over again except someone who loves the wealth itself, rather

---

5. Sūrat al-Ḥashr (59):19
6. *Al-Kāfī* 2/130
7. *Al-Khiṣāl* 1/282
8. Sūrat al-Jumuʿah (62):10
9. Sūrat al-Jumuʿah (62):11

than someone who aims to spend it in on those things Allāh has recommended for His servant.

7. Derision from comrades

One of the things that causes a person to come back from falsehood in the Qurʾān is the derision from their comrades. In this *sūrah* we read, in addition to the invocation of woe which itself is a kind of derision and censure:

- "He will surely be cast..." which means to throw something away, as if he is something useless which one wants to dispose of.
- "...into the Crusher" which is the fire that crushes and tears apart whatever is thrown into it.

Add to all of the above the lowliness of their own souls which seem unable to grasp the simplest of truths. They actually believe that their money can buy them immortality, which is perhaps the most foolish thought a person can entertain!

8. Hellfire

The expression "And what will show you..." is usually used in descriptions of the resurrection and its terrors, such as the besieger (*al-Ḥāqqa*)[10] and the catastrophe (*al- Qāriʿa*).[11] The fact that it appears in this *sūrah* with its description of hellfire as the crusher "which will overspread the hearts" is a severe warning against this sin which is something common and ordinary for many people!

This shows us that we must avoid all kinds of forbidden things whose true spiritual form is hidden until we enter that realm ("but what will the admonition avail him?"[12]). We should note how appropriate this crushing fire in the hereafter is as a punishment for the sins of those consigned to it because their words have crushed the hearts of others in this world.

---

10. Sūrat al-Ḥāqqah (69):3
11. Sūrat al-Qāriʿah (101):3
12. Sūrat al-Fajr (89):23

9. Slandering and scandal-mongering

If we define a major sin (*kabīra*) as "something for which Allāh has decreed Hellfire as a recompense in the Qurʾān," then in its plainest sense this includes the sins of slandering and scandal-mongering. The problem with most verbal sins such as these is that people find them easy to do because nothing visibly disgraceful happens on account of their claims, unlike fornication, theft, and murder, for example!

In fact, verbal sins are the source for many of these other sins. A person might become enraged and kill someone because of words such as these, just as another might be aroused to fornicate by them.

10. Burning to the core

The punishment mentioned in Allāh's words "which will overspread the hearts" (even if some take it to mean that a person will burn not just from the outside but from within) can be explained as follows: This punishment will reach a person's true core, meaning their soul and not just the inside of their body, for it is this core that is the source of all evil. We can see the burning of sinners' hearts in the hereafter reflected in this world, for they are burnt by these fires even now. This is what causes them to become vexed and annoyed, just as the Qurʾān describes them: "whomever He desires to lead astray, He makes his breast narrow and straitened as if he were climbing to a height."[13] It is this that explains their attachment to various kinds of enjoyment and pleasure to relieve this vexation and angst they feel.

11. Hell closing

In this world, the greatest hope for someone imprisoned is to escape the prison, but the Qurʾān deprives the inmates of the hellfire of this fanciful wish in various verses saying that the gates of hellfire are firmly shut and sealed upon its inmates. For example,

13. Sūrat al-Anʿām (6):125

Allāh says, "upon them will be a closed Fire."[14] Elsewhere, He says, "Whenever they seek to leave it, they will be turned back into it, and they will be told: 'Taste the punishment of the Fire....'"[15] And in this *sūrah*, we read, "Indeed it will close in upon them."

Obviously, being punished and feeling that there is no escape or relief from punishment will inflict upon a person psychological torment in addition to their physical torment, which is why the word 'distress' (*ghamm*) is used to describe the punishment of one in hellfire in Allāh's words "Whenever they desire to leave it out of anguish, they will be turned back into it...."[16]

12. Wealth

In this *sūrah* it is interesting to note the juxtaposition of a wealthy person who imagines that their wealth will eternalize them ("He supposes his wealth will make him immortal!") and the one who is cast into "the Crusher." How this must dash the hopes of one who sees their wealth, which they fancy will give them eternal life, become a cause for them to be cast headlong into hellfire!

It is also interesting to note the juxtaposition between wealth which he "counts it over" and the column of flame that looms "outstretched" over him, as it was by his obsessive counting of wealth that he extended this column of flame for himself in hellfire!

14. Sūrat al-Balad (90):20
15. Sūrat al-Sajdah (32):20
16. Sūrat al-Ḥajj (22):22

Sūrat al-Fīl (no. 105: The Elephant)

Verses 1–5

In the name of Allāh, the All-Beneficent, the All-Merciful

105:1 *Have you not regarded how your Lord dealt with the Companions of the Elephant?*

105:2 *Did He not make their plots go awry,*

105:3 *and send against them flocks of birds*

105:4 *pelting them with stones of shale,*

105:5 *thus making them like chewed-up straw?*

1. Rhetorical questions

The expression "Have you not regarded...?" instead of "Do you not know...?" indicates that this is something so obvious that it can almost be seen. It is well-known that the events of the elephant occurred at about the same time as the Prophet's birth, so it is as if the Qur'ān means to say that the occurrence of this event is so certain that the Prophet (s) can be asked about is as if he saw it with his own eyes!

This expression suits the peculiarity of this event and the kind of fate suffered by the army of the elephant, which has no parallel in history. So it is necessary to use a rhetorical question like this. The Qur'ān sometimes uses them in relation to realities clearly perceptible to human beings ("Have you not regarded that Allah sends down water from the sky...?"[1]) and sometimes for subtle realities that are hidden from them ("Have you not regarded that

1. Sūrat al-Ḥajj (22):63

to Allāh prostrates whoever is in the heavens and whoever is on the earth..."[2]). But the ultimate reason why Allāh uses these rhetorical questions in both cases is so that people will discover realities from them, like the unveiling of the spiritual realities that are with Him.

2. Pondering

In His words "Have you not regarded how your Lord dealt..." Allāh wants the audience to ponder the way in which Allāh acted, not with the mere fact of the action itself. This is because when simple-minded folk consider the destruction of the army of the elephant, this does not in itself have an effect on them or cause them to take a moral lesson from it. When it comes to seeing the act itself, both intelligent and unintelligent observers are one and the same, but Allāh wants those people with intellects to investigate and analyze these actions and to apply the lessons they learn from the past to what will happen in the future. This is the fundamental reason for Allāh relating the accounts of earlier people as Allāh says, "Travel over the land, and then observe how was the fate of the deniers."[3] We can see this command has three components: First, to travel; second, to look; and third to draw a lesson from the kind of fate the deniers suffered.

3. "Your Lord"

The expression "your Lord" addressed to prophets and other persons appears more than two hundred times in the Qur᾿ān, even though Allāh belongs to all existence equally. This should be more fitting for the station of lordship because His relation to the whole is more worthy than His relation to any one part. So He cannot have eschewed this except for a good reason, such as we find in this *sūrah*. The context here is invoking the greatness of the Lord who exacts retribution upon His enemies in ways that no man can even conceive. So saying "your Lord" to the Prophet (s), with this dominant attribute in mind, should steady the latter's heart and the hearts of the faithful who were with him.

2. Sūrat al-Ḥajj (22):18
3. Sūrat al-Anʿām (6):11

It should not be forgotten the favor that this address shows the Prophet (s) as well—directing it to him alone amongst all creatures is an act of great honor and kindness—great enough, surely, to relieve any worries caused by calling people to Allāh!

4. The word 'companion'

The word 'companion' (*ṣāḥib*) is usually used in the context of homogeneity (*tajānus*) in nature, such as a human being with other members of his species, whether they are of the same religion ("But they called their companion, and he took [a knife] and hamstrung [her]."[4]) or not ("His companion said to him, as he conversed with him..."[5]), but using the term 'companion' to connect a human to something non-rational, such as "the Companions of the Elephant" is only correct for rhetorical purposes, as is intended by this *sūrah*: Because of his rebelliousness, the rider of the elephant became like that animal in his violence, with the difference that the former wanted to destroy the Kaʿba intentionally and purposefully, while his mount only wanted to do so as a result of the nature with which Allāh had endowed it and as a result of its subjugation to His servants. It is even said that it refused to destroy the Kaʿba!

5. Depending only on Allāh

Using the expression "Companions of the Elephant" alludes to the fact that these renegades depended on material means for their success, such as bringing along a powerful and frightening war elephant! Their dependency upon this elephant also justifies calling them its companions.

By contrast, in all the ups and downs of their lives, the faithful depend only upon the Almighty and All-Powerful, as we understand from Allāh's words "That is because Allah is the protector of the faithful, and because the faithless have no protector."[6] What a difference there is between a true protector who defends His

4. Sūrat al-Qamar (54):29
5. Sūrat al-Kahf (18):37
6. Sūrat Muḥammad (47):11

subjects and someone who has no protector, or a protector who cannot protect him!

6. Plots

When Allāh describes the actions of the faithless as plots (*kayd*), as He does here with regards to Abraha and his army, this alludes to their moral degeneracy as a plot is the use of cunning and treachery rather than a straightforward confrontation, in which case the act is even more distasteful! From this, we can know that this was not merely a matter of destroying the Kaʿba. In fact, they had evil intentions that were known only to Allāh. For example, we know that they wanted to divert the pilgrims from the Kaʿba to Abraha's own false Kaʿba that he had built in Yemen.

7. Plots of the faithless

The plots of the faithless are not something trifling. The Qurʾan describes them as "even if their schemes are such as to dislodge the mountains."[7] The severity of these plots meant that they might cast feelings of fear and weakness into the hearts of the faithful, so Allāh must say something to remove these feelings. For example:

- "Indeed your Lord is in ambush."[8]
- "Allah indeed defends those who have faith."[9]
- "O you who have faith! If you help Allah, He will help you and make your feet steady."[10]
- "Those who were before them schemed. Then Allah razed their edifice from the foundations..."[11]
- "Their plotting shall come to naught."[12]
- And we find another example of this in the present *sūrah.* Their plots to misguide others were futile and did not

7. Sūrat Ibrāhīm (14):46
8. Sūrat al-Fajr (89):14
9. Sūrat al-Ḥajj (22):38
10. Sūrat Muḥammad (47):7
11. Sūrat al-Naḥl (16):26
12. Sūrat Fāṭir (35):10

> succeed. Things did not go as they intended despite their careful planning. Equally, their supplications in hellfire will not have the intended effect of eliciting a response. Allāh says, "the invocations of the faithless only go awry."[13]

It is interesting to note that here Allāh says that it is their plots that went awry (*ḍalāl*), but that same expression is used for their own persons when Allāh says, "nor those who are astray."[14] Nothing comes from one who is astray (*ḍāll*) except more error (*ḍalāl*), whether in words or deeds, both at the time and in their final outcomes.

8. Attribution of actions

The Qurʾān combines two statements in this *sūrah* and in doing so solves the problem of how actions can be attributed to anyone besides Allāh. This is by distinguishing between an original owner of property (*aṣīl*) and the one to whom it is entrusted (*wakīl*). At the beginning of the *sūrah*, Allāh attributes how He dealt with the army of the elephant to Himself ("Did He not... send against them flocks of birds") but then says that the birds were "pelting them" and attributes the action to the birds. Clearly there is no contradiction between these two statements because there is no contradiction between property having an indigenous owner while being in the care of another. This principle applies in all instances where a being performs an action by Allāh's leave, such as: "Allah takes the souls at the time of their death..."[15] which goes with the verse "You will be taken away by the angel of death, who has been charged with you."[16]

This is made even more explicit when Allah says, "...you did not throw when you threw, rather it was Allah who threw...."[17] Here, Allāh unequivocally negates the effectuation of any action by the thrower himself, even though it emanated from him.

---

13. Sūrat al-Raʿd (13):14
14. Sūrat al-Fātiḥah (1):7
15. Sūrat al-Zumar (39):42
16. Sūrat al-Sajdah (32):11
17. Sūrat al-Anfāl (8):17

Everything that we have mentioned here should suffice to remove the peculiarity of some of the extraordinary things that appear from Allāh's righteous servants, for these are in the same position as "pelting them" after "Did He not... send against them flocks of birds...."

9. Divine will

This *sūrah* contains an exquisite contrast between the elephant and the flock of birds, which refers to the different groups of birds that attacked the army, for it is a contrast between a tiny bird and the largest land animal in the world. Its great size did not avail it, nor did the mass of soldiers that surrounded it, so long as it was the divine will that it should perish.

There is a lesson in this for all confrontations between the faithful and other people throughout history. No one can count on their numbers or preparations if Allāh wishes to destroy them with even the simplest means, such as the wind, a thunderclap, or a flock of birds.

10. Challenging the Lord

The Quraysh had been intent on worshipping idols since time immemorial. This state of belief was no better in Allāh's eyes than the state of desiring to ruin the Kaʿba. Yet He did not send upon them a similar punishment. Perhaps the crucial difference was the fact that the army of the elephant was opening and deliberately challenging the Lord of the Kaʿba rather than acting out of ignorance or some other shortcoming. Not to mention the fact that Abraha was aggressing against the rights of other people, even sinners, for they were in a place of divine sanctuary and had security because of that. So what about when there were righteous persons there such as ʿAbd al- Muṭṭalib, who left the affair of the Kaʿba to its protector, saying, "As a man will protect his camel, so you protect your possession! Their strength and their schemes never shall triumph against your stratagem."

11. Birds aware of divine inspiration

The lethal pelting carried out by the birds was not something easy or simple. Whence did they find these stones of shale? How did their attack reduce the enemy to be like chewed-up leaves? Whence did these flocks come from and where did they go? From all of these questions we know that these creatures have an awareness of and capacity to receive divine inspiration. In this they are like all other birds, as Allāh has described in them the Qurʾān: "Have they not regarded the birds disposed in the air of the sky."[18]

What a shame it is that the birds in the sky are at Allāh's disposal, but the son of Adam who rebels against his Lord and challenges Him is not!

12. Psychological warfare

The plan to attack the Kaʿba and destroy it did not depend solely on bringing the elephant to Makkah. They could have just as easily attacked with horsemen and then destroyed it with tools instead. Rather, these men wanted to strike fear in the hearts of the people of Makkah with an animal they had not encountered before—the elephant. This is a kind of psychological warfare that is commonplace in military conflicts. But nevertheless, Allāh destroyed the army of the disbelievers, even with their terrifying beast. Therefore, no one should ever rely solely on military power so long as the belief remains that "power, altogether, belongs to Allah..."[19]

13. Different kinds of punishment

Divine retribution in this world is proportional to the gravity of the crime, such that Allāh varies the different kinds of punishment He sends down: "So We seized each [of them] for his sin: among them were those upon whom We unleashed a rain of stones, and among them were those who were seized by the Cry, and among them were those whom We caused the earth to swallow, and

18. Sūrat al-Naḥl (16):79
19. Sūrat al-Baqarah (2):165

among them were those whom We drowned. It was not Allah who wronged them, but it was they who used to wrong themselves."[20] The essence of punishment is that the bodies of those punished took on different forms. There were those like trunks of palm trees uprooted from the ground ("so that you could have seen the people lying about therein prostrate as if they were hollow trunks of palm trees"[21]), and there were those who died in their homes without moving ("and they lay lifeless prostrate in their homes."[22]).

But in the case of the army of the elephant, Allāh describes a fate like no other: ("making them like chewed-up straw") bits and pieces of crops that are blown away by the wind after their seeds have been consumed or eaten by words, such that nothing remains of them, unlike someone who dies a corpse in his home. Perhaps the reason for this rare punishment amongst others is the fact that the army of Abraha directly threatened the sanctity of Allāh's sacred house, so Allāh effaced them from existence just as they would have effaced His house, which is the symbol of His divine unity.

---

20. Sūrat al-ʿAnkabūt (29):40

21. Sūrat al-Ḥāqqah (69):7

22. Sūrat al-Aʿrāf (7):78

Sūrat Quraysh (no. 106: The Quraysh)

Verses 1–4

106:1 *For solidarity among the Quraysh,*

106:2 *their solidarity during winter and summer journeys,*

106:3 *let them worship the Lord of this House,*

106:4 *who has fed them from a hunger, and secured them from a fear.*

1. Feuding

A society that is united and far removed from serious disagreements is one that is close to attaining social and spiritual happiness, which is why the Final Prophet (s) could not sow the seeds of the divine mission in Medina except through this social togetherness, which is why Allāh counts this as a blessing He bestowed upon them when He says, "and united their hearts. Had you spent all that is in the earth, you could not have united their hearts, but Allah united them together."[1] Moreover, He warns them against disuniting again until the Day of Resurrection: "...and do not dispute, or you will lose heart and your power will be gone."[2]

It is known that internal feuding and disagreements, as well as being harmful in of themselves, also give power to the enemies who beset the *umma*.

2. Uniting Quraysh

Assuming that this *sūrah* is connected to the one immediately before it (Sūrat al-Fīl) (as is understood from the jurisprudential

1. Sūrat al-Anfāl (8):63
2. Sūrat al-Anfāl (8):46

ruling that they should be recited together in prayer), then the destruction of the army of the elephant became a step towards the unity of the Quraysh and the land in which they lived because were it not for this divine intervention and the removal of fear, they would have scattered through the land seeking sustenance and security and become like the Jews ("We dispersed them into communities around the earth..."[3]). If this happened, they would have lost the rank and nobility they had earned through their service of the Holy Sanctuary at Makkah.

In addition to this, the destruction of Abraha's army was also a preliminary to another blessing, namely, their ability to travel safely in the summer to Syria and in the winter to Yemen. Were it not for this safety, they would not have dared leave their homes and delve into the desert wilderness in search of profit. Rather they would have remained in their settlement coveting safety and thereby lost the blessings of living in the vicinity of the Holy Sanctuary.

3. Uniting

Traveling and moving about in different seasons to seek a living is a decent thing to do or else Allāh would not have counted it as a blessing for the Quraysh by mentioning their ability to move safely. This complements His blessing of establishing them in the vicinity of the House, which depends on their wealth and safety.

Now, if the Quraysh needed this unity for a worldly affair, such as traveling in the winter and summer seeking wealth and profit, then the Muslim *umma* is in even greater need of unity and peace of mind for the affair of the hereafter and spreading the message of Islām to people's hearts, just as the individual needs that to attain nearness to Allāh.

4. Enumeration of blessings

Hearing the blessings of Allāh enumerated should cause us to wake up and pay attention to the source of these blessings. This

3. Sūrat al-Aʿrāf (7):168

is something instinctive even for animals when they receive the care of their owners. It is in this context that we see Allāh highlight several of His blessings over the Quraysh, including unity, their ease of travel in the summer and winter, their food and security, as a precursor to summoning them to worship the Lord of the house.

We can rely on this principle as well in people's interactions with one another. Why should a father not enumerate the blessings he has given to his son to motivate him to be dutiful and kind to him, rather than holding this over him and declaring him to be in his debt!?

5. Worshipping

The House occupies a special place of honor in Allāh's eyes. Sometimes He attaches it to Himself ("purify My House"[4]), and sometimes He attaches Himself to it ("the Lord of this House"). By using more than one mode of attachment, He also demonstrates the greatness of this Sanctuary.

It is clearly fitting to mention the House in this *sūrah* because the Lord who repelled tribulation from this House, and from those living around it, is worthy of being worshiped exclusively. Worship here is ultimately a matter of giving thanks for blessings which is something everyone can understand, not worshipping purely for its own sake, which is only known to the elect of Allāh's servants.

6. How to show kindness

Reason dictates that avoiding harm comes before seeking benefit, so Allāh first shows the Quraysh how He kept them safe from harm, first by destroying Abraha and his army, and second He shows them how He brought them the benefits of safety and sustenance. This shows us the logical order of this *sūrah* and the one before it.

Therefore, a person should learn from Allāh how he should treat those whom he wishes to show kindness—first by keeping them safe from harm and then by bringing them benefit.

---

4. Sūrat al-Ḥajj (22):26

7. Kindness to Quraysh

The Quraysh, despite their faithlessness and evil conduct (such as fighting, raiding, and persecuting the Prophet (s), even after many years of resisting the prophetic mission) were still shown kindness by Allāh through the things mentioned in this *sūrah* such as feeding them and keeping them safe:

- In order to magnify His Holy Sanctuary because they had lived in its vicinity so long that others called them "Allah's people"
- To magnify those who lived amongst them, like ʿAbd al-Muṭṭalib, because Allāh honors a land with the presence of a righteous servant therein and repels harm from them through him
- Out of respect for the one who would be born amongst them later, a prophet from themselves

And why should Allāh not show favor to an earlier person because of the nobility of a later one? This is why ʿAlī (as) would spare the lives of those in whose future offspring he saw light!

8. Worshipping Allāh after provision

Worshipping Allāh requires a soul that has gathered its strength, is secure in its livelihood, and that finds its provision near at hand. Something that obstructs this is suffering hunger and insecurity, which is why the Lord in His wisdom asks His servants to worship Him after blessing them with sustenance and safety so that they have no excuse not to!

This is supported by something that Imām al-Ṣādiq (as) relates from Salman, "Do you not know, O ignorant ones! The soul is slow to obey its master if it lacks reliable sustenance, for when it has secured its livelihood it is content. As for Abu Dharr, he had a few she-camels and sheep which he would milk and slaughter if his family desired meat or if he had a guest."[5]

---

5. *Al-Kāfī* 5/68

9. The act of feeding

The act of feeding is in and of itself a praiseworthy attribute that Allāh joins to the act of creation when He says, "Shall I take for guardian anyone other than Allah, the originator of the heavens and the earth, who feeds and is not fed?"[6] This is also an attribute of Allāh's friends (*awliyā*ʾ), for there is no prophet or *walī* save that he displays the utmost generosity in feeding others and other things. But when Allāh mentions that this is from hunger and deprivation, this serves to emphasize it further, and the verse specifically mentions this: "who fed them from a hunger," especially when we notice that the verse uses the indefinite for fear and hunger ("from a hunger... from a fear...") which aggrandizes them. The Qurʾān also mentions this as a means of overcoming obstacles, "or feeding on a day of starvation."[7]

10. Hunger and fear

Hunger and fear are generally forms of tribulation, a common feature of creation, such that Allāh says, "We will surely test you with a measure of fear and hunger...."[8] Here we must note that sometimes a person faces these as a form of punishment and retribution, as happened to the secure and peaceful town that was ungrateful for Allāh's blessings ("So Allah made it taste hunger and fear."[9]). But a person might also face hunger and fear as a means to awaken them to worship Allāh, for it is the nature of the low self (*nafs*) to be heedless and distracted, so this kind of tribulation is a way to set right the self. One form of this can be found in this *sūrah* when Allāh says, "who has fed them from a hunger, and secured them from a fear" so being free from hunger and fear is a step towards worshipping the Lord of the House.

---

6. Sūrat al-Anʿām (6):14
7. Sūrat al-Balad (90):14
8. Sūrat al-Baqarah (2):155
9. Sūrat al-Naḥl (16):112

11. Safety and security

The blessing of security and being free from the fear of external threats is one of the most important blessings that Allāh can single out His servants for in this world, and also in the hereafter, because a heart that is free from every distraction is a sound heart that can then receive the divine lights of beauty and majesty. This is supported by a narration from Imām al-Ṣādiq (as) about the verse "except him who comes to Allah with a sound heart."[10] He (as) says, "A sound heart which receives its Lord without anyone else being within it."[11]

As for the evidence that this blessing will be granted to the faithful in this world, it is Allāh's saying "Allah has promised those of you who have faith and do righteous deeds that He will surely make them successors in the earth, just as He made those who were before them successors, and He will surely establish for them their religion which He has approved for them, and that He will surely change their state to security after their fear, while they worship Me, not ascribing any partners to Me. Whoever is ungrateful after that — it is they who are the transgressors."[12] As for in the hereafter, Allāh says, "Those who have faith and do not taint their faith with wrongdoing — for such there shall be safety, and they are the guided ones."[13] So the faithful are given glad tidings of safety and security in both worlds.

12. Supplication for the future

When the supplications of the prophets (as) are granted, these extend for many centuries. For example, the supplication of Abraham (as) for the inhabitants of Makkah, when he said, "My Lord, make this a secure town, and provide its people with fruits...,"[14] the things mentioned in this *sūrah* are the fulfilment of his supplication in that the blessing of fruit is not restricted only to the righteous inhabitants of Makkah but includes all of them so

10. Sūrat al-Shuʿarāʾ (26):89
11. *Al-Kāfī* 2/16
12. Sūrat al-Nūr (24):55
13. Sūrat al-Anʿām (6):82
14. Sūrat al-Baqarah (2):126

as to establish Allāh's authority over them. So why do people not follow the example of Abraham (as) when supplicating to Allāh by not only supplicating for all the people in their own time but for the people in future times as well?

Sūrat al-Māʿūn (no. 107: Aid)

Verses 1–7

In the name of Allāh, the All-Beneficent, the All-Merciful

107:1 Did you see him who denies the Dīn?

107:2 So that is the one who drives away the orphan,

107:3 and does not urge the feeding of the needy.

107:4 Woe to them who pray,

107:5 —those who are heedless of their prayers,

107:6 those who show off

107:7 but deny aid.

1. Losing practices

The question "Did you see...?" implies amazement at one who manages to accept matters of belief while simultaneously going astray in matters of practice, as if this is some kind of anomaly amongst all the creatures in existence such that it is worthy of being highlighted with surprise like a rare specimen! In fact, the truth is that the majority of people, because they have become accustomed to various forms of deviance, are used to it and do not see anything wrong with it, which is why such a strong emphasis is placed on keeping apart from faithless people and not living in their lands if one fears losing his or her religion or weakening it as a result thereof.

2. *Dīn*

The word *dīn* in "Did you see him who denies the *dīn*?" could mean the religion (*dīn*) of Islām as Allāh restricts the correct religion to Islām when He says, "Indeed, with Allah religion is Islam..."[1] but it could also mean divine retribution (*dīn*), as in Allāh's saying "and we used to deny the Day of Retribution"[2] which means the resurrection as that is when this retribution is meted out, and the Qur'ān uses words derived from the root of *d-y-n* to signify recompense. For example, Allāh says, "when we are dead and have become dust and bones, we shall indeed be brought to retribution?"[3]

The reason why Allāh focuses on this fundamental doctrine of the religion and condemns those who reject it is that denying the resurrection frees human beings from every restraint because they see no ultimate recompense for their actions. This leaves them free to do whatever they want, especially when their innate nature (*fiṭra*) flickers out and their conscience dies.

3. Abandoning prayer and failing to feed the needy

The one who fails to give Allāh His full due (while He is the ultimate source of blessings, in fact, there is no source besides Him) will also fail to give other creatures their full due because when someone is blinded to the ultimate duty they have towards their Creator, how can they attend to that of those lower than Him?

This is why the Qur'ān draws a connection between abandoning prayer and failing to feed the needy in the verse "We were not among those who prayed. Nor did we feed the poor"[4] and why it also connects a lack of belief in Allāh to failing to encourage others to feed the needy ("Indeed he had no faith in Allah, the All-supreme, and he did not urge the feeding of the needy."[5]). It is in this same vein that this *sūrah* draws a similar connection between

1. Sūrat Āle ʿImrān (3):19
2. Sūrat al-Muddaththir (74):46
3. Sūrat al-Ṣāffāt (37):53
4. Sūrat al-Muddaththir (74):43–44
5. Sūrat al-Ḥāqqah (69):33–34

a lack of faith in the resurrection and failing to encourage others to feed the poor.

4. Humble acts of obedience

Servants should never treat any act of obedience lightly, just as they should never underestimate the gravity of any sin, however trivial they might think it, for Allāh's pleasure and anger and that of His *walī* could lie in something servants do not expect, as some traditions intimate. This is why when the inmates of hellfire are asked how they ended up in the pits of hell, they will answer that they abandoned humble acts of obedience such as feeding the poor ("Nor did we feed the poor"[6]) and performing subtle sins such as gossiping ("We used to gossip along with the gossipers"[7]). This *sūrah* mentions similar issues, like failing to urge others to feed the poor ("does not urge the feeding of the needy") which is even more subtle than merely failing to feed them personally when describing the attributes of those who deny the retribution ("Nor did we feed the poor.").

5. All wealth is Allāh's

In numerous instances, the Qurʾān says that all wealth ultimately belongs to Allāh and that He has merely deputized His servants to spend it. Allāh says, "and spend out of that wherein He has made you deputies"[8] and elsewhere, "and give them out of the wealth of Allah which He has given you."[9] The consequence of this is that anyone who denies Allāh's dependents that which He has commanded to be spent upon them has betrayed Allāh's trust, and it is narrated in a *qudsī* tradition: "All wealth is my wealth, the poor are my dependents, the wealthy are my trustees; and should my trustees be stingy, I will take my wealth back from them without compunction."[10]

---

6. Sūrat al-Muddaththir (74):43–44
7. Sūrat al-Muddaththir (74):45
8. Sūrat al-Ḥadīd (57):7
9. Sūrat al-Nūr (24):33
10. *Jāmiʿ al-akhbār* 80

The present *sūrah* also highlights this reality from another dimension because, in the Arabic, it actually uses the word for 'food' (*taʿām*) rather than the word for 'feeding' (*iṭʿām*) to describe the act of giving food to the poor. This is as if to suggest that feeding the poor is merely conveying the food to its rightful owner, as one partner in a business returns the share of another to him. This is supported by something we read in another verse, namely, "and there was a share in their wealth for the beggar and the deprived."[11] So what pride is there in that?

6. Discouraging others from feeding others

It is interesting to note that this *sūrah* at one point uses the phrase "Have you seen the one who denies the *dīn*?" and at another uses the word 'woe' (*wayl*) to rebuke something that is not necessarily forbidden (*ḥarām*) in the jurisprudential sense, namely, not encouraging others to feed the needy and withholding help from others. We can resolve this peculiarity as follows:

- The core of what is being censured here is denying the Day of Retribution, which naturally engenders such behavior and that is prefixed with the causal conjunction "So that is the one..." (*fa*).
- This act actually reveals the vileness that is contained in the soul being rebuked for it, for a person might be excused for not feeding others, but he will not be excused from discouraging others from doing so.

7. Neglecting prayers

'Woe,' which is a word expressing the severity of punishment a person will experience on the Day of Resurrection, is directed towards the one who denies the Day of Retribution on more than ten occasions, and in this *sūrah* we can interpret this denier to be the one who is neglectful of their prayers, which is different than one who abandons them. In which case, we should ask ourselves, if this is the punishment for one who neglects their prayers, how

11. Sūrat al-Dhāriyāt (51):19

can we conceive of the punishment awaiting one who abandons them completely!?

8. Neglecting prayers

When Allāh says "Woe to those who pray" in this *sūrah*, it is directed towards those who neglect (*sahw*) their prayers but not to those who suffer lapses (*sahw*) within their prayers, as this happens even for the believer—this means those who attach little importance to their prayers and squander them, either by performing them intermittently, delaying them for no reason, or performing them to show off. A natural corollary of this attitude is a lack of concern for the needs of others ("but deny aid"). How can someone who has no concern for their own well-being be concerned for the needs of others? This shows us the connection between the two verses.

9. Seeking recompense from other creatures

It is only natural that someone who denies the resurrection will seek their recompense from other creatures, as it the nature of the carnal soul to yearn for rewards and praise, which is why these people take recourse to showing off in their acts of worship—to curry favor with the inhabitants of this world. This a continuous mode of behavior for them, as Allāh says "who show off" using the present tense of verb (*muḍāriʿ*). By contrast, fear of the hardships a person will face during the resurrection directs our concern towards seeking the pleasure of our Master who will grant us the best kind of reward—which the Qurʾān describes in the following verse, referring to the Prophet's Household (as): "We feed you only for the sake of Allāh. We do not want any reward from you nor any thanks. Indeed we fear from our Lord a day, frowning and fateful."[12]

Therefore, anyone who is mindful of the fact that their ultimate return shall be to Allāh and lives this reality with all of their being, will not have to struggle to devote themselves to the Lord in every instance. In fact, merely being aware of this reality at all times will make it easy for them to be devoted.

---

12. Sūrat al-Insān (76):9–10

10. Avoiding serving other people

Islām is a religion that combines many varieties of moral duty (*taklīf*), including:

- those connected to the Creator, represented first and foremost by the obligatory prayers and the injunction to avoid showing off to other people in them (those who show off").
- those connected to other creatures, which this *sūrah* elaborates in a number of verses such as not driving away the orphan ("drives away the orphan"), encouraging others to feed the needy ("does not urge the feeding of the needy"), and giving assistance to others ("and denies aid").

Therefore, anyone who uses worship to avoid serving other people has indeed strayed far from the spirit of the authentic and complete Islām.

11. Aid

Some people are very tolerant of deviant beliefs in others and see this as a matter of personal choice and freedom. Perhaps they do not see anything wrong with a person who holds these beliefs if they engage in some humanitarian work! In fact, these deviant beliefs are a source of moral and practical deviance, some of which are enumerated in the verses of this *sūrah* after it mentions the denial of the resurrection (such as driving off the orphan harshly, even to the extent that a person leaves the bounds of common decency). That is if we understand aid (*māʿūn*) in this *sūrah* to refer to something other than *zakāh*, meaning something that includes all the things necessary for a home, such as pans, tools, plates, and anything else that a person usually borrows. Imām al-Ṣādiq (as) explains this in the following words "It is a loan he gives, a provision he lends or a good deed that he does."[13]

13. *Al-Kāfī* 3/498

12. Permissive *sharīʿa*

This *sūrah*, when explaining solidarity, does not mention something affirmative that goes back to people themselves. Rather it calls on them not to drive away the orphan and not to withhold help—both of these are negative actions. It also calls on them to encourage others to feed the poor, which does not require that they do so from their own property. From all of this we understand that the *sharīʿa* is very permissive and wants us to not be evil in some areas and encourage others to do good in others.

13. Hard-heartedness

There might be times when people are afflicted by a dulling of feelings towards those orphans and needy persons around them. The cure for this state is concealed in this *sūrah*—it is to visit the orphans and stroke their heads to rouse such feelings, to feed the needy and encourages others to do so. But if this state persists, then it is the result of hard-heartedness.

It is toward this persistent state that the voice of rebuke is directed in this *sūrah*, as such a state indicates that a person has become devoid of feeling, not merely dulled in them. This is why expressions such as "drives away...," "does not urge...," and "denies..." appear in this *sūrah*, as all of these indicate a continuous state because they are in the present tense!

14. Denying aid

When one person asks another for something to help him (e.g., the aid that is understood to mean things like salt, water, and fire; basic provisions), this causes him to lose face. Even asking the simplest questions such as asking directions, involves humbling oneself. This is why refusing to help, especially in small matters, is such a reprehensible quality! This is why Allāh calls down woe upon such people when the Qurʾān does not do this anywhere else except in matters of gravity. It has been narrated that the Prophet (s) said, "Whoever denies aid to his neighbor, Allah will deny him His goodness on the Day of Resurrection and leave him to his own devices, and whomsoever Allah leaves to his own devices, what a terrible state he is in!"[14]

15. Prayer and *zakat*

The Qurʾān frequently draws a connection between prayer and *zakat*. What both of these have in common is that they involve stopping a person from being absorbed by other things. In prayer, human beings forsake other things in their heart, represented by different thoughts, to turn all their being towards their Creator. In *zakat*, they forsake other things in the outside world, as represented by wealth, to turn their attention and concern towards other creatures.

This *sūrah* also alludes to this relation between prayer and *zakāh* because Allāh mentions "their prayers" and "aid" but also brings out their clearest instances and those that most inspire empathy, for it talks about food which is one of the essential substances of life and about the needy person who is one of the lowest levels of the poor, before mentioning encouraging others to feed them, which is the easiest duty imaginable!

16. Hypocrites

One of the marks of hypocrites is that they are disinterested in all personal human dimensions. So in matters of belief, they have no solid argument against those with arguments, in which case they resort to denial which is something easy that does not require any forethought ("who denies the dīn"). In matters of worship, they are neglectful and inattentive towards them, often, if not always, missing them ("those who are heedless of their prayers"), and when they do undertake them, they do so ostentatiously seeking praise and worldly rewards ("those who show-off"). In matters of interacting with other people, they have no empathy for their suffering, nor do they encourage others to feed them ("does not urge the feeding of the needy") and refuse to give others aid, no matter how meager it is ("but deny aid"). They even drive the

---

14. *Man lā yaḥḍuruhu al-faqīh* 4/14

orphan away from them. So what trait of humanity remains in them? Anyone who finds such traits in them is attached to them in the hereafter, even if he is nominally counted amongst the ranks of the Muslims!

17. Society's success

The ultimate lesson of this *sūrah* is that the way to a society's success rests on two principles that those in authority must heed in every age:

- Concern for matters of education and upbringing—most importantly, prayer, as this prevents indecencies and wrongdoing which is why another verse says that one of the main priorities of those whom Allāh has established upon the earth is maintaining the prayer ("Those who, if We granted them power in the land, maintain the prayer, give the zakat, and bid what is right and forbid what is wrong. And with Allah rests the outcome of all matters."[15]).
- Concern for matters of livelihood—most importantly, looking after the needs of orphans and the weakest members of society, the needy, especially for their nourishment which is something all people need in this life.

15. Sūrat al-Ḥajj (22):41

Sūrat al-Kawthar (no. 108: Kawthar)

Verses 1–3

In the name of Allāh,, the All-Beneficent, the All-Merciful

108:1 *Indeed We have given you abundance.*

108:2 *So pray to your Lord, and sacrifice.*

108:3 *Indeed your enemy is the one without posterity.*

1. Qurʾān's miraculous inimitability

This *sūrah*, which is one of the smallest *sūrahs* in the Qurʾān, does not differ in its formulation or style from other longer *sūrahs*, so it is included in the Qurʾānic challenge: "Say, 'Then bring a surah like it, and invoke whomever you can, besides Allah, should you be truthful.'"[1] This *sūrah* is one of those that demonstrate the Qurʾān's miraculous inimitability (*iʿjāz*) as it challenges the most eloquent speakers of the Arabs to produce three verses like those in this *sūrah*.

2. Unique words

This *sūrah* is distinguished insofar as it uses words we do not find anywhere else in the Qurʾān, such as *kawthar* (lit. "abundance"), *naḥr* (lit. "sacrifice"), *shāniʾ* (lit. "enemy"), and *abtar* (lit. "without posterity"). It is the Prophet's due that Allāh should address him with this *sūrah* made unique by the words used in it, foremost amongst which is the word *kawthar*, meaning all kinds of abundant goodness.

1. Sūrat Yūnus (10):38

3. Sagacious use of words

The Qurʾān is extremely precise and sagacious in how it uses words throughout its text, including its use of the first person pronoun that refers to the divine essence. Sometimes this pronoun appears in the singular ('I'), as in "I am indeed the All-forgiving, the All-merciful"[2] and "I am indeed nearmost"[3] which is supposed to give a sense of Allāh's nearness and immanence to His servant. This necessitates a feeling of familiarity, as is clear in Allāh's address to Moses (as), "Indeed I am Allah — there is no god except Me. So worship Me, and maintain the prayer for My remembrance."[4] But sometimes it also appears in the plural ("we"), and this includes the opening verses of four *sūrahs* of the Qurʾān:

- "Indeed We have inaugurated for you a clear victory"[5]
- "Indeed We sent Noah to his people..."[6]
- "Indeed We sent it down on the Night of Ordainment."[7]
- "Indeed We have given you abundance."[8]

What unites all these *sūrahs* is a sense of the great act being attributed to Allāh, whether:

- granting a clear victory,
- sending the first of the great prophets who occupies the position of a second father to all humanity,
- sending down the final divine message to mankind, or
- granting an abundance of good.

There is a clear connection between all of these instances—the prophethood of the great prophets, divine scripture, the Holy Household (as) equal to it, and outward victory that guarantees the success of the prophetic mission.

---

2. Sūrat al-Ḥijr (15):49
3. Sūrat al-Baqarah (2):186
4. Sūrat Ṭa Ha (20):14
5. Sūrat al-Fatḥ (48):1
6. Sūrat Nūḥ (71):1
7. Sūrat al-Qadr (97):1
8. Sūrat al-Kawthar (108):1

4. Bestowing ownership

It is possible to honor someone generously without actually making them the owner of something, as when one person grants another the usufruct (*manfaʿa*) of a thing without giving him the thing itself. But the act of giving here is manifestly bestowing ownership, which is the utmost honor, in addition to the fact that the person being addressed in the words "We gave you" is the Final Prophet (s), which suggests that his being has a special quality in this gift that entitles him to the abundant good contained within this gift, as the readiness of the receiver engenders the act of the giver as well.

5. Prophecies

It is striking that as many as twenty-six different explanations have been offered for the term *kawthar* ('abundance'), all united by the idea that this *kawthar* contains abundant good. But the most appropriate interpretation in the broader context of this *sūrah* is "an abundance of offspring" firstly because *kawthar* is contrasted with *abtar* ("without posterity") (which is a like a recompense for those who first accused the Prophet (s) of being without issue) and secondly because of the command to sacrifice, according to one interpretation, which refers to the practice of offering a sacrifice when one is granted offspring.

It should be remembered that this *sūrah* is an instance in which the Qurʾān is divulging knowledge of the unseen. These instances are known collectively as the prophecies of the Qurʾān (*malāḥim al-Qurʾān*). This glad tiding came in Makkah while the Prophet (s) had few supporters and scant resources, while his enemy was a person of importance and influence. And yet, events would confirm the veracity of the Qurʾān's prophecy, as was the case with all other prophecies, for no lineage in history has been preserved like that of the final messenger (s).

6. *Kawthar*

The ambiguity of the word *kawthar*, which has produced such disagreement amongst different commentators, could be intended to illustrate the breadth of the scope of this abundant goodness. Some interpretations of this word have gone to great lengths: from those who say it refers to the scholars of the *umma* to others who say it is a river in paradise and yet others who say it means wisdom (*ḥikma*), which another verse also describes as abundant good![9]

It is the habit of the Qur'ān to leave some words ambiguous in their meaning in order to prompt people to use their intellects and ask questions from one angle and to ultimately refer those questions to the companion of the Qur'ān represented by the Prophet's Household (as) from another!

7. Maleness and femaleness

It was the divine will to realize the abundant good contained within the descendants of the Prophet (s) through his daughter, Fāṭimah (as). Remember this was at a time when having a daughter was considered ill-fated ("When one of them is brought the news of a female, his face becomes darkened and he chokes with suppressed agony."[10]). Just as Allāh willed to realize His word and spirit, Jesus (as), through the Virgin Mary (as). This contains a powerful lesson for us—that blessings are directed to the spiritual realm, while maleness and femaleness are attributes of the physical one, and these have no relation to receiving the divine effusion of munificence.

8. Fulfilment of a divine promise

We can see this *sūrah* as the fulfilment of the divine promise contained in Sūrat al-Ḍuḥā: "Soon your Lord will give you [that with which] you will be pleased."[11] This is because dedicating an entire *sūrah* to the promise to give him abundant good (*kawthar*) implies that there was something important that the Prophet (s)

9. Sūrat al-Baqarah (2):269: "...and he who is given wisdom, is certainly given an abundant good."
10. Sūrat al-Naḥl (16):58
11. Sūrat al-Ḍuḥā (93):5

was awaiting, something that would grant him utter happiness and satisfaction.

There is no doubt that the divine gift represented by Fāṭimah (as) contained the satisfaction of Allāh's messenger because her influence in this world was plainly manifested in the form of an abundance of offspring, and in the hereafter it was manifested in the form of intercession for this *umma.*

9. *Kawthar*

When Allāh blessed His prophet (s) with the conquest of Makkah, He commanded him to glorify Him and plead forgiveness ("and you see the people entering Allah's religion in throngs, then celebrate the praise of your Lord, and plead to Him for forgiveness..."[12]) as a kind of thanksgiving to the One who granted him this victory. But when He granted him the blessing of *kawthar*, He commanded him to pray ("so pray") which contains both glorification and pleading forgiveness.

This shows that this *kawthar* has a great effect in bringing people to Allāh's religion in droves and that is throughout all ages, not just at the time of Makkah's conquest.

10. "Your Lord"

It is inconceivable that the prayer of the Prophet (s) should be for anyone except the Lord. But in spite of that, the verse affirms that this prayer is directed towards "your Lord" and is only for Allāh, because it is obvious that any deed not done seeking His countenance, no matter how great the deed or its doer, is ultimately without substance.

11. Sūrat al-Kawthar and Sūrat al-Takāthur

There is a contrast, which is clear to anyone who reflects, between Sūrat al-Kawthar and Sūrat al-Takāthur, even though the two words are derived from the same root (*k-thr-r*):

12. Sūrat al-Naṣr (110):2–3

- In the first, we see an abundance that causes a person to worship Allāh ("so pray to your Lord") while in the second we see an abundance that causes a person to forget the remembrance of Allāh ("rivalry distracted you..."[13]).
- In the first, the call to pray brings Allāh's servants to their prayer niches, while in the second, rivalry drives them to the graves to count the deceased of their tribe ("until you visited the graves"[14]).
- *Kawthar* is represented by an abundant good given by Allāh to His beloved prophet (s), which is a real (rather than imagined) good that lasts across generations, while the kind of rivalry being censured in Sūrat al-Takāthur is actually something illusory and imagined. In and of itself, an abundance of children is not something valuable, not to mention that this thing of imaginary value loses its worth to a person who dies in this world, let alone in the hereafter.
- The *kawthar* given by Allāh is an emanation of Allāh's overflowing munificence, and it is well-known that everything that comes from Allāh and everything that is for Allāh's sake grows. On the other hand, the source of immoral rivalry is the love of this world, being deceived by it and feeling proud of it in front of one's peers. Of course, whatever is for the sake of someone other than Allāh will fade and disappear.

12. Kindling hearts

There is a clear connection between the statement "We have given you..." and the command "So pray..." that follows it. Recalling one of Allāh's gifts should motivate someone to pray to Him, which is something that confers awe and humility upon the worshiper. This is one of the ways in which people's hearts can be kindled—they should "pray" whenever they see themselves slipping. Equally, one of the ways in which people can be called towards Allāh is by

13. Sūrat al-Takāthur (102):1
14. Sūrat al-Takāthur (102):2

reminding them of the blessings that came before the call to obey Him. It has been narrated in a *qudsī* tradition: "Allah revealed to Moses (as): 'Endear me to my creation, and endear my creation to me.' Moses asked, 'My Lord, how should I do that?' He said, 'Remind them of by blessings and gifts that they might love Me.'"[15]

13. *Kawthar*

By attaching the Lord to the Prophet (s) in the phrase "...to your Lord," the Qurʾān suggests that the very same divine favor that this and other *sūrahs* mention flows from the station of lordship. Were it not for the fact that the Lord of the Worlds undertook to exalt the name of His beloved prophet, Muḥammad (s), this honor would never have stretched through the ages.

One of the interpretations offered by Fakhr al-Rāzī for the word *kawthar* is that it refers to his sons, to which he appends, "Because this sūrah only came down to refute those who mocked the Prophet (s) for his lack of male progeny. So this means that Allāh will give him a lineage that will endure with the passage of time; see how many members of the Prophet's Household (as) were slain, and yet the world is filled with them, while not a single worthy descendent of the Umayyad clan remains! Then look how many great scholars came from his offspring: al-Bāqir, al-Ṣādiq, al-Kāḍhim, al-Riḍā, the Pure Soul (*al- nafs al-zakiyya*),[16] and the like of them."[17]

14. *Sūrah* addressing the Prophet (s)

Despite this *sūrah*'s brevity, being only three verses long, it addresses the Prophet (s) directly five times, whether using the explicit pronoun ("to your Lord") or the implicit one ("and sacrifice")[18] as if the axis around which this *sūrah* revolves is none other than the

---

15. *Al-Jawāhir al-sunniyya fī al-aḥādīth al-qudsiyya* 525

16. This is Muḥammad b. ʿAbd Allah b. al-Ḥasan al-Muthannā b. al-Ḥasan b. ʿAlī b. Abī Ṭālib (d. 145/762), who led an unsuccessful uprising against the ʿAbbāsid Caliph, al-Mansūr, in Medina, while his brother, Ibrāhīm, led a parallel uprising in southern Iraq.

17. *Mafātīḥ al-ghayb* 32/313

18. This is because in Arabic grammar, the pronoun "you" is treated as implicit in imperative commands.

Prophet (s) himself, even if its purpose is to expound the blessings of *kawthar* in response to the reproach of his enemy who sought to disparage to most noble and honored of Allāh's creatures.

15. "And sacrifice"

"And sacrifice" is explained to mean the sacrifice of a she-camel, whether on the two Eid days, or generally, and it fits within the context of the Qur'ān's emphasis on the correspondence between fulfilling the rights of the Creator and fulfilling the rights of the creation, as we also can see in how the Qur'ān repeated the combination of the injunction to pray and the injunction to give *zakāh* and its forbiddance on neglecting prayers and refusing to help others.

It is from this perspective that the Qur'ān bids the Prophet (s) to give thanks for the blessing of *kawthar* sometimes by praying and others by feeding the needy—neither one removes the need for the other.

16. "And sacrifice"

Another interpretation of the injunction *wanḥar* ("and sacrifice") is to raise one's hands level to one's neck when reciting the *takbīr* that begins the prayer.[19] If this is the case, then mentioning this after the injunction to pray suggests that this fundamental component of prayer is very important. After all, this *takbīr*:

- accompanies the very beginning of a person's prayer and symbolizes their entry into the divine presence through their ascent in prayer.
- consists of one of the most important Islamic invocations (*dhikr*), as the utmost praise of the station of lordship is conceding one's inability to adequately describe or praise

19. The command *wanḥar* comes from the root *n-ḥ-r* which relates to the throat (*naḥr*). It is this which makes both interpretations of the word possible; an animal is sacrificed by cutting its throat, and a worshiper raises his hands so that his palms are level with his throat when pronouncing *takbīr* ("*allāhu akbar*") in prayer.

the Lord, which is the essence of the words of the *takbīr* ("*allāhu akbar*" – "Allah is greater").

17. Best ways to give thanks

One could say, based on the ideas gleaned from this *sūrah*, that one of the best gifts Allāh can bestow upon His servants is righteous children, and some of the best ways to give thanks are:

- to offer prayers before Allāh that are attached to that blessing, as indicated by the conjunction "So..." (*fa*) in the phrase "So pray to your Lord...."
- to offer sacrifices seeking nearness to Him, based on Allāh's command to His prophet (s) "And sacrifice."

18. Allāh defending Prophet Muḥammad (s)

Allāh wastes no opportunity to defend His favorite prophet (s). He generally defends the faithful ("Allah indeed defends those who have faith..."[20]), so what about His chosen messenger? When the idolaters accused him of being insane, Allāh responded, "...you are not, by your Lord's blessing, crazy."[21] When they denied that he was a messenger ("You have not been sent [by Allah]"[22]), Allāh responded, "and you are indeed one of the messengers."[23] When they accused him of being a poet ("for a crazed poet"[24]), Allāh responded in his defense, "We did not teach him poetry, nor does it behoove him."[25]). We see this pattern continued in this *sūrah* when they claimed he was without issue, whereat Allāh defended him with the words "Indeed it is your enemy who is without posterity."

This was not idle talk on Allāh's part. Rather He demonstrated to everyone in practice the truthfulness of this description, and he had a great many offspring, not least amongst which were the *imāms* of the Prophet's Household (as).

---

20. Sūrat al-Ḥajj (22):38
21. Sūrat al-Qalam (68):2
22. Sūrat al-Raʿd (13):43
23. Sūrat al-Baqarah (2):252
24. Sūrat al-Ṣāffāt (37):36
25. Sūrat Yā Sīn (36):69

19. A lack of posterity

Divine recompense always reflects the actions of the person, whether this recompense is meted out in this world or the hereafter. So it is very fitting that the person who disparaged the Prophet (s) for having no male heir, especially after the loss of his sons Qāsim and ʿAbd Allāh, should be rewarded with the same kind of fate—a lack of posterity (*batr*), which is explained to mean someone who has no religion or lineage. This is what ultimately happened—the enemy of the Prophet (s) has no exalted reputation, nor any surviving heirs, unlike the Prophet himself. Allāh exalted his reputation and granted him abundant and blessed progeny until the Day of Resurrection.

20. Ostentation

Any important action that is not attached to Allāh is without issue (*abtar*), whether it concerns a person's connection to their Lord, such as prayer, or their connection to others, such as slaughtering a sacrificial animal. Hence the words "to your Lord" are positioned between those of "So pray..." and "...sacrifice" to demonstrate the positive aspect of this, just as the words "...those who show off..." are positioned between those of "their prayers" and "deny aid" to demonstrate the negative one.

Based on this, we can say that ostentation and showing off (*riyāʾ*) obliterates every kind of good deed, just as dedication (*ikhlāṣ*) yields every act of obedience.

21. Being an enemy of the Prophet (s)

When Allāh threatens the Prophet's enemy with a lack of posterity, it is as if he is to be the only person in history without offspring, because Allāh says, "Your enemy is the one without posterity." This phrasing suggests either emphasis or specification. However, this threat is not restricted to this person in particular for the meaning of the revelation is not restricted to the person about whom it was originally revealed. Everyone who hates the Prophet (s) will suffer the same fate and be without issue in all times. This is especially clear because the Arabic uses the noun of the active participle (*fāʿil*) rather than that of the verb that indicates that this recompense is for anyone who possesses this attribute (i.e., being the enemy of the Prophet) in any context.

Sūrat al-Kāfirūn (no. 109: The Faithless Ones)

Verses 1–6

In the name of Allāh, the All-Beneficent, the All-Merciful

109:1 *Say, 'O faithless ones!*

109:2 *I do not worship what you worship,*

109:3 *nor do you worship what I worship;*

109:4 *nor will I worship what you have worshiped*

109:5 *nor will you worship what I worship.*

109:6 *To you your religion, and to me my religion.'*

1. Intractable disbelievers

The address to the faithless ones in this *sūrah*, even if it is unqualified (*muṭlaq*), is directed towards a specific group of people in the time of the Prophet (s). This group were some of the most intractable disbelievers in history because they were both ignorant and obstinate! These verses convey the utter hopelessness of this group ever believing. However, it does not apply to all the faithless, for there are often those who give up their disbelief, like those who found faith after Makkah was conquered, and become good Muslims, or those magicians who believed in Moses (as) after they had long been his opponents!

2. Agreements with the faithless

This *sūrah* affirms, in four verses whose fundamental ideas are very similar, an essential truth—there is no common worship between the two sides of faith and disbelief because of the importance of belief in the personality of a believer, especially with regards to divine unity (*tawḥīd*). All of his practices are affected by this most fundamental of principles.

But just because there can be no compromise about this central principle does not mean that people cannot come to agreements for their mutual benefit in those matters not directly affected by beliefs, which is why the Prophet (s) made treaties with the faithless, such as that of Ḥudaybiyya. In fact Allāh commanded the Prophet to seek treaties where appropriate with the words "And if they incline towards peace, then incline towards it [also]...."[1]

3. No compromise on matters of doctrine

Using the Arabic particle *lā* (translated as "shall not") signifies a future negation. This both illustrates the position of the Prophet (s) in relation to worshipping their deities and that of the faithless in relation to worshipping Allāh, which in turn demonstrates that there could never be any reconciliation between the Prophet (s) and those who opposed him.

This is why there can be no compromise on matters of doctrine, even if there can be compromise in matters of warfare. The Qurʾān settles this decisively when it says, "Never will the Jews be pleased with you, nor the Christians, unless you followed their creed,"[2] meaning that surrendering one's principles is the only way to truly please others—may it never come to pass!

4. The pronoun 'what'

The pronoun 'what' (*mā*), which is commonly employed for non-rational beings, is used for the gods of faithless in the verse "I do not worship what you worship" because these gods are idols that cannot comprehend anything. But why is the same pronoun then used for the One True God in the verse "nor do you worship what I worship"? To resolve this, we must say either that it is mirroring the expression in the previous verse, that it is referring to the

1. Sūrat al-Anfāl (8):61
2. Sūrat al-Baqarah (2):120

method of worship, or it is referring to the worship itself (i.e., "Nor do you worship my worship.").

5. Worship

The disagreement between the Prophet (s) and the faithless of his time did not concern Allāh's status as the Creator because they did not deny this. The Qurʾān says, "those who take guardians besides Him [claiming,] 'We only worship them so that they may bring us near to Allah....'"[3] So the disagreement is in the method of worshipping Allāh, and the practice of associating partners with Him (*shirk*), namely, divine unity in worship (*al-tawḥīd fī al-ʿibāda*), which is why these verses revolve around worship and its derivatives.

Let it be known that those who worship ostentatiously, even though they believe in Allāh, suffer from the same kind of defect as these faithless ones, for what is the point of worship that is not solely dedicated to Allāh?

6. Goal of repetition

One of the goals of repetition in these clear verses is to firmly establish this truth, namely, that neither party can turn aside from what it worships. Although the expression used for the Prophet (s) varies between "I do not worship..." which uses a verb and "Nor am I a worshiper..." which uses the active participle, these two expressions, when taken together, are more forceful in their rejection!

7. Repetition explained

We can explain the repetition in this *sūrah* as follows:

- The repetition in the two verses is addressed to the offer of the faithless to the Prophet (s) that he would worship their gods in one year and they would worship his God in another,

3. Sūrat al-Zumar (39):3

so the negation is repeated for the number of alternating years of worship.

- The pronoun 'what' in the first two verses refers to the object of worship, thus negating the worship of each other's deity, while in the last two verses, 'what' refers to the method of worship. In this case, the verses mean that the two sides disagree not only about the objects of worship but about the very method of worship itself.
- When the Qurʾān says, "I do not worship what you worship," this applies to the present because it contains a verb in the present continuous tense, while "nor will I worship what you have worshiped" contains a verb in the past tense; so, taken together, these verses negate the act of worship at all times.

8. The religion of the faithless has nothing to do with the Prophet (s)

Placing the preposition and the noun it governs before the subject of the sentence in the verse "To your religion, and to me my religion" signifies that the religions of truth and falsehood only belong to their followers. So the religion of the faithless has nothing to do with the Prophet (s) and vice versa! This declaration also affirms that there is no common ground between the two, and there is no room for compromise in fundamental beliefs.

9. Religion other than Islām

There is no room to suppose that these verses which indicate that each group should be left to follow their own religion also indicate that people should be free to believe whatever they want, whether true or false, which is a concept promoted by misguided people in every era in order to escape the bonds of the *sharīʿa*. The Qurʾān in its totality calls people to divine unity (*tawḥīd*) and declares false any religion other than Islām. In other words, these verses should actually be understood as a threat—follow your religion and see what becomes of you! What we have said here also applies to the verse "Our deeds belong to us, and your deeds belong to you."[4]

10. Adopting a stance

Believers adopt their stance according to the person they are confronted with:

- With a believer who has fallen into heedlessness, they take a stance of reminding them ("And remind, for reminding indeed benefits the faithful."[5]).
- With a believer who sins openly, they take a stance of enjoining good and forbidding evil ("There has to be a nation among you summoning to the good, bidding what is right, and forbidding what is wrong. It is they who are the felicitous."[6]).
- With a believer who mistreats them, they take a stance of seeking reconciliation ("If two groups of the faithful fight one another, make peace between them. But if one party of them aggresses against the other, fight the one which aggresses until it returns to Allah's ordinance."[7]).
- With a disbeliever who attacks them, they takes a fighting stance ("Fight in the way of Allah those who fight you..."[8]).
- But with a disbeliever who seeks peace, they take a stance of compromise ("Allah does not forbid you in regard to those who did not make war against you on account of religion and did not expel you from your homes, that you deal with them with kindness and justice. Indeed Allah loves the just."[9]).

---

4. Sūrat al-Qaṣaṣ (28):55
5. Sūrat al-Dhāriyāt (51):55
6. Sūrat Āle ʿImrān (3):104
7. Sūrat al-Ḥujurāt (49):9
8. Sūrat al-Baqarah (2):190
9. Sūrat al-Mumtaḥanah (60):8

11. The Qur'ān's use of repetition

The Qur'ān's use of repetition is a familiar device to hone in on a concept to which its Author wants to call attention (and Allāh knows best what He means and what will benefit His servants).

- One example of this is when it repeats the words "So which of your Lord's bounties will you both deny?"[10] more than thirty times in Sūrat al-Raḥman to firmly embed the idea of thanksgiving.
- The words "woe to the deniers on that day"[11] is repeated more than ten times in Sūrat al-Mursalāt to drive home the threat to the deniers.
- The words "Perish he, how he decided!"[12] is repeated in Sūrat al-Muddaththir to underline the invocation against them.
- The words "No indeed! Soon you will know!"[13] is repeated in Sūrat al-Takāthur to impress upon them the fear of the Day of Resurrection.

This *sūrah* is another example of this, in that it categorically rejects the idea that the Prophet (s) will forsake any part of his religion to conform to the wishes of the faithless because it repeats this idea, albeit through two different expressions: "I do not worship..." and "Nor will I worship...."

12. A call to a form of disassociation from the faithless

The Qur'ān exhorts the faithless to take Allāh's friends as their allies and disassociate themselves from His enemies. One of the clearest instances of this is found at the beginning of Sūrat al-al-Tawbah: "a repudiation by Allah and His Messenger to the polytheists with whom you had made a treaty."[14]

---

10. Sūrat al-Raḥman (55):13
11. Sūrat al-Ṭūr (52):11
12. Sūrat al-Muddaththir (74):19
13. Sūrat al-Takāthur (102):3
14. Sūrat al-al-Tawbah (9):1

In this *sūrah*, we also find a call to a form of disassociation from the faithless, namely by refusing to compromise with them on matters of religion. Obviously, this discourse is directed in particular to the leaders of the *umma*, particularly the Final Prophet (s), as compromise begins with those who occupy a position of leadership if they are not distinguished by their being God-fearing persons.

Sūrat al-Naṣr (no. 110: Divine Help)

Verses 1–3

110:1 *When Allah's help comes with victory,*

110:2 *and you see the people entering Allah's religion in throngs,*

110:3 *then glorify the praise of your Lord, and plead to Him for forgiveness. Indeed He is all-clement.*

1. Allāh's help and victory

It is customary for the seeker to pursue the object of his desire, but sometimes, to display the utmost honor to the seeker, the object of his desire comes to him, just as a bride comes in procession to her husband, despite the fact that he desires her. An example of this in the Qurʾān is that paradise, which is promised to its inhabitants, comes towards them: "and paradise will be brought near for the Godwary."[1] Another example of this can be found in this *sūrah*, for those who struggle for the sake of Allāh usually strive to attain Allāh's help and victory, but here we see that Allāh's help comes to the Prophet (s) and not the other way around ("When Allah's help comes with victory...").

2. The source of help

The source of help, even though it is attributed to Allāh just as all good is attributed to Him, lies in the hand of Allāh's servant, and He alludes to this fact through His words "If you help Allah, He will help you...."[2] It is known that helping Allāh, in a general sense, entails:

1. Sūrat al-Shuʿarāʾ (26):90
2. Sūrat Muḥammad (47):7

- first, helping in all arenas of struggle, great or small, and
- second, fixing one's gaze on the object of one's assistance, namely Allāh, without any ulterior motives, or else it is not counted as helping Him.

3. Cutting roots of sedition

Mentioning victory over Makkah after mentioning Allāh's help in general shows that tearing out the sources of corruption and the axis of injustice is essential to the success of the mission of calling others towards Allāh. The fight between the Prophet (s) and his enemies did not end with the Battles of Badr, Uḥud, or the Trench, they only ended when he took Makkah and left no remnant of them.

This means that the faithful must use whatever strength they have been given to cut the roots of sedition (*fitna*) in every time, lest they stumble upon the path to their victory.

4. Blessings for Prophet Muḥammad (s)

Allāh's blessings are mentioned abundantly in the final *sūrahs* of this section (*juzʾ*) of the Qurʾān:

- In some instances, the Lord recalls the blessings that He bestowed upon His prophet, such as opening his breast in Sūrat al-Sharḥ.[3]
- In another, He promises him a gift that will please him, which refers to his power of intercession (*shafāʿa*) as a gift in Sūrat al-Ḍuḥā.
- In Sūrat al-Kawthar, He informs him that He has granted him abundant good.[4]
- In Sūrat al-Qadr, the revelation of the Qurʾān to His chosen prophet (s) is counted as a blessing.[5]

---

3. Sūrat al-Sharḥ (94):1: "Did We not open your breast for you?"
4. Sūrat al-Kawthar (108):1: "Indeed We have given you abundance."
5. Sūrat al-Qadr (97):1: "Indeed We sent it down on the Night of Ordainment."

- And in this *sūrah*, Allāh mentions His assistance to His beloved prophet (s) and the great victory that resulted from this assistance.

5. Help and victory

There is a difference between help (*naṣr*) and victory (*fatḥ*), namely, that Allāh might grant help to His servant in the form of support against the enemy by thwarting their plans and warding off their stratagems without decisively ending the conflict with them. So in the Battle of Badr, there was divine assistance for the faithful,[6] but this did not spell victory for them, which is why they then suffered the setback of Uḥud. But Allāh granted His prophet both help and victory when he conquered Makkah in what was called "the victory of victories" because with that victory his conflict with faithlessness and its followers was decisively resolved.

This distinction that exists in the external world also exists in the world of the soul: Allāh might help His servant in the greater struggle (*al-jihād al-akbar*) in some stages of his life without handing him complete victory, which is represented by being firmly established at the level of the contented soul and entering the kingdom ("enter among My servants, and enter My paradise!"[7]).

6. "The people"

The verse refers to those entering the religion of Allāh in droves as "the people" which makes it seem as though those who do not enter the final religion are not even people! After all, the Qur'ān refers to those who have strayed from obedience to Allāh as "just like cattle; rather they are further astray from the way."[8] This is supported by a narration from Imām al-Ḥasan (as) about the people in which he says, "We are the people, our followers are semblances of the people, our enemies are neanderthals (*nasnās*)."[9]

---

6. Sūrat Āle ʿImrān (3):123: "Certainly Allah helped you at Badr..."
7. Sūrat al-Fajr (89):29–30
8. Sūrat al-Furqān (25):44
9. *Jawāmiʿ al-Jāmiʿ* 15/556

7. Entering the religion

There is a difference between people entering the religion by themselves individually and entering the religion in groups and droves. This is nearer to the ultimate goal of the *sharīʿa* and more pleasing to the Lord! This is why this state in particular is singled out for mention.

Therefore, someone who does something to bring people to the religion is thereby closer to divine assistance and victory. Equally, someone who does something to drive people away from the religion carries a clear burden, and this is what will come to pass in one of the *umma*'s stages of life, as it has been narrated from the Prophet (s) that he said, "People entered the religion in droves, and they shall leave it in droves."[10]

8. *Fiṭra*

The original nature (*fiṭra*) upon which humankind was originated calls them to turn towards Allāh's religion which is in complete harmony with this original nature, which is why the *sharīʿa* is called "upright" (*hanīfiyya*), which means it turns away from the path of falsehood. But the hegemony of the enemy stands in the way of this, just as Pharaoh and others like him have done throughout history. Allāh says, "So he misled his people and they obeyed him."[11] But when the regime of falsehood vanishes, this obstacle will be removed and man's original nature will be able to have its effect, which is why the conquest of Makkah was such a great victory—it removed the most important barrier to the success of the prophetic mission in that age.

9. Worldly success

Help and victory only attain their value and nobility if they lead to people entering Allāh's religion in droves. In fact, it could be said generally that any merit in this world must be seen in the context of its connection with the merits of the unseen world. Something

10. *Jawāmiʿ al-Jāmiʿ* 15/555
11. Sūrat al-Zukhruf (43):54

is only praiseworthy insofar as it brings someone closer to Allāh, or else it becomes a burden for its possessor. If the people of this world implemented these criteria in their lives, they would not be so pleased by worldly success, whether it took the form of victory over their enemies or the most opulent of fleeting enjoyments.

10. Honoring the Prophet (s)

When Allāh mentions help in this *sūrah*, He calls attention to His essence at the same time ("Allah's help"), and He does the same for religion ("Allah's religion") because this is within the context of expounding the greatness of the help and the religion. In this situation, it is appropriate to mention the most noble of Allāh's names. Yet when it comes to mentioning His beloved prophet (s), He attaches him to Himself by invoking lordship "your Lord." We should not miss the subtlety and favor contained in this expression, namely:

- by attaching His prophet (s) to Himself to honor him.
- by using the title "Lord" (*rabb*), alluding to Allāh's aspect of lordship (*rubūbiyya*) from whence this divine assistance came, after honoring the Prophet (s) by attaching him to Himself.
- by the Qurʾān employing a direct second person address ("you") which demonstrates concern and intimacy.

11. Remembrance

The need for remembrance (*dhikr*) is greater still when there are things that distract the human being from remembering the Lord, including fighting in battle for the nature of attacking the enemy and retreating from them could cause someone to forget much remembrance. This is why the divine ordinance came in the Qurʾān: "O you who have faith! When you meet a host [in battle], then stand firm, and remember Allah greatly so that you may be felicitous."[12] People also become heedless because they are preoccupied with

12. Sūrat al-Anfāl (8):45

some of the results of divine help, such as worldly booty and the exuberance of victory. That is why this *sūrah* enjoins glorifying Allāh's praise and pleading forgiveness from Him after divine help and victory.

12. Glorification

We can interpret glorifying Allāh's (*tasbīḥ bil-ḥamd*) praise in a number of ways, including:

- Combining glorification and praise together (*alḥamdulillāh* and *subḥānallāh*) just as we are commanded to combine *lā ilāha ill allāh* with *allāhu akbar* without any connection between them.
- That this celebration (*tasbīḥ*) means to exalt Him above any deficiency. This is through praising and extolling Him, as an object of praise does not deserve to be praised unless it is free from faults in its essence and attributes.
- That the primary goal is to glorify, but this is supported by praising Allāh and His favor, just as one attaches all good deeds to oneself by praising Allāh (e.g., "Alḥamdulillāh, I prayed.").

13. Glorification

Glorification (*tasbīḥ*) is mentioned in the Qur'ān more than *tahlīl,*[13] *takbīr,*[14] or praise (*taḥmīd*).[15] Perhaps the reason for this is that a person's disobedience towards his Lord in many of His commands and prohibitions causes him to suffer many stumbles and falls, whereat it is appropriate for a person to exalt his Lord above having any fault attributed to Him, including wrongdoing (*ḍhulm*). Namely, a person sees in himself some effects of his actions that do not please him and actually attributes the fault to himself (rather than Allāh). This is how Jonah (as) entreated his Lord ("There is no god except You! You are immaculate! I have indeed been among

13. Meaning to say "*Lā ilāha ill allāh*"
14. Meaning to say "*Allāhu akbar*"
15. Meaning to say "*Alḥamdulillāh*"

the wrongdoers!"[16]). This glorification became a means of his salvation, just as it became a means for the apology of the angels to be accepted (Immaculate are You! We have no knowledge except what You have taught us."[17]).

14. Help

A corollary of completely exalting and glorifying Allāh is believing that Allāh will never abandon His friends in this world or the hereafter ("Indeed We shall help Our Messengers and those who have faith in the life of the world and on the day when the witnesses rise up."[18]). It is clear that because one good deed begets another, Allāh will help those who listen to and obey Him because He has said in a verse containing several forms of emphasis, "Allah will surely help those who help Him."[19] The pages of history bear witness to this fact, namely, that sooner or later, Allāh will always help His friends and thwart His enemies!

15. Forgiveness

When the Prophet (s) pleads for forgiveness, and when Allāh commands him to do so, as we see in this *sūrah* or in the verse "...plead for forgiveness of your sin and for the faithful, men and women,"[20] this could be for a number of reasons:

- To set an example for those who follow the Prophet (s) as a role model. This is an idea we often see in educating others; a teacher might reprimand a hard-working student to call other students' attention to their own mistakes and the fact that they are more worthy of such a reprimand.
- For not doing what was most appropriate or best, but this act does not conflict with infallibility (*ʿisma*), despite that it calls for a feeling of embarrassment before Allāh when

---

16. Sūrat al-Anbiyāʾ (21):87
17. Sūrat al-Baqarah (2):32
18. Sūrat Ghāfir (40):51
19. Sūrat al-Ḥajj (22):40
20. Sūrat Muḥammad (47):19

observing oneself sternly, which in turn calls for real repentance to Allāh.

- It could be a requirement of traversing the spiritual stations when wayfaring towards Allāh, for when someone ascends from a high level to an even higher one, they see themselves as though they were deficient and lacking in their previous state, which requires them to seek forgiveness from the One towards whom they are ascending.

16. Etiquette of supplication

Pleading for forgiveness (*istighfār*) is a kind of supplication with which servants turn to their Lord, and they must therefore observe the etiquette of supplication, including preceding with praise and adulation as we see in this *sūrah* because Allāh instructs His prophet (s) to glorify and praise Him before He instructs him to plead for forgiveness. This is etiquette we should observe in all forms of supplication and in all states.

17. Victory

Success and victory naturally breed feelings of conceit and vainglory, which are famous qualities of conquerors. However, this *sūrah* came to remind them to plead for forgiveness after remembering their Lord, contrary to what one might expect from this situation. Perhaps the reason for this is to first remove this conceit, and second to dispel the illusion that their success belongs to them in any real sense, for Allāh actually directly attributes it to Himself by saying, "Victory comes only from Allah."[21]

18. Forgiveness

In this *sūrah*, Allāh does not qualify pleading for forgiveness with many stipulations as He does in other verses of repentance, such as ignorance, its being near at hand, or avoiding persistently sinning before it. After all, pleading for forgiveness here comes in the context of Allāh's help in response to His servants helping Him, so

21. Sūrat al-Anfāl (8):10

this does not need many stipulations. In fact, this verse mentions clemency as a direct result of this pleading using a number of kinds of emphasis including:

- prefixing the sentence with "indeed" (*inna*) for emphasis (*ta'kīd*),
- using the noun form of intensification (*mubālagha*) in describing the scope of His clemency ("all-clement" (*tawwāb*)), and
- expressing the sureness of this clemency by using the explicit copula "is" (*kāna*).[22]

19. Clemency

It is well-known that using the expression "all-clement" (*tawwāb*) instead of all-forgiving (*ghaffār*) contains a subtle implication in the context of this discussion of divine assistance insofar as clemency (*tawba*) means that the Lord returns to His servant, turning to him with kindness and mercy, and this inspires the servant to return to Him also, as Allāh says, "He turned clemently toward them so that they might turn [to Him]."[23] This meaning is distinct from that of mere forgiveness, for Allāh might forgive His servant in the sense of effacing his bad deeds without actually turning towards him.

22. In most Arabic sentences, the copula ("is") is implicit. But this verse uses the verb *kāna* (lit. "to be") to emphasize the certainty of this statement.
23. Sūrat al-al-Tawbah (9):118

Sūrat al-Masad (no. 111: The Palm Fiber)

Verses 1–5

In the name of Allāh, the All-Beneficent, the All-Merciful

111:1 *Perish the hands of Abu Lahab, and perish he!*

111:2 *Neither his wealth availed him, nor what he had earned.*

111:3 *Soon he will enter a fire of flames,*

111:4 *and his woman, the firewood carrier,*

111:5 *with a rope of palm fibre around her neck.*

1. Perish

Using the expression "Perish...!," which means either to inform the audience of his ruin and loss, or to call down ruin upon him, is sometimes used in connection with a person's hand, which is the limb through which one executes his will and at others used for the person himself, the owner of that hand.

The divine language, which conforms to this style, nullifies the deeds of the faithless just as these deeds ruin their persons! After this divine threat, which includes all wrongdoers like Abū Lahab throughout history, why should there remain any fear in the hearts of the faithful?

2. Abū Lahab

One of the very closest relatives to the noblest of Allāh's creatures was Abū Lahab. Even today in Arab and other societies, a paternal uncle (*ʿamm*), is second only to a child's father in importance, and he often he will take on the responsibilities of a father in the event of the former's loss. This is why Abraham (as) addressed his paternal uncle, Azar, as his father ("When Abraham said to Azar, his father..."[1]). Therefore, is it right for one of the Prophet's closest kin to decide that he is going to do whatever he wants? In fact, the rebuke and threat issued here to the Prophet's uncle is almost without compeer in the Qurʾān because an entire *sūrah* has been set aside to rebuke him and his wife, Umm Jamīl.

3. Abū Lahab's persecution of the Prophet (s)

There are some people who refuse to curse (*laʿn*) others or make invocations that they be removed from the sphere of divine mercy, while we see that the Qurʾān invokes curses in more than forty different locations with various expressions, including the formula we find in this *sūrah* which is also a curse and an invocation for someone to be denied mercy. This one is specifically directed against Abū Lahab because he was outstanding in his persecution of the Prophet (s) to an almost unbelievable degree. He would stalk the Prophet (s) like a shadow, and whenever a delegation came to see him (s), they would first ask about him from his uncle, Abū Lahab, because of the latter's seniority, kinship, and importance. Abū Lahab would tell them he is a magician, so then they would go back without meeting him. But then there came a delegation to him who said, "We will not leave without seeing him." So he told them, "We are still trying to cure him of his madness, the unfortunate wretch!" One of them said of the Prophet (s), "While I was in a covered market, there was a young man who came saying, 'O people! Say there is no god but Allah (*lā ilāha ill allāh*) and be successful!' There came a man behind him, pelting him with stones until he had bloodied his thighs and calves saying, 'O people! He is a liar, so don't believe him!'"[2]

4. Effects of curses

Supplications against the faithless, represented as they are by curses and invocations to expel them from divine mercy, usually

1. Sūrat al-Anʿām (6):74
2. *Tafsīr al-mīzān* 20/386

have their effect on the Day of Resurrection, but these verses allude to these curses have consequences and effects in this world as well, namely:

- The waste of their efforts opposing the prophetic mission ("Perish the hands of Abu Lahab, and perish he!")
- It is Allāh Himself who will undertake to fight them, and who can possibly stand against the sovereign of the heavens and the earth? ("May Allah assail them, where do they stray?!"[3])
- The utter destruction of their riches, as happened with Pharaoh's clan ("Our Lord! Blot out their wealth...!"[4])
- The ruin of their edifice ("Then Allah razed their edifice from the foundations and the roof collapsed upon them from above..."[5])

5. Allāh's enemies

A person who reads the Qur'ān lives with what Allāh has sent down as though it was sent down for his own time. They yearn for the bliss of paradise when it is mentioned and seek refuge from the punishment of hellfire as though they hear its cries ringing in their ears. They give thanks whenever Allāh reminds them of one of His blessings and disassociate themselves from Allāh's enemies when they see them mentioned with ill- repute.

An instance of living with the Qur'ān in this manner can be found in this *sūrah*. It is appropriate to supplicate against those whom Allāh has rebuked in the harshest terms, and this too is a form of disassociation from the wrongdoers in the Qur'ān. This is what has been narrated from Imām al-Sādiq (as): "When you recite 'Perish the hands of Abū Lahab and perish he!" then supplicate against Abū Lahab, for he was indeed one of the deniers who denied the Prophet (s) and what he brought from Allah."[6]

3. Sūrat al-al-Tawbah (9):30
4. Sūrat Yūnus (10):88
5. Sūrat al-Naḥl (16):26
6. *Wasāʾil al-shīʿa* 6/73

6. Manifestations of bounty and power

All manifestations of bounty and power of this world will not avail a person if they are not blessed by Allāh for He is the giver of all bounties just as He is the one who blesses them. This is why there are numerous verses demonstrating that the things the wealthy rely on in this world will not avail them, including:

- wealth and children, which Allāh nullifies with His words "neither their wealth nor their children shall avail them anything against Allah."[7]
- friends and those whom a person relies upon in attaining his goals, which Allāh nullifies with His words "the day when a friend will not avail a friend in any way."[8]
- guile and plotting, which Allāh nullifies with His words "the day when their guile will not avail them in any way...."[9]
- the intercession of the faithless, which Allāh invalidates with the words "Shall I take gods besides Him? If the All-beneficent desired to cause me any distress their intercession will not avail me in any way, nor will they rescue me."[10]
- amassing a numerous and well-equipped host, which Allāh invalidates by saying, "your troops will never avail you though they should be ever so many...."[11]

7. Wealth and what is earned

One could say that the difference between "his wealth" and "what he earned" is that the first refers to a person's possessions, even if he has not earned it, such as inherited property, while the second refers to his efforts, assuming that "what" (*mā*) conveys the meaning of a verbal noun.

---

7. Sūrat Āle ʿImrān (3):10
8. Sūrat al-Dukhkhān (44):41
9. Sūrat al-Ṭūr (52):46
10. Sūrat Yā Sīn (36):23
11. Sūrat al-Anfāl (8):19

Therefore, the divine wrath encompasses all of this entity, as represented by his efforts ("hands"), his person ("Abū Lahab", his "wealth," and his efforts in life ("what he earned"). So what will become of such a person when Allāh's curse surrounds all aspects of his being?!

8. Plots of the faithless

In a number of verses, the Qur'ān refers to the guile of the faithless and their plotting, but it does so with contempt and derision in order to strengthen the hearts of the faithful when they see plots from the faithless so severe as to move mountains. One example of this is when Allāh says, "But the stratagems of the faithless only go awry"[12] and "[know] that Allah undermines the stratagems of the faithless."[13] We find yet another instance in this *sūrah* when Allāh describes the ruin of the foremost opponent of the Prophet, Abū Lahab, and says that whatever wealth he has at his disposal to persecute the Prophet (s) will not only not avail him but actually kindle a blazing fire for him in hell.

9. Abū Lahab's wife

Allāh's punishment in the hereafter will correspond to how a person was in this world. So Abū Lahab's recompense in the hereafter will be rooted in his own being, and his wife's punishment will be rooted in her deeds. She used to carry firewood and thorns and throw them in front of the Prophet (s), so it is only right that this will become fuel for a blazing fire whose intensity is too great to be known, as indicated by the use of the indefinite "a fire with flames" to inspire terror. After all, every fire has flames.

10. Spouses

The word 'wife' (*zawja*) implies a kind of bond and affection that Allāh places between spouses which is why the Qur'ān does not use this relationship (i.e., marriage) to denote someone whose fate

12. Sūrat Ghāfir (40):25
13. Sūrat al-Anfāl (8):18

is hellfire, which is why we read in this *sūrah*: "and his woman, the firewood carrier." This is the way in which Allāh refers to the wives of Noah and Lot [to disassociate His prophets from them]: "Allah draws an example for the faithless: the woman of Noah and the woman of Lot."[14] Conversely, He uses the same expression for Pharaoh's wife [to disassociate her from her husband]: "Allah draws an example for those who have faith: the woman of Pharaoh, when she said, 'My Lord! Build me a home near You in paradise, and deliver me from Pharaoh and his conduct....'"[15]

- So in the first case is an example of a corrupt woman in the company of a corrupt man.
- The second is an example of a corrupt woman with a righteous man.
- The third is an example of a righteous woman with a corrupt man.
- As for the fourth case, namely, that of a righteous wife in the care of a righteous husband, this is the best match between spouses in existence. This match is idealized in the marriage of ʿAlī and Fāṭimah (as) insofar as "He merged the two seas, meeting each other. There is a barrier between them which they do not overstep. So which of your Lord's bounties will you both deny? From them emerge the pearl and the coral."[16]

11. Connection between two spouses

The essential connection between two spouses is an obvious social reality. So the appositeness of a carrier of firewood to Abū Lahab (of the fire with flames) is not something arbitrary. Generally speaking, a husband and a wife support one another, for good or for evil, because of the essential connection they share. If there were any seeds of goodness in the wife of Abū Lahab, she might have chided her husband or tried to curb his cruelty. This is why it

14. Sūrat al-Taḥrīm (66):10
15. Sūrat al-Taḥrīm (66):11
16. Sūrat al-Raḥman (55):19–22

is so important to be careful in choosing a spouse—a person should look to where they are putting themselves!

12. Humiliation in hellfire

One form of punishment in hellfire is the humiliation of its inhabitants in various ways, such as what we read in this *sūrah* concerning the carrier of firewood, the wife of Abū Lahab, for she has been portrayed repulsively in hellfire. Normally a woman wears a necklace of gold, but this unfortunate woman has a rope of palm-fiber around her neck, rough to the touch, wound from fibers, carrying firewood—the fuel for her own punishment in hellfire. This, in its entirety, is nothing less than the physical manifestation of how she was in this world, for it is not unlikely that she wore around her neck a vessel fastened with a rope wound from fibers, which she had filled with thorns to throw in front of the Prophet (s).

13. Prophecy about Abū Lahab and free will

This *sūrah* is one of the prophecies of the Qurʾān that impart knowledge of the unseen. It was revealed while Abū Lahab was still alive and a disbeliever. Had he wanted to, he could have challenged the Qurʾān by believing in the Prophet (s) and proving this prophecy to be false! And yet, because Allāh knew that this would never happen, He sent down this *sūrah* containing the exposition of a general rule, whose upshot is that even when Allāh foretells the deeds of His servants, this does not remove free will from them. Whatever deeds of theirs are described are only mentioned assuming that they will have free will. Otherwise, if these prophecies left them without free will, there would be no punishment for their deeds!

Sūrat al-Ikhlāṣ (no. 112: Devotion)

Verses 1–4

In the name of Allāh, the All-Beneficent, the All-Merciful

112:1 *Say, 'He, Allah, is One.*

112:2 *Allah is the All-embracing.*

112:3 *He neither begat, nor was begotten,*

112:4 *nor has He any equal.'*

1. Absolute oneness of essence

The significance of this *sūrah* is the same as that of Ayat al-Kursī insofar as it describes the Lord and styles Him with the most exalted attributes, namely, absolute oneness of essence (*aḥadiyya*), the absence of any equal to Him, whether in essence, attributes, or deeds, the logical corollary of which is that He alone is worthy of turning to in every matter, and that He is exalted above any composition such that He would need any other being or that would require Him to take on a physical form.

This is why this *sūrah* has acquired such a special place of honor—because it expounds the loftiest realities of existence in a few short verses. In a narration from Imām al-Ṣādiq (as) about the miʿrāj, we read that Allāh said to the Prophet (s), "Recite [the *sūrah*] 'Say Allah, He is One' as it came down, for it is My attribution and My description."[1] Which is why it is appropriate to affirm the contents of this *sūrah* by saying, "Thusly is Allah, my Lord!" (*kadhālik allāhu rabbī*) after we recite it in prayer.

1. *ʿIlal al-Sharīʿa* 2/315

2. Equal to a third of the entire Qurʾān

Narrations[2] state explicitly that this *sūrah* is equal to a third of the entire Qurʾān, and this has been explained in a number of ways:

- This is with regards to the doctrinal teachings of the Qurʾān as represented by divine unity (*tawḥīd*), prophethood (*nubuwwa*), and resurrection (*maʿād*). This *sūrah* undertakes to expound the first of these three.
- This is because the very foundation of the *sharīʿa* is knowing Allāh in three dimensions, namely, with regards to His essence, His attributes, and His actions. This *sūrah* also undertakes to explain the first of these three.
- Insofar as the Qurʾān in its entirety revolves around beliefs, morality, and parables of peoples past, this *sūrah* undertakes to explain the first of these three.

3. Four *sūrahs*

There is a certain affinity between the four *sūrahs* towards the end of the Qurʾān that begin with the command "Say...!" (*qul*), namely Sūrat al-Nās, Sūrat al-Falaq, Sūrat al- Ikhlāṣ, and Sūrat al-Kāfirūn:

- In al-Ikhlāṣ, the aspect of affirmation is dominant, namely, that of turning to the aspect of lordship and all of its corollaries such as relying only upon Allāh in seeking one's needs.
- In al-Kāfirūn, the aspect of negation is dominant, namely that of turning towards any object of worship besides Him, and both of these *sūrahs* are connected to the actions of the heart.
- As for al-Nās and al-Falaq, they both expound the way to being saved from the evil of every whisperer (*muwaswis*) who bars the way to obeying Allāh and the evil of every envier who envies one's blessings and the harm of every evil thing,

2. See, for instance *al-Kāfī* 4/644; *Wasāʾil al-shīʿa* 6/225

whether the darkness of the night or a sorcerer's witchcraft. All of this is connected to the actions of the limbs.

4. Allāh's magnificent name

Allāh's magnificent name (*lafḍh al-jalāla*)[3] appears in more than one-thousand five-hundred locations throughout the Qur'ān. This is the name used to denote all of Allāh's attributes of magnificence and perfection in their totality, as opposed to those names which signify one attribute amongst many, such as the All-Generous (*al-karīm*), the Knower (*al-ʿālim*) etc.

All the parts that make up this blessed name appear in the Qur'ān, beginning with *Allāh* itself, then *lillāh*, *lahu* and ending with the pronoun that refers to Him: *huwwa.*

5. Referring to Allāh with the pronoun 'he'

Referring to Allāh with the pronoun 'he' (*huwwa*) as a metonymy for Him (*kināya ʿanhu*), not, as some have suggested, a the subject of the sentence, followed by the magnificent name itself, conveys some deep ideas insofar as:

- It refers first to that dimension of Allāh which, in its perfection and elusiveness, is above specification and description, using the word 'he.'
- Then it refers to Him with the name that signifies His attributes, using the word *Allāh.*
- Then it refers to Him with one of His attributes ("One"), then another ("the All- Embracing").

To grasp the awesomeness of the reference to this first dimension without specifying any name or description, we must look to the words narrated from the Commander of the Faithful (as): "I saw Khiḍr (as) in a dream on the night before [the Battle of] Badr. I told him, 'Teach me something which will help me against the enemy!' He said, 'Say: "O He! – O He whom there is no He except He!"' So

3. Meaning the name: "Allāh"

when I awoke I related this to Allāh's messenger (s), who told me, 'O ʿAlī! You have been taught the greatest name!' So it was upon my lips on the Day of Badr."[4]

6. Divine unity

The practical outcome of believing in the divine unity of the divine essence, attributes, and acts is divine unity in worship for when someone believes these things, how can they even think of worshipping anyone else? This is how we know that deepening one's theoretical understanding will help them dedicate their practical worship to Him, for it is human nature to show concern for that which will fulfil one's needs. When a person sees no efficient cause (*muʾaththir*) in existence except Him, and this is a logical corollary of the theory of divine unity, it is only natural that they will only take recourse to Allāh, even if this is only because they want to attain their goals through Him rather than Him being worthy of worship!

7. Etymology of the name "Allāh"

The etymology of the name "Allāh" denotes a state of perplexity and seeking refuge. When the Arabs use the verb *aliha*, they mean that the subject of the verb has become perplexed by something and does not know what it is, and when they use the verb *walaha*, this means that its subject has taken refuge in its object from something which it fears.

In this context, we can turn to the following narration from the Commander of the Faithful (as): "Allāh means: The object of worship about whom all creation is perplexed, and in whom all creation seeks refuge. Allāh is veiled from apprehension by sight and secluded from all thoughts and suppositions."[5] Likewise from Imām al-Bāqir (as): "Allāh means the object of worship about whom, in trying to grasp His quiddity and encompass His quality, all creation becomes confused."[6]

4. *Tawḥīd* 89
5. Ibid.
6. Ibid.

8. *Wāḥid* and *aḥad*

There is a clear difference between the Arabic terms *wāḥid* and *aḥad*. Both are translated as "one," but it is the second which best befits the divine station. This is because when we negate *wāḥid*, this does not negate the possibility of a number above one. If you say, "One person did not come to me" (*mā jāʾanī wāḥid*), this leaves open the possibility that two or more people did. However, when we negate *aḥad,* this negates all numbers, whether in the mind or in the external world. This negation negates multiplicity in all of its forms, which is why we only use the description "the One" (*al-aḥad*) for the divine essence.[7]

This subtle use of language makes this *sūrah* an object of intense interest for those who love plumping the depths of meaning. It is narrated that Imām al-Sajjād (as) said, "Allah knew that in the end times there would be peoples of deep understanding (*awqām mutaʿammiqūn*) so Allah sent down the verse 'Say: "He, Allah, is One. Allah is the All- Embracing..."' and the first verses in Sūrat al-Ḥadīd up until His words '...and He knows best what is in the breasts.'[8] So whoever conjectures beyond what is there will perish."

9. Multifaceted words

The Qurʾānic approach rests upon awakening people's intellects, so it brings words that are multifaceted and could apply to numerous meanings, words such as "*kawthar*."[9] Another example is the use of a third person pronoun in this *sūrah*, expressing an ambiguous concept: "Say: 'He...'" then clarifying it "...Allah, is One." So we see a succession of predicates for that which is hidden in the utmost with regards to its essence, even if it is manifest in the utmost with regards to its effects.

---

7. So the same sentence using *aḥad* (*mā jāʾanī aḥad*) would be translated as "Not a single person came to me." The implications of this are clear in English. [Translator]
8. Sūrat al-Ḥadīd (57):6
9. Sūrat al-Kawthar (108):1

10. The word 'All-Embracing'

The word 'All-Embracing' applies to that which people resort to and rely upon for the satisfaction of their needs, as is narrated from Imām al-Jawwād (as) when he was asked: "What is the All-Embracing (*al-ṣamad*)?" He replied, "The master to whom people turn (*maṣmūd ilayh*) in all matters, great and small."[10] This term cannot truly be applied to anyone not imbued with the attribute of Absolute Oneness (*aḥadiyya*), such that there is no equal to Him in essence, attributes, or acts.

"The All-Embracing" has been applied to Allāh in this verse, taking the magnificent name as the subject of the sentence, just as the attribute "One" is predicated to the magnificent name too. So each verse expounds a single aspect of the divine with a single tenor insofar as the former "Allah is the All-Embracing" expounds the aspect of divine acts while the latter "He, Allah, is One" expounds the aspect of the divine essence. It is well-known that the perfect conception of divine unity encompasses both of these dimensions.

11. Absolute oneness

The verses of this *sūrah* are arranged in the best manner possible insofar as:

- The logical consequence of absolute oneness (*aḥadiyya*) is that Allāh is the All- Embracing (*al-ṣamad*) to whom everything turns because He alone possesses all the attributes of magnificence and perfection.
- The logical consequence of His being All-Embracing is the negation of any composition (*juzʾiyya*) from Him, such as being a father or a son, because every compound needs its components, and the negation of His being a trinity because a negation such as this cannot be attained unless He is completely without need of any presumed partner, whether at the level of the divine essence, attributes, or actions.

10. *Al-Kāfī* 1/91

12. The word 'All-Embracing'

The word 'All-Embracing' has been explained in this *sūrah* to mean that which has no inner cavity (*jawf*). It is narrated from Imām Ḥusayn (as): "The All-Embracing is that which is without a cavity." So 'All-Embracing' here means something totally solid, which of course must be a metaphorical expression referring to either:

- the fact that He is not affected by other beings, as corporeal beings can be compressed because of the spaces they contain within themselves or
- the absence of a womb in which to beget offspring, as exists in His creatures, in which case the words "He neither begat, nor was begotten" serve as an explanation of this dimension to Him.

13. The false ascription of fatherhood to Allāh

The false ascription of fatherhood to Allāh was widespread in earlier peoples, such as the claim that either Jesus or Ezra was His son as in His words "The Jews say, 'Ezra is the son of Allah,' and the Christians say, 'Christ is the son of Allah.'"[11] Or the claim that the angels are His sons and daughters, as in the verse "they... carve out sons and daughters for Him...."[12] This is why the verse first negates fatherhood from Him ("He neither begat...") before His being begotten, as it was uncommon to claim, as a few idolaters did, that He had been begotten by another deity.

14. Exclusivity

In Arabic rhetoric, placing something earlier in word order when it normally appears later yields the meaning of exclusivity (*ḥaṣr*). So when the Qurʾān places 'has He' (*lahu*) before 'any equal,' this indicates that only Allāh is without equal, because it is possible to conceive of an equal to everything besides Him, as all contingent beings are equal in the fact of their originatedness (*ḥudūth*) and potentiality (*qābiliyya*). Another verse that yields this exclusivity

11. Sūrat al-al-Tawbah (9):30
12. Sūrat al-Anʿām (6):100

is "Look! In Allah's remembrance do the hearts find rest!"[13] So this indicates that the hearts only find rest in His remembrance, the Most High—the One who has no equal in His essence has no equal in His effects, and one of these is giving tranquility to human hearts through His remembrance!

15. Equality

Equality in essence cannot apply to any being in the sense of their being two beings whose existence is necessary (*wājib al-wujūd*), but equality in action has many instances throughout history. Some give the attribute of arrangement (*tadbīr*) to other beings independently of Allāh, as did the idol worshipers or those who worshiped human beings, like those who believed that Pharaoh was the highest lord, for example!

Accepting this equality in the arrangement of worldly affairs could be a subtle form of polytheism for those who rely on anyone besides Allāh in looking after their affairs, even if they do not actually believe in that.

16. Divine unity in legislation and governance

One of the effects of a deeply rooted belief in divine unity, in addition to divine unity in worship, is divine unity in legislation and governance. This is the social dimension of divine unity, in addition to the individual dimension that is sometimes mentioned. How can someone who believes in a singular, all-embracing deity who is without equal possibly allow anyone else to rule over them unless they have been appointed by the True Ruler or to promulgate legislation in some affair whose knowledge they have not been inspired with by the All-Embracing source of revelation?

This is why the Qurʾān counts those who do not rule according to what Allāh has sent down amongst the faithless ("Those who do not judge by what Allah has sent down — it is they who are the faithless."[14]).

13. Sūrat al-Raʿd (13):28
14. Sūrat al-Māʾidah (5):44

Sūrat al-Falaq (no. 113: The Dawn)

Verses 1–5

In the name of Allāh, the All-Beneficent, the All-Merciful

113:1 *Say, 'I seek the protection of the Lord of the dawn*

113:2 *from the evil of what He has created,*

113:3 *and from the evil of a dark night when it settles,*

113:4 *and from the evil of the witches who blow on knots,*

113:5 *and from the evil of an envious one when he envies.'*

1. Seeking protection

Every act of seeking protection (*isti'ādha*) means to seek refuge from any source of harm by taking recourse to another being. This involves three fundamental elements, namely:

- The one seeking protection, accompanied by a sense of fear towards something that threatens them or else they would not be seeking protection.
- The one whose protection is sought, accompanied by a sense of trust in their ability to give assistance and protection.
- The thing from which protection is sought, which is that source of evil from which a person seeks refuge out of fear that they might come to harm because of it.

When these three fundamental elements are present, it is expected that a person will seek refuge in another, and that is assuming that the one seeking protection is serious in their entreaties.

This *sūrah* came to establish these three elements, so the one to whom the command "Say...!" is addressed is the one seeking refuge, the Exalted Lord ("the Lord of the dawn") is the one whose refuge is sought, and the objects of fear from which refuge is being sought are those evil things mentioned below in this *sūrah*.

2. Seeking refuge

The command to seek refuge (by saying "I seek refuge from Satan, the Outcast") when reciting the Qurʾān, relies on the magnificent name that signifies the divine essence ("When you recite the Qurʾan, seek the protection of Allah against the outcast Satan."[1]). But here, the command to seek refuge relies on a name signifying an attribute ("I seek protection in the Lord of the Dawn."). This could be an allusion to the gravity of Satan's whispering when reciting the Qurʾān, hence requiring the reciter to invoke their Master with the greatest of His names. That situation is nothing less than looking to repel evil in the realm of nearness to Allāh, unlike the situation of seeking refuge from the evils of darkness, witchcraft, and envy, whose harm could be restricted to this world alone.

3. Seeking refuge before a calamity occurs

Seeking refuge with Allāh is proper before a calamity occurs. In fact, it repels calamities, and, obviously, it is easier to repel a calamity than to alleviate one! So the Prophet (s) would protect his own self with this *sūrah*, and Imāms Ḥasan and Ḥusayn (as) would frequently seek protection with this *sūrah* and the one after it (Sūrat al-Falaq and Sūrat al-Nās),[2] which is especially significant considering the belief that the Prophet (s) could not fall victim to witchcraft as this would show a weakness in him that was incompatible with the rank of divine messengership, so there is no harm in seeking refuge even from evils that will not occur.

1. Sūrat al-Naḥl (16):98
2. *Majmaʿ al-bayān* 10/686

4. Doing good deeds to seek refuge

Seeking refuge accompanies fear, and fear requires one to seek safety from that which they fear. We can see this in what the Qurʾān relates about the Prophet's Household (as) when they gave food as charity and said, "Indeed we fear from our Lord a day, frowning and fateful."[3] In doing so, they combined "We feed you only for the sake of Allah..."[4] with the fear that required them to seek refuge.

Therefore, if someone is truthfully seeking refuge, this means genuinely taking recourse with Allāh, and taking genuine recourse to Allāh is through doing good deeds that will bring about salvation.

5. Seeking refuge at dawn

There is a clear appositeness between using the expression "the Lord of the Dawn" and seeking refuge from the various kinds of evil mention in this *sūrah*. After all, what could prevent Allāh from removing the darkness of evil with the light of relief when someone seeks refuge with Him, while each and every day He is the one who splits the darkness of the night with the light of the dawn?

The appositeness of this could be those intimate moments of mercy that accompany the hours of dawn at which time we witness those "pleading forgiveness at dawns"[5] at which time the angels of the night are met by those of the day, whereat the recitation of the Qurʾān at *fajr* is witnessed by both sets of angels ("Indeed the dawn recital is attended [by angels]."[6]). So seeking refuge with the Lord connected to this blessed time is more likely to receive a favorable response!

6. The word 'dawn'

The word 'dawn' here is like 'abundance'[7] and 'dawn'[8] and other terms about whose meaning the commentators disagree because

---

3. Sūrat al-Insān (76):10
4. Sūrat al-Insān (76):9
5. Sūrat Āle ʿImrān (3):17
6. Sūrat al-Isrāʾ (17):78
7. Sūrat al-Kawthar (108):1
8. Sūrat al-Fajr (89):1

they are multifaceted and can apply to multiple meanings. At the same time, these serve to reveal the depth of this scripture and demonstrate the need for someone to specify which of these meanings is correct. Here, a number of possible meanings are suggested:

- It is the dawn that splits the darkness.[9]
- It is the bringing forth of every being into existence by splitting its seed[10] whether a plant or animal, as Allāh says, "Indeed Allah is the splitter of the grain and the pit."[11]
- It is the bringing forth of everything from the darkness of non-existence into the light of existence, for He splits the veil of non-existence as well.

7. Evil from creation

Some people express amazement at how we seek refuge with Allāh from the "the evil of what He has created" while He is its creator, as if we are seeking refuge with Him from Himself!

The answer to this is that sometimes evil comes from someone who deliberately intends evil, like the evil of human beings, and sometimes evil comes from non-thinking beings, like the evil of natural disasters. In both cases, Allāh created that being itself and endowed it with the power to enact whatever good or evil it does. Whereat we say that whatever comes forth from that being, whether because of a character flaw, as with human beings, or rather as some consequence of its nature, like animals, it is proper for a person to seek refuge in their Lord who looks after all the affairs of this universe, good and evil, to remove from that person the flaw in their character or from that animal the consequence of its nature.

---

9. *Muʿjam maqāyīs al-lugha* 4/452
10. *Taḥqīq fī kalimāt al-Qurʾān* 9/136
11. Sūrat al-Anʿām (6):95

8. Darkness

"A dark night when it settles" is a night without light when it descends and sets in.[12] It is as though this night facilitates evildoing by spreading darkness. The sinner can sin therein without discovery or disgrace, and an assailant can take his opponent by surprise without leaving him any chance to escape. This is in addition to the fact that some people are afraid of the darkness itself, especially when this darkness of the night is combined with the darkness of the ocean, and this is the reason it is singled out for mention after evil itself. Perhaps the ease with which certain sins can be committed under cover of darkness is one of the most important sources of the evil it contains. What a difference there is between a night in which evil is done and the night described by the Qurʾān: "...they recite Allah's signs in the watches of the night..."[13]!

9. Invisible evils

This universe is composed of things both visible and unseen, so just as there is visible evil that can be seen with the eye (such as a dangerous animal) or through specialist equipment (such as microscopic germs), there are also invisible evils represented by those things not directly connected to the senses, such as the effects of witchcraft ("the witches who blow on knots") and the evil eye ("the evil of an envious one when he envies"). The Qurʾān affirms that such things do exist in other verses. For example, it mentions:

- magic ("...it was the devils who were faithless — teaching the people magic..."[14]),
- the evil eye ("Indeed the faithless almost devour you with their eyes when they hear the Reminder..."[15]), and

12. *Tahdhīb al-lugha* 8/31
13. Sūrat Āle ʿImrān (3):113
14. Sūrat al-Baqarah (2):102
15. Sūrat al-Qalam (68):51

- jinn ("Indeed some persons from the humans would seek the protection of some persons from the jinn."[16]).

Therefore, rushing to deny those things not subject to the senses makes no sense so long as the intellect deems it possible and there is some evidence for it.

10. Witchcraft

The ascription of witchcraft to women who blow on knots, if we do not treat it as a reference to specific witches in the time of the Prophet (s), could allude to some women in every time either:

- with regards to their weakness when confronted by adversaries, which causes them to take recourse to plots that do not involve man-to-man confrontations because of the strength it requires or
- with regards to their emotional power in ensnaring the hearts of men. So they resort to means of kindling affection even if through means forbidden because they cause harm to others.

11. Alternative meaning for witchcraft

It could be said that the subject of this verse is not actually witchcraft practiced by women by blowing on knots tied in threads or the like. Rather it is their natural efforts to win the hearts of men. By using their God-given physical and emotional qualities, they take hold of men's hearts, as if they are blowing into their hearts things that sap their willpower and discipline!

This meaning is plain to see in intimate moments of seclusion in which men will often act against their principles and common sense as if they have been truly bewitched. So it is appropriate to warn against such women as one would warn against a witch, for the danger is one and the same. This is supported by what Allāh has said about women, even if this is about a person's wife: "Indeed

---

16. Sūrat al-Jinn (72):6

among your spouses and children you have enemies; so beware of them."[17]

12. Indefinite usages

The use of the indefinite for "a dark night" and "an envious one" could be used to:

- magnify their evil compared to that of the witches who blow on knots because the evil of those witches is something coincidental that only happens rarely, unlike the night which descends upon us every day or the problems of human relations which we suffer in every group!
- diminish their evil compared to the witches who blow on knots from the angle that evil does not necessarily result from the night or from human envy. How many a night is free from evil! How many an envious person does nothing evil! So it is appropriate to use the indefinite for them in this sense in contrast to the witches because evil necessarily results from practicing witchcraft.

13. Not acting on envy

When an envious person conceals their envy and does not display it, and actually is troubled by their feelings, this could place them in the compass of divine mercy. For just as the Lord turns night to day, He can change this person's state too! Evil is only kindled when an envious person acts upon their envy, which is why refuge is sought from their evil with the proviso that they enact their envy ("and from the evil of the envious one when he envies"). This is either through the evil eye (for it has been narrated from the Prophet (s): "Envy almost outstrips destiny!"[18]) or through their actions when they plot against the object of their envy and do things that displease they Lord, in which case the words of the

17. Sūrat al-Taghābun (64):14
18. *Wasā'il al-shī'a* 15/365

Prophet (s) apply to them: "Beware of envy! For envy devours good deeds as fire devours kindling!"[19]

14. Repugnance of envy

The fact that envious people are singled out for mention after the witch, out of all the evil things in existence, shows the repugnance of this condition because:

- they are miserly to the utmost, as they do not seek good for themselves but rather hope that someone else will be deprived of it.
- they are ignorant to the utmost, for they do not seek good from Him in whose hand are the treasuries of the heavens and the earth and who tells His servants to ask for His grace "And ask Allah for His grace."[20]).
- they are audacious to the utmost, even if they do not realize it, as they are practically objecting to Allāh's actions while Allāh is the One who says, "Or do they envy the people for what Allah has given them out of His grace?"[21]

19. *Al-Kāfī* 2/306
20. Sūrat al-Nisā' (4):32
21. Sūrat al-Nisā' (4):54

Sūrat al-Nās (no. 114: Mankind)

Verses 1–6

In the name of Allāh the All-Beneficent, the All-Merciful

114:1 *Say, 'I seek the protection of the Lord of mankind,*

114:2 *Sovereign of mankind,*

114:3 *God of mankind,*

114:4 *from the evil of the whisperer who withdraws*

114:5 *who whispers into the breasts of men,*

114:6 *from among the jinn and men.'*

1. Evil from imperceptible sources

Allāh connects two *sūrahs* to call on His servants to seek refuge in Him, for in all of his life the human being is never free from things that scare him. The previous *sūrah,* Sūrat al-Falaq, is distinguished in its mention of perceptible sources of harm, such as the night, the envious person, and the witch, while this *sūrah* is distinguished by its focus on imperceptible sources of harm such as whispers in the hearts of men, whether these come from jinn or other men. No one is fully protected from evil unless they are saved from physical and spiritual sources of harm together.

2. Taking refuge with Allāh

Some people suffice themselves with verbally seeking Allāh's protection before reciting the Qur'ān, acting in accordance with Allāh's saying "When you recite the Qur'an, seek the protection of

Allāh against the outcast Satan"[1] because the hounding of the devils intensifies when a person does good deeds! But this verbal action will not render a person needless of truly seeking protection, for what is being enjoined by the words "Say: I seek the protection..." is not merely the utterance of some words, but first and foremost the heartfelt sensation that one is taking refuge with Allāh, followed by acting outwardly in a way that accords with seeking divine protection, such as giving up the pre-Islamic customs of the Arabs after emigrating [to Islamic lands] when seeking protection from the corruption of one's religion. In fact, one must give up any behavior that conflicts with seeking divine protection—like a person seeking Allāh's protection from wild animals while there is a fortified castle standing in front of him, but he does not enter it!

3. Divine protection

The one whose protection is sought in this *sūrah* is mentioned from various dimensions. From one angle, divine protection is sought from:

- "The Lord of mankind" – This is an independent reason for seeking protection in its own right because Allāh is the refuge of everyone who seeks protection. He is the Lord who arranges everything and in whose hand rests all of His servants affairs.
- "The Sovereign of mankind" – This is another independent reason, as Allāh is the sovereign whose authority over His servants is absolute and who can do whatever He likes to whomever He likes and however He likes.
- "The God of mankind" – This is, again, an independent reason, for He is the object of worship to whom everything returns in all affairs and upon whom rests the fulfilment of all needs.

1. Sūrat al-Naḥl (16):98

From all of the above, it is clear that a person must seek the protection of someone who combines all of these reasons in his being.

4. Seeking protection from Allāh

In numerous verses are phrases that highlight:

- Allāh's divine aspects of lordship and godhood ("Lord of the east and the west, there is no god except Him, so take Him for your trustee"[2])
- His divine aspect of sovereignty ("To Him belongs the kingdom of the heavens and the earth, and to Allah all matters are returned."[3]) and
- there is a single verse that highlights all three divine aspects together, namely, His words "That is Allah, your Lord! To Him belongs all sovereignty. There is no god except Him. Then where are you being led away?"[4] which combines lordship, godhood, and sovereignty.

Here, we ask: If someone believes they are seeking the protection of a being that combines all three of these dimensions, then how can they have any fear left in their heart when facing the evils of this life?

5. The Lord, the Sovereign, the God

The first three verses gradually introduce the giver of protection, who is Allāh, by mentioning the Lord, then the Sovereign, and finally the God. We can suppose that it is the ideas these designations contain that necessitates this gradual arrangement:

- The station of lordship is the nearest to the lives of Allāh's servants because they can see the effects of His arrangement of the creation, which belongs to the dimension of lordship, in even the tiniest details of their lives.

---

2. Sūrat al-Muzzammil (73):9
3. Sūrat al-Ḥadīd (57):5
4. Sūrat al-Zumar (39):6

- This is followed by a sense of the sovereignty that permeates all existence. Of course, recognizing this station is only for those who truly live with the knowledge that there is none to suffice them save Him, in accordance with His words "Does not Allah suffice His servant?"[5]
- This, in turn, is followed by a sense of spiritual immanence, represented by the connection of devoted servanthood between a person and the God besides whom there is no object of worship!

So this shows that the gradual development of this *sūrah*'s opening verses reveals the gradation that exists between the different stations of a person's connection to the Origin of all things, in whom it befits them to seek protection from spiritual evils. As for in Sūrat al-Falaq, protection is sought from "the Lord of the Dawn" alone, and this befits worldly evils which are less dangerous than those mentioned in this *sūrah*.

6. Different reasons for seeking His protection

This *sūrah* commands people to seek security with Allāh through His three manifestations (*tajalliyāt*), meaning lordship, sovereignty, and divinity, without using any particle of conjunction in the Arabic and repeating the word 'mankind' with each mention of Allāh. What we understand from this is that each verse provides us with different reasons for seeking His protection.

It is interesting to note that human beings also make these various dimensions reasons for seeking one another's protection. Anyone who suffers some injustice will first take recourse to whomever looks after their affairs, such as their father, then to someone who has power and authority, such as a ruler, and when they despair of these, they will turn to whichever deity they worship beyond mankind!

5. Sūrat al-Zumar (39):36

7. The whispers

The devastating influence of the whispers (*waswās*) by devils and men alike on the human soul is demonstrated by the fact that there are three formulas of seeking protection (from the Lord, Sovereign, and God of mankind) from a single evil, unlike in Sūrat al-Falaq where a single formula of seeking protection was used for four evils. The reason for this could be:

- These insinuations are subtle and a person might not notice them, for they belong to the realm of being cast into men's hearts ("into the breasts of men").
- They come from various sources ("from among the jinn and men").
- The whisperer whispers continuously, as indicated by the use of a present continuous verb ("who whispers...").
- Because this whisperer never gives up and returns to whisper time and again, for he is the one "who withdraws."

This is why such great protection must be sought with a great Lord from this great evil!

8. Purifying the hearts from the influence of Satan

Purifying the hearts from the influence of Satan is a way of purifying one's limbs, for the human being is exposed to the influence of these insinuations which are sometimes so intense that they almost overwhelm his own will so long as there is one whispering in his heart. So whatever force pushes a person internally could reach an intensity where it could push him externally, like a shove.

It is well-known that just as Allāh has given free reign to the one who whispers evil into men's hearts, He has reserved for Himself the right, through a superior means, to inspire His friends with that which contains good. This happens quite frequently, as the Qurʾān mentions in numerous locations. For example, Allāh says, "Then We revealed to your mother whatever was revealed."[6]

6. Sūrat Ṭa Ha (20):38

Another instance of this is what happened to the companions of the cave: "They were indeed youths who had faith in their Lord, and We had enhanced them in guidance."[7]

9. Escaping whispers

When a person conceives of how Satan watches over the human heart and hovers around it, and when they remember that Satan flows through the son of Adam as blood flows in their veins, and they recall that whenever Allāh is mentioned, Satan withdraws, as is mentioned in this *sūrah*...all of this should make them eager to be in a state of constant remembrance, for the only way to break the continuous whispering, as mentioned by the present continuous verb "who whispers...", is through continuously seeking divine protection ("I seek the protection of...").

Hence we must know that the default state of the human being is to be exposed to Satan's gnawing upon they heart, and we cannot escape this except by realizing that which will repel Satan from him. The best way for us to imagine this situation is what has been narrated from the Prophet (s) who said, "Satan places his snout upon the heart of the son of Adam; if he remembers Allāh, Satan withdraws; but if he forgets, Satan swallows his heart; that is the whisperer who withdraws!"[8]

10. Influencing hearts

If we say that the description "the whisperer who withdraws" applies to both "jinn and men," as this verse would appear to suggest, then this shows that some people have the ability to influence the hearts of others in their species. Satan's subtle influence on the hearts of men is something to be expected, but the power of one person over another normally does not go beyond their physical being. For some people to penetrate to the level of other's hearts requires a special kind of power, which is why people should beware them as they beware the devils themselves! But know also

7. Sūrat al-Kahf (18):13
8. *ʿIlal al-sharāʾi* 2/566

that the description "who withdraws" applies to them as well, so they will not give up their prize at the first sign of resistance, for their nature is like that of the devils in their determination to drag their victim down into moral depravity.

11. Attacking and retreating

Connecting the expression "the whisperer" to "who withdraws" suggests that there is a state of attacking and retreating between the human soul and the devils from amongst the jinn and men, which is why an expression is used which implies that they hide once more after emerging ("who withdraws") but that this battle continues until the "whisperer" ultimately triumphs, for this affair ultimately goes beyond withdrawing to the level of a person's heart being impressed ("They are the ones on whose hearts Allah has set an impressure"[9]) and sealed ("Allah has set a seal on their hearts and their hearing, and there is a blindfold on their sight"[10]) which is the level that the Commander of the Faithful (as) described as follows: "It is there that Satan takes control of his allies."[11]

12. Impregnable armor

So long as this whispering is connected to the realm of the hearts, and not every person has control over that which is hidden from the realm of senses, this affirms the desperate need for people to take refuge with the One who holds in His hand the keys of the hearts, for "People's hearts rest between two fingers of the All-Beneficent."[12] It is He who "intervenes between a man and his heart..."[13] and it is He who "knows the treachery of the eyes, and what the breasts hide."[14] This *sūrah* came down in order to push the human being towards this dimension, for only it has the power to place the one who seeks protection in its impregnable armor.

9. Sūrat al-Naḥl (16):108
10. Sūrat al-Baqarah (2):7
11. *Al-Kāfī* 8/159
12. *Al-Kāfī* 2/353
13. Sūrat al-Anfāl (8):24
14. Sūrat Ghāfir (40):19

13. Difference between satanic whispering

There is a difference between the satanic whispering (*waswasa*) directed into the breasts of people in general ("into the breasts of men") (from whence emerge false thoughts, then an inclination towards to forbidden, followed by the response of the limbs to this) and the satanic whispering to which the elect (*khawāṣṣ*), namely, the prophets (as), are exposed, as happened to Adam (as) ("Then Satan whispered to him..."[15]) and what befalls the Godwary of Allāh's servants ("When those who are Godwary are touched by a visitation of Satan, they remember and, behold, they perceive."[16]). The difference is that these latter whisperings are fleeting and do not remain in the hearts, nor is it feared that the possessors of these hearts will fall into forbidden things as a result.

14. Men being evil

Placing a conjunction between human beings and devils ("from among the jinn and men") signifies that there is a kind of commonality between them. So just as we find we have an inner prophet, represented by the intellect (*ʿaql*), that assists the outer prophet, there are also people who are, in their own way, outward representations of the inner devil, which is why the Qurʾān joins them together in a single verse "...the devils from among humans and jinn...."[17]

It is of interest to note that there is a class of people who, in a few short years, can learn what it took the devils many long ones to learn. In fact, they can even reach a level where they and the devils inspire one another to obstruct the path of the prophets (as): "That is how for every prophet We appointed as enemy the devils from among humans and jinn, who inspire each other with flashy words, deceptively."[18]

15. Sūrat Ṭa Ha (20):120
16. Sūrat al-Aʿrāf (7):201
17. Sūrat al-Anʿām (6):112
18. Sūrat al-Anʿām (6):112

15. Protecting the heart

The take-home message of this, the final *sūrah* of the Qurʾān, is that a person must protect the very core of their being, namely, the heart (which is called the breast here), lest it fall into the grasp of their enemies who lie in wait—the devils amongst the jinn and men who whisper temptations to them. It is well-known that unless a person fortifies this castle, which contains the governing force of their entire body, then their bodily acts of worship will not be able to help them in the slightest when it comes to repelling the besiegers of this citadel.

The best means to make tangible the war being waged between the soul and its enemies, which this *sūrah* hints at, is the tradition narrated from Imām al-Ṣādiq (as) in which he says, "The heart is Allah's sanctuary, so do not let anyone reside in Allah's sanctuary except Allah."[19] This sentence, in its succinctness and brevity, perfectly encapsulates the view of the Prophet's Household (as) when it comes to the purification and refinement of the human heart.

---

19. *Biḥār al-anwār* 25/67

Made in the USA
Lexington, KY
20 December 2019

58792151R00275